Future Outlooks on Corporate Finance and Opportunities for Robust Economic Planning

Siraj Kariyilaparambu Kunjumuhammed
Modern College of Business and Science, Oman

Nithya Ramachandran
University of Technology and Applied Science, Oman

IGI Global
PUBLISHER of TIMELY KNOWLEDGE

A volume in the Advances in Finance, Accounting, and Economics (AFAE) Book Series

Published in the United States of America by
IGI Global
Business Science Reference (an imprint of IGI Global)
701 E. Chocolate Avenue
Hershey PA, USA 17033
Tel: 717-533-8845
Fax: 717-533-8661
E-mail: cust@igi-global.com
Web site: http://www.igi-global.com

Library of Congress Cataloging-in-Publication Data

Names: Kunjumuhammed, Siraj, 1978- editor. | Ramachandran, Nithya, 1980- editor.
Title: Future outlooks on corporate finance and opportunities for robust economic planning / Siraj Kunjumuhammed, and Nithya Ramachandran, editors.
Description: Hershey, PA : Business Science Reference, [2023] | Includes bibliographical references and index. | Summary: "This book will disseminate knowledge on corporate response during the covid-19 crisis, which will help readers to understand the relevance of each adjustment and strategic intervention on firm value, addressing challenges on both the demand and supply side and the firm value chain"-- Provided by publisher.
Identifiers: LCCN 2022023428 (print) | LCCN 2022023429 (ebook) | ISBN 9781668453421 (hardback) | ISBN 9781668453438 (paperback) | ISBN 9781668453445 (ebook)
Subjects: LCSH: Corporations--Finance. | Corporations--Valuation. | Organizational effectiveness. | Strategic planning. | COVID-19 Pandemic, 2020---Influence.
Classification: LCC HG4026 .F88 2023 (print) | LCC HG4026 (ebook) | DDC 658.15--dc23/eng/20220714
LC record available at https://lccn.loc.gov/2022023428
LC ebook record available at https://lccn.loc.gov/2022023429

This book is published in the IGI Global book series Advances in Finance, Accounting, and Economics (AFAE) (ISSN: 2327-5677; eISSN: 2327-5685)

British Cataloguing in Publication Data
A Cataloguing in Publication record for this book is available from the British Library.

Advances in Finance, Accounting, and Economics (AFAE) Book Series

ISSN:2327-5677
EISSN:2327-5685

Editor-in-Chief: Ahmed Driouchi Al Akhawayn University, Morocco

MISSION

In our changing economic and business environment, it is important to consider the financial changes occurring internationally as well as within individual organizations and business environments. Understanding these changes as well as the factors that influence them is crucial in preparing for our financial future and ensuring economic sustainability and growth.

The **Advances in Finance, Accounting, and Economics (AFAE)** book series aims to publish comprehensive and informative titles in all areas of economics and economic theory, finance, and accounting to assist in advancing the available knowledge and providing for further research development in these dynamic fields.

COVERAGE

- Finance
- Stock Market
- Economics of Intellectual Property Rights
- Behavioral Economics
- Accounting information systems
- Corporate Finance
- Internet Banking
- Finance and Accounting in SMEs
- Microeconomics
- Investments and Derivatives

IGI Global is currently accepting manuscripts for publication within this series. To submit a proposal for a volume in this series, please contact our Acquisition Editors at Acquisitions@igi-global.com or visit: http://www.igi-global.com/publish/.

The Advances in Finance, Accounting, and Economics (AFAE) Book Series (ISSN 2327-5677) is published by IGI Global, 701 E. Chocolate Avenue, Hershey, PA 17033-1240, USA, www.igi-global.com. This series is composed of titles available for purchase individually; each title is edited to be contextually exclusive from any other title within the series. For pricing and ordering information please visit http://www.igi-global.com/book-series/advances-finance-accounting-economics/73685. Postmaster: Send all address changes to above address.

Titles in this Series

For a list of additional titles in this series, please visit:
www.igi-global.com/book-series/advances-finance-accounting-economics/73685

Considerations of Territorial Planning, Space, and Economic Activity in the Global Economy
Helmuth Yesid Arias Gomez (Masaryk Institute of Advanced Studies (MIAS), Czech Technical University in Prague, Czech Republic) and Gabriela Antošová (Institute of Education and Communication, Czech University of Life Sciences in Prague, Czech Republic)
Business Science Reference • © 2023 • 356pp • H/C (ISBN: 9781668459768) • US $250.00

Transforming Economies Through Microfinance in Developing Nations
Yahaya Alhassan (University of Sunderland in London, UK) and Uzoechi Nwagbara (University of Sunderland in London, UK)
Business Science Reference • © 2023 • 263pp • H/C (ISBN: 9781668456477) • US $250.00

Advanced Machine Learning Algorithms for Complex Financial Applications
Mohammad Irfan (CMR Institute of Technology, India) Mohamed Elhoseny (American University in the Emirates, UAE) Salina Kassim (International Islamic University of Malaysia, Malaysia) and Noura Metawa (University of Sharjah, UAE)
Engineering Science Reference • © 2023 • 292pp • H/C (ISBN: 9781668444832) • US $270.00

Exploring the Dark Side of FinTech and Implications of Monetary Policy
Sheraz Ahmed (LUT University, Finland) John Agyekum Addae (LUT University, Finland & Ghana Communication Technology University, Ghana) and Kwame Simpe Ofori (International University of Grand-Bassam, Côte d'Ivoire & University of Electronic Science and Technology of China, China)
Business Science Reference • © 2023 • 300pp • H/C (ISBN: 9781668463819) • US $250.00

Blockchain Applications in Cryptocurrency for Technological Evolution
Atour Taghipour (Normandy University, France)
Business Science Reference • © 2023 • 308pp • H/C (ISBN: 9781668462478) • US $250.00

For an entire list of titles in this series, please visit:
www.igi-global.com/book-series/advances-finance-accounting-economics/73685

IGI Global
PUBLISHER of TIMELY KNOWLEDGE

701 East Chocolate Avenue, Hershey, PA 17033, USA
Tel: 717-533-8845 x100 • Fax: 717-533-8661
E-Mail: cust@igi-global.com • www.igi-global.com

Table of Contents

Preface xiv

Acknowledgment xix

Chapter 1
A Study on the Linage Between Business Continuity Plans and Corporate Finance During COVID-19 1
Siraj Kariyilaparambu Kunjumuhammed, Modern College of Business and Science, Oman

Chapter 2
Global Systemic Risk Interdependencies and Transitory Connectedness Networks 21
Onur Polat, Bilecik Seyh Edebali University, Turkey

Chapter 3
Corporate Financing Decisions During a Crisis: An Empirical Review 48
Padmalosani Dayalan, University of Technology and Applied Sciences, Oman

Chapter 4
Impact of Gender Diversity on the Board of Directors on the Financial Performance of the Chinese Private Water Companies 68
Rajibur Reza, Griffith University, Australia
Lan Sun, CQUniversity, Australia

Chapter 5
Corporate Response to Macroeconomic Shocks 99
Anitha Narayanan Nair, Modern College of Business and Science, Oman

Chapter 6
Corporate Financial Management Decisions During COVID-19......................115
Rengarajan Veerasamy, Arab Open University, Oman
Kabaly Subramanian, Arab Open University, Oman
Subrahmaninan Muthuraman, Arab Open University, Oman

Chapter 7
Does Financial Attitude Impact Trading Activity of Retail Investors During the COVID-19 Pandemic in the Sultanate of Oman?..129
Shanmuga Pria, University of Technology and Applied Sciencce, Oman
VenkataVara Prasad, University of Technology and Applied Science, Oman

Chapter 8
Corporate Governance Practices During COVID-19...149
Kavitha Govindaraj, PSGR Krishnammal College for Women, India
Bala Thripurasundari Venkatesh, PSGR Krishnammal College for Women, India

Chapter 9
The Impact of Corporate Social Responsibility (CSR) on Firm Performance During the COVID-19 Pandemic: Evidence From Oman.................................170
Essia Ries Ahmed, Faculty of Business, Karabük University, Turkey
Jawaher Hamdan Al-Alawi, University of Nizwa, Oman
Hajar Saeed Al-Rissi, University of Nizwa, Oman

Chapter 10
COVID-19 Pandemic Jolt: Qualitative Research on Investor Behavior Toward Mutual Funds Investment With Special Reference to Tamilnadu......................187
Radhamani K., P.K.R. Arts College for Women, Gobichettipalayam, India

Chapter 11
Impact of COVID-19 on the Financial Management of MSMEs: An Analytical Review...203
Abhijit Sharad Kelkar, University of Fujairah, UAE
Nithya Ramachandran, University of Technology and Applied Sciences, Oman

Chapter 12
Impact of COVID-19 on Capital Structure Towards Maruti Suzuki India Limited 224
Janaki P., Vellalar College for Women (Autonomous), India
Mounaarthi K., Vellalar College for Women (Autonomous), India

Compilation of References 238

About the Contributors 272

Index 276

Detailed Table of Contents

Preface xiv

Acknowledgment xix

Chapter 1
A Study on the Linage Between Business Continuity Plans and Corporate Finance During COVID-19 1
Siraj Kariyilaparambu Kunjumuhammed, Modern College of Business and Science, Oman

This chapter discusses the linkage between business continuity plans (BCP) and corporate finance during the COVID-19 pandemic. Unlike the previous financial crises, such as the global financial crisis of 2008-09, the COVID-19 pandemic significantly impacted the corporate sector from both the demand and supply perspectives. The precautionary lockdown and social distancing measures to prevent the spread of the virus resulted in declining household earnings and wealth, consumer spending (demand-side), production and supply chain disruptions, and closure of business activities (supply-side). Corporate organizations set business continuity plans to mitigate the crisis's impact and sustain their business operations, focusing on the mission-critical functions and validating a plan for maintaining business operations during and after the crisis.

Chapter 2
Global Systemic Risk Interdependencies and Transitory Connectedness Networks 21
Onur Polat, Bilecik Seyh Edebali University, Turkey

This work examines the connectedness of financial stress index (FSI) categorical indicators indicating the US, other advanced economies, and emerging economies. In this context, the authors implement two pioneering methodologies, the Diebold-Yilmaz and the frequency connectedness, and compute spillovers among the FSI categorical indicators between January 3, 2000 and January 22, 2021. In doing so, they estimate global financial stress interdependence during financial turbulent episodes such as the global financial crisis (GFC) and the recent COVID-19 pandemic. Furthermore, they compute overall connectedness of FSI categorical indicators in the short-, medium-, and long-cycle. Overall spillover indexes computed by both methodology create proper signs to prominent financial/geopolitical incidents. Finally, they concentrate on the network connectedness of pairwise spillovers indicating the GFC and the COVID-19 pandemic epochs. The network analysis highlights the key role of equity and volatility channels in catalyzing total spillovers for both of the episodes.

Chapter 3
Corporate Financing Decisions During a Crisis: An Empirical Review 48
Padmalosani Dayalan, University of Technology and Applied Sciences, Oman

This chapter reviews the literature on corporate financing decisions during a crisis. The COVID-19 pandemic impacted all walks of life: individual, corporate, and government. Decisions on corporate finance influence a firm's survival and growth and are influenced by many factors, like the investment opportunities, cost of capital, firm age, current capital structure, availability of funds, etc. This chapter sheds light on the factors that influence corporate financing during a crisis. Various crises, including the global financial crisis and COVID-19 crisis, influenced the corporate world, and corporate responses to these crises were detailed. The chapter reviews the empirical literature on the subject. It is observed that though the availability of external funds during a crisis is affected, corporates prefer to increase their leverage during a financial crisis when funds are required for operations. Similarly, the study also found that firms utilized retained earnings and deferred dividend payments during the crisis to make funds available to meet contingency and maintain sustainability.

Chapter 4
Impact of Gender Diversity on the Board of Directors on the Financial Performance of the Chinese Private Water Companies 68
Rajibur Reza, Griffith University, Australia
Lan Sun, CQUniversity, Australia

China is facing an acute portable water problem and presents a picture of severe supply constraints. Thus, China's water crisis offers attractive business opportunities for foreign water companies as well as domestic private water companies. Hence, the private sector participation in the Chinese water sector is a hot topic. This chapter investigates the impact of gender diversity on board of directors on the financial performance of the Chinese private water companies using ordinary least squares (OLS) and unbalanced panel (random effects) regression models, which are estimated as the baseline approach on a sample of 19 Chinese private water companies for the period of 2010-2017. The OLS and random effects results show that number of women on board (WB), percent of women on board (%WB), number of female executives (FE), and percent of female executives (%FE) affect the Chinese water companies' financial performance. The results of this chapter are important for researchers, regulators, and policymakers to benefit from policies that encourage board varieties at an individual water company level.

Chapter 5
Corporate Response to Macroeconomic Shocks..99
Anitha Narayanan Nair, Modern College of Business and Science, Oman

COVID-19 has bought its fair share of troubles to the world when it came unannounced in late December 2019. Nobody was spared, and the corporate sectors bore the brunt of it along with the common man. Globally, almost all industries were affected by the pandemic due to lockdowns and restrictions which further intensified the problems of the corporate sectors. Many sectors faced shocks from both the demand side and the supply side. Unemployment, instabilities in the financial markets, and uncertainties prevailing in almost all sectors of the economy were predominant throughout the world. This chapter is an attempt to see how the demand shocks and supply shocks impacted the different industries and what measures were taken up by the governments and the corporate sectors to wade through this period of uncertainty and ambiguity.

Chapter 6
Corporate Financial Management Decisions During COVID-19......................115
Rengarajan Veerasamy, Arab Open University, Oman
Kabaly Subramanian, Arab Open University, Oman
Subrahmaninan Muthuraman, Arab Open University, Oman

Financial decisions such as investment and financing will have to be made in accordance with the environmental conditions prevailing in a particular time. This chapter will focus on the corporate financial decisions during the current pandemic situation. In financing decisions, cost of capital is the determining factor, and accordingly, financing modes are preferred by the organizations. Financial decisions made in a difficult time are resulting in negative cash profits in most of the cases. With the ongoing COVID-19 crisis, the stock markets suffered a severe shock resulting in negative returns, and the stock market crash risk has become higher than normal. COVID-19 has made the financing and investment markets more challenging. Financing decisions are the hardest decisions that companies could make during COVID-19 times as the cost of capital might skyrocketed and the companies themselves would find their profits declining significantly. Corporates must now be thinking seriously about alternative sources of funding for their business requirements.

Chapter 7
Does Financial Attitude Impact Trading Activity of Retail Investors During the COVID-19 Pandemic in the Sultanate of Oman? 129
Shanmuga Pria, University of Technology and Applied Sciencce, Oman
VenkataVara Prasad, University of Technology and Applied Science, Oman

The purpose of this research is to find out whether retail investor trading activity was influenced by their financial attitude during the COVID-19 pandemic. The research follows the descriptive and causal research design on a sample size of 87 retail investors obtained through snowball sampling method in which respondents were first identified with the help of financial advisors from five brokerage companies in Oman. The identified respondents were requested to forward the Google survey form to other participants. The study results reveal that the majority of the respondents were in agreement that they can be optimistic regardless of the current COVID-19 situation. There was found to be no difference in the mean rating given by Omanis and non-Omanis towards financial anxiety, optimism, financial security, precautionary savings, financial literacy, financial satisfaction, and risk involvement. Nationality matters only for investor confidence as the mean ratings given for it differ between Omanis and non-Omanis.

Chapter 8
Corporate Governance Practices During COVID-19...149
Kavitha Govindaraj, PSGR Krishnammal College for Women, India
Bala Thripurasundari Venkatesh, PSGR Krishnammal College for Women, India

The novel coronavirus (COVID-19) that emerged in December 2019 did not only cause health problem to people but also disrupted the entire global economic condition. COVID-19 is one of the most prominent issues in the 21st century. The COVID-19 pandemic has brought unusual challenges to corporates and their boards. COVID-19 raised the sphere of corporate governance practices. All listed companies look for effective and qualitative corporate governance practices by conscientiously integrating transparency, accountability, responsibility, and control. Distancing, travel restrictions, forbidding events for controlling the spread of COVID-19 have had bad impacts on economic conditions in the world. The crises occurred in corporates as well. The corporates where at risk in the time of pandemic, and it raised serious apprehension to corporate governance practices. The objective of this study is to assess the effect of corporate governance practices during COVID-19 and provide insight regarding the opportunities and challenges faced by corporates during the COVID-19 pandemic.

Chapter 9
The Impact of Corporate Social Responsibility (CSR) on Firm Performance During the COVID-19 Pandemic: Evidence From Oman 170
Essia Ries Ahmed, Faculty of Business, Karabük University, Turkey
Jawaher Hamdan Al-Alawi, University of Nizwa, Oman
Hajar Saeed Al-Rissi, University of Nizwa, Oman

This study investigates the impact of corporate social responsibility's features as predictor variables of firm performance with a sample of firms belonging to financial and industrial sectors in the Muscat Stock Exchange (MSX) in the Sultanate of Oman. This study analysed data for 75 financial and industrial firms. It used annual reports for the physical years 2019 and 2020 to analyze the impact of CSR features on firm performance during COVID-19 pandemic. The present study tested the hypotheses and utilised variables via utilizing the Smart-PLS for data analysis. The results found that CSR has a positive impact on firm performance in the financial and industrial sectors in the Sultanate of Oman.

Chapter 10
COVID-19 Pandemic Jolt: Qualitative Research on Investor Behavior Toward Mutual Funds Investment With Special Reference to Tamilnadu..................... 187
Radhamani K., P.K.R. Arts College for Women, Gobichettipalayam, India

Due to high instability in the markets and a situation similar to the year 2008, investors are worried about their investments and want to make quick decisions regarding the investments. Due to COVID-19, financial health has recessed. Investors are finding it difficult to decide whether they should continue their investment or redeem all and keep the cash aside for an emergency because life is unpredictable. In this context, secure monitoring and evaluation of mutual funds has become essential.

Chapter 11
Impact of COVID-19 on the Financial Management of MSMEs: An Analytical Review 203
Abhijit Sharad Kelkar, University of Fujairah, UAE
Nithya Ramachandran, University of Technology and Applied Sciences, Oman

With the advent of advanced information technology and related tools in late 1990s, the scope, nature, and avenues of the business opportunities and its financial perspectives changed. Stabilization and equating of the demand and supply for the sources of inflows and outflows of funds remained the challenges across the industry. The struggling players during this time remained MSMEs due to their limited scale and more importantly limited cushioning capacity to absorb the shocks of financial downs. The micro, small, and medium enterprise (MSME) sector has emerged as a highly vibrant and dynamic sector of the Indian economy over the last five decades. It contributes significantly to the economic and social development of the country by fostering entrepreneurship and generating many employment opportunities at comparatively lower capital cost, next only to agriculture. MSMEs are complementary to large industries as ancillary units, and this sector contributes significantly to the inclusive industrial development of the country.

Chapter 12
Impact of COVID-19 on Capital Structure Towards Maruti Suzuki India Limited 224

Janaki P., Vellalar College for Women (Autonomous), India
Mounaarthi K., Vellalar College for Women (Autonomous), India

The purpose of the study is to analyse the change in capital structure of Maruti Suzuki India Limited during the time of COVID-19. The main objective of the study is to analyse the key determinants of capital structure of a company before and during pandemic period. In order to analyse the capital structure of Maruti Suzuki India Limited, the ratio analysis has been used. The ratio includes capital gearing ratio, leverage, debt equity ratio, total investment to long-term liabilities, ratio of fixed assets to funded debt, ratio of current liabilities to proprietors' funds, ratio of reserve to equity capital, and interest coverage ratio. The study covers the period of five years, and it is based on secondary data obtained from the published annual report of Maruti Suzuki India Limited. From the analysis, it shows that the overall capital structure of the company is satisfactory during the study period. However, the company performance in the pandemic period is good.

Compilation of References 238

About the Contributors 272

Index 276

Preface

The COVID-19 pandemic has profoundly impacted the global economy, and the corporate sector has been no exception. Companies have had to adapt quickly to the new challenges posed by the pandemic, including changes in the cost of capital, performance crisis, lockdown and recessionary pressures, supply chain disruptions, and economic uncertainty. The financial markets underwent severe disruptions, and corporates utilized for alternative funding sources to meet their financial requirements. Despite these challenges, the financial sector has played a crucial role in supporting businesses and helping them navigate the crisis. This edited book brings together experts from various backgrounds to examine the impact of the pandemic on corporate financing and explore the key developments and trends in this dynamic and ever-changing field. With insights from leading practitioners and academic researchers, this book provides a comprehensive overview of the corporate financing landscape during the pandemic and opportunities for robust planning.

The path towards a brighter future demands innovative solutions to organizations' challenges. During the pandemic, corporate organizations faced turbulent times from both demand and supply perspectives. A unique set of challenges necessitated solutions that required out-of-the-box strategic thinking. Every crisis offers a lesson to learn, and corporates experiment with several turnaround strategies to come out of it. A crisis brings inherently abnormal, unstable and complex situations. Learning how corporates respond to financial crises is essential for corporate finance professionals to enhance their strategic thinking. The book 'The future outlooks on corporate finance and opportunities for robust planning' shed light on corporate finance decisions during COVID-19 times and brought forward best practices that helped corporates to withstand the challenges. The chapters in this edited book brought forward the extensive research experiences of experts in the specialization and focused on several critical elements of corporate finance during the last few years. Several themes on corporate finance during a crisis and the opportunities for robust planning are discussed.

The target audience of *Future Outlooks on Corporate Finance and Opportunities for Robust Economic Planning* includes finance professionals, academicians, students, financial analysts and policymakers in corporate finance. This book would be highly useful for anyone interested in corporate finance and who would like to know about corporate resilience during the pandemic. Additionally, the book may also be a valuable resource for academic researchers and instructors in finance and business-related fields.

A significant theme that requires attention and has been brought forward in the introductory chapters is the alignment of corporate finance functions to business continuity plans (BCP). Business continuity initiatives drive a business's mission-critical functions during a crisis. The chapter brought in the relevant empirical literature and business continuity practices on corporate finance during COVID-19. Both the demand and supply shocks were addressed in the business continuity plans. Crises also posed opportunities and led to financial innovation. New practices emerge and create innovative solutions to existing problems. It calls for critically evaluating the financial activities during a crisis and their role in ensuring business continuity.

During a crisis, several factors influence investment, financing and dividend decisions. The authors attempted to answer these questions. For instance, in the introductory chapters based on the empirical review, the authors concluded that corporate firms maintained their dividend payments during the crisis to instill investor confidence in the business prospects. Similarly, regarding the financing decisions, stock market volatility due to lockdown and social restrictions resulted in investors disposing of risky asset portfolios. Syndicated loans were also opted for by firms to bolster their cash buffers and liquidity shortfalls. COVID-19 created severe stress on cashflows; unlike previous crises, economics with a stable government and central bank interventions showcased corporate resilience more than other economies.

The pandemic has underlined the interdependencies and connectedness in the global financial system. The pandemic has caused significant systematic risks, for instance, recessionary pressures in economic activity due to lockdown, social distancing and temporary suspension of commercial activities, supply chain disruptions, and stock market volatility. These risks are interdependent and have the potential to transmit across countries and markets, creating transitory connectedness. The book also showcased researchers' interest in global systematic risk interdependencies and transitory connectedness. Contagion of financial bursts and financial connectedness are tightly related. Based on empirical review and data from the US and other major economies, the authors provided empirical evidence on the share market reactions to COVID-19 and valuable insights into the interdependence of categorical indicators.

The pandemic significantly impacted corporate financing decisions. Due to reduced revenue and profitability, many corporate organizations faced severe cashflow difficulties in addressing their working capital requirements. Chapter 3 focused on corporate financing decisions during the crisis. The chapter explored the relative weightage of debt and equity in financing corporates' demand for funds.

Corporations met their financial needs from various sources; however, they are influenced by factors like size, Industry, region, existing capital structure, and access to funding sources. Other strategies deployed by organizations include deferring loan payments, seeking government support, reevaluating investment priorities, cutting costs through layoffs, and reducing investments.

Highlighting the significance of an effective oversight body on firm performance, Chapter 4 investigated the impact of gender diversity on the board of directors on the financial performance of Chinese private water companies using ordinary least squares (OLS) and unbalanced panel (random effects) regression models. The models are estimated using the baseline approach on a sample of 19 Chinese private water companies from 2010-2017. The chapter has implications for corporate governance research and its application to Investment in the Chinese private water industry. Furthermore, the results of this chapter are significant for researchers, regulators and policymakers for getting benefits from policies that encourage board varieties at an individual water company level.

Chapter 5, "Corporate Response to Macroeconomic Shocks," explains government policy initiatives and measures worldwide to mitigate the crisis and its impact on the corporates. The pandemic disrupted the smooth functioning of all the economies around the world. Through the central bank interventions using monetary and fiscal policies, the government provided direct and indirect support to maintain liquidity and resilience during the crisis. The chapter provides an in-depth review of these measures and their impact on corporate performance during the crisis.

Corporate finance decisions are influenced by the economic outlook and the environmental conditions prevailing at a particular time. Chapter 6 focussed on corporate financial decisions during the recent COVID-19 pandemic. Corporate decisions are challenging because of the significant shock on profitability, the stress in the capital markets, etc. The authors explained that the financing decisions were the most challenging during this period as the cost of capital might have skyrocketed and declined profitability. The chapter provided insight into companies' responses to the shocks and how they addressed these challenges in corporate financing decisions.

Chapter 7 furthered the discussion on the impact of COVID-19 on retail investors' trading activity with a specific focus on the Sultanate of Oman's capital market. The study utilized a descriptive and causal research design on a sample size of 87 retail investors, using the snowball sampling method. The results confirmed previous empirical results that the two variables, optimism and financial satisfaction, affect investors' trading activity during the pandemic. The authors concluded that the investors were optimistic during the pandemic, actively involved in trading activity, and did not view the pandemic as a financial threat to their Investment.

With a specific focus on the Indian corporate sector, Chapter 8 discussed the corporate governance practices during the pandemic. The authors reviewed the Indian corporate governance framework and the seven pillars of corporate governance. The focus of the chapter was to review the robustness of the corporate governance framework and sustainable CG practices and to address the impact of a pandemic on corporate governance. A descriptive methodology is followed in the chapter and offers helpful insight into corporate governance practices to address macroeconomic challenges in the corporate sector.

Chapter 9 investigated the impact of corporate social responsibility features as predictor variables of firm performance with a sample of firms belonging to financial and industrial sectors in the Muscat Stock Exchange (MSX) in the Sultanate of Oman. The research utilized audited annual statements of 75 financial and industrial firms. The results showed a positive relationship between corporate social responsibility practices and firm performance in the Financial and Industrial sectors in the Sultanate of Oman.

Chapter 10 investigated investors' behavior toward mutual funds Investment during the pandemic. Various factors influenced the decisions of retail investors, such as the worrying corporate performance, the prevailing uncertainty in the market, and the recessionary pressures affecting the economy. The authors reviewed the investors' behavior and showcased investors appreciation towards mutual funds, to diversify investment risk and to allow rational decisions.

With the advent of advanced information technology and related tools in the late 90s, the scope, nature and avenues of the business opportunities and its financial perspectives changed. Stabilization and equating the demand and supply for the sources of inflows and outflows of funds remained the challenge across the Industry. The most struggling players during this time remained to be MSMEs due to their limited scale and, more importantly, limited cushioning capacity to absorb the shocks of financial downs. The Micro, Small and Medium Enterprises (MSME) sector has emerged as a highly vibrant and dynamic sector of the Indian economy over the last five decades. While adjusting to the emerging and consistently emerging business environment, MSMEs started playing a considerably quantifiable role in the GDP of India. The position of India's Micro, Small and medium enterprises (MSME) is the largest in the world after china. MSME plays a significant role in accelerating the growth of the Indian economy. Chapter 11 sheds light on the impact of the pandemic on the financial management of MSMEs in India. The chapter highlights various challenges MSMEs face and recommendations to improve MSMEs in India.

Chapter 12 analyzed the changes in the capital structure of companies in India, using a case study on Maruti Suzuki India Limited during COVID-19, using ration analysis. The selected ratios include the capital gearing ratio, leverage, debt-equity ratio, total Investment to long-term liabilities, fixed assets to funded debt, current liabilities to proprietors' funds, the reserve to equity capital ratio, and interest coverage ratio. The research provided insights into Maruti Suzuki India Limited's capital structure and financial position.

The COVID-19 pandemic has significantly impacted corporate financing, forcing companies to adapt to new challenges and find innovative solutions. Despite the difficulties, the financial sector has been resilient and has played a crucial role in supporting businesses and helping them navigate the economic downturn. To conclude, the book reports empirical research outcomes from authors across the globe on the impact of the pandemic on corporate finance. The book "Future outlook on corporate finance and opportunities for robust planning" is worth reading to know the corporate response to the pandemic challenges, specifically focusing on corporate financing decisions. This book provides a comprehensive overview of the corporate financing landscape during the pandemic and highlights the key developments and trends. The way forward is promising, and the learnings from the pandemic offer new insights into planning and implementing corporate finance activities. As the world begins to recover, companies must continue to carefully evaluate their financing options and take advantage of their opportunities to build a solid and sustainable future.

Siraj Kariyilaparambu Kunjumuhammed
Modern College of Business and Science, Oman

Nithya Ramachandran
University of Technology and Applied Science, Oman

Acknowledgment

The publication of the edited book *Future Outlooks on Corporate Finance and Opportunities for Robust Economic Planning* would not have been possible without the contributions of many individuals. We would like to extend our heartfelt gratitude to all authors who shared their expertise and wrote chapters on various topics on corporate finance in challenging times. We would also like to thank IGI and the publishing team, who worked tirelessly to bring this project to fruition, and the reviewers, who provided valuable feedback and helped improve the book's quality. Finally, we would like to acknowledge the support of family and our colleagues at work for their support during this journey. Your support has been invaluable and has made this project a reality.

Chapter 1
A Study on the Linage Between Business Continuity Plans and Corporate Finance During COVID-19

Siraj Kariyilaparambu Kunjumuhammed
https://orcid.org/0000-0002-7314-8677
Modern College of Business and Science, Oman

ABSTRACT

This chapter discusses the linkage between business continuity plans (BCP) and corporate finance during the COVID-19 pandemic. Unlike the previous financial crises, such as the global financial crisis of 2008-09, the COVID-19 pandemic significantly impacted the corporate sector from both the demand and supply perspectives. The precautionary lockdown and social distancing measures to prevent the spread of the virus resulted in declining household earnings and wealth, consumer spending (demand-side), production and supply chain disruptions, and closure of business activities (supply-side). Corporate organizations set business continuity plans to mitigate the crisis's impact and sustain their business operations, focusing on the mission-critical functions and validating a plan for maintaining business operations during and after the crisis.

INTRODUCTION

The coronavirus pandemic took the world by storm, affected every walks of life and impacted economies worldwide. The severe acute respiratory syndrome (SARS-

DOI: 10.4018/978-1-6684-5342-1.ch001

2) and COVID -19, the disease it causes, was first identified in Wuhan, China, in December 2019. Since the World Health Organization (WHO) declared a public health emergency at the end of 2020, severe measures, including a complete lockdown, were imposed by many governments to prevent the spread of the virus. Severe disruptions occurred in economic activities, labor force movements, supply chain, and production and distribution of goods and services. Unlike the previous global financial crisis of 2008-09, the pandemic has shaken the global economy from both the demand and supply sides. Most of the previous financial crises were rooted in financial institutions and affected specific sectors of the economy. The precautionary lockdown measures adversely affected the production of goods and services (the supply side) and customers' income and earnings, resulting in declining household wealth and consumer spending(the demand side). In addition, the supply chain disruptions affected the movement of goods and services and resulted in the closure of business activities.

A crisis refers to an inherently abnormal, unstable and complex situation threatening an organization's strategic objectives, reputation or existence (PAS 200:2011). The relevant question is; How did the corporates respond to the crisis that had an overarching impact on all elements in the value chain? What critical activities did they focus on that enabled them to continue and sustain their business performance? What core competencies of corporates helped them to be resilient to the crisis? Since the COVID-19 pandemic was reported in China in December 2019, businesses have initiated several plans to respond to the crisis. However, as economies initiated strict measures such as lockdowns and closure of activities to reduce the virus spread, businesses realized the significant stress the pandemic has on revenue shortfalls, liquidity and business operations. Several corporates failed to be resilient during the crisis; however, examples of successful business continuity plans also exist. Though all elements of business continuity plans and strategies deployed are relevant, this chapter doesn't focus on them entirely. Instead, the focus vests on the role of corporate finance in enabling business continuity plans and organizational resilience.

Literature on the impact of the pandemic on organizational performance sheds light on a common conclusion. The basic premise of this chapter is that COVID-19 exerted a significant negative jolt on the demand and supply side of business operations. The extant literature supports the basic premise. For instance, Shafi et al. (2020) researched the performance of Pakistan's micro, small and medium-sized enterprises (MSME) and found that MSMEs were severely affected by financial, supply chain disruption, decrease in demand, and reduction in sales and profit. Xu and Abbasov (2021) reported a similar finding in their study on Azerbaijans' small and medium enterprises (SMEs). Although Thukal (2021) offered an analogous finding on SMEs, the author further emphasized the relevance of creativity and innovation to seize opportunities during a crisis. Given this inference, the empirical reviews strongly recommended government interventions to support SMEs in recovering from the crisis and revitalizing the entrepreneurship ecosystem.

Managing corporate finance in a crisis is challenging. The severe strain on cash flows, the risk-conscious attitude of creditors and lenders, near-term and long-term debt overhang, equity shortfalls, and stress on liquidity, leverage and solvency are challenges that corporate financial managers deal with during crises. COVID-19 and consequent uncertainty shock required extraordinary measures to continue and sustain business performance. The business model, the nature of the business, the financial position, and the existing capital structure composition shaped the corporate finance responses. The extant literature supported various corporate responses, including cash conservation strategies, controlling operating and capital expenditure, capital rationing, securing access to funds and government support, and reducing fixed liability obligations by infusing more equity. Given the uncertainty and disruption of business activities, the corporate response essentially involves identifying the business interruption and critical financial risks and defining strategic moves to respond to and mitigate them. As Li et al. (2020) reported in the early part of the pandemic, corporates ' dash for cash' due to liquidity demands resulted in substantial borrowing by drawing lines of credit from banks and accessing the public markets. However, the responses differed as the pandemic progressed; several firms experienced long-term financial difficulties, leading to financial distress.

This chapter focuses on the question; how do corporate finance activities influence the business continuity plans of an organization during a crisis? Specifically, the chapter reviews the empirical literature on corporate responses to manage the crisis during COVID-19. The pandemic exerted unprecedented challenges for the corporate sector; consequently, crisis management took measures to address the challenge. The chapter hypothesizes that the financing, dividend and working capital management decisions during the pandemic focus on business continuity and disaster management rather than other considerations typically considered during corporate finance decision-making. Business risks and uncertainties during the pandemic were unprecedented, and how businesses managed them also has no precedence. The liquidity shortfalls, with constraints on near-future cash inflows and significant turmoil in the capital market, created a shift of focus and required instantaneous replies to remain resilient. This chapter examines the different strategies and tactics deployed by the corporate sector in addressing these issues.

BACKGROUND

Business Continuity

Business continuity is defined in many ways. Supriadi and Pheng (2017) defined business continuity as anticipating incidents affecting mission-critical functions and processes and ensuring that it responds to any incident in a planned and rehearsed manner. Alshammari and Alwan (2016) explained a business continuity plan (BCP) as a procedure used to establish and validate a plan for continuously maintaining the operations of a business before, during, and after disasters and disruptive events. Venclova and Urbancova (2013) referred to business continuity as an effort to ensure that critical business functions would be available to customers, suppliers and other entities so that the entity had access to their functions within an organization when the risk occurred. Over the years, BCP has evolved into a process that identifies an organization's exposure to internal and external threats and synthesizes strengths and weaknesses to focus on prevention and effective recovery after a crisis (Herbane, Elliott, & Swartz, 2004). BCP sets the right people in the right places and performs business in different modes by involving the shareholders through different stations until everything returns to normal. Business continuity plans are proactive strategies that enable the business to respond quickly during adverse situations and ensure its smooth running and continuity of operations. A business continuity plan helps businesses become resilient and commercially operational during turbulent times. Castillo (2004), based on the 9/11 attack, explained disaster management and preparedness and pointed out that Boeing has integrated disaster management preparedness with the business continuity model, which helped the development of robust plans to serve employees, customers, stakeholders and the community at turbulent times.

The empirical literature offers contrasting evidence on the implementation of business continuity plans. The majority of empirical literature available in the last decade mentioned a lack of awareness of implementing BCP in organizations. Low et al. (2010) observed that corporates do not have any business continuity plan (BCP) as they are unaware of what constitutes a BCP. Fani and Subriadi (2019) observed that many organizations have not realized that BCP is essential to their business continuity and are more concerned about profit and market growth than business continuity.

One of the most significant reasons for business failure during crises is the lack of business continuity and disaster management plans. The absence of BCP forces corporates to take harsh measures to mitigate the crisis, like layoffs, unpaid leaves, termination of employees, etc. These measures affect the stakeholder sentiments and eventually threaten business continuity. On the other hand, a business continuity plan means a corporate commitment to the stakeholders; shareholders, suppliers, customers, and employees. BCP allows corporates to outperform others, as it is a strategic resource to lead competitive advantage during a crisis (Freeman, 2010).

However, firms also realized that the existing business continuity plans are not adequate to meet the unique challenges created by the pandemic. Each business is unique; hence, the business continuity framework should focus on critical features of the organization, its business model and business activities. As discussed, the pandemic brought in a common outlook among the organizations that the existing business continuity plans are inadequate to handle the pandemic. The pandemic creates waves, each one lasting many weeks. The chance of multiple occurrences, the spread of the virus in a short time, the need for continuous testing, and the complete closure or temporary suspension of business activities are critical challenges faced by organizations which in turn create the business continuity plans a unique one.

Business Continuity Plans and Pandemic

Deloitte (2020) classified the corporate response to the pandemic into four areas

1. Talent and Strategy
2. Customer Engagement
3. Business Continuity and Finance
4. Supply Chain

Talent and Strategy focus on workforce management, employment contracts, safety, and working conditions. Several companies opted for work-from-home (WFH) during the pandemic to prevent the spread of the virus. Other strategies include flexible working hours and paid leaves. These strategies allowed businesses to continue their business during a crisis. However, several businesses laid off their employees and temporarily suspended business activities due to the lack of BCP and the demand and crisis. Customer engagement strategy focus on engaging with key customers to maintain business continuity. Retaining customers and continuing business with them are essential for survival during crises. Though the supply chains were disturbed during the pandemic, several businesses developed alternative plans to continue operating with customers.

Business Continuity and Finance is the third key area that focuses on managing working capital liquidity requirements during a crisis. The emphasis is primarily on managing both operating and capital expenditures. The financial management decisions – investment, financing, dividend and working capital management- follow a precautionary operating model to mitigate the crisis. Relationships with creditors, lenders, shareholders and customers are crucial to addressing the working capital and

Figure 1. Corporate finance and business continuity plans

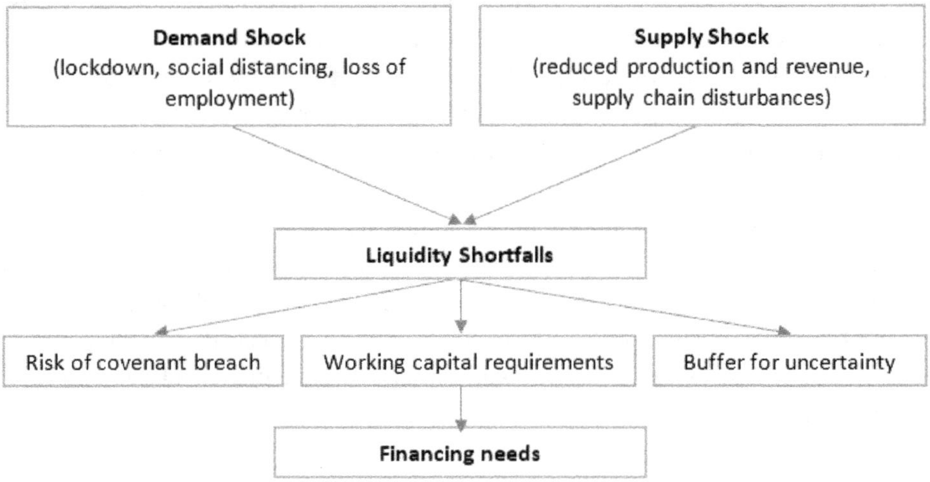

liquidity shortfalls. The supply chain is the fourth concern for corporates during the pandemic. During the coronavirus pandemic, the supply chain was the worst affected segment, as several countries announced lockdown measures and social distancing. Successful businesses addressed the challenge by introducing alternate strategies, utilizing technology in managing the supply chain, developing contingency plans, and managing inventory and cash flows through mutual consent.

Corporate Finance During the Pandemic

How does the pandemic impact business continuity? The key learnings from empirical reviews and the author's personal experience are summarized in the following figure.

Further, to maintain shareholder confidence, dividend decisions are of paramount importance. Interestingly, dividend decisions are considered by other stakeholders, such as the prospective investors and creditors, as an indication of firms' prospects. Business continuity plans also consider dividend decisions while prioritizing the strategies to manage the crisis and remain resilient.

Financial planning is critical during a crisis to maintain business continuity. The various corporate finance decisions, capital structure, dividend, working capital and investment decisions form part of business continuity decisions. Corporate finance decisions during the pandemic depend on several considerations, for instance, the current liquidity condition and the probable impact of the pandemic. Khalfan and Sturluson (2018) observed that capital structure decisions are influenced by the need to maintain financial flexibility and the cost associated with financial distress.

Similarly, investment practices avoid capital rationing associated with the financial crisis. Crises also pose opportunities and lead to financial innovation. New practices emerge and create innovative solutions to existing problems. It calls for critically evaluating the financial activities during a crisis and their role in ensuring business continuity.

The social and economic consequences of the pandemic vary across industries, economies, and geographical areas. The impact of finance shock is reportedly severe among small and medium enterprises. Kennickell et al. (2015), in their empirical research, found that tight credit constraints severely affected the vast majority of SMEs during great financial crises and recessions. Since the advent of the crisis, many startups terminated contracts with full-time employees while social entrepreneurship gained momentum. Reports also cited corporate layoff, downsizing, bankruptcy, and temporary closure of activities in developing and developed economies. However, the corporate sector also exhibited resilience and took strategies to mitigate the pressure, for instance, investment in digital technologies and ICT tools (Acciarini et al., 2021). While examining the severity of COVID-19 on the corporate sector, in terms of average stock-price change, Agarwal et al. (2020) found a decline in stock prices by 46% for commercial aerospace companies, 44% for air and travel companies, 42% for oil and gas companies, while the insurance carriers stock prices reduced by 29%. Though the listed sectors were adversely affected, the way the pandemic impacted each of these sectors was different. For instance, commercial aerospace companies face challenges due to high fixed costs, near-term cash flow issues, and uncertainty about long-term growth. On the other hand, companies in the air and travel industry faced near-time demand erosion due to travel restrictions and higher operational expenses. Fr oil and gas companies, a sharp decline in oil prices and the impact on short-term demand worsened the situation.

Deloitte (2020) presented a framework guiding firms to address finance during the pandemic. Two primary components influence the strategy. The first and foremost is the level of liquidity (low and high), and the next is the probability of impact (low and high). Accordingly, the following framework is presented.

During a financial crisis and economic downturn, financial institutions tighten the credit allocation process, and the investors opt to sell risky portfolios and abstain from the capital market. Bernanke (1983) pointed out that financial crises disrupt the credit allocation process, leading to restricted credit supply and higher borrowing costs. The drop in the supply of bank credit stems from shocks to borrowers' collateral, which affect firms' ability to raise capital if agency and information problems are significant (Hassan, Politsidis, & Sharma, 2020). Importantly, in such a situation, corporates focus on obtaining finance to manage liquidity shortfalls and a buffer against future uncertainties using other sources of finance such as the capital market, syndicated loans and bond market. Hence, a financial crisis often results

Figure 2. COVID 19 and corprorate vulnerabilty: strategies

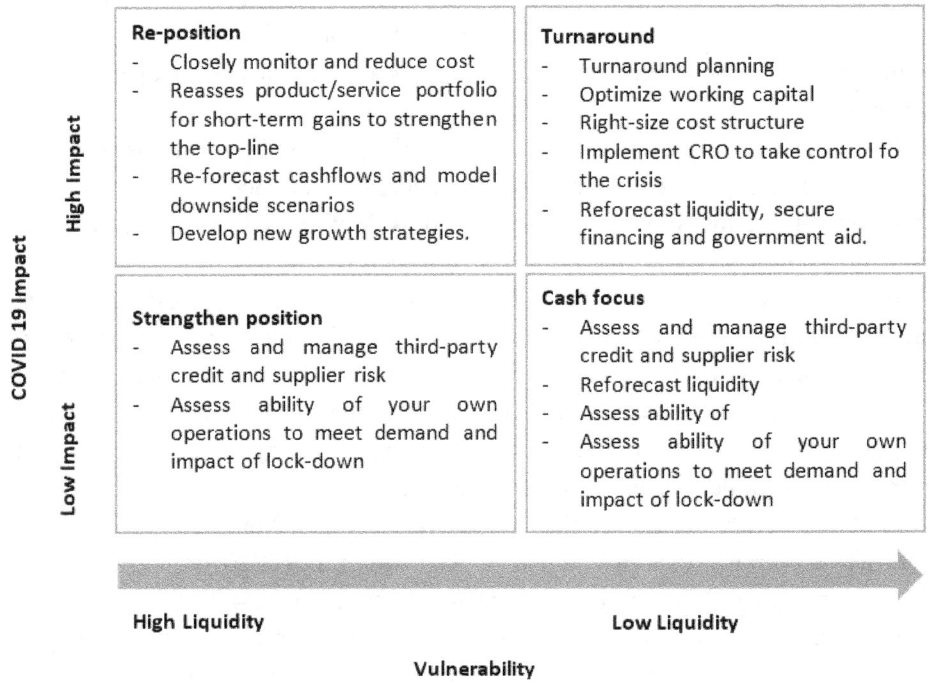

in firms' capital structure decisions (Wrongska & Mazurkiewicz, 2018). However, COVID-19 posed a unique situation wherein the supply and demand for funds were significantly affected. Though empirical research identified firm behavior during the financial crisis, the pertinent question is whether firm behavior during COVID-19 is similar to firm behavior in earlier financial crises. How did firms manage their financial shortage and liquidity shortfalls during the pandemic? Did it create any changes in the capital structure? It is also relevant in working capital management decisions and dividend decisions. The financial crisis and recessionary pressures also influence corporate investment decisions. Overall, corporate finance decisions during a pandemic are perplexing. It requires a detailed review of the existing literature to address the strategies companies followed to mitigate the challenges using better financial decisions.

RESEARCH METHODOLOGY

Corporate's Business continuity plans during COVID-19 focus on anticipating mission-critical functions and processes and responding to any incident in a planned and rehearsed manner. An essential mission-critical function is the corporate finance activities, which include anticipating the near-future and long-term cash flows, any liquidity concerns, the future working capital and investment requirements, and managing the funds to ensure the smooth functioning of the entity.

In this chapter, the author examines the BCP during COVID-19 and its linkage with corporate finance. Specifically, the chapter conceptualizes and addresses the results of empirical findings on strategies employed by resilient companies to manage corporate finance during the pandemic. Only a few empirical studies on this topic are available; hence, this chapter proposes a conceptual design based on available literature for further research deliberations. As the pandemic continues to impact the economy with new variants of the virus, the outcome of this chapter is highly relevant and of practical significance.

Raising Capital During the Pandemic – Learnings

Business continuity and corporate finance are closely related. The pandemic resulted in an unexpected demand shock as firms' cashflows were dramatically affected by plummeting revenues. Thus, firms' faced severe challenges in meeting fixed expenses, current debt obligations and building precautionary buffers. Many industries' cash flows were heavily impaired, with adverse implications for corporate liquidity and solvency (Deghi, Seneviratne, Tsuruga, & Vandenbussche, 2021). Similarly, the pandemic created significant stress on firms' balance sheets and the value of the collateral that the firms can borrow against (Siregar et al., 2021; Hassan et al., 2020). Above all, the liquidity shortfalls in financial markets that firms' depended on before the crisis forced firms to look for alternate sources to meet their financial needs.

Unlike the previous crises, the financial markets also faced large outflows of funds resulting from panic selling by investors. In their report, the Financial Stability Board (2020) classified the crisis into two phases. The first phase, categorized as a flight to safety, saw investors selling riskier assets and buying less risky ones. The second phase, the dash for cash phase, saw investors selling risky and safer assets to obtain cash or cash-like instruments (FSB, 2020). A similar observation was made by Karger et al. (2020), who explained the deteriorating liquidity conditions in the corporate bond market that limits the ability of firms to raise debt. The corporate bond, loan, and prime money market funds witnessed large cash outflows. These developments led corporates to look for finance from other sources, for instance, bank lending, syndicated loan issuance, and capital markets using non-conventional practices. Financial crisis results in a drop in the value of assets in banks' portfolios, eventually cutting down lending and/or charging higher interest rates. The role of central bank interventions, for instance, using reverse repo and asset purchases in the secondary market, is vital in this context.

Organizations follow different strategies as part of BCP to source, use and manage the funds. The vital question addressed here is; What sources did corporates utilize to raise funds for meeting liquidity, working capital and solvency needs during the pandemic? Before the pandemic, the capital markets, in general, were bullish and equity financing was relatively easy. Sabetti (2020) shared a similar view in a study on the Canadian stock market. Sabettil (2020) pointed out that the uncertainty precipitating the equity market during the pandemic forced investment banks away from underwriting equity offerings. A possible alternative that corporates deployed is to undertake a hybrid offering, a combination of underwriting and 'best efforts' agency basis. Thus it aligns the interest of the issuer and the investment bank as both parties, in all likelihood, want to increase the size of the offering if there is market demand. Another strategy to raise funds is through non-brokered private placement. In both cases, the relevant laws need to be acknowledged, and stockholders' permission should be obtained in some cases. This poses difficulty in raising funds. Successful corporates could gain the confidence of stockholders during the pandemic and thereby be able to raise funds either through public offering or private placement based on the fund requirements. OECD (2022), based on a study on the Asian market, supported the above view and explained the significant role of the capital market in financing companies during the pandemic. In response to the pandemic, Asian economies adopted various measures, from regulatory adjustment to direct and indirect financial support.

Bank Credit

A discussion on bank credit during COVID-19 requires specific attention, as the crisis posed differed from the earlier financial crises. Hassan et al. (2021) observed similarities to the 2008-09 crisis since both put a severe strain on global economies (through widespread bankruptcies, liquidity shortages, significant losses, etc.), but unlike the 2008-09 crisis, the pandemic contributed an aggregate demand and supply shock for both lenders and borrowers.

Banks were adequately capitalized and liquid when the pandemic erupted worldwide. Banking system indicators were relatively robust during the pre-COVID period. In a study by International Monetary Fund (2020), the pre-COVID period was considered a period of high profitability and stricter regulatory requirements to preserve financial stability. Banks had built up ample capital and liquidity buffers. Typically, the sharp tightening in financial conditions, the heightened funding stress, and the significant repricing of risky assets have tested their resilience and the momentum of bank lending (Altavilla et al., 2020). IMF (2020), based on their study of seven major economies, reported an increase in bank credit to firms during the crisis attributable mainly to the sizeable credit line drawdowns. On average, listed companies' drawdowns increased more than 40 percent compared with the first half of 2019 (Deghi et al., 2021). Higher drawdowns show firms' desire to secure funds while still in compliance with their maintenance covenants and because they expected a sharp deterioration in cash flow during the second quarter. Li et al. (2020) examined bank credit during COVID-19 and concluded that firms in the U.S. turned to their banks during COVID-19 and drew funds from pre-existing lines of credit at an unprecedented scale. As mentioned earlier, banks were on a safer net, as policy interventions after the global financial crisis led to safe bank balance sheets when the pandemic hit.

Many governments implemented programs- such as off-budget credit guarantees and targeted longer-term refinancing operations- to pump bank credit into the economy. Altavilla et al. (2020) also observed a similar view. The authors observed that the coordinated intervention by monetary and prudential authorities amplified the effects of the individual measures in supporting liquidity conditions and helping sustain the flow of credit to the private sector. These measures were inevitable, as otherwise, the impact of the pandemic on firms' employment should have been a significant concern. Further, as Altavilla et al. (2020) observed, in the absence of such pandemic response measures, persistent impairment in access to market-based funding, coupled with a substantial surge in demand for loans to meet the emergency liquidity needs, would have seriously undermined the bank's intermediation capacity. Hassan et al. (2021) noted the intervention of central banks in adjusting the price and liquidity of securities by repo operations and asset purchase activities in the secondary market.

However, as Siregar et al. (2021) observed, the potential vulnerabilities due to deteriorating asset quality is a matter of concern for banking across the world. Likewise, IMF (2020) projected that if the pandemic leads to a more profound and prolonged recession together with renewed disruptions in the financial market and another round of currency depreciation, nonfinancial corporate performance could deteriorate further, and the banks could face a substantial increase in non-performing loans, and their profitability and capital adequacy would come under renewed pressure. OECD (2021) shared a similar view and explained that if the impact of the pandemic persists, the non-performing loans will increase due to the rise in household and company defaults and, thereby, a rise in the loan loss provisions and allowance.

As liquidity is a significant concern, it may be concluded that firms in countries with a robust banking systems could develop and implement a sustainable business continuity plan to mitigate the challenges posed by the pandemic. Unlike the previous crises, the pandemic necessitated timely support from government and non-government institutions to maintain liquidity and financial needs, thereby implementing business continuity plans.

Syndicated Loans

Typically, a syndicated loan is provided by a group of lenders and is structured, arranged and managed by a lead arranger, which may be a bank, investment house or a group of lenders. Firms often use syndicated loans to finance medium and long-term financial needs (Tampakoudis et al., 2022). A common advantage of syndicated loans is the ability to raise significant funds and share risk among groups of lenders. Goel and Serena (2020) observed an increasing trend among nonfinancial firms to dash to debt markets – bond and syndicated loan markets – to secure funds for covering operational expenses and possibly buttress their cash buffers. While examining the firm-level trends, the authors observed that large firms had better access to the booming bond market while syndicated loan markets trailed in comparison. Nevertheless, the certification of multiple lenders' loans conveys a positive signal for the borrowers' creditworthiness during the pandemic-driven economic meltdowns (Tampakoudis et al., 2022). Empirical reviews also draw similar conclusions on earlier financial crises (Gasbarro et al., 2017; Li and Ongena, 2015).

Stock and Bond Market

Liu et al. (2022), while evaluating the effect of the pandemic on the stock market and bond market using data collected from 26 countries, revealed that the fiscal policy has a more positive impact on the stock market while the monetary policy has brought more positive impact on the bond market. The fiscal policy has brought more volatility to the bond market than the stock market. In a similar study comparing the stock and bond market, Chen et al. (2021) applied Vector Autoregressive Model to the Chinese Stock Market. They found that the pandemic had a significant negative impact on the stock market and a significant positive impact on the bond market. During the COVID-19 pandemic, firms choose to issue bonds with longer maturities, contrary to the previous financial crises (Halling et al., 2020). Research also indicated different funding strategies followed by firms. The BBB-rated and non-investment-grade firms utilized credit lines with banks. In contrast, the AAA to A-rated firms managed to secure funds from the capital market and issued bonds and equities (Acharya and Steffen, 2020).

Baker et al. (2020) observed that the government restrictions on commercial activity and voluntary social distancing measures mainly drove the US Stock market volatility during the pandemic. These measures have created panic and resulted in significant cash outflows in the market.

Business Continuity Plan and Corporate Funding

COVID-19 resulted in firm vulnerabilities, a unique situation that was never experienced before. Firms implemented business continuity plans to remain active and meet stakeholder expectations. However, the crises posed several challenges, the most among them being liquidity shortfalls, near-term and long-run financial obligations and uncertainty in demand and supply conditions.

The discussion on corporate financing presented a comprehensive view of how financial markets reacted to the pandemic. As observed from the reviews, the large corporates could obtain funds to meet liquidity shortages and a buffer for uncertainties using bank credits, bond market and syndicated loans. However, small and medium enterprises could not access the funds as effectively as large firms. Based on their empirical investigation, Goel and Serena (2020) observed that large firms significantly increased their borrowing, while the rest faced bottlenecks due to their reliance on a strained syndicated loan market and hurdles in switching to bond markets. Any business continuity plan requires an alternative funding source to meet the contingencies for which COVID-19 poses a significant challenge. As the demand for funds surged while the supply of funds was restricted, many firms could not access adequate funds, forcing them to take severe measures, including layoffs and closure of business activities.

Viewing business continuity plans from the perspective of corporate finance, the effect of country-specific characteristics, firm-specific characteristics and governmental support played a significant role in business performance, disaster management and business continuity plans. A similar view is expressed by Golubeva (2021), confirming the significance of country-specific factors such as sector, size, participation in exports, and market demand for firm products as significant for firm performance. In addition, the author also cited the relevance of country-specific factors, such as the level of economic development, as significant in firm performance during the pandemic.

Dividend Policy and Business Continuity Plan

Ali (2022) examined the impact of COVID -19 on dividend decisions using a sample of 8,889 firms listed in G-12 countries and found that though the proportion of dividend cuts and omissions was significantly higher during the COVID-19 times, the majority of the firms could either maintain or increase dividends. Technically, dividend decisions essentially connect business continuity plans to shareholders during a crisis. By doing so, firms could build and sustain investor confidence and signal their financial prospects at adverse times. However, as Mili et al. (2017) reported, dividend decisions during a crisis are influenced by many factors, such as the corporate ownership structure and board characteristics. Because BCP focuses on measures to meet stakeholder expectations during a crisis, dividend decisions are paramount to maintaining investor confidence in corporate performance.

FUTURE RESEARCH DIRECTIONS

This chapter examined the linkage between corporate finance and business continuity plans. Business continuity plans are essential in a crisis. This chapter took a macro perspective in understanding the relevance of corporate finance decisions – financing and dividend decisions – on business continuity plans. The financing decisions ensure that the firms obtain adequate funds to meet liquidity shortfalls, near-term and long-term debt obligations and a buffer for uncertainties. Without adequate funds, firms may be unable to exercise their business continuity plan. Firms must maintain their dividend payout during turbulent times to instill investor confidence and gain perspective investors' attention.

As outlined, the chapter looks at the linkage from a macro perspective; however, more detailed studies are required to examine the linkage from an industry perspective. Also, the role of regulatory intervention in promoting an active financial market is explained. More specific studies focusing on developed and developing countries are required to understand the influence of regulatory bodies' intervention in BCP during a crisis.

CONCLUSION

Business continuity plans are critical to managing the business under uncertainty. Unlike the previous financial crises, the pandemic has shaken the corporate sector from both the demand and supply perspectives. For some firms, the effect was temporary; for others, the effect was long-term, leading to financial distress. The lockdown and social distancing measures were not incompatible for some firms and created severe stress on cashflows. The liquidity challenges triggered primary concerns, which firms addressed through equity and debt sources. Corporate set business continuity plans to mitigate the impact of the crisis, focusing on mission-critical functions and validating a plan for maintaining business operations during and after the crisis. Successful businesses maintained BCP and implemented strategies to manage uncertainty and build stakeholder confidence during the pandemic. However, a critical analysis of the current situation, liquidity and probable impact of the pandemic are required to be effective. The strategies may include turnaround strategies, mergers, right-sizing and so on. A turnaround strategy is a crisis management strategy that focuses on prioritizing the activities based on forecasted goals and implementing it.

The pandemic resulted in revenue shortfalls that created stress on liquidity and near-term and long-term debt obligations and required a buffer to meet uncertain future. Access to credit at turbulent times is a strategic priority in BCP to maintain operations and sustain stakeholder confidence. A review of the extant literature on the subject was undertaken to verify the corporate responses and BCP during the crisis. The financial institutions took a cautious approach during the crisis, but the literature showed increased bank credit. However, such growth is mainly attributed to the central banks' government interventions and policy initiatives. The growth, hence, was not common across all economies. Economies with significant central bank interventions - such as off-budget credit guarantees, targeted longer-term refinancing operations, repo transactions and asset purchase activities in the secondary market – could support the corporate funding needs better than other economies. However, financial analysts predict stress on banks – higher levels of non-performing loans and pressure on capital adequacy norms – if the pandemic leads to a more profound and prolonged recession.

The empirical literature concluded that the bond market played a more significant role than the stock market in providing funds to corporates during the crisis, attributed to the government's monetary policy initiatives. Stock market volatility due to lockdown and social restrictions resulted in investors disposing of risky asset portfolios. Syndicated loans were also opted by firms to bolster their cash buffers and liquidity shortfalls. The chapter concludes that to implement BCP successfully during a crisis, firms require access to funds, which are influenced by the policy decisions of central banks and governments. As COVID-19 stressed deep stress on cashflows, unlike the other crises, economies with a stable government and central bank interventions showcased corporate resilience more than other economies. Further, the chapter observed empirical literature supporting the argument that firms maintained their dividend payments during the crisis to instill investor confidence in the business prospects. These measures showcased the linkage of corporate finance with BCP and the corporate responses during a crisis.

REFERENCES

Acciarini, C., Boccardelli, P., & Votale, M. (2021). Resilient companies in the time of Covid-19 pandemic: a case study approach. *Journal of Entrepreneurship and Public Policy, 10*(3), 336-351. doi:10.1108/JEPP-03-2021-0021

Acharya, V., & Steffen, S. (2020). The risk of being a fallen angel and the corporate dash for cash in the midst of COVID. *Review of Corporate Finance Studies, 9*(9), 430–471. doi:10.1093/rcfs/cfaa013

Agarwal, A., Chandra, K., Maloney, M., & Tam, M. (2020). *Planning for uncertainity: Performance management under COVID-19.* Strategy and Corporate Finance McKinsey & Company. Retrieved from https://www.mckinsey.com/business-functions/strategy-and-corporate-finance/our-insights/planning-for-uncertainty-performance-management-under-covid-19

Ali, H. (2022). Corporate dividend policy in the time of COVID-19: Evidence from the G-12 countries. *Finance Research Letters, 46*, 1–9. doi:10.1016/j.frl.2021.102493 PMID:34658678

Alshammari, M. M., & Alwan, A. A. (2016). *IT disaster recovery and business continuity based on VMware SRM solution for Kuwait Oil Company (KOC).* IEEE.

Altavilla, C., Barbiero, F., Boucinha, M., & Burlon, L. (2020). *The great lockdown: pandemic response policies and bank lending conditions.* European Central Bank (No. 2465).

Baker, S. R., Bloom, N., Davis, S. D., Kost, K. J., Sammon, M. C., & Viratyosin, T. (2020). *The unprecedented impact of stock market impact of COVID-19.* NBER Working Paper No. 26945. Retrieved from https://www.nber.org/system/files/working_papers/w26945/w26945.pdf

Bernanke, B. S. (1983). *Non-monetary effects of the financial crisis in the propagation of the Great Depression.* National Bureau of Economic Research (No. W1054).

Castillo, C. (2004). Disaster preparedness and Business Continuity Planning at Boeing: An integrated model. *Journal of Facilities Management, 3*(1), 8–26. doi:10.1108/14725960510808365

Chen, X., Wang, Z., Li, X., Liu, Z., & Li, K. (2021). The impact of COVID-19 on the Securities Market: Evidence from Chinese Stock and Bond Markets. *Procedia Computer Science, 187*, 294–299. doi:10.1016/j.procs.2021.04.065

Deghi, A., Seneviratne, D., Tsuruga, T., & Vandenbussche, J. (2021). *Corporate funding and the COVID-19 crisis.* IMF Working Paper, WP/21/86, 1-36.

Fani, S. V., & Subriadi, A. P. (2019). Business continuity plan: Examining of multi-usable framework. *Procedia Computer Science*, *161*, 275–282. doi:10.1016/j.procs.2019.11.124

Financial Stability Board. (2020). *Holistic Review of the March Market Turmoil*. Financial Stabilility Board. Retrieved from https://www.fsb.org/wp-content/uploads/P171120-2.pdf

Freeman, R. E. (2010). *Strategic Management: A Stakeholder Approach*. Cambridge University Press. doi:10.1017/CBO9781139192675

Gasbarro, D., Le, K. S., Schwebach, R. G., & Zumwalt, J. K. (2017). An analysis of syndicated loan announcements during the global financial crisis. *Journal of Financial Research*, *40*(4), 535–565. doi:10.1111/jfir.12134

Goel, T., & Serena, J. M. (2020). Bonds and syndicated loans during the Covid-19 crisis: decoupled again? *BIS Bulletin, 29*(1). Retrieved from https://www.bis.org/publ/bisbull29.pdf

Golubeva, O. (2021). Firm performance during the COVID-19 outbreak: International evidence from 13 countries. *Corporate Governance*, *21*(6), 1011–1027. doi:10.1108/CG-09-2020-0405

Halling, M., Yu, J., & Zechner, J. (2020). How did COVID-19 affect firms access to public capital markets? *Review of Corporate Finance Studies*, *9*(9), 501–533. doi:10.1093/rcfs/cfaa008

Hassan, I., Politsidis, P. N., & Sharma, Z. (2020). Global syndicated lending during the COVID-19 pandemic. *Journal of Banking & Finance*. Advance online publication. doi:10.1016/j.jbankfin.2021.106121

Herbane, B., Elliott, D., & Swartz, E. (2004). Business Continuity Management: Time for a Strategic Role? *Long Range Planning (Long Range Plan), 37*(6), 386-386. . doi:10.1016/j.lrp.2004.07.010

IMF. (2020). *Assessing the impact of COVID-19 pandemic on the corporate and banking sectors in Latin America*. International Monetary Fund. Retrieved from https://www.imf.org/-/media/Files/Publications/REO/WHD/2020/Oct/English/CorporateFinancial.ashx

Karger, M., Lester, B., Lindsay, D., Liu, S., Weill, P. O., & Zuniga, D. (2020). *Corporate bond liquidity during the COVID-19 crisis (Paper No. 27355)*. National Bureau of Economic Research.

Kennickell, A. B., Kwast, M. L., & Pogach, J. (2015). Small Businesses and Small Business finance during the financial crisis and the great depression: New evidence from the survey of consumer finances. Federal Research Organization - Center for Financial Research.

Khalfan, T., & Sturluson, J. P. (2018). Corporate finance approaches of Icelandic private firms after the financial crisis. *Managerial Finance*, *44*(11), 1274–1291. doi:10.1108/MF-05-2017-0167

Li, L., Strahan, P., & Zhang, S. (2020). Bank as lenders of first resort: Evidence from the crisis. *Review of Corporate Finance Studies*, (9), 472–501.

Li, C., & Ongena, S. (2015). Bank loan announcements and borrower stock returns before and during the recent financial crisis. *Journal of Financial Stability*, *21*, 1–12. doi:10.1016/j.jfs.2015.09.006

Li, L., Strahan, P. E., & Zhang, S. (2020). Banks as Lenders of First Resort: Evidence from the COVID-19 Crisis. *The Review of Corporate Finance Studies*, *9*(3), 472–500. doi:10.1093/rcfs/cfaa009

Liu, F., Kong, D., Xiao, Z., Zhang, X., Zhou, A., & Qi, J. (2022). Effect of economic policies on the stock and bond market under the impact of COVID-19. *Journal of Safety Science and Resilience*, *3*(1), 24–38. doi:10.1016/j.jnlssr.2021.10.006

Low, S. P., Liu, J., & Sio, S. (2010). Business continuity management in large construction companies in Singapore. *Disaster Prevention and Management*, *19*(2), 219–232. doi:10.1108/09653561011038011

Mili, M., Sahut, J.-M., & Teulon, F. (2017). Do corporate governance and ownership structure impact dividend policy in emerging markets during the financial crisis? *Journal of Applied Accounting Research*, *18*(3), 274–293. doi:10.1108/JAAR-07-2014-0079

OECD. (2021). *The COVID-19 crisis and banking system resilience: simulation of losses on non-performing loans and policy implications*. OECD.

OECD. (2022, June 24). *Corporate Finance in Asia and the COVID-19 Crisis*. Retrieved from Corporate Finance in Asia and the COVID-19 Crisis: https://www.oecd-ilibrary.org/sites/87861cf0-en/index.html?itemId=/content/publication/87861cf0-en

Sabetti, J. M. (2010, May 13). *Corporate Finance During COVID-19: Considerations For Raising Capital During A Time Of Crisis*. Retrieved from Corporate Finance During COVID-19: Considerations For Raising Capital During A Time Of Crisis: https://www.mondaq.com/canada/securities/932868/corporate-finance-during-covid-19-considerations-for-raising-capital-during-a-time-of-crisis

Shafi, M., Liu, J., & Ren, W. (2020). Impact of COVID-19 pandemic on micro, small, and medium-sized enterprises in Pakistan. *Research in Globalization*, *2*(2), 1–15. doi:10.1016/j.resglo.2020.100018

Siregar, R. Y., Gunawan, A. H., & Saputro, A. N. (2021). Impact of the COVID-19 shock on banking and corporate sector vulnerabilities in Indonesia. *Bulletin of Indonesian Economic Studies*, *57*(2), 147–173. doi:10.1080/00074918.2021.1956397

Supriadi, L. S., & Peng, L. S. (2018). Business Continuity Management (BCM). In *Business Continuity Management in Construction. Management in the Built Environment* (pp. 41–73). Springer. doi:10.1007/978-981-10-5487-7_3

Tampakoudis, I., Noulas, A., & Kiosses, N. (2022). The market reaction to syndicated loan announcements before and during the COVID-19 pandemic and the role of corporate governance. *Research in International Business and Finance*, *60*, 1–25. doi:10.1016/j.ribaf.2021.101602 PMID:34975188

Tampakoudis, I., Noulas, A., & Kiosses, N. (2022). The market reaction to syndicated loan announcements before and during the COVID-19 pandemic and the role of corporate governance. *Research in International Business and Finance*, *60*, 1–25. doi:10.1016/j.ribaf.2021.101602 PMID:34975188

Thukral, E. (2021). COVID-19: Small and medium enterprises challenges and responses with creativity, innovation and entrepreneurship. *Strategic Change*, *30*(2), 153–158. doi:10.1002/jsc.2399

Venclova, K., & Urbancova. (2013). Advantages and disadvantages of Business Continuity Management. *International Journal of Industrial and Systems Engineering*, *7*(4).

Wronska-Bukalska, E., & Mazurkiewicz, K. (2018). Corporate Capital Structure Changes during financial crisis: Case of Polish Companies. *Managing Global Transitions - International Research Journal, 16*(1), 19-35. doi:10.26492/1854-6935.16_1

Xu, Q., & Abbasov, S. (2021). Impact of COVID-19 pandemic on small and medium sized enterprises (SMEs) in Azerbaijan. *Open Journal of Business and Management*, *9*(6), 2759–2771. doi:10.4236/ojbm.2021.96153

Chapter 2
Global Systemic Risk Interdependencies and Transitory Connectedness Networks

Onur Polat
https://orcid.org/0000-0002-7170-4254
Bilecik Seyh Edebali University, Turkey

ABSTRACT

This work examines the connectedness of financial stress index (FSI) categorical indicators indicating the US, other advanced economies, and emerging economies. In this context, the authors implement two pioneering methodologies, the Diebold-Yilmaz and the frequency connectedness, and compute spillovers among the FSI categorical indicators between January 3, 2000 and January 22, 2021. In doing so, they estimate global financial stress interdependence during financial turbulent episodes such as the global financial crisis (GFC) and the recent COVID-19 pandemic. Furthermore, they compute overall connectedness of FSI categorical indicators in the short-, medium-, and long-cycle. Overall spillover indexes computed by both methodology create proper signs to prominent financial/geopolitical incidents. Finally, they concentrate on the network connectedness of pairwise spillovers indicating the GFC and the COVID-19 pandemic epochs. The network analysis highlights the key role of equity and volatility channels in catalyzing total spillovers for both of the episodes.

DOI: 10.4018/978-1-6684-5342-1.ch002

INTRODUCTION

Systematic risk is often defined as the risk relevant to the entire financial system, explicable to economic, geopolitical, or market-related incidents. The recent COVID-19 pandemic sets an example for this and the devastative effects of the pandemic has spread out across the globe expeditiously since the emergence of the pandemic. The systemic risk has notably soared following the COVID-19 outbreak, and the pandemic has vehemently hit global financial markets (Goodell, 2020; Corbet et al., 2020; Zhang and Ji, 2020; Albilescu, 2021).

The new type of coronavirus first emerged in the Chinese municipality Wuhan in late 2019 and rapidly spilled across the globe. The total number of identified COVID-19 cases has dramatically surged thenceforth and surpassed 110,000,000 as of the second week of February 2021 with more than 2,431,794 deaths[1]. The COVID-19 pandemic exemplifies a unique outcome in regards to its global scope as a pandemic since the pandemic of 1918 influenza (Goodell, 2020), keeps its geometric increasing trend despite more than 20 countries having launched vaccination and the cumulative number of doses has surpassed 7.7 bn as of February 24th, 2021[2].

The financialization era has accompanied by the severe and prolonged crises such the 1987 Black Monday, the 1994 Mexican crisis, the 1997 Asian flu, the 1998 Russian financial crisis, the 2002 stock market crash, and the last global financial crisis (GFC). Among these economic turbulences, the most acute one is unarguably the GFC and the crisis propelled the world entering the first collective recession since the World War II (Chandy et al., 2009). Notwithstanding, the debate on the grounds behind the GFC persists, the global economy has not completely recovered from the crisis despite more than a decade.

In the post-GFC period, the world economy has frequently witnessed imbalances, yet the more recent Covid pandemic has sorely harmed the world economic system. Since the emergence of the pandemic in late 2019, it has yielded devastative effects on primary and secondary sectors of the economy (Susskind and Vines, 2020). Despite monetary/fiscal stimulus packages launched by both emerging and advanced economies, the deleterious impacts of the crisis have not completely ceased (Casado et al., 2020; Furceri et al., 2020).

Contagion of financial bursts and financial connectedness are tightly related, and a plethora of studies report a noticeably intensified financial interdependence around financial/geopolitical turmoils (Minoiu et al., 2015; Demirer et al., 2018; Zhang and Broadstock, 2018; Barigozzi et al., 2020). Particularly, recent studies have noted a remarkable surge in the financial connectedness in the wake of the COVID-19 pandemic (Adekoya and Oliyide, 2020; Bouri et al., 2020; So et al., 2020, Lin and Su, 2021).

In light of the noticeable amplified global systemic risk connectedness, this work investigates the connectedness of financial stress for the US, other advanced economies (Eurozone, and Japan), and emerging markets. To this end, we use the daily financial stress index (FSI) constructed by the Office of Financial Research (OFR), which distills information engrained more than 30 financial indicators. The FSI is decomposed of five categories as credit, equity, funding, safe assets, and volatility and developed by a dynamic factor model (Monin, 2019). We employ the Diebold-Yilmaz (DY) and frequency connectedness (BK) methods to compute interdependencies among categorical market components between January 3, 2000, and January 22, 2021. As a consequence, we estimate connectedness of systemic risk corroborating emerging and advanced economies during financial calm and turbulent times. Furthermore, we provide the network structure of systemic risk connections for the GFC and the COVID-19 pandemic and compare them.

Our contribution to the extant literature three folds. Firstly, we estimate systemic risk contagion among advanced and emerging economies by employing two novel approaches over a timeline that covers two global economic imbalances. Secondly, we estimate short-, medium-, and long-term global systemic risk connectedness, and thereby focus on frequency dynamics of systemic risk spillovers. Finally, we examine the short-term network connectedness of systemic risk spillovers during the GFC and the COVID-19 epochs and hence compare pairwise spillovers indicating them. To our knowledge, this is the first study to examine systemic risk contagion using the categorical FSI indicators as input and estimating the spillovers by employing the DY and BK methodologies during the aforementioned financial upheavals.

We proceed with as follows. Section 2 delineates the contexts on financial stress and reviews studies on financial stress indexes. Section 3 provides a review of financial connectedness studies. Section 4 presents the empirical model and the data of the work. Section 5 presents empirical findings of the study and discusses about them. Section 6 concludes the study.

THEORETICAL FRAMEWORK FOR FINANCIAL STRESS AND FSIS

Financial stress is an essential concept in the financial economics field, yet scholars have no conciliation on the notion. Still, studies assert some key phenomena to delineate financial stress. In this vein, Illing and Liu (2006) describe "*financial stress as a continuous variable*" and state that it amplifies with expected financial loss, or with uncertainty. Hakkio and Keaton describe features of financial stress as "*increased uncertainty about the fundamental value of assets*", "*increased uncertainty about the behavior of other investors*", "*increased asymmetry of information*", "*Decreased*

Table 1. FSI/FCI studies for advanced/emerging economies

Study	Country – FSI/FCI	Frequency	Data Period	Methodology
Hakkio and Keaton (2009)	US – Kansas City FSI (KCFSI)	Monthly	Feb, 1990 – Mar, 2009	Principal Component Analysis (PCA)
Kliesen and Smith (2010)	US – St. Louis FED FSI (STLFSI)	Weekly	Dec 31, 1993 – Dec 11, 2009	PCA
Brave and Butters (2011)	US - FCI	Weekly	1971:w1-2008:w45	PCA
Oet et al. (2015)	US – Cleveland FED FSI (CFSI)	Daily	Jan 18, 1970 – Jun 30, 2015	PCA
Monin (2019)	US – OFR FSI	Daily	Jan 1, 2000 – Aug 31, 2017	PCA
Holló et al. (2012)	Euro – Composite Indicator of Systemic Stress (CISS)	Daily	Jan 2, 1987 – Jun24, 2011	Portfolio-Theoretic Aggregation
Angelopoulou et al. (2014)	Euro – 3 FCIs	Annual	Jan, 2003 – Dec, 2011	PCA
Islami and Kurz-Kim (2014)	Euro - FSI	Daily	Jan 1, 2007 – Apr 30, 2013	Variance Equal Weight (VEW)
Koop and Korobilis (2014)	Euro - FCI	Quarterly	1971:Q1 – 2013Q3	TVP-FAVAR
van Roye (2014)	Germany - FSI	Monthly	Apr, 1970 – Dec, 2012	PCA
Hoatori (2015)	Finland - 3 FSIs	Monthly	Jan, 1987 – Dec, 2014	VEW, PCA, and the CISS Methodology
Cambón and Estévez (2016)	Spain - FMSI	Daily	Apr 1, 1987 – Mar, 6 2015	CISS Methodology
Balakrishnan et al. (2011)	Emerging Markets – EM-FSI	Monthly	Jan, 1997 – Jan, 2009	VEW
Cevik et al. (2013)	Turkey - TFSI	Monthly	Jan, 1997 – Mar, 2010	PCA
Park and Mercado (2014)	25 Emerging Markets - FSI	Quarterly	1992:Q1 – 2012:Q4	VEW
Çamlıca (2016)	Turkey - FSI	Monthly	Jan, 2005 – Oct, 2015	CISS Methodology
Stolbov and Shchepeleva (2016)	14 Emerging Economies - FSI	Monthly	Feb, 2008 – Sep, 2015	PCA, VEW
Chadwick and Ozturk (2019)	Turkey – 15 FSIs	Monthly	Apr, 2005 – Dec, 2016	VEW, Portfolio Theory, PCA, and the Bayesian Dynamic Factor Model
Polat and Ozkan (2019)	Turkey - FSI	Daily	Jan 11, 2005 – Nov 17, 2016	CISS Methodology
Ishrakieh et al. (2020)	Lebanon - IFEFSI	Monthly	Jan, 1998 – Jan, 2018	VEW
Sahoo (2021)	India - FSI	Monthly	Mar, 2007 – Dec, 2016	VEW

willingness to hold risky assets (flight to quality)", "*Decreased willingness to hold illiquid assets (flight to liquidity)*" (Hakkio and Keaton, 2009: 6-10). Likewise, Balakrishnan et al. (2011) assert that "*substantial movements in asset prices, a sudden surge in risk and/or uncertainty, liquidity scarcities, and scrutinizes about the banking sector's health*" are the stylized facts of financial stress.

Despite it is hard to find a common definition for the financial stress, studies have attempted to construct the FSI or financial conditions indexes (FCIs) to gauge the financial stress, and hence to determine early warning indicators (EWI) of financial stress episodes. In this context, scholars combine indicators from financial markets and develop FSIs or FCIs by employing various econometric models. For example, Illing and Liu (2006) proposed three alternative measures (standard, refined, and GARCH estimations) for financial stress and developed a timely FSI for Canada.

The construction of financial stress indexes has gained further prominence by the scientific community following the global financial crisis (GFC), and researchers have developed the FSIs or FCIs for the US (Hakkio and Keaton, 2009; Kliesen and Smith, 2010; Brave and Butters; 2011; Oet et al., 2015; Monin, 2019), Euro area (Holló et al., 2012; Angelopoulou et al., 2014; Islami and Kurz-Kim, 2014; Koop and Korobilis, 2014; van Roye, 2014; Huotari, 2015; Cambón and Estévez, 2016), developing economies (Balakrishnan et al., 2011; Cevik et al., 2013; Park and Mercado, 2014; Çamlıca, 2016; Stolbov and Shchepeleva, 2016; Chadwick and Ozturk, 2019; Polat and Ozkan, 2019; Ishrakieh et al., 2020; Sahoo, 2021). Table 1 summarizes the aforementioned studies that have developed the FSI or FCI for emerging/advanced economies

THE LITERATURE ON THE FINANCIAL CONNECTEDNESS

Analysis of connectedness among financial assets serves important insights and implications for investors and policymakers. First, the dynamic interdependence of cross-markets can affect portfolio management in the sense of hedging or rebalancing. Particularly, the dynamic connectedness of return and volatility can improve the portfolio diversification effects, which is the main issue for portfolio managers. Second, the linkage among financial assets provides the basis for explaining risk propagation in markets. It could be argued that the premised methodologies have been popular among researchers to unveil the characteristics of financial interdependence, yet a comprehensive study introduced a novel approach to detect linkages between the variables. Diebold and Yilmaz (2009) introduced the Diebold-Yilmaz connectedness, thenceforth the DY, which relies on the forecast error decompositions of a VAR model. The study computed the H-step forecast ahead connectedness between 19 global stock markets by employing the DY approach. Diebold and Yilmaz computed connectedness between several financial indicators by utilizing the DY methodology[3] (Diebold and Yilmaz, 2012, 2014, 2015).

It should be worth noting that interdependencies among financial variables are prone to intensify during financial turmoil episodes. Thereupon, scholars attempted to gauge connectedness between financial variables by implementing different approaches such as the correlation analysis (Lang and Stulz, 1992; Lee and Kim, 1993; Calvo and Reinhart, 1996; Karolyi and Stulz, 1996; Baig and Goldfajn, 1999; Edwards and Susmel, 2001), the ARCH or GARCH models (Hamao et al., 1990; Chou et al., 1994; Susmel and Engle, 1994; Edwards, 1998), spillovers obtained by the multivariate-GARCH models (Baur, 2003; Chancharoenchai and Dibooglu, 2006; Beirne et al., 2013; Choudhry and Jayasekera, 2014; Wang et al., 2018; Sarwar et al., 2020).

The DY methodology has received overwhelming interest from scholars and studies have estimated connectedness among financial markets by employing this approach. A plethora of recent literature computes stock market connectedness by utilizing the DY methodology. For example, Barunik et al. (2016) estimated the volatility connectedness between 21 most liquid US stocks between August 2004 and December 2011 and detected asymmetry that dominates the volatility spillovers. Abbas et al. (2019) examined volatility connectedness among G-7 stock markets between July 1985, and June 2015, and found a strong interdependence reflecting the volatility transmissions among the stock markets. Along similar lines, Wu (2020) analyze financial interaction between stock markets for ASEAN-5 countries and China between June 23, 1999, and June 26, 2019, and found a strong interdependence mainly caused by the global equity market.

Other financial connectedness studies focus on the connectedness among bond markets (Cronin and Dunne, 2019; Mensi et al., 2020; Karkowska and Urjasz, 2021; Umar et al., 2021), foreign exchange markets (Baruník et al., 2017; Fasanya et al., 2020; Huynh et al., 2020; Wen and Wang, 2020); banking sectors (Demirer et al., 2018; Hernandez et al., 2020), cryptocurrency markets (Corbet et al., 2018; Balli et al., 2020); Aslanidis et al., 2021), commodity markets (Diebold et al., 2017, Yoon et al., 2019; Polat, 2020).

Despite abound financial connectedness studies, only a few studies estimated connectedness among FSIs or FCIs by implementing the DY approach. Cipollini and Mikaliunaite (2020) used monthly FSIs for 27 Euro states developed by Duprey et al. (2017), and estimated connectedness among the core and periphery Euro states. The authors argued that the interdependence among Euro states is mainly dominated by financial stress and declines aftermath of the Eurozone crisis. Likewise, Magkonis and Tsopanakis (2020) developed weekly FSIs for GIIPS countries by employing the PCA approach between January 2001 and September 2013. Then, the authors computed connectedness among the FSIs and determined a significant role of Spain and Italy in propagating financial stress, particularly in terms of banking and equity markets.

Aspired to gauge frequency-dependent linkages among financial variables, Baruník and Křehlík (2018) developed a novel methodology, *the frequency connectedness*, hereafter the BK, based on the spectral representation of the VAR. This groundbreaking approach has received interest in the recent literature, and scholars have computed connectedness among different financial markets by utilizing the BK methodology (Luo and Ji, 2018; Baruník and Kocenda, 2019; Kang et al., 2019; Polat, 2019; Naeem et al., 2020; Ferrer et al., 2021).

A body of studies focuses on financial connectedness during a financial/geopolitical crisis period and calm episodes. Within this strand, a strand of literature has investigated the connectedness of financial markets before and during the COVID-19 health crisis. A plethora of studies has examined how the COVID-19 pandemic influenced the interdependencies of global financial markets by employing the spillover effect between financial markets. First, some studies compared the spillover impacts between the stock indices of different countries before and during the COVID-19 pandemic (Abuzayed et al., 2021; Samitas et al., 2022; Choi, 2022). These studies gauge the volatility spillovers between various stock markets and determined that the risk contagion tends to be stronger during the COVID-19 pandemic. Likewise, some studies examined the impact of the COVID-19 pandemic on the relationship between asset markets including commodity, foreign exchange (FX), and cryptocurrency markets. Borgards et al. (2021) analyzed the overreaction behavior of various commodity futures in terms of the effects of the COVID-19 pandemic. The authors asserted that the overreactions are significantly amplified in both the number and the amplitude during the pandemic. Additionally, this excess overreaction can serve as a profitable trading opportunity. Some studies examined the impact of the COVID-19 pandemic on the connectedness among various fx rates (Wei et al., 2020; Fasanya et al., 2021b; Gunay, 2021). These studies used the volatility spillover index in the sense of the DY framework, and based on their findings, the total volatility spillover surged remarkably during the pandemic compared to the pre-COVID-19 episode. In this vein, Gunay (2021) found that the total volatility spillover index (SOI) during the pandemic period is higher than the volatility SOI in GFC. Furthermore, Naeem et al. (2021) and Narayan et al. (2022) examined the spillover impact between various cryptocurrencies during the COVID-19 pandemic. The total connectedness index amplified during the COVID-19 pandemic. In their turn, Narayan et al. (2022) found that the return and volatility spillovers between cryptocurrencies are more sensitive to crisis periods over the short-term (one day to one week) than over longer horizons (one month and above) by employing a frequency-based connectedness methodology.

A strand of literature has examined the spillovers between different asset classes during the COVID-19 pandemic. For example, Corbet et al. (2020), Mensi et al. (2021) and Li et al. (2021) applied the spillover analysis using different asset classes from China. Sakurai and Kurosaki (2020) and Adekoya and Oliyide (2021) from the United States, and Narayan et al. (2020) from Japan, Rai and Garg (2021) from BRICS. These studies detected that the connectedness between the financial assets is stronger during the COVID-19 pandemic than the linkages among the same financial assets before.

A vast number of studies indicated that despite the COVID-19 pandemic has substantially harmed the entire financial system, the shocks could be positive or negative depending on the industry. For instance, the tourism industry suffered a noteworthy damage, while IT-related industries have benefited greatly from telecommunicating during the COVID-19 pandemic. As a consequence, some studies focused on how the COVID-19 pandemic impacted each industry through the spillover effect (Laborda and Olmo, 2021; Si et al., 2021; Shahzad et al., 2021). In the studies of Laborda and Olmo (2021) and Choi (2022a), volatility spillovers among the US stock market sectors during the COVID-19 pandemic were examined. Their results propose that the pandemic has intensified the volatility spillover. They commonly showed that among several sectors, energy sectors played an important role in the transfer of volatility. In addition, Si et al. (2021) investigated the effect of the COVID-19 pandemic on the volatility spillovers among Chinese energy industry. To this end, they used nine energy sub-sectors in China. The authors stated that the pandemic has remarkably influenced the Chinese energy sectors, and the effect for each-subsector is distinct. Likewise, Shahzad et al. (2021) concentrated on the inter-sectoral volatility linkage in the Chinese stock market. In particular, the authors investigated the asymmetric volatility spillovers during the pandemic. Their findings reveals that the asymmetric impact of good and bad volatilities was extensively enhanced during the pandemic period.

Lastly, some studies examined the spillover effect between the COVID-19 news-related indices (Coronavirus Media Coverage Index, sentiment index, media type heat index, fake news index, panic emotion index, and contagion index) and financial assets (Zhang et al., 2022; Umar et al., 2022). Common to both studies, total interdependence among them was found to be strong when impactive events occur.

EMPIRICAL FRAMEWORK

The DY Methodology

Let the $VAR\left(q\right)$ model is defined as follows:

$$y_t = \sum_{i=1}^{q} \varphi_i y_{t-i} + \varepsilon_t \tag{1}$$

where, $\varepsilon_t \sim (0, \Omega)$ are i.i.d. error terms. The MA representation of the $VAR(q)$ is defined as $y_t = \sum_{i=0}^{\infty} B_i \varepsilon_{t-i}$

Assume that the H-step-ahead forecast error variance decomposition $\psi_{ij}^{g}(H)$, for $H = 1, 2, \ldots$ is defined as:

$$\psi_{ij}^{g}(H) = \frac{\sigma_{jj}^{-1} \sum_{h=0}^{H-1} \left(e_i' B_h \Omega e_j\right)^2}{\sum_{h=0}^{H-1} \left(e_i' B_h \Omega e_i\right)} \tag{2}$$

Here, Ω represents the variance vector of ε, σ_{ii} is the standard deviation of ε_t for the ith equation and e_i takes 1 as the ith element, 0 o.w. We normalize each component of the variance decomposition matrix as:

$$\tilde{\psi}_{ij}^{g}(H) = \frac{\psi_{ij}^{g}(H)}{\sum_{j=1}^{N} \psi_{ij}^{g}(H)} \tag{3}$$

The total volatility spillover is defined as:

$$S^{g}(H) = \frac{\sum_{\substack{i,j=1 \\ i \neq j}}^{N} \tilde{\psi}_{ij}^{g}(H)}{\sum_{i,j=1}^{N} \tilde{\psi}_{ij}^{g}(H)} \cdot 100 = \frac{\sum_{\substack{i,j=1 \\ i \neq j}}^{N} \tilde{\psi}_{ij}^{g}(H)}{N} \cdot 100 \tag{4}$$

"The directional volatility spillovers received by market i from all markets j" (Diebold and Yilmaz, 2012):

$$S_{i.}^{g}(H) = \frac{\sum_{\substack{j=1 \\ j \neq i}}^{N} \tilde{\psi}_{ij}^{g}(H)}{\sum_{i,j=1}^{N} \tilde{\psi}_{ij}^{g}(H)} \cdot 100 = \frac{\sum_{\substack{j=1 \\ j \neq i}}^{N} \tilde{\psi}_{ij}^{g}(H)}{N} \cdot 100 \tag{5}$$

"The directional volatility spillovers transmitted by market i to all markets j" (Diebold and Yilmaz, 2012):

$$S_{.i}^{g}\left(H\right)=\frac{\sum_{\substack{j=1\\j\neq i}}^{N}\tilde{\psi}_{ji}^{g}\left(H\right)}{\sum_{i,j=1}^{N}\tilde{\psi}_{ji}^{g}\left(H\right)}\cdot 100=\frac{\sum_{\substack{j=1\\j\neq i}}^{N}\tilde{\psi}_{ji}^{g}\left(H\right)}{N}\cdot 100 \tag{6}$$

"The net volatility spillover from market i to all markets j" (Diebold and Yilmaz, 2012):

$$S_{i}^{g}\left(H\right)=S_{.i}^{g}\left(H\right)-S_{i.}^{g}\left(H\right) \tag{7}$$

"The net pairwise volatility spillover" (Diebold and Yilmaz, 2012):

$$S_{ij}^{g}\left(H\right)=\frac{\tilde{\psi}_{ji}^{g}\left(H\right)-\tilde{\psi}_{ij}^{g}\left(H\right)}{N}\cdot 100 \tag{8}$$

The BK Methodology

The BK methodology is defined based on the $VAR\left(q\right)$ model given in (1).

The MA form of the $VAR\left(q\right)$ is introduced as $y_t=\phi\left(\mathrm{L}\right)\varepsilon_t$ with $\varphi\left(L\right)=\left[\phi\left(\mathrm{L}\right)\right]^{-1}$.

We define the frequency response function as $\phi\left(e^{-iw}\right)=\sum_{h}e^{-iwh}\phi_h$.

Generalized variance decompositions can be introduced as:

$$\theta\left(\left(w\right)\right)_{j,k}=\frac{\sigma_{kk}^{-1}\sum_{h=0}^{H}\left(\left(\phi_h\Omega\right)_{j,k}\right)^2}{\left(\phi_h\right)\Omega\phi_h{}'\right)_{jj}} \tag{9}$$

The spectral density of x_t at frequency w is defined as:

$$S_X\left(W\right)=\sum_{h=-\infty}^{\infty}E\left(x_t x_{t-h}^{'}\right)e^{-iwh}=\phi\left(e^{-iw}\right)\Omega\phi^{'}\left(e^{+iw}\right) \tag{10}$$

The generalized causation spectrum over frequencies $w\in\left(-\pi,\pi\right)$ is defined as:

$$\upsilon\left(\left(w\right)\right)_{j,k}=\frac{\rho_{kk}^{-1}\left|\left(\phi\left(e^{-iw}\right)\Omega\right)_{j,k}\right|^2}{\left(\phi(e^{-iw}\right)\Omega\phi'\left(e^{+iw}\right)_{jj}} \tag{11}$$

where $\phi\left(e^{-iw}\right)=\sum_h e^{-iwh}\phi_h$, and $\rho_{kk}=\left(\Omega\right)_{kk}$.

Scaled generalized variance decompositions on the frequency band $d=\left(a,b\right):a,b\in\left(-\pi,\pi\right),\ a<b$ is defined as $\left(\tilde{\theta}_d\right)_{j,k}=\left(\theta_d\right)_{j,k}/\sum_k\left(\theta_\infty\right)_{j,k}$, where

$$\left(\tilde{\theta}_d\right)_{j,k}=\frac{1}{2\pi}\int_a^b\frac{\left(\phi(e^{-iw}\right)\Omega\phi'\left(e^{+iw}\right)_{jj}}{\frac{1}{2\pi}\int_{-\pi}^{\pi}\left(\phi(e^{-i\lambda}\right)\Omega\phi'\left(e^{+i\lambda}\right)_{jj}d\lambda}\left(\upsilon\left(w\right)\right)_{j,k}dw \tag{12}$$

and

$$\left(\theta_\infty\right)_{j,k}=\frac{1}{2\pi}\int_{-\pi}^{\pi}\frac{\left(\phi(e^{-iw}\right)\Omega\phi'\left(e^{+iw}\right)_{jj}}{\frac{1}{2\pi}\int_{-\pi}^{\pi}\left(\phi(e^{-i\lambda}\right)\Omega\phi'\left(e^{+i\lambda}\right)_{jj}d\lambda} \tag{13}$$

The frequency connectedness on d is defined as:

$$C_d^f=100.\left(\frac{\Sigma\tilde{\phi}_d}{\Sigma\tilde{\phi}_\infty}-\frac{Tr\left(\tilde{\phi}_d\right)}{\Sigma\tilde{\phi}_\infty}\right)=C_d^w\frac{\Sigma\tilde{\phi}_d}{\Sigma\tilde{\phi}_\infty} \tag{14}$$

Data

We collect the OFR FSI categorical indicators data between January 3, 2000, and January 22, 2021 from the Office of Financial Research website[4]. The OFR FSI incorporates five categories of indicators and reflects stress contributions by three regions such as the US, Japan, the Eurozone, and emerging economies (Monin, 2019).

EMPIRICAL RESULTS

Dynamics of FSI Categorical Indicators

Figure 1 exhibits FSI categorical indicators from January 3, 2000 to January 22, 2021.

As Figure 1 clearly shows the FSI categorical indicators noticeably soars during financial turmoil times such as the GFC, the European Sovereign Debt Crisis (ESDC), the Brexit referendum, and the recent COVID-19 pandemic. Except for safe assets, all series peak in October 2008 shortly after the Lehman Brother's collapse on September 15, 2008. Distinctively, safe assets indicator peaks on February 4, 2003.

The DY and the BK Connectedness Analysis

We estimate the total interdependencies between the FSI categorical variables5 in a 200-day rolling window with 10-day forecast ahead6 by employing the DY methodology. Figure 2 exhibits the total interdependencies between the FSI categorical indicators with prominent turmoil incidents.

The total spillover index (SOI) fluctuates between 23% and 70% between October 2000 and January 2021. The SOI peaks on March 12, 2020, shortly after the official declaration of Covid pandemic by the WHO[7], and reaches its trough on December 2, 2005. The index markedly escalates around prominent financial stress incidents and alleviates during financial calm periods. The SOI reaches its first peak on January 1, 2002 (54%), which pertains to the early 2000s dot-com bubble. The index accurately captures prominent incidents of the GFC such as BNP Paribas' redemption of three investment funds on August 9, 2007 (43.26%) and Lehman Brother's collapse on September 15, 2008 (43.05%). The SOI precipitously surges during the ESDC that covers the Greece bailout, the Ireland bailout, the Portugal bailout, the Long-Term Refinancing Operation (LTRO) announcement of ECB, and reaches its second highest value on November 8, 2011 (65.19%). The index gradually declines following the Eurozone crisis, yet it steeply hikes around the stock market downturn in August 2015 due to huge selloffs and around the Brexit referendum on June 23, 2016. With the COVID-19 pandemic, the SOI hits its apex and peaks on March 12, 2020 (69.23%).

Next, we compute overall connectedness among FSI categorical indicators on different frequency bands[8] by implementing the BK methodology. Furthermore, we perform the VAR-LASSO with automatic selection of the LASSO penalty using

Figure 1. FSI Categorical Indicators in January 3, 2000 to January 22, 2021

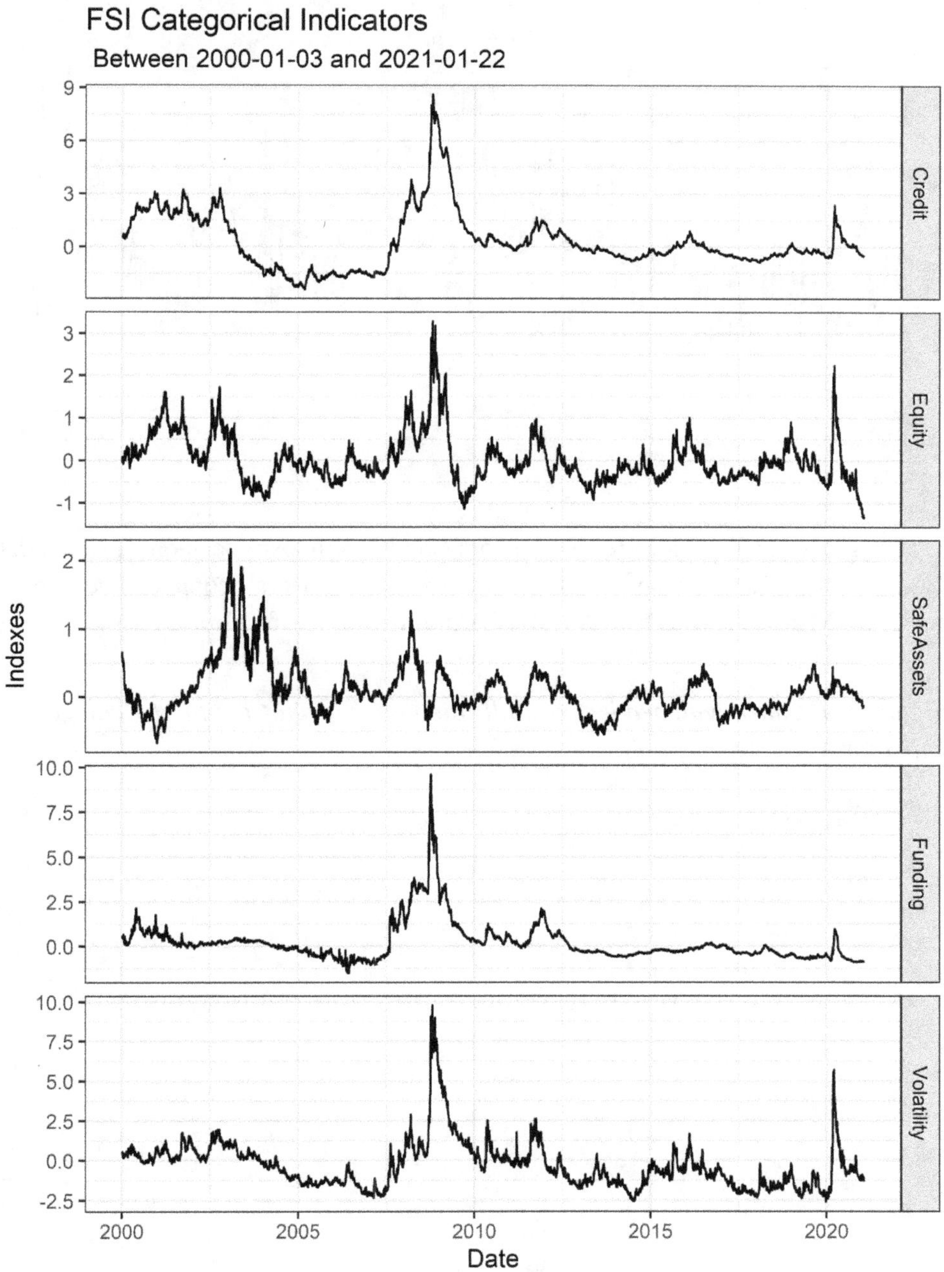

cross-validation. Figure 3 displays the overall frequency connectedness between FSI categorical indicators.

Figure 2. Overall Spillover Index vs. Prominent Incidents

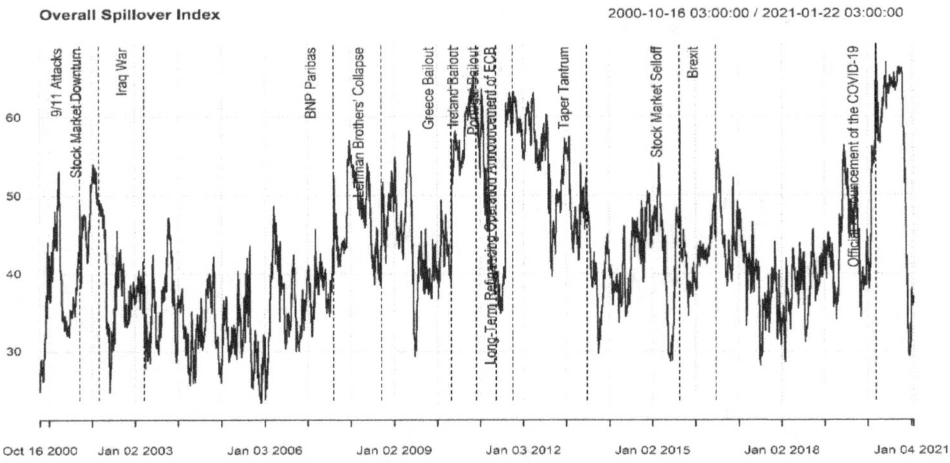

The short-, and medium-term total connectedness indexes peak on April 6, 2020 (80.21%, and 81.84%, respectively), while long-cycle overall connectedness index peaks on March 12, 2020 (74.99%). Sharing a common feature, all three indexes

Figure 3. Frequency-dependent overall interdependencies for the fsi categorical indicators

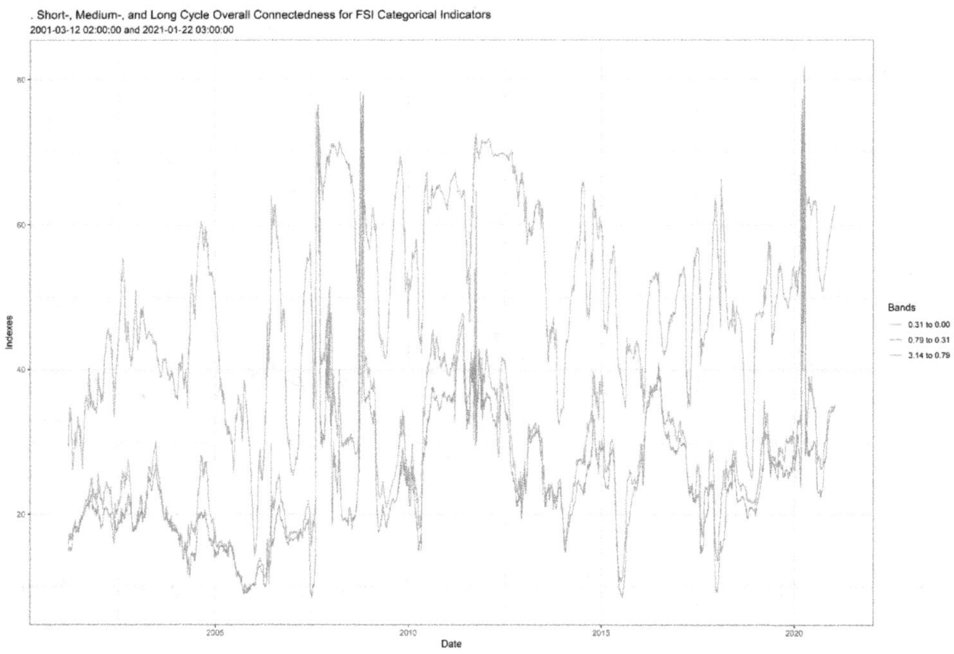

hit their apexes during the ongoing pandemic. Furthermore, the indexes extensively elevate around financial/geopolitical turmoil episodes.

Diagnostic Check

We follow Yoon et al. (2019), we compute overall connectedness in alternative N -day rolling windows and the alternative h -day forecast days. Figure 4 provides the diagnostic check for the DY SOIs in 200-day, and 250-day rolling windows with 2-, 5-, and 10-day forecast horizons.

Figure 4. Diagnostic check for the DY overall connectedness

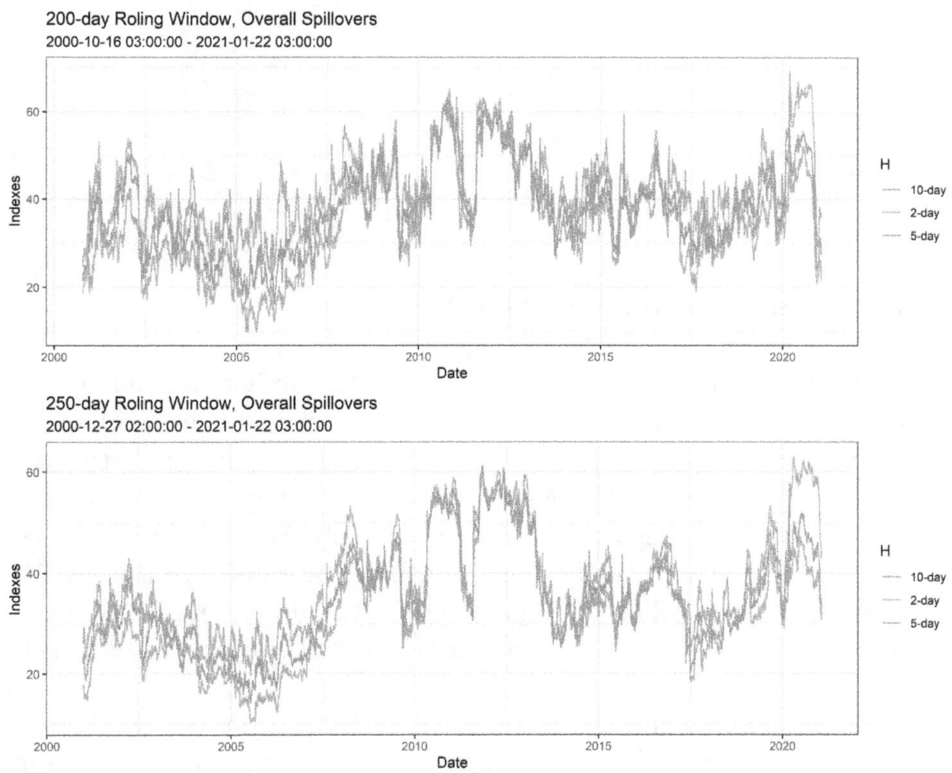

Overall spillovers exhibited in Figure 4 display similar patterns stating that the DY results are insensitive to the window length or forecast horizons.

Figure 5. Transitory connectedness network for the FSI categorical indicators

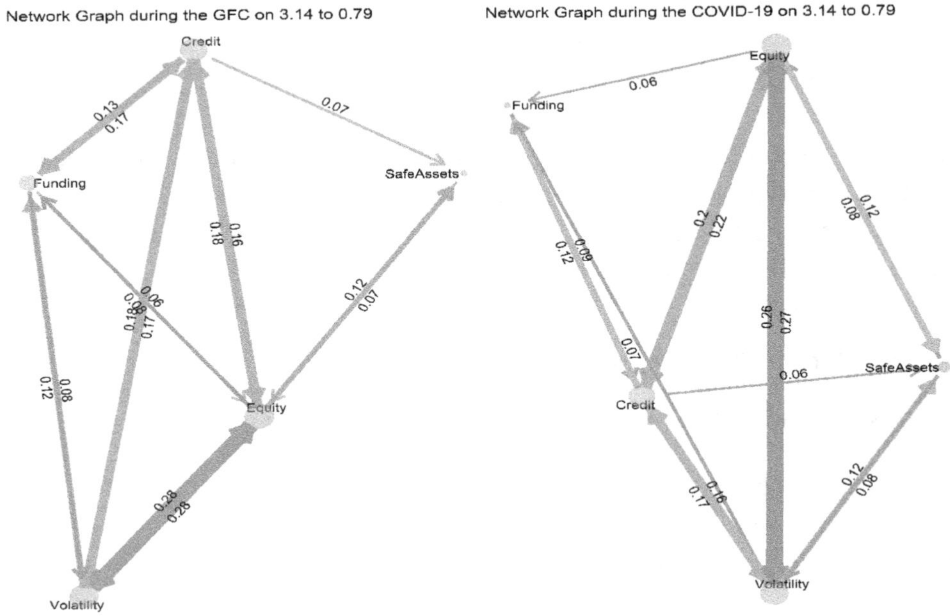

Network Structure of the Connectedness

The next phase of the study explicitly focuses on the transitory network linkages among the FSI categorical indicators, since a vast amount of systematic risk spreads in the short-run (Diebold and Yilmaz, 2014). Consequently, we estimate the transitory connectedness network for FSI categorical indicators reflecting two financial turmoil periods the GFC, and the ongoing pandemic, respectively. We select the GFC episode as 2007/08/01 – 2009/11/01 by following the Bank for International Settlements (BIS, 2009). We select the timeline for the pandemic as 2020/01/01-2021/01/21[9]. Figure 4 presents the short-cycle network connectedness of FSI categorical indicators for the GFC and COVID-19 pandemic episodes.

Network topologies provide valuable insights on the connectedness between FSI categorical indicators during two financial bursts. First, equity and volatility indicators catalyst the largest total spillovers (66.3%, and 63.6%, respectively), and followed by the credit indicator (56.5%). This finding highlights the essential role of equity, and volatility channels in propagating spillovers during the GFC and in line with the previous studies (Dungey and Gajurel, 2014; Luchtenberg and Vu, 2015). Contrariwise, the safe assets indicator transmits the lowest amount of total spillovers (15.9%) as expected. Second, the volatility/equity pair has the tightest connectedness and followed by volatility/credit, equity/credit, and credit/funding pairs. On the other hand, the pair credit/safe assets have the weakest interdependence.

Equity and volatility indicators keep their leading roles in transmitting spillovers during the COVID-19 pandemic (66.7%, and 62.6%, respectively) and followed by the credit indicator (54.6%). On the contrary, the funding indicator propagates the least amount of total spillovers (21.2%). Likewise, the volatility/equity pair has the strongest interdependence for the pandemic episode and followed by the equity/credit pair. The rest pairs are characterized by moderate connectedness, and hereby signify the essential role of the COVID-19 on the connectedness among the FSI categorical indicators.

CONCLUSION

The new type of coronavirus SARS-Cov-2 emerged in late 2019 and expeditiously spilled across the globe. The catastrophic impacts of the pandemic have sorely hit the world economy, and it has witnessed the worst economic downturn since the GFC (Ozili and Arun, 2020).

In this work, we implement two novel methodologies to examine connectedness among the FSI categorical indicators (credit, equity, funding, safe assets, and volatility) between 2000/01/03 and 2021/01/22. Furthermore, we unveil the transitory connectedness network for two financial/geopolitical bursts.

The findings of study can be summarized as follows: First, the SOIs estimated by both methodologies properly captures prominent incidents. Second, sharing a common feature, all indexes peak in March or April 2020, which coincidence with the ongoing pandemic. This result highlights the significant impact of the COVID-19 pandemic on the financial contagion and in line with the previous studies (Gunay, 2021). Third, the transitory connectedness network provides valuable insights for the interdependence of FSI categorical indicators. In consistent with the related literature, we determine that the equity and volatility indicators catalyst the largest total spillovers for the both of the periods. This result underlines the key roles of the equity and volatility channels in two burst episodes. Contrariwise, the safe assets and the funding indicators transmit the lowest shocks. Furthermore, our results assert that the strongest interdependence exist among the equity and the volatility indicators for both periods, and the rest of the pairs are characterized by moderate or strong connectedness.

Precipitously intensified interdependence between FSI categorical indicators during the recent COVID-19 pandemic highlights the severity of the crisis. Despite fiscal/monetary stimulus enacted by the governments' aftermath of the outbreak and launching vaccination in early 2021, the devastating effects of the crisis continue to disperse around the globe. In the light of this, authorities should continue to launch fiscal/monetary stimulus and high-income countries and international organizations can allocate funds for low-income and medium-income countries (LMICs) in alleviating the harmful effects of the pandemic on real/financial-economic activity.

Future research can focus on the connectedness among the FSIs of emerging and advanced economies by implementing newly engineered connectedness methodologies. In this context, the time-varying parameter-VAR-based connectedness approaches could be helpful.

REFERENCES

Abuzayed, B., Bouri, E., Al-Fayoumi, N., & Jalkh, N. (2021). Systemic risk spillover across global and country stock markets during the COVID-19 pandemic. *Economic Analysis and Policy*, *71*, 180–197. doi:10.1016/j.eap.2021.04.010

Adekoya, O. B., & Oliyide, J. A. (2020). How COVID-19 drives connectedness among commodity and financial markets: Evidence from TVP-VAR and causality-in-quantiles techniques. *Resources Policy*, 101898. PMID:34173426

Albulescu, C. T. (2021). COVID-19 and the United States financial markets' volatility. *Finance Research Letters*, *38*, 101699. doi:10.1016/j.frl.2020.101699 PMID:32837380

Angelopoulou, E., Balfoussia, H., & Gibson, H. D. (2014). Building a financial conditions index for the euro area and selected euro area countries: What does it tell us about the crisis? *Economic Modelling*, *38*, 392–403. doi:10.1016/j.econmod.2014.01.013

Aslanidis, N., Bariviera, A. F., & Perez-Laborda, A. (2021). Are cryptocurrencies becoming more interconnected? *Economics Letters*, *199*, 109725. doi:10.1016/j.econlet.2021.109725

Baig, T., & Goldfajn, I. (1999). Financial market contagion in the Asian crisis. *IMF Staff Papers*, *46*(2), 167–195.

Balakrishnan, R., Danninger, S., Elekdag, S., & Tytell, I. (2011). The transmission of financial stress from advanced to emerging economies. *Emerging Markets Finance and Trade, 47*(sup2), 40-68.

Balli, F., de Bruin, A., Chowdhury, M. I. H., & Naeem, M. A. (2020). Connectedness of cryptocurrencies and prevailing uncertainties. *Applied Economics Letters*, *27*(16), 1316–1322. doi:10.1080/13504851.2019.1678724

Barigozzi, M., Hallin, M., Soccorsi, S., & von Sachs, R. (2021). Time-varying general dynamic factor models and the measurement of financial connectedness. *Journal of Econometrics, 222*(1), 324–343. doi:10.1016/j.jeconom.2020.07.004

Baruník, J., Kočenda, E., & Vácha, L. (2017). Asymmetric volatility connectedness on the forex market. *Journal of International Money and Finance, 77*, 39–56. doi:10.1016/j.jimonfin.2017.06.003

Baruník, J., & Křehlík, T. (2018). Measuring the frequency dynamics of financial connectedness and systemic risk. *Journal of Financial Econometrics, 16*(2), 271–296. doi:10.1093/jjfinec/nby001

Baur, D. (2003). Testing for contagion—Mean and volatility contagion. *Journal of Multinational Financial Management, 13*(4-5), 405–422. doi:10.1016/S1042-444X(03)00018-5

Beirne, J., Caporale, G. M., Schulze-Ghattas, M., & Spagnolo, N. (2013). Volatility spillovers and contagion from mature to emerging stock markets. *Review of International Economics, 21*(5), 1060–1075. doi:10.1111/roie.12091

BIS. (2009). *The international financial crisis: Timeline, impact and policy responses in Asia and the Pacific. BIS Papers No 52*. Bank for International Settlements.

Borgards, O., Czudaj, R. L., & Van Hoang, T. H. (2021). Price overreactions in the commodity futures market: An intraday analysis of the Covid-19 pandemic impact. *Resources Policy, 71*, 101966. doi:10.1016/j.resourpol.2020.101966 PMID:36569184

Bouri, E., Cepni, O., Gabauer, D., & Gupta, R. (2021). Return connectedness across asset classes around the COVID-19 outbreak. *International Review of Financial Analysis, 73*, 101646. doi:10.1016/j.irfa.2020.101646

Brave, S. A., & Butters, R. A. (2011). Monitoring financial stability: A financial conditions index approach. *Economic Perspectives, 35*(1), 22.

Calvo, S., & Reinhart, C. (1996). *Capital Flows to Latin America: Is there Evidence of Contagion Effects?* World Bank Policy Research Working Paper Series 1619.

Cambón, M. I., & Estévez, L. (2016). A Spanish financial market stress index (FMSI). *The Spanish Review of Financial Economics, 14*(1), 23–41. doi:10.1016/j.srfe.2016.01.002

Çamlıca, F. (2016). Responsiveness of monetary policy to financial stress in Turkey. *Central Bank Review, 16*(4), 143–150. doi:10.1016/j.cbrev.2016.11.003

Casado, M. G., Glennon, B., Lane, J., McQuown, D., Rich, D., & Weinberg, B. A. (2020). *The Effect of Fiscal Stimulus: Evidence from COVID-19 (No. w27576).* National Bureau of Economic Research.

Cevik, E. I., Dibooglu, S., & Kenc, T. (2013). Measuring financial stress in Turkey. *Journal of Policy Modeling*, *35*(2), 370–383. doi:10.1016/j.jpolmod.2012.06.003

Chadwick, M. G., & Ozturk, H. (2019). Measuring financial systemic stress for Turkey: A search for the best composite indicator. *Economic Systems*, *43*(1), 151–172. doi:10.1016/j.ecosys.2018.09.004

Chancharoenchai, K., & Dibooglu, S. (2006). Volatility spillovers and contagion during the Asian crisis: Evidence from six Southeast Asian stock markets. *Emerging Markets Finance & Trade*, *42*(2), 4–17. doi:10.2753/REE1540-496X420201

Chandy, L., Gertz, G., & Linn, J. (2009). *Tracking the global financial crisis: An analysis of the IMF's world economic outlook.* Wolfensohn Center for Development at Brookings. http://www. brookings. edu/reports/2009/05_financial_crisis _linn. aspx.

Choi, S. Y. (2022). Volatility spillovers among Northeast Asia and the US: Evidence from the global financial crisis and the COVID-19 pandemic. *Economic Analysis and Policy*, *73*, 179–193. doi:10.1016/j.eap.2021.11.014

Chou, R., Ng, V., & Pi, L. (1994). Cointegration of International Stock Market Indices. *IMF Working Paper*, *94*(94), i. doi:10.5089/9781451950700.001

Choudhry, T., & Jayasekera, R. (2014). Returns and volatility spillover in the European banking industry during global financial crisis: Flight to perceived quality or contagion? *International Review of Financial Analysis*, *36*, 36–45. doi:10.1016/j.irfa.2014.05.003

Cipollini, A., & Mikaliunaite, I. (2020). Macro-uncertainty and financial stress spillovers in the Eurozone. *Economic Modelling*, *89*, 546–558. doi:10.1016/j.econmod.2019.11.017

Corbet, S., Larkin, C., & Lucey, B. (2020). The contagion effects of the COVID-19 pandemic: Evidence from gold and cryptocurrencies. *Finance Research Letters*, *35*, 101554. doi:10.1016/j.frl.2020.101554

Corbet, S., Meegan, A., Larkin, C., Lucey, B., & Yarovaya, L. (2018). Exploring the dynamic relationships between cryptocurrencies and other financial assets. *Economics Letters*, *165*, 28–34. doi:10.1016/j.econlet.2018.01.004

Cronin, D., & Dunne, P. G. (2019). How effective are sovereign bond-backed securities as a spillover prevention device? *Journal of International Money and Finance*, *96*, 49–66. doi:10.1016/j.jimonfin.2019.05.001

Demirer, M., Diebold, F. X., Liu, L., & Yilmaz, K. (2018). Estimating global bank network connectedness. *Journal of Applied Econometrics*, *33*(1), 1–15. doi:10.1002/jae.2585

Diebold, F. X., Liu, L., & Yilmaz, K. (2017). *Commodity connectedness (No. w23685)*. National Bureau of Economic Research. doi:10.3386/w23685

Diebold, F. X., & Yilmaz, K. (2009). Measuring financial asset return and volatility spillovers, with application to global equity markets. *Economic Journal (London)*, *119*(534), 158–171. doi:10.1111/j.1468-0297.2008.02208.x

Diebold, F. X., & Yilmaz, K. (2012). Better to give than to receive: Predictive directional measurement of volatility spillovers. *International Journal of Forecasting*, *28*(1), 57–66. doi:10.1016/j.ijforecast.2011.02.006

Diebold, F. X., & Yılmaz, K. (2014). On the network topology of variance decompositions: Measuring the connectedness of financial firms. *Journal of Econometrics*, *182*(1), 119–134. doi:10.1016/j.jeconom.2014.04.012

Diebold, F. X., & Yilmaz, K. (2015). Trans-Atlantic equity volatility connectedness: US and European financial institutions, 2004–2014. *Journal of Financial Econometrics*, *14*(1), 81–127.

Dungey, M., & Gajurel, D. (2014). Equity market contagion during the global financial crisis: Evidence from the world's eight largest economies. *Economic Systems*, *38*(2), 161–177. doi:10.1016/j.ecosys.2013.10.003

Duprey, T., Klaus, B., & Peltonen, T. (2017). Dating systemic financial stress episodes in the EU countries. *Journal of Financial Stability*, *32*, 30–56. doi:10.1016/j.jfs.2017.07.004

Edwards, S. (1998). *Interest rate volatility, capital controls, and contagion* (No. w6756). National Bureau of Economic Research.

Edwards, S., & Susmel, R. (2001). Volatility dependence and contagion in emerging equity markets. *Journal of Development Economics*, *66*(2), 505–532. doi:10.1016/S0304-3878(01)00172-9

Fasanya, I. O., Oyewole, O., Adekoya, O. B., & Odei-Mensah, J. (2020). Dynamic spillovers and connectedness between COVID-19 pandemic and global foreign exchange markets. *Economic Research-Ekonomska Istraživanja*, 1-26.

Furceri, D., Ganslmeier, M., Ostry, J. D., & Yang, N. (2021). *Initial Output Losses from the Covid- 19 Pandemic: Robust Determinants (No. 2021/018)*. International Monetary Fund.

Goodell, J. W. (2020). COVID-19 and finance: Agendas for future research. *Finance Research Letters, 35*, 101512. doi:10.1016/j.frl.2020.101512 PMID:32562472

Gunay, S. (2021). Comparing COVID-19 with the GFC: A shockwave analysis of currency markets. *Research in International Business and Finance, 56*, 101377. doi:10.1016/j.ribaf.2020.101377 PMID:36540770

Hakkio, C. S., & Keeton, W. R. (2009). Financial stress: What is it, how can it be measured, and why does it matter? *Economic Review (Kansas City, Mo.), 94*(2), 5–50.

Hamao, Y., Masulis, R. W., & Ng, V. (1990). Correlations in price changes and volatility across international stock markets. *Review of Financial Studies, 3*(2), 281–307. doi:10.1093/rfs/3.2.281

Hernandez, J. A., Kang, S. H., Shahzad, S. J. H., & Yoon, S. M. (2020). Spillovers and diversification potential of bank equity returns from developed and emerging America. *The North American Journal of Economics and Finance, 54*, 101219. doi:10.1016/j.najef.2020.101219

Holló, D., Kremer, M., & Lo Duca, M. (2012). *CISS-a composite indicator of systemic stress in the financial system* (No. 1426). ECB Working Paper.

Huotari, J. (2015). *Measuring financial stress–A country specific stress index for Finland*. Bank of Finland Research Discussion Paper, (7).

Huynh, T. L. D., Nasir, M. A., & Nguyen, D. K. (2020). Spillovers and connectedness in foreign exchange markets: The role of trade policy uncertainty. *The Quarterly Review of Economics and Finance, 79*, 1–14. doi:10.1016/j.qref.2020.09.001 PMID:33052186

Illing, M., & Liu, Y. (2006). Measuring financial stress in a developed country: An application to Canada. *Journal of Financial Stability, 2*(3), 243–265. doi:10.1016/j.jfs.2006.06.002

Islami, M., & Kurz-Kim, J. R. (2014). A single composite financial stress indicator and its real impact in the euro area. *International Journal of Finance & Economics, 19*(3), 204–211. doi:10.1002/ijfe.1483

Ji, Q., Bouri, E., Lau, C. K. M., & Roubaud, D. (2019). Dynamic connectedness and integration in cryptocurrency markets. *International Review of Financial Analysis, 63*, 257–272. doi:10.1016/j.irfa.2018.12.002

Karkowska, R., & Urjasz, S. (2021). Connectedness structures of sovereign bond markets in Central and Eastern Europe. *International Review of Financial Analysis*, *74*, 101644. doi:10.1016/j.irfa.2020.101644

Karolyi, G. A., & Stulz, R. M. (1996). Why do markets move together? An investigation of US-Japan stock return comovements. *The Journal of Finance*, *51*(3), 951–986. doi:10.1111/j.1540-6261.1996.tb02713.x

Kliesen, K. L., & Smith, D. C. (2010). *Measuring financial market stress. Economic Synopses*. Federal Reserve Bank of St. Louis.

Koop, G., & Korobilis, D. (2014). A new index of financial conditions. *European Economic Review*, *71*, 101–116. doi:10.1016/j.euroecorev.2014.07.002

Laborda, R., & Olmo, J. (2021). Volatility spillover between economic sectors in financial crisis prediction: Evidence spanning the great financial crisis and Covid-19 pandemic. *Research in International Business and Finance*, *57*, 101402. doi:10.1016/j.ribaf.2021.101402

Lang, L. H., & Stulz, R. (1992). Contagion and competitive intra-industry effects of bankruptcy announcements: An empirical analysis. *Journal of Financial Economics*, *32*(1), 45–60. doi:10.1016/0304-405X(92)90024-R

Lee, S. B., & Kim, K. J. (1993). Does the October 1987 crash strengthen the co-movements among national stock markets? *Review of Financial Economics*, *3*(1), 89–102. doi:10.1002/j.1873-5924.1993.tb00574.x

Li, X., Li, B., Wei, G., Bai, L., Wei, Y., & Liang, C. (2021). Return connectedness among commodity and financial assets during the COVID-19 pandemic: Evidence from China and the US. *Resources Policy*, *73*, 102166. doi:10.1016/j.resourpol.2021.102166 PMID:34539034

Lin, B., & Su, T. (2021). Does COVID-19 open a Pandora's box of changing the connectedness in energy commodities? *Research in International Business and Finance*, *56*, 101360. doi:10.1016/j.ribaf.2020.101360 PMID:36540766

Magkonis, G., & Tsopanakis, A. (2020). The financial connectedness between Eurozone core and periphery: A disaggregated view. *Macroeconomic Dynamics*, *24*(7), 1674–1699. doi:10.1017/S1365100518000998

Mensi, W., Al-Yahyaee, K. H., Vo, X. V., & Kang, S. H. (2020). Dynamic spillover and connectedness between oil futures and European Bonds. *The North American Journal of Economics and Finance*, 101342.

Mensi, W., Reboredo, J. C., & Ugolini, A. (2021). Price-switching spillovers between gold, oil, and stock markets: Evidence from the USA and China during the COVID-19 pandemic. *Resources Policy*, *73*, 102217. doi:10.1016/j.resourpol.2021.102217 PMID:36567727

Minoiu, C., Kang, C., Subrahmanian, V. S., & Berea, A. (2015). Does financial connectedness predict crises? *Quantitative Finance*, *15*(4), 607–624. doi:10.1080/14697688.2014.968358

Monin, P. J. (2019). The OFR financial stress index. *Risks*, *7*(1), 25. doi:10.3390/risks7010025

Naeem, M. A., Qureshi, S., Rehman, M. U., & Balli, F. (2022). COVID-19 and cryptocurrency market: Evidence from quantile connectedness. *Applied Economics*, *54*(3), 280–306. doi:10.1080/00036846.2021.1950908

Narayan, P. K., Devpura, N., & Wang, H. (2020). Japanese currency and stock market—What happened during the COVID-19 pandemic? *Economic Analysis and Policy*, *68*, 191–198. doi:10.1016/j.eap.2020.09.014 PMID:33012962

Oet, M. V., Dooley, J. M., & Ong, S. J. (2015). The financial stress index: Identification of systemic risk conditions. *Risks*, *3*(3), 420–444. doi:10.3390/risks3030420

Ozili, P., & Arun, T. (2020). *Spillover of COVID-19: Impact on the Global Economy (No. 99317).* University Library of Munich.

Park, C. Y., & Mercado, R. V. Jr. (2014). Determinants of financial stress in emerging market economies. *Journal of Banking & Finance*, *45*, 199–224. doi:10.1016/j.jbankfin.2013.09.018

Polat, O. (2019). Systemic risk contagion in FX market: A frequency connectedness and network analysis. *Bulletin of Economic Research*, *71*(4), 585–598. doi:10.1111/boer.12197

Polat, O. (2020). Measuring dynamic connectedness networks in energy commodities: Evidence from the D-Y and frequency connectedness approaches. *OPEC Energy Review*, *44*(4), 404–428. doi:10.1111/opec.12188

Polat, O., & Ozkan, I. (2019). Transmission mechanisms of financial stress into economic activity in Turkey. *Journal of Policy Modeling*, *41*(2), 395–415. doi:10.1016/j.jpolmod.2019.02.010

Rai, K., & Garg, B. (2021). Dynamic correlations and volatility spillovers between stock price and exchange rate in BRIICS economies: Evidence from the COVID-19 outbreak period. *Applied Economics Letters*, 1–8.

Sahoo, J. (2021). Financial stress index, growth and price stability in India: Some recent evidence. *Transnational Corporations Review, 13*(2), 222–236. doi:10.1080/19186444.2020.1768789

Sakurai, Y., & Kurosaki, T. (2020). How has the relationship between oil and the US stock market changed after the Covid-19 crisis? *Finance Research Letters, 37*, 101773. doi:10.1016/j.frl.2020.101773 PMID:33046963

Samitas, A., Kampouris, E., & Polyzos, S. (2022). Covid-19 pandemic and spillover effects in stock markets: A financial network approach. *International Review of Financial Analysis, 80*, 102005. doi:10.1016/j.irfa.2021.102005 PMID:36536788

Sarwar, S., Tiwari, A. K., & Tingqiu, C. (2020). Analyzing volatility spillovers between oil market and Asian stock markets. *Resources Policy, 66*, 101608. doi:10.1016/j.resourpol.2020.101608

Shahzad, S. J. H., Naeem, M. A., Peng, Z., & Bouri, E. (2021). Asymmetric volatility spillover among Chinese sectors during COVID-19. *International Review of Financial Analysis, 75*, 101754. doi:10.1016/j.irfa.2021.101754 PMID:36568735

Si, D. K., Li, X. L., Xu, X., & Fang, Y. (2021). The risk spillover effect of the COVID-19 pandemic on energy sector: Evidence from China. *Energy Economics, 102*, 105498. doi:10.1016/j.eneco.2021.105498 PMID:34898735

So, M. K., Tiwari, A., Chu, A. M., Tsang, J. T., & Chan, J. N. (2020). Visualizing COVID-19 pandemic risk through network connectedness. *International Journal of Infectious Diseases, 96*, 558–561. doi:10.1016/j.ijid.2020.05.011 PMID:32437929

Stolbov, M., & Shchepeleva, M. (2016). Financial stress in emerging markets: Patterns, real effects, and cross-country spillovers. *Review of Development Finance, 6*(1), 71–81. doi:10.1016/j.rdf.2016.05.004

Susmel, R., & Engle, R. F. (1994). Hourly volatility spillovers between international equity markets. *Journal of International Money and Finance, 13*(1), 3–25. doi:10.1016/0261-5606(94)90021-3

Umar, Z., & Gubareva, M. (2021). Faith-based investments and the Covid-19 pandemic: Analyzing equity volatility and media coverage time-frequency relations. *Pacific-Basin Finance Journal, 67*, 101571. doi:10.1016/j.pacfin.2021.101571

Umar, Z., Riaz, Y., & Zaremba, A. (2021). Spillover and risk transmission in the components of the term structure of eurozone yield curve. *Applied Economics, 53*(18), 2141–2157. doi:10.1080/00036846.2020.1856322 van Roye, B. (2014). Financial stress and economic activity in Germany. *Empirica, 41*(1), 101–126. doi:10.100710663-013-9224-0

Wang, G. J., Xie, C., Zhao, L., & Jiang, Z. Q. (2018). Volatility connectedness in the Chinese banking system: Do state-owned commercial banks contribute more? *Journal of International Financial Markets, Institutions and Money, 57*, 205–230. doi:10.1016/j.intfin.2018.07.008

Wang, Y., Pan, Z., & Wu, C. (2018). Volatility spillover from the US to international stock markets: A heterogeneous volatility spillover GARCH model. *Journal of Forecasting, 37*(3), 385–400. doi:10.1002/for.2509

Wei, Z., Luo, Y., Huang, Z., & Guo, K. (2020). Spillover effects of RMB exchange rate among B&R countries: Before and during COVID-19 event. *Finance Research Letters, 37*, 101782. doi:10.1016/j.frl.2020.101782 PMID:33013238

Wen, T., & Wang, G. J. (2020). Volatility connectedness in global foreign exchange markets. *Journal of Multinational Financial Management, 54*, 100617. doi:10.1016/j.mulfin.2020.100617

Wu, F. (2020). Stock market integration in East and Southeast Asia: The role of global factors. *International Review of Financial Analysis, 67*, 101416. doi:10.1016/j.irfa.2019.101416

Yoon, S. M., Al Mamun, M., Uddin, G. S., & Kang, S. H. (2019). Network connectedness and net spillover between financial and commodity markets. *The North American Journal of Economics and Finance, 48*, 801–818. doi:10.1016/j.najef.2018.08.012

Zhang, D., & Broadstock, D. C. (2018). Global financial crisis and rising connectedness in the international commodity markets. *International Review of Financial Analysis*, 101239.

Zhang, D., Hu, M., & Ji, Q. (2020). Financial markets under the global pandemic of COVID- 19. *Finance Research Letters, 36*, 101528. doi:10.1016/j.frl.2020.101528 PMID:32837360

Zhang, H., Chen, J., & Shao, L. (2021). Dynamic spillovers between energy and stock markets and their implications in the context of COVID-19. *International Review of Financial Analysis, 77*, 101828. doi:10.1016/j.irfa.2021.101828 PMID:36570866

ENDNOTES

1 See https://www.worldometers.info/coronavirus.
2 See https://ourworldindata.org/covid-vaccinations.

3 See https://financialconnectedness.org/.

4 See https://www.financialresearch.gov/financial-stress-index/ for details about the categorical FSI indicators.

5 We perform the ADF, the PP, and the KPSS unit root tests for FSI categorical indicators. Except the credit indicator, all series are I(0) at %1 significance level, thereby we omit the credit indicator for the estimations of overall spillover index. The unit root tests estimations are not covered to save space and available upon request.

6 We select the optimal order of the VAR as 25 by the Akaike Information Criterion (AIC) and the Bayesian Information Criterion (BIC).

7 See https://www.euro.who.int/en/health-topics/health-emergencies /coronavirus-covid-19/news/news/2020/3/who-announces-covid-1 9-outbreak-a-pandemic.

8 $(\pi, \pi / 4)$, $(\pi / 4, \pi / 10)$, and $(\pi / 10, 0)$ correspond to 1 days to 4 days, 4 days to 10 days, and 10 days to infinity days connectedness, respectively.

9 The total identified cases of the pandemic have an exponential growth on the study date (2021/01/21).

Chapter 3
Corporate Financing Decisions During a Crisis:
An Empirical Review

Padmalosani Dayalan
University of Technology and Applied Sciences, Oman

ABSTRACT

This chapter reviews the literature on corporate financing decisions during a crisis. The COVID-19 pandemic impacted all walks of life: individual, corporate, and government. Decisions on corporate finance influence a firm's survival and growth and are influenced by many factors, like the investment opportunities, cost of capital, firm age, current capital structure, availability of funds, etc. This chapter sheds light on the factors that influence corporate financing during a crisis. Various crises, including the global financial crisis and COVID-19 crisis, influenced the corporate world, and corporate responses to these crises were detailed. The chapter reviews the empirical literature on the subject. It is observed that though the availability of external funds during a crisis is affected, corporates prefer to increase their leverage during a financial crisis when funds are required for operations. Similarly, the study also found that firms utilized retained earnings and deferred dividend payments during the crisis to make funds available to meet contingency and maintain sustainability.

INTRODUCTION

Corporate finance decisions are crucial to value creation. Corporate financing is a part of financial management decisions that include investment, dividend and working capital management decisions. All these decisions are interrelated; for

DOI: 10.4018/978-1-6684-5342-1.ch003

instance, investment decisions influence the financing decisions and vice versa, and the dividend decisions are influenced by the investment decisions. (Bhabra, 2008) pointed out the following factors like tangible assets, size, profitability, and growth opportunities have a significant effect on the performance of the company. (Frank, 2009) suggested that the following factors are reliable for explaining market leverage: median industry leverage, market-to-book assets ratio, asset tangibility, profits, asset log, and expected inflation Several firm-specific factors, such as firm age, the complexity of business, existing capital structure, risk and return expectations, influence corporate finance decisions. During pandemic investors tried different strategies like changing their management portfolios in various ways by allocating less to stocks (Guiso, 2018) and due to ambiguity investors' sentiments had an influence on volatility and market returns were considered very important (Lee, 2002). Besides the firm characteristics, macroeconomic factors and stakeholders' sentiments also significantly affect corporate finance decisions. For instance, investors' sentiments influence their investment decisions, overreaction and underreaction, overconfidence and herd behavior (Metawa, Hassan, Metawa, & Safa, 2019). Macroeconomic conditions result in changes in investors' sentiments, affecting the availability of funds and the demand for securities that corporations offer. (Jess Benhabib, 2016). Thus, corporate finance decisions are complex and influenced by firm-specific, investor-specific, and macroeconomic factors.

Many factors influence financing decisions and are debated extensively in academic and empirical literature. Corporate financing decisions focus on the supply side, and the decisions are broadly termed capital structure decisions. Capital structure is the composition of debt and equity financing a firm's assets (Titman & Wessels, 1988). A firm can obtain funds to finance its assets and operations from equity and debt. In addition, a firm may also utilize retained earnings to finance its operations. Each source of finance has its characteristics. Firms leverage when they utilize borrowed funds to maximize shareholder wealth. Borrowed funds carry fixed obligations.

On the other hand, the issue of common stock dilutes ownership (Bui, 2022). Firms consider many factors while considering financing options. For instance, the maximum usage of internal sources of financing is mostly affected by its accessibility, risk problems, and tax factors (Santos & Cincera, 2021). A firm's financing decisions are closely related to investment decisions (Chirella, 1992). Hirsh and Walz (2009) explained that pecking and tradeoff theories are pivotal in explaining firms' financing decisions.

Corporate leaders gauge the influence of many factors, for instance, the firm size, existing capital structure, and business growth prospects, while making financial management decisions. However, corporate financing decisions in a crisis are complex. A crisis, for instance, the recent crisis created by the COVID-19 pandemic, poses significant stress on the demand and supply paradigm, the availability and utilization of funds, the utilization of assets and the presence of high fixed costs.

The decisions which affect the capital structure are planned and permanent business decisions at difficult times (Porumboiu, 2020). From a macroscopic view, there are differences in corporate finance behavior during regular and crisis periods. Planning is a complex process due to unclear economic conditions and demand and supply cycles. Corporations revise the existing plans and priorities in a crisis to accommodate the changes in macroeconomic and microeconomic characteristics. The availability of funds, the investment avenues, the behavior of investors and the uncertainty of crisis etc., are critical in capital structure decisions during a crisis period. Financial strategy is the foundation for competitive business models (Alejandra, 2012). Panjaitan and Simbolon (2020) explained that firms exhibit a herding behavior during a crisis, wherein the decisions are not based on their perspective but rather a group behavior. The financial decision-making behavior of firms is explained by the "pecking order" view of capital structure (Abdulla, 1998). Obtaining funds from financial institutions and other corporates is not daunting during inflationary periods. However, banks and other financial institutions follow a precautionary approach during a crisis, so obtaining borrowed funds becomes quite difficult.

In a recent IMF working paper, Deghi et al. (2021) mentioned severe disruptions to corporate funding markets during COVID-19 in advanced economies as corporate bond funds, loan accounts, and major capital market reserves had faced more spendings. This led to the breakdown in the issuing of nonfinancial corporate bonds, syndicated loans, and commercial paper and to a jump in corporate spreads. This chapter reviews the empirical literature on corporate financing during the crisis, specifically to discuss the factors that corporations evaluate while selecting corporate financing decisions during a crisis.

BACKGROUND

The pandemic impacted businesses across the globe, irrespective of their size and business models. The pandemic created almost the worst impact on all levels of the firms (Andrew Ellul, 2020). The economic situation was down. Both the supply and demand sides got affected. The risk of debt increased, resources were not mobilized, high currency inflation, the unemployment rate increased, and many issues were created due to this pandemic (Engidaw, 2022). Some firms were struggling to sustain themselves in the long run. Some firms sustained due to their business models during the pandemic period. They redesigned the business models in response to the external environment changes, for instance, moving online. The lockdown and social distancing requirements significantly dented business activities; the supply chain was mostly affected. This has significantly affected the repayment of loans and other obligations (Andrew Ellul, 2020; Zou, 2020). The most affected businesses were the construction sector, hotels, transportation, and restaurant business. (Fairlie, 2020).

Michael Halling (2020) observed that firms tried to use internal sources to manage difficult situations during the crisis. There was a high demand for external capital. Liquidity was challenging during the pandemic situation. The lockdown and suspension of business activities prolonged further in many countries and has significantly affected the demand for all the products. Internally generated funds affected the firm's debt and equity issues. While enterprises in other industry segments try to reorganize toward measures aimed at boosting perseverance, such as explaining away production and SKUs, redeploying talents, rerouting governance roles in the context of teleworking, shifting processes, and introducing new business models, uncertainty appears to be the only confirmation for some sectors that have been severely impacted by the pandemic, such as travel, tourism, hospitality, or the arts. Companies considered trying to recover profits and reworking operations, looking to change the organization, accelerating industrialization, and integrating agile marketing responses. (Pinzaru, 2020)

The pandemic's circumstances of uncertainty aided in stimulating innovation. It resulted in a mass migration of gaining knowledge from traditional face-to-face communication to internet interaction. (Badran, 2021)

New business processes include in business processes and operations, intensive use of technology, adaptability, and green jobs can all become prominent. Corporate strategies are expected to be revised in the context of complex conditions. Emergency procedures and business continuity, Sustainability, and working hours are all major determinants. Business needs new paradigms to be more equipped, adaptable, great thinker, compassionate, groundbreaking, and entrepreneurial. (Alpaslanoğlu, 2021)

In order to develop the finest techniques for managing their organizations and industries, people need to rethink, redesign, and think creatively. To succeed under the current conditions, HR must continue to nurture workers that are creative, proactive, devoted, and dedicated to their employer. They must also maintain enthusiasm and productivity in this challenging environment. The need for restructured and redefined work roles, as well as resource reskilling, is urgent. (Kaushik, 2020)

MAIN FOCUS OF THE CHAPTER

Decisions in Finance

Financial management is defined as planning, organizing, directing, and managing financial aspects of the organization (Ahood & Nobanee, 2021). It ensures how the financial assets are being utilized and managed in the proper utilization of it. Financial management aims to achieve some of its goals. Firstly, it will ensure that enough sources of funds are available to the organization. Second, it concentrates on the application of funds. Third, on the efficient utilization of resources and finally finding the investment opportunities available. Financial management acts as a base for the business in various ways. It helps establishments with financial preparation and fund procurement; it helps organizations make maximum use of the sourced cash. It strengthens businesses in making important financial decisions on time, helps grow business cash flow, increases an organization's total value, and guarantees financial prosperity. The company must consider having an effective financial management system, which leads to the company's success.

Companies generally employ debt and equity finance to generate funds for their operations, but each has advantages and disadvantages. Businesses usually utilize financing according to what the firm requires at any given time. Debt finance entails issuing bonds with the responsibility to repay them later with interest. One of the principal advantages of debt financing is that a corporation will not have to give someone else control of the property and that there are various tax incentives. Ownership is riskier and more expensive than borrowed money; however, the corporation is not required to repay the money. One disadvantage of financial leverage is that the firm might give up some of its interest to the investor assisting in raising capital. (Ghimire, 2021)

Profitability considers long-term funding mechanisms such as debt and equity financing. The corporate structure is a combination of different forms of funding, mainly classified as stocks and bonds. As a result, a firm's capital structure is referred to as its 'Debt To equity ratio Mix.' The potential costs associated with debt versus raising capital are distinct. From the standpoint of the organization raising cash, debt is considered a less expensive type of capital than financial assets. Debt, on the other hand, increases the company's financial risk and may be the source of an increase in ownership prices.

The significance of creating a proper capital structure is vital for every company. Capital Structure increases the market price of a company, i.e., in a company with an appropriately structured capital structure, The cumulative value of the assertions and the equity interests of the shareholders are maximized. It is designed to reduce the business's cost of capital. Identifying the right mix of funding sources allows a company's current capital cost to be kept as low as possible. An increase in the earnings per share can be an advantage for the business. The capital structure will boost the market price through earnings per share. It will also positively impact the number of dividends by the shareholders. It will also improve the new ventures, yielding investment opportunities for the business. It will help build trust among the debt suppliers with correct capital pitching. The country's investment and growth rate will help to get wealthy project investments for the business. (Usman, 2019)

Capital Structure Decisions

Capital structure is an important topic in corporate finance for any commercial organization. Proper capital structure determinations would boost the value of businesses. (Tongkong, 2012). A better understanding of the corporate decision during the crisis will ease the difficulties in obtaining the funds to run their operations. Knowing the association between the firm's value and the capital structure decisions adds value to the business's overall functioning (Asif, 2016). The various theories like tradeoff theory, pecking order theory, and market timing theory help the development of a scientific viewpoint for conceptualizing the major influencing factors of capital structure decisions.

Successful corporations may gain more from debt financing and suffer significantly less during a crisis. The advantages of taxation from debt payments make financial leverage attractive because it eliminates numerous debt finance costs. According to the tradeoff theory, profitability and leverage ratio have a relationship. If the leverage ratio is higher, the better the business performance, and hence it will result in good future investment opportunities. Successful firms generate good cashflows, so they prefer to take on more debt to take advantage of tax benefits and the higher likelihood of a refund. (Ismail, 2007). The tradeoff theory also suggests that the leverage ratio of companies with more significant investment potential in intangible assets that cannot be safeguarded is the lowest (Gropp, 2010). However, in a study on UK, France, and Germany firms, Iqbal and Kume (2014) pointed out that firms' leverage ratio increases during a crisis and then decreases the post-crisis. This observation referred firm's behavior during the financial crisis in 2008. Additionally, they discovered that enterprises with capital structure ratios in the pre-crisis period that were below the industry average gradually increased their leverage both during and after a crisis. On the other hand, companies with capital structure ratios that were greater than the industry average before the crisis saw a considerable drop in their leverage ratios, especially after the crisis.

Successful businesses employ more leverage. The pecking order theory describes how corporations make financing decisions, with retained earnings taking precedence over debt and debt taking precedence over equity. When the companies issue securities, they prefer debt to equity. This theory suggests that profitability should explain a company's leveraging level and that the high-profit enterprises may result in lesser leverage. Due to the reality that a company's financial status fluctuates over time; the concept of market timing has recently gained traction. This theory highlighted how companies decide when they need finance and decide on debt or equity. Firms prefer stock over debt when the cost of equity is less. Stock market conditions should explain the firm's leverage level; in a bullish equity market, companies prefer equity issuance to debt funding. (Tongkong, 2012). The pecking order hypothesis establishes a hierarchy for enterprises' choices regarding the issuance of start - up capital rather than determining an ideal capital structure. (Myers and Majluf, 1984).

In a study on the relationship between the financial crisis and capital structure, Santa (2021) found that financial crisis negatively mapct the total debt ratio of SMEs, and firms decreased their leverage the most after the crisis. The impact of the drivers of the debt maturity ratios varies depending on the kind of company, i.e. large/small enterprises, and the economic cycle, when determining capital structure decisions. (Neves et al., 2020). Firm-specific variables include company growth, size, tangibility, and debt-to-equity ratio, all of which are directly connected to profitability. Several empirical research pointed out that size and profitability have a good relationship (Smirlock, 1985).

The extant literature pointed out that there exist three kinds of impacts on "enterprise value" side by side: approach or "value" effects, based on the formation of the future organizational direction; firm-specific effects, based on the subject matter of the institution's core competencies; and organization-wide implications, based on the business structure applied. The statistical study underlines the "business model" function as a significant moderating mechanism and the complementing impact of "corporate structure".

Economic theories use the cost of capital as a key tool to promote more saving, as higher inflation empowers more savings. At the same time, low rates motivate companies to buy for yet another financing that will yield a greater return. (Murungi, 2014). Similarly, Akers (2014) pointed out that the inflation rate acts basis on the price index and reflects on the changes in the average price level. GDP deflator and consumer price index are the two indicators to quantify inflation better. Different factors influence capital structure decisions, and includes interest rates, political stability, inflation, internal harmony, and governance quality mostly influence the exchange rate in the country. (Egbunike, 2018). Other considerations include age, financial restrictions, tax shelters, market circumstances, agency costs, ownership structure, profitability, size, growth, industry practice, tangibility, and orientation to financial markets. The profitability, asset tangibility, and firm size were the most significant variables influencing capital structure decisions, while the growth and age of the firm do not significantly influence capital structure (Mueller & Sensini, 2021).

However, Salam et al. (2021) observed that the firm's performance is not influenced by the funding decision, the relative share of debt or equity in the capital structure. Huang and Ritter (2021) argued that the anticipated near-future cash needs and fixed financing costs explain the fraction of firms' proceeds (net income) retained.

This argument supports that firm depends on internally generated funds to meet the financing needs during a crisis or when a crisis is anticipated.

A company's assets are classified into two divisions: tangible and intangible. Companies with more physical assets tend to have more debt since they are liable to repay the investors in a short time with small asset value. Companies with more physical assets will rely on more debt, resulting in quicker repayment to the lenders with the available assets. According to the tradeoff theory, the leverage ratio is influenced by the share of tangible assets. Because management engages in suboptimal investment, which exposes debtholders to high risks, there may be a conflict of interests between shareholders and debt holders. (Bukair, 2018). Liquidity is a term used to describe the bank's ability to deal with short-term obligations and unusual withdrawals. Earlier it was also pointed out that the tradeoff perspective has a considerable impact on the leverage ratio and the business liquidity. That paves the way for the companies with a high degree of liquidity (excellent short-term assets) that have reduced financial resources risks and can have access to more debt because they are stable to repay it. Most studies have revealed that the liquidity ratio negatively impacts capital structures. (Sundarajan, 2002)

Factors Influencing Capital Structure Decisions

(Ngoc Bao Vuong, 2022) and (Killins, 2019) pointed out the factors affecting the corporate financing decisions which is given in the above framework. However, such conceptual underpinning may not hold about the capital structure decisions during a crisis. The factors that may influence capital structure decisions may also differ among firms of different sizes, age, and business models. Wronska-Bukalska and Mazurkiewics (2018), in their study based on Polish companies, established that polish companies did not change their capital structure during the crisis. However, they also noted that companies with higher debt ratios before the crisis increased their debt ratio despite the financial crisis.

Covid 19 and Capital Structure Decisions

Globally, the Covid-19 shock has mostly had a negative effect on company profitability and leverage. The median business saw a 2% fall in revenues and earnings, an increase in debt and leverage ratios, and a two-percentage point decline in the interest coverage ratio (ICR), a crucial measure of solvency. (Puy and Rawdanowicz, 2021). The closure of the business operations and travel restrictions within and between the countries wreaked havoc on the global economy. COVID-19 has caused global financial markets to plummet due to the confusion and public fear it has sparked. (He Huang, 2021). Research reveals that capital raising was exceptionally high

Figure 1. Factors influencing capital structure decisions

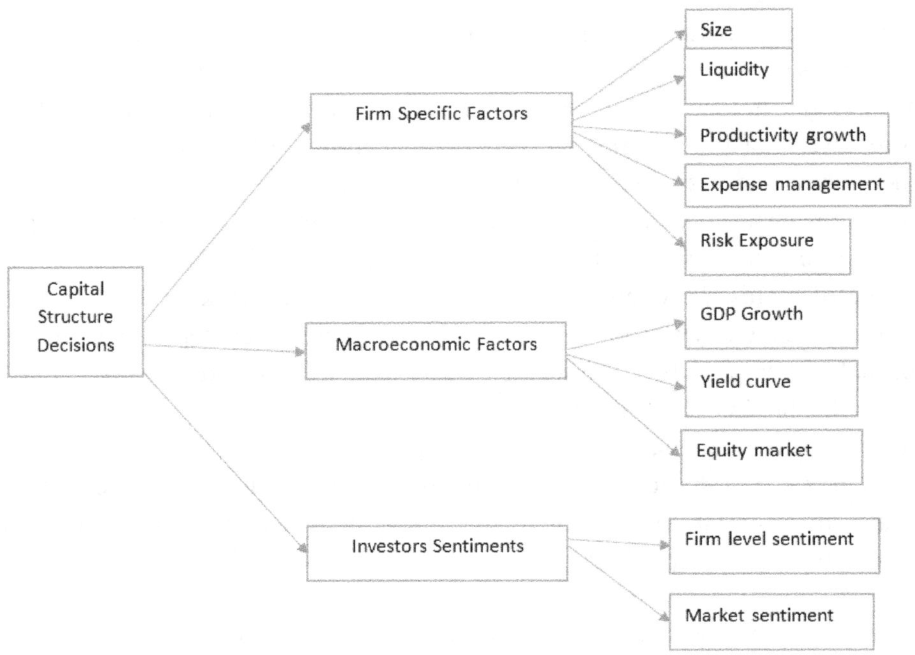

among enterprises most affected by the pandemic, demonstrating that much of the additional issuance reflected demand for capital to replace cash flows lost because of the economic disruption because of the pandemic. (Hotchkiss, 2020). It was discovered that in the early phases of the crisis, listed enterprises with poorer liquidity or solvency positions before the beginning of COVID-19, as well as smaller firms, incurred relatively more financial stress in various economies. (Deghi, 2021)

During the pandemic, companies with high value, more new lines of credit, fewer short-term debt, and more profitability had led to better performance related to stock price. Moreover, major corporation stocks outperformed smaller corporation equities. Large firms, on the other hand, have longer time horizons and better access to money. The pandemic situation has an impact on a company's operations as well as its capital structure and financing decisions. (Ding, 2021). The term premium is affected by nominal factors such as inflation and fundamental factors such as predicted output growth. Lenders are hesitant to lock down funds for long-term commitments. The long-term debt is less attractive for the investors; hence the business could not get more investment which affects the business's profitability. (Dick, 2013).

Mirza (2020) examined the consequences of the Covid 19 impact on the selected American countries struggling to cope with risk-adjusted equity fund performance.

The researchers revealed that the exceptional performance of greater human capital productivity ranked funds over their counterparts using 2019 as the base year. Similarly, Dimson (2020) and Eggers (2020) found that because of a perceived vulnerability of efficiency and because resources are not used properly, many small and medium-sized businesses were more badly affected by the pandemic situation compared with the large businesses.

Corporate Financing Decisions During a Crisis Period

Access to finance is of fundamental importance to a business's survival, and it involves working capital needs or long-term capital projects (Hourvouliades, 2022). The COVID-19 shock harmed corporate liquidity and performance due to a decline in revenue, earning volatility, and deteriorating stock prices. Governments reacted quickly and appropriately by deploying liquidity-ensuring procedures. Several tools, including short-term working allowances, tax breaks, cheap loans, and subsidies, are aimed at bridging the crisis's amplification phase, allowing businesses to continue functioning through and after the crisis without incurring significant financial and investment losses. Even when there is no large wave of insolvencies that stresses the financial industry (Demary and Hüther, 2020), firms' capital will continue suffering substantial consequences.

Many crises have erupted in the corporate world in the past. The great depression in 1932, the global financial crisis in 2008 and the oil price crash in the Middle East in 2014 are examples of the financial crisis in the past. Corporate responses to the crisis depended on many factors; however, the decision vests mainly on preference on equity financing over debt financing, long term financing than short term financing. However, the financial market is also influenced by the crisis. For instance, Kahle and Stulz (2013) mentioned that due to the supply shock caused by the financial crisis, it was expensive for high-levered corporations to issue new stock.

The financial crisis disproportionately affects the small, medium, and large enterprises (Zubair, et al., 2020); hence the size of a business also influences the financing decisions during a crisis period. Similarly, de la Torre (2020) observed that private SMEs face additional restrictions and costs in gaining access to finance relative to large, listed firms during a financial crisis. Firms differ in business model, performance, accessibility to the capital market, firm age, information asymmetry and growth opportunities.

Financial flexibility is the capacity to raise funds on acceptable terms in the case of poor economic situations. A consistent monetary base is essential to support sustainable performance. When the financial crisis restricts the money supply and when a firm is experiencing operational problems, capital providers prefer to advance cash to enterprises with a strong, sound fiscal and operational position.

(BODEA, 2014). This is from a supplier perspective.On the other hand, a capital structure choice can be challenging for corporates when evaluating the prices and advantages of debt and equity securities. Financially distressed firms suffer the most significant credit crunch consequences (Bhaird, 2013). Graham et al. (2014) observed that during the crisis, there are few opportunities to invest, which makes it difficult to raise outside cash, which lowers enterprises' leverage ratios.

Akbar et al. (2017), referring to the global financial crisis of 2008, mentioned that while managing through the potential adverse effects of the financial crisis, companies generally increased the use of internal finance and deferred the dividends payments for financing during the crisis. A similar view is expressed by Killincarian (2021) in a study on the global financial crisis and financial stability, researcher observed that the financial crisis negatively impacts dividend payments and leads to a tendency to adjust dividends immediately in response to earning changes. However, a differing view is presented by Ali (2022) based on dividend policy among G-12 countries. In the study, Ali (2022) concluded that even though the fraction of dividend reductions and omissions increases dramatically during the outbreak, most companies were able to keep or raise dividends.

Any incorrect capital requirements choice ultimately leads to economic trouble or insolvency (Seetanah, 2014). Similarly, Dao (2020), while examining the link between capital structure and organizational performance, observed that capital selections negatively impact corporate performance. The observation supports the tradeoff model with agency problems and expectancy theory. Gul (2019), on the relationship between short- and long-term debt, mentioned that the risk of failure rises as short-term debt to assets increases, but the chance of failure declines as long-term debt to assets increases. The volume, liquidity, and interest margin, according to the authors, are also significant drivers of credit risk. Using statistical models, a favorable association exists between debt to assets and short-term debt to total assets. (Arbor, 2005)

A profitable corporation usually finds capital to finance its projects even if its financial structure is in debt. Furthermore, if the total rate of return is higher than the return, the leverage effect will increase the industry's earnings. (Toma, 2003). These are some of the board's responsibilities to devise suitable adaptable funding plans to meet the variable demands for cash support arising from the company's growth while maintaining the investor's risk ratio. Simultaneously, the utilization of long-term equity entails satisfying creditors' requirements and, preferentially, paying stockholders with higher returns than expected. (Helfert, 2006)

The investment strategy achieves the best balance of risk and revenue while maximizing the company's worth. Stakeholders or the company's associates' profit from the capital requirements adjustment if and only if the company's value rises, therefore. As a result, to benefit the firm's owners, strategic members need to adopt a corporate structure that they feel would raise the industry's worth. (Hoanţă, 2003)

The capital structure was assessed by the earnings ratio, while the net profit performs the firm's evaluation before the tax to total assets ratio. According to the findings, companies with significant financial leverage have relatively low productivity and growth, and there is a negative relationship between credit risk and debt ratio to efficiency. They also discovered that firms that work in market-based bank lending outperform businesses operating in financial institution structures. (Al-Azzam, 2022)

Organization productivity is an overall demand statistic that reflects the employment of manufacturing components. As a result, operating margin is an established industrial measure that reflects the use of the enterprise's material and financial resources to accomplish maximum efficiency. Estimating and monitoring business results is among the most contentious and debated problems in financial planning. (Hung,2020)

Capital structure is one of the considerations that a corporation will make, together with management and payout strategies, to maximize its value. A business's capital structure is a subject that is influenced by asymmetric knowledge. Market imperfections are a circumstance in corporate finance in which internal persons, such as supervisors, have a greater understanding of their firm's worth and financing prospects than market investors. (Klein, 2002)

Numerous theories have been proposed to explain business funding behavior. The cost-benefit theory was one of the first ideas in this area and is regarded as a prominent theory in working capital research. According to this theory, an ideal borrowing mix would result in a corporation achieving the highest benefit; the borrowing mix is established by comparing the amount of tax shelter against various prices of financial stress, transaction cost, and systemic risk. (Myers S. C., 1984)

In organizations where ownership and management are divided, debt is a common means of settling disagreements. Companies can enhance the value of their company since the higher the value, the more power, prestige, and income they will receive. Debt is used as a disciplinary tool to reduce monitoring costs, according to the 'control hypothesis,' by aligning the shareholders' interests and administration. (Jensen, 1976) Most of the studies reveal that, regardless of ownership structure, higher levels of holding concentration relate to higher levels of debt. (Driffield, 2007). Merlo (2013) suggested that it would be critical for firms to utilize the appropriate model to compile and analyze their capital requirements since it is a crucial factor for borrowing capital at better rates and therefore maintaining an optimal portfolio.

FUTURE RESEARCH DIRECTIONS

This chapter reviewed existing literature on corporate financing and capital structure decisions during a crisis. Covid 19 crisis, unlike the previous global financial crisis, has impacted all walks of life and created a significant dent in the supply and demand profile. Corporate revenue declined, and the liquidity and debt coverage were significantly affected. This chapter has examined examples from various parts of the world on how they managed corporate financing during the various crises in the past. Not many studies were reviewed on the impact of Covid-19 as the availability of such studies was limited. Future studies should address this gap, specifically on how the Covid-19 crisis impacted each source of financing. A country-specific or region-specific research initiative with both primary and secondary data is required to develop more understanding of the topic.

CONCLUSION

Covid-19 shook the corporate from both demand and supply perspectives. The lockdown and social distancing announced by governments worldwide followed corporate losses, liquidity, and debt coverage crisis, and so on. However, there are examples of successful business models during the crisis. Decisions on corporate finance influence a firm's survival and growth and are influenced by many factors, like the investment opportunities, cost of capital, firm age, current capital structure, availability of funds, etc. There are many theories on corporate financing and capital structure. This chapter sheds light on the factors that influence corporate financing during a crisis. Various crises, including the global financial crisis and the pandemic, influenced the corporate world and corporate responses to these crises were detailed. The chapter reviews the empirical literature on the subject. Based on the reviews, it is observed that though the availability of external funds during a crisis is affected, corporate prefer to increase their leverage during a financial crisis when funds are required for operations. Using an appropriate model to meet the capital structure requirements is essential for any business. Estimating and monitoring business results is very crucial to handle but the corporations which tried were paid off during the critical situation. Companies with high levels of financial leverage are less productive and grow slower, and efficiency and credit risk are negatively correlated. Most of the corporations are hesitant to take initiative. Instead, they frequently take the easiest route and accept shortcomings. Important implications for corporate finance result from this. When companies are proficient at predicting the market through their financial choices, then their selection of debt or equity ought to be a good indicator of future stock returns. Similarly, the study also found that firms utilized retained earnings and deferred dividend payments during the crisis to make funds available to meet contingency and maintain sustainability.

REFERENCES

Abdullah, A. A. B. (2018). Factors Influencing Islamic Banks' Capital Structure in Developing Economies. *Journal of Islamic Accounting and Business Research.*

Ahood & Nobanee. (2021). Main Functions of Financial Management. Academic Press.

Akbar, S., Rehman, S., Liu, J., & Ali Shah, S. Z. (2017). Credit supply constraints and financial policies of listed companies during the 2007–2009 financial crisis. *Research in International Business and Finance, 42*, 559–571. doi:10.1016/j.ribaf.2017.07.001

Akers, H. (2014). *Key macroeconomic variables.* EHow Contributor.

Al-Azzam, B. A.-D. (2022). *Factors influencing the capital structure of Industrial Firms during the Covid 19: Evidence from Jordanian firms.* Academic Press.

Alpaslanoğlu, A. (2021). The Effects of COVID-19 Pandemic on Business Areas and Post COVID-19 Management Trends. *Turkish Studies - Social Sciences, 16*(1), 131–156. doi:10.47356/TurkishStudies.47192

an Bhaird, C. M. (2013). Demand for debt and equity before and after the financial crisis. *Research in International Business and Finance, 28*, 105–117. doi:10.1016/j.ribaf.2012.10.001

Andrew Ellul, I. E. (2020). The COVID-19 Pandemic Crisis and Corporate Finance. *The Review of Corporate Finance Studies, 9*(3), 421–429. doi:10.1093/rcfs/cfaa016

Arbor, J. (2005). The effect of capital structure on profitability: An empirical analysis of listed firms in Ghana. *The Journal of Risk Finance, 6*(5), 438–444. doi:10.1108/15265940510633505

Asif, A. &. (2016). *Impact of Capital Structure on Firm Value Creation-Evidence from the Cement Sector of Pakistan.* Academic Press.

Audil Rashid Khaki, A. A. (2020, March). Factors affecting the capital structure: New evidence from GCC countries. *Journal of International Students, 13*(1), 9–27. doi:10.14254/2071-8330.2020/13-1/1

Badran, O. (2021). Business analysis in post-pandemic era. *Academy of Strategic Management Journal., 20*, 2021.

Bhabra, H. L., Liu, T., & Tirtiroglu, D. (2008). Capital structure choice in a nascent market: Evidence from listed firms in China. *Journal of Financial Management, 37*(2), 341–364. doi:10.1111/j.1755-053X.2008.00015.x

Bodea, N. B.-M.-F. (2014). The Role of Capital Structure in Company's Financing. *Economics and Applied Informatics*.

Bui, T. (2022). The determinants and evolution of corporate ownership structure: Evidence from spinoffs. *Scenarios Not Adequately Addressed by Economic Theories, 1*, 10.

Chatzoglou, P. C., Chatzoudes, D., Sarigiannidis, L., & Theriou, G. (2018). The role of firm-specific factors in the strategy-performance relationship: Revisiting the resource-based view of the firm and the VRIO framework. *Management Research Review, 41*(1), 46–73. doi:10.1108/MRR-10-2016-0243

Chirella. (1992). The interaction of the financing and investment decisions: Preliminary results in the Australian context. *Asia Pacific Journal of Management*.

Dao, T. T., & Ta, T. D. N. (2020). A meta-analysis: Capital structure and firm performance. *Journal of Economic Development, 22*(1), 111–129. doi:10.1108/JED-12-2019-0072

de le Torre, A., Martinez Peria, M., & Schmulker, S. (2010). Bank involvement with SMEs: Beyond relationship lending. *Journal of Banking & Finance, 34*(9), 2280–2293. doi:10.1016/j.jbankfin.2010.02.014

Deghi, A. D. (2021). *IMF Working Paper, WP/21/86*. IMF.

Demary & Hüther. (2020). *Why the COVID-19 Pandemic Could Increase the Corporate Saving Trend in the Long Run*. Academic Press.

Dick, C. S., Schmeling, M., & Schrimpf, A. (2013). Macro-expectations, aggregate uncertainty, and expected term premia. *European Economic Review, 58*, 58–80. doi:10.1016/j.euroecorev.2012.11.005

Dimson, J. M. (2020). *COVID-19 and European small and medium-size enterprises: How they are weathering the storm*. https://www.mckinsey.com/industries/public-and-social-sector/our-insights

Ding, W. e., Levine, R., Lin, C., & Xie, W. (2021). Corporate immunity to the COVID-19 pandemic. *Journal of Financial Economics, 141*(2), 802–830. doi:10.1016/j.jfineco.2021.03.005 PMID:34580557

Dinh. (2020). The Effect of Capital Structure on Financial Performance of Vietnamese Listing Pharmaceutical Enterprises. *Journal of Asian Finance, Economics and Business, 7*(9), 329–340.

Driffield, N. L., Mahambare, V., & Pal, S. (2007). How does ownership structure affect capital structure and firm value? Recent evidence from East Asia. *Economics of Transition, 15*(3), 535–573. doi:10.1111/j.1468-0351.2007.00291.x

Egbunike, C. F. (2018). *Macroeconomic factors firm characteristics and financial performance*. Emerald. doi:10.1108/AJAR-09-2018-0029

Eggers, F. (2020). Masters of disasters? Challenges and opportunities for SMEs in times of crisis. *Journal of Business Research, 116*, 199–208. doi:10.1016/j.jbusres.2020.05.025 PMID:32501306

Engidaw, A. E. (2022). Small businesses and their challenges during COVID-19 pandemic in developing countries: in the case of Ethiopia. *Journal of Innovation and Entrepreneurship*.

Fairlie, R. (2020). The impact of COVID-19 on small business owners. *Journal of Economics & Management Strategy*. PMID:32904856

Frank, M., & Goyal, V. K. (2009). Capital structure decisions: Which factors are reliably important? *Financial Management, 38*(1), 1–37. doi:10.1111/j.1755-053X.2009.01026.x

Ghimire, A. M. (2021). Analysis of the Impact of Capital Structure in the Innovation of a Firm Using the Techniques of Financial Engineering. *Proceedings of the International Conference on Industrial Engineering and Operations Management*.

Graham, J. R., Leary, T. M., & Roberts, M. R. (2014). *A century of capital structure; the leveraging of corproate America.* NBER Working Paper Series 19910.

Gropp, R., & Heider, F. (2010). The Determinants of bank capital structure. *Review of Finance, 14*(4), 587–622. doi:10.1093/rof/rfp030

Guiso, L. P., Sapienza, P., & Zingales, L. (2018). Time varying risk aversion. *Journal of Financial Economics, 128*(3), 403–421. doi:10.1016/j.jfineco.2018.02.007

Gul, S. (2019). Capital Structure and Default Risk: Evidence from Korean Stock Market. *Journal of Asian Finance, Economics and Business, 6*(2), 15–24.

He Huang, Y. Y. (2021). Rethinking capital structure decision and corporatesocial responsibility in response to COVID-19. *Accounting and Finance*, *61*(3), 4757–4788. doi:10.1111/acfi.12740

Helfert, E. (2006). *Tehnici de analiză financiară*. BMT.

Hirsch, J., & Walz, U. (2009). *Financing decisions along a firm's life cycle: Debit as a commitment device*. German Research Foundation.

Hoanţă, N. (2003). *Finanţele firmei*. Economica.

HotchkissE. S. (2020). *Corporate Capital Raising During the COVID Crisis*. doi:10.2139/ssrn.3723001

Hourvouliades, N. L. (2022). Financing Small Businesses: The Agony of Securing Funding. In K. Biginas, S. Sindakis, A. Koumproglou, V. Sarantinos, & P. Wyer (Eds.), Small Business Management and Control of the Uncertain External Environment (pp. 229-258). Emerald Publishing Limited.

Huang, R., & Ritter, J. R. (2021). Corporate cash shortfalls and financing decisiosn. *Review of Financial Studies*, *34*(4), 1789–1833. doi:10.1093/rfs/hhaa099

Iqbal, A., & Kume, O. (2014). Impact of financial crisis n firms' capital structure in the UK, France and Germany. *Multinational Finance Journal*, *18*(3/4), 1–33. doi:10.17578/18-3/4-3

Ismail, W. A. (2007). *Islamic bank performance and capital structure*. MPRA Paper No. 6012.

Jensen, M. C. (1976). Theory of the Firm: Managerial Behaviour, Agency Costs and Ownership Structure. *Journal of Financial Economics*, *3*(4), 305–360.

Jess Benhabib, X. L. (2016). Sentiments, financial markets, and macroeconomic fluctuations. *Journal of Financial Economics*, 420–443.

Kahle, K. M., & Stulz, R. M. (2013). Access to capital, investment, and the financial crisis. *Journal of Financial Economics*, *110*(2), 280–299.

Kaushik, M. (2020). The Impact of Pandemic COVID -19 in Workplace. *European Journal of Business Management and Research.*, *12*, 10. doi:10.7176/EJBM/12-15-02

Killins, R. N. (2019). Firm-specific, industry-specific and macroeconomic factors of life insurers' profitability: Evidence from Canada. *The North American Journal of Economics and Finance*, *101068*. Advance online publication. doi:10.1016/j.najef.2019.101068

Klein, L. S. (2002). *Debt vs. Equity and Asymmetric Information*. Academic Press.

Lee, W. C. (2002). Stock market volatility, excess returns, and the role of investor sentiment. *Journal of Banking & Finance*, *26*(12), 2277–2299.

Merlo, P. D.-D. (2013). *Probabilistic and statistical methods of risk analysis in the investments effectiveness evaluation and their application in business practice*. Academic Press.

Metawa, N., Hassan, M. K., Metawa, S., & Safa, M. F. (2019). Impact of behavioral factors on investors' financial decisions: Case of the Egyptian stock market. *International Journal of Islamic and Middle Eastern Finance and Management*, *12*(1), 30–35.

Michael Halling, J. Y. (2020). How Did COVID-19 Affect Firms' Access to Public Capital Markets. *The Review of Corporate Finance Studies*, *9*(3), 501–533.

Mirza, N. H. (2020). The impact of human capital efficiency on Latin American mutual funds during Covid-19 outbreak. *Schweizerische Zeitschrift für Volkswirtschaft und Statistik*, *156*(1), 16.

Mueller, A., & Sensini, L. (2021). Determinants of financing decisions of SMEs: Evidence from hotel industry. *International Journal of Business and Management*, *16*(3), 117–127.

Murungi, D. (2014). *Relationship between macroeconomic variables and financial performance of insurance companies in Kenya*. Academic Press.

Myers, S. C. (1984). The capital structure puzzle. *The Journal of Finance*, *39*(3), 574–592.

Myers, S. C., & Majluf, N. S. (1984). Corporate financing and investment decisions when firms have information the investors do not have. *NBER Working Paper Series*, *1396*(38), 3295-3296.

Neves, M. E., Serrasqueiro, Z., Dias, A., & Hermano, C. (2020). Capital structure decisions in a period of economic intervention: Empirical evidence of Portuguese companies with panel data. *International Journal of Accounting & Information Management*, *28*(3), 465–495.

Panjaitan, R., & Simbolon, I. P. (2020). Financing and Herd behavior in financial crises: Invesstment decision. *International Journal of Economics and Business Administration*, *8*(4), 1089–1096.

Pinzaru, F. &. (2020). *The Impact of The COVID-19 Pandemic on Business. A Preliminary Overview.* Academic Press.

Porumboiu, C. (2020). *The importance of emerging industries: The case of biopharma*. European Business Perspective, Springer Open.

Puy, D., & Rawdanowicz, L. (2021, June 21). *Covid-19 and the corporate sector: Where we stand*. Retrieved from https://voxeu.org/article/covid-19-and-corporate-sector-where-we-stand

Salam, A. F., Ikmat, H., Haquei, I., Badariah, F., Nurjaya, E., Manan, A., ... Purwanto, A. (2021). The influence of share ownership, funding decisions, CSR and financial performance of Food Industry. *Annals of RSCB*, *25*(4), 12698–12710.

Santa, J. F. (2021). Financial crisis and capital structure decisions. *BMEP*, 67-96.

Santos, A., & Cincera, M. (2021). Determinants of financing constraints. *Small Business Economics*, 1-13. doi:10.1007/s11187-021-00449-w

Seetanah, B. S. (2014). *Capital structure and firm performance: Evidence from an emerging economy*. Academic Press.

Smirlock, M. (1985). Evidence on the (Non) Relationship between Concentration and Profitability in Banking. *Journal of Money, Credit, and Banking*, *17*(1), 69-83.

Sundarajan, V. a. (2002). Islamic financial institutions and products in the global Financial System: Key Issues in Risk Management and Challenges Ahead. *IMF Working Paper*, *2*, 1–27.

Titman, S., & Wessels, R. (1988). The determinants of capital structure Choice. *The Journal of Finance*, *43*(1), 1–19.

Toma, M. (2003). *Finanţe şi gestiune financiară*. Economica.

Tongkong, S. (2012). Key factors influencing capital structure decision and its speed of adjustment of Thai listed real estate companies. *Procedia: Social and Behavioral Sciences*, *40*, 716–720.

Usman, M. (2019). The Impact of Capital Structure on Financial Performance of Consumer Goods Industry in Nigeria. *Open Journal of Accounting*, *8*, 47–62.

van Wees, H. H. (2020). Global health beyond geographical boundaries: Reflections from global health education. *BMJ Global Health*, *5*(5), 3.

Vuong. (2022). Investor sentiment, corporate social responsibility, and financial performance: Evidence from Japanese companies, Borsa Istanbul Review, 22(5), 911-924.

Wronska-Bukalska, E., & Mazurkiewicz, K. (2018). Corproate capital structure changes during crisis times: Case of Polish companies. *Managing Global Transitions - International Research Journal, 16*(1), 19-35.

Zou, P. H. (2020). The impact of the COVID-19 pandemic on firms: a survey in Guangdong Province. *China. Glob Health Res Policy*, *5*, 41.

Zubair, S., Kabir, R., & Huang, X. (2020). Does the financial crisis change the effect of financing or investment? Evidence from private SMEs. *Journal of Business Research*, (110), 456–463.

Chapter 4
Impact of Gender Diversity on the Board of Directors on the Financial Performance of the Chinese Private Water Companies

Rajibur Reza
Griffith University, Australia

Lan Sun
CQUniversity, Australia

ABSTRACT

China is facing an acute portable water problem and presents a picture of severe supply constraints. Thus, China's water crisis offers attractive business opportunities for foreign water companies as well as domestic private water companies. Hence, the private sector participation in the Chinese water sector is a hot topic. This chapter investigates the impact of gender diversity on board of directors on the financial performance of the Chinese private water companies using ordinary least squares (OLS) and unbalanced panel (random effects) regression models, which are estimated as the baseline approach on a sample of 19 Chinese private water companies for the period of 2010-2017. The OLS and random effects results show that number of women on board (WB), percent of women on board (%WB), number of female executives (FE), and percent of female executives (%FE) affect the Chinese water companies' financial performance. The results of this chapter are important for researchers, regulators, and policymakers to benefit from policies that encourage board varieties at an individual water company level.

DOI: 10.4018/978-1-6684-5342-1.ch004

INTRODUCTION

Water is one of the finite resource and fundamental commodity to human well-being and survive the human lives (Reza, 2017; UN, 2015). However, China is facing an acute portable water problem and presents a picture of severe supply constraints because of over use of water, pollution and lots of people living in places that don't have much water (Jiang & Zheng, 2014; Reza, 2017). It is important to note that there are limitations of water supply over 100 cities in China; approximately 60% of China's 661 cities have been facing seasonal water shortages, and around 20% of the water produced at the water treatment plant has been losing through leaky distribution pipes (Browder et al., 2007). Currently, water supply shortages in China an estimated 40 billion cubic meters. Thus, China has water shortfall cost of $39 billion[1] a year because of lost crops, lower industrial production and stalled economic output. It is noted that China is one of the top countries in terms of water scarcity ranked (Sullivan et al., 2008). China one of the 13 countries most affected by water scarcity. China accounts 20% of the world population with only 7% of is fresh water (World Economic Forum, 2016). Recently, it has been predicted by the Chinese government that water consumption will be increased and 1068 billion tons consumed by 2030 (ASRIA, 2007). The economy of China has been growing day by day. Currently, the Chinese economy is the second largest economy around the world[2]. Thus, the Chinese economy practically now effect the global economy. Water has accepted as a vital natural resource for the continuing economic development of China should be noted (Asia Society Report, 2009). If China is to meet future water challenges, the Chinese water utilities must be dramatically improved (Browder et al., 2007). Hence, the urgent need to increase water supply through government or private sector participation in the Chinese water sector (Lee, 2007). A huge amount of investment is required to improve the infrastructure of the Chinese water industry which is one of the most highly capital and water infrastructure intensive (Olstein et al., 2009). Usually, it is very difficult to provide sufficient financing by the government alone. Hence, private sector investors can contribute to improve the Chinese water sector which is previously discussed in numerous news, articles and research reports inside and outside in China.

In order to achieve this, the Chinese government can do much better the investment in water sector by improving the rules, regulation, policies, and practising good corporate governance. The practice of corporate governance (with gender diversity on board of directors) is strongly influenced by the firm management, shareholders, investors, creditors, employees, and government. Thus, good corporate governance (with gender diversity on board of directors) is expected to provide a better much required reforms regarding investment issues and increase water companies' performance.

The global financial crisis (GFC) has challenged academic and conventional wisdom, and may have caused the beginning of a dramatic shift in international relations. The governance of water industry is part of that bigger picture. Governance in the broad sense is open for debate-the role of the state, international cooperation, the scope of prudential regulation, the role of boards of directors and in particular risk management procedures and capital adequacy requirements are all being questioned. In the past some research has been done on the link between governance and performance. Perhaps the present emphasis should be more on the link between good corporate governance and performance. It is noted that research on corporate governance, board gender diversity and corporate performance is still going on throughout the world. Most studies to date show different result from different countries. The relationship between profitability indicators which act as cumulative predictors of financial position. But, corporate governance can be well observed after proper exploration of the relationship between board gender diversity and female executives, and financial performance of the of water companies in China.

The fundamental motivation for this study is that the seeming lack of elementary explanation the relationship between corporate governance and performance of water industry, and therefore this study finds a scenario of corporate governance of water industry. GFC was triggered largely by the collapse end of September 2008 of the investment bank, Lehman Brothers. Financial scandals not only arose in American enterprises but also other countries enterprises as well. Highly concentrated ownership and poor corporate governance system lead to the financial crisis in world. Accordingly, poor corporate governance system indeed has adverse impact on the performance of enterprises and it even causes enterprises fall into a big danger of financial crisis. Moreover, there is a gender gap in water management leadership at levels of government and private sector of water utilities around the world (Jalal, 2014). As women's participation in corporate governance in China is low (Horak and Cui, 2017), percentage of women on board of the Chinese private water sector should be examined. Additionally. the association between corporate governance, women participation on board and performance of water industry is still not clear and varies'. Hence, female representative has been becoming a more important topic for the water industry. Thus, the water company management and researchers give the more emphasis on the topic entitled "board gender diversity- issues and problems". Hereafter, our motivation would be of particular relevance to the board gender diversity which is very important for good corporate governance practice in the water industry.

The contributions of this chapter to the literature are threefold. Building on the agency theory (Jensen and Meckling, 1976), this chapter seeks to add to the existing literature on water company management by examining whether the board size and composition and the board gender diversity of the Chinese water industry affect firms' decisions and how they impact on performance. Due to the lack of research on the relationships between corporate governance, board gender diversity, female executives and water companies' performance, our study makes a number of significant contributions to the current literature. To the best of our knowledge, this is the first study to examine the relationship between board gender diversity, female executives and the financial performance of the Chinese water industry. Second, this chapter is also the first attempt to use board gender diversity and female executives to find out the effect of water companies' performance in the Chinese private water industry. Thus, this study sheds new light on the Chinese water industry boardroom dynamics. Third and most importantly, as the government, policy makers and regulators are thoughtful about board gender diversity, our study provides an empirical guidance to Chinese policy makers and regulators on the water investment issue.

The objective of this chapter is to empirically examine the association between diversity on board, female executives and the financial performance of the Chinese private water companies in order to find out the nature of impact on firm's decision during the period of 2010-2017. Specifically, this chapter investigates the reciprocal relationship between, women on the board, female executives and the performance of the Chinese water industry. Hence, this study asks, "do gender diversity on board of directors affect the Chinese private water companies to improve the financial performance more precisely?"

PARTICIPATION IN THE CHINESE WATER INDUSTRY

Prior to 1979 and under the old command economy, public utilities such as water, electricity, solid and liquid waste, and public transportation were all run by State Owned Enterprises (SOEs). In 1992, first time the Chinese urban water supply sector was opened to private investment (Li, 2018; Wang et al., 2011). However, it was for only foreign private investors; began with Sino French Water (a joint venture between Suez Group and Hong Kong based NWS holding Limited) and the water utility of Zhongshan City jointly established Zhongshan Tanzhou Water Supply Company Limited, the first Sino-foreign joint venture in water supply in the city of Zhongshan, China (Li, 2018; Wang et al., 2011).

Again, in the late 1990s, the central government of China began to pursue a huge program such as Public-Private partnerships (PPPs) Build-Operate-Transfer (BOT) approach, Franchise Pilot Projects with Foreign Investment, urban water supply pipeline network etc. for water supply privatization by allowing private capital, both domestic and foreign to invest in the China water sector in the hope of improving the water productivity (Yu & Danqing, 2006)

In 2004, Chinese government reformed the water supply and water sewage sector to privately owned companies by following the worldwide trend. It is important to note that two French companies, Suez and Veolia Water (previously Vivendi Water), and a U.K. company, Thames Water, are the best-known foreign companies that have profited from Chinese market development (Jin et al., 2019) and domestic private water companies such as Beijing Capital Group, General Water of China, and Shenzhen Water Group actively participated in the China water market of through share transfer, joint venture, Build-Operate-Transfer (BOT), Transfer-Operate-Transfer (TOT), Build-Transfer (BT), Renovate-Operate-Transfer (ROT), Build-Own-Operate(BOO), Operation & Maintenance Contract, Operation Outsourcing, share transfer, joint venture etc. (Fu & Chang, 2006; Li, 2018; Wang et al. 2011;).

To sum up, it can be seen that private sector participation (PSP) in the China water sector is a hot topic and has been discussed inside and outside of China because of China's water crisis offers attractive business opportunities for foreign water companies as well as domestic private water companies (Lee, 2007; Hutterer, 2008).

THEORETICAL FRAMEWORK AND LITERATURE REVIEW

Several theories in the literature have established the conceptual frameworks for the research of gender diversity and firm performance. One popular theoretical framework is the agency theory from Fama and Jensen (1983) which define the role of the board of directors is an internal corporate governance mechanism and boards are in place to supervise and monitor managers, protect shareholder interests, implement incentives to motivate managers to act in the best interest of shareholders and replace those who do not. However, the agency theory did not provide a clear-cut prediction on how board diversity will add value to firm. The resource dependence theory is another influential theory which posits that a firm is an open system that is dependent on external resources and the role of the board of directors is to provide access to capital, information, network, skills, talent and other important resources that a firm could not obtain from the managers (Pfeffer & Salancik, 1978; Stiles & Taylor, 2001). The resource dependence theory implies that board diversity is useful to improve economic outcome because a more diverse board will bring a valuable set of resources that is useful to decision-making and problem-solving (Hillman et al., 2000). According to the social identity theory and social categorization theory, male directors would prefer themselves to be identified and categorised as 'directors' (Ashforth & Mael, 1989; Tajfel, 1981). The perception that directors are dominated by men creates boundaries and barriers for female to get into the business and these two theories have been used to explain why women directorship has been very low in many countries (Singh & Vinnicombe, 2004).

Another most frequently cited theory in explaining the connection between gender diversity and firm performance perhaps is the upper echelons theory. This theory suggests that directors are different in their experiences, knowledge and values. Such differences define their different cognitive functions - the processes of information-seeking, evaluation and interpretation, and eventually decision-making (Hambrick & Mason, 1984; Hambrick, 2007).

Robinson and Dechant (1997) suggest that demographic factors such as age, race and gender are the cause for different cognitive functions, attitudes and beliefs. Gender diversity implies cognitive diversity. Women tend to have different experiences, knowledge, values and perspectives as compared to men (Simpson et al., 2010; Adams & Funk, 2012; Perryman et al., 2016). Women are more likely to add value to a male-dominated boardroom by providing new perspectives and by asking different questions (Farrell &Hersch, 2005; Burgess & Tharenou, 2002). Female directors are likely to bring different cognitive frames to a board. For example, Carter et al. (2010), Hillman, Cannella & Harris (2002), Hillman et al. (2000) report that female directors tend to hold more university degrees than their male counterparts. Groysberg and Bell (2013), Simpson et al. (2010) find the female directors are more experienced in marketing, sales and socialisation, they tend to have unique social networks, and they have a more diverse interests especially in philanthropy and community service. Buress and Tharenou (2002), Post and Byron (2015) argue that female directors have a different risk attitude as compared to male directors, that is, female directors are more risk averse and they have a strong sense to commit to corporate social responsibility. Moreover, female directors are more likely to value interdependence, benevolence and tolerance (Adams & Funk, 2012). Post and Byron (2015) suggest that female directors are prone to value different views and promote team working and collaboration. Female directors tend to make fair and better decisions because they praise a cooperative decision-making approach, which stimulates collaboration and in-depth discussions among all board members (Bart & McQueen, 2013; Post & Byron, 2015). In contrast, male directors tend to make decisions based on rules, regulations and traditions (Bart & McQueen, 2013).

Moreover, Cox and Blake (1991) and Robinson and Dechant (1997) propose that company needs diversity because the variety of perspectives and skills will encourage creativity and innovation and enhance problem-solving within the company. Diversity also allows top managers to gain a better understanding of the complex environment and cultural differences and therefore produces effective corporate leaderships. Firms may gain benefit from female directors who are able to share distinct backgrounds, experiences, skills, perspectives, knowledge and social networks (Hillman et al.,2007) and female directors may help firms to improve the ability to generate profit from business and investment activities (Miller & del Garmen Triana, 2009). A gender diverse board is more likely to welcome different perspectives in solving a problem, so that the firm will have a broader and complete understanding of the needs of multiple stakeholders (Conyon & Mallin, 1997; Carter et al., 2003). A gender diverse board as compared a male only board is more likely to make better decisions leading to positive financial performance when female directors embrace deliberativeness and multiple perspectives (Miliken & Martins, 1996; Post & Byron, 2015).

So, does gender diversity always lead to good firm performance and what did the empirical evidence say? A growing number of studies have examined board diversity especially gender diversity and their impact of firm performances (Terjesen et al., 2009; Hillman, 2015; Post & Byron, 2015) and the results are inconclusive. Jurkus et al. (2011) investigate a sample of Fortune 500 firms and find that the integration of female to top management team will reduce agency costs significantly. Using S&P listed firms as a sample, Carpenter (2002) argues that gender as one of the demographic characteristics is likely to influence organisational outcomes like performance. Post and Byron (2015) compare the results from 140 studies from different judiciaries and argue that countries with strong shareholder protection tend to give boards the ability to highly value and utilize female directors' knowledge and experience and they find a positive association between gender diversity and accounting performance existed in these countries. Adams and Ferreira (2009) report several findings on gender diversity and firm performance in a sample of US firms. They find that female directors as compared to their male counterparts, are less likely to have attendance problems, more likely to hold monitoring-related committee roles such as the member of audit committee. Moreover, a diverse board with more female directors tend to hold CEOs accountable for poor stock price performance. However, Adams and Ferreira (2009) show a negative relationship between the percentage of women on boards and firm performance and they argue that board diversity is harmful to firms with strong corporate governance mechanisms because a more diverse board tends to introduce unnecessary and excessive monitoring. Dwyer et al. (2003) study 535 US banks and find female representation is more likely to have a positive impact on firm performance in an organsiation with a culture that values teamwork, commitment, employee loyalty, and ethics, because such a culture unifies a diverse team and strengthens contributions of female members. Cater et al. (2003) examine US boards and find that the presence of a woman director on board and the percentage of female directors are positively associated with firm performance as measured by Tobin's Q. Shrader et al. (1997) examine 200 *Fortune* 500 firms and find a significant negative relationship between the percentage of women on the board and firm performance as measured by ROA and ROE. Carter et al. (2010) study US boards and find that gender diversity has no impact on firm financial performance. Farrell and Hersch (2005) document abnormal returns for the Fortune 500 firms on the date when the news is announced that a female director is appointed, however, it is insignificant.

Among other countries, for example, Ahern and Dittmar (2012) study Norwegian boards and find that the 40% female board representation mandatory gender quota is negatively associated with firm performance. They explain that the appointment of younger and less experienced female directors to the boardroom contributes to the poor performance. Diversity may foster social categorization and tokenism that destroys board effectiveness. In a Canadian sample, Francoeur et al. (2008) find no evidence suggesting that the percentage of female directors is associated with stock returns. The relationship between gender diversity and firm value turns out to be a U-shape in a study of German boards, Joecks et al. (2013) explore that initially firm performance (measured by ROE) decreases as the percentage of women on board increases, however after a 'critical mass' of about 30% female directors, firm performance starts to increase as the percentage of women on board increases. The authors interpret this break point as a magic number that at least three women should be appointed in a boardroom. Nguyen et al. (2015) find a similar nonlinear relationship between gender diversity and firm value existed in Vietnamese boards; however, it is invert U-shaped with the break point occurred at 20% of female directors. The authors suggest there is a trade-off between the costs and benefits of gender diversity, the firm performance (measured by Tobin's Q) first increases as the number of female directors increases, and once the percentage of female directors reaches 20% the firm value starts to decrease as the number of female directors increases. They suggest that boards with at least two female directors seem to perform the best. Low et al. (2015) investigate boards in Hong Kong, South Korea, Malaysia and Singapore and they find that the number of female directors is positively associated with firm performance as measured by ROE, however this relationship is weakened in countries with high female economic participation and empowerment. Abdullah et al. (2016) study Malaysian boards and find that gender diversity is positively associated with accounting performance but negatively associated with market performance. Moreover, the relationship is significant for government-controlled firms and insignificant for family-owned firms. In Australia, Chapple and Humphrey (2014) compare the performance of portfolios of firms with gender diverse boards to those without and overall, they find no evidence suggesting that having women on board will improve firm performance.

In China, the legal institutions for corporate governance and shareholder protections are less developed than those of the western countries (Allen et al., 2005). The current state of corporate governance system tends to be weak and it has undergone a significant change in the reform of state-owned enterprises. In 2006, the government introduced the *Company Law* and the *Securities Law* which provides the regulatory framework for corporations. The China Securities Regulatory Commission (CSRC) has set the Code of Corporate Governance of Listed Companies. Conyon & He (2011) suggest that listed companies in China have increasingly adopted Anglo-Saxon style of corporate governance system. China also implemented regulations in promoting women's participation in top management team. According to China National Program for Women's Development issued by the State Council, the board of directors should increase the proportion of women in the top management level. The Program for the Development of Chinese Women (2001-2010) develops the guidelines for state-owned enterprises to foster women for senior managers and members of board of directors. Li and Chen (2018) provide statistics showing the number of female directors on the board is increased from 1,000 in 2001 to 3,000 in 2012. The number of female executives in increased from 2,000 before 2007 to 6,000 in 2012. The female participation in top management is about 12.9% in 1999 and by the end of 2012 it increased to 16%. There is an extensive literature review of Chinese corporate governance by Jiang and Kim (2015) which covers almost every internal and external corporate governance mechanisms. From the review it is also evident that gender diversity has not been well studied in China and the empirical evidence is limited. Liu et al. (2014) document a 'critical mass' points that boards with three or more women tend to have a positive influence on firm performance. However, such as positive effect is significant in firms owned by legal person but insignificant in state-owned companies. Horak and Cui (2017) investigate the relationship between gender diversity and firm performance in the Chinese automotive firms and the results show that firms that include women on their boards perform better in asset growth and sales growth, and these firms are more risk averse with lower level of debt and R&D expenditure than firms with male-only boards. Li and Chen (2018) find that gender diversity has a positive impact on firm performance for small and median sized firms. For large firms, gender diversity is more likely to yield negative performance. The authors explain that small firms as compared to large firms tend to have less bureaucratic procedure in the system, the organisational structure is more flexible, which strengthens the positive impact of female directors on firm's strategic management and decision making.

In water finance and economics, the majority of past research has focused on the use of literature feedback or factor analysis as metrics for performance of the water companies. Previous researches have investigated a range of factors potentially associated with public ownership, institutional ownership, foreign ownership, leverage, asset size and profitability (see, for instance, Peda et al., 2013; Reza, 2017). However, unfortunately, in spite of its importance to the water company management, a very few studies have been conducted on the relationship between corporate governance (board size, board composition and % of women on board) and financial performance of the water companies. In Italy, only the influence of board directors, board size and ownership on public and private water companies' performance has been examined previously. The study of Romano and Guerrini (2014) examine the effects of ownership, board size, board composition and % of women on board and the performance of 72 Italian water utilities using ordinary least squares regression analysis for the period of 2011 only. They find that board size impacts on the profitability, and politically connected directors dominate the boards of Italian water utilities whereas % of women on board does not affect the profitability. Furthermore, Romano et al. (2015) study the relationship between the corporate governance and efficiency of 85 Italian water utilities for the period of 2010-2012 using DEA and panel regression model. They find out that board size negatively impacts on the efficiency of water utilities. However, their results show that ownership, % of women on board and average age of board members do not affect the efficiency.

These two studies do not focus on the relationship between gender diversity on board of directors and the financial performance of the Italian water utilities. Hence, there is a literature gap concerning the relationship between gender diversity on board of directors and the financial performance of the water companies. This study fills this gap by investigating in depth the relations between gender diversity (Number of women on board, % of women on board) and female representative (Number of female executives, % of female executives) and the financial performance in the water industry for the period of 2008 to 2017 using unbalanced panel (random effects) regression model. It is noted that this study is first time going to find out the relationships between board gender diversity on board of directors and the financial performance of the private water companies. Board diversity is very important for good corporate governance practice in the water industry.

Based on the theoretical framework and literature review we test the following four hypotheses:

The first hypothesis is:

H01: There is no relationship between financial performance and number of women on board.

H1a: There is a positive relationship between financial performance and number of women on Board.

H1b: There is a negative relationship between financial performance and number of women on board.

The second hypothesis is:

H02: There is no relationship between financial performance and % of women on board.

H2a: There is a positive relationship between financial performance and % of women on board.

H2b: There is a negative relationship between financial performance and % of women on board.

The third hypothesis of this study is as follows:

H03: There is no relationship between financial performance and number of female executives.

H3a: There is a positive relationship between financial performance and number of female executives.

H3b: There is a negative relationship between financial performance and number of female executives.

The fourth hypothesis of this study is as follows:

H04: There is no relationship between financial performance and % of female executives.

H4a: There is a positive relationship between financial performance and % of female executives.

H4b: There is a negative relationship between financial performance and % of female executives.

DATA AND METHODOLOGY

Data

In this study, firm performance, gender diversity, female executives and control variables data are obtained from the Bloomberg database. Initially, we have selected 22 listed water companies at the Shanghai Stock Exchange for which Bloomberg measures financial and governance data in the 10 years from 2008 to 2017 (n=22 organizations). However, we have excluded 3 water companies because of these 3 water companies are not actual water companies. Later, we also eliminated 2008-2009 data sample as board characteristics- Board Size, Board Duration and #Board Meetings data for control variables were not available for these two years. At last, the final sample consists of 152 observations across 19 Chinese water companies for the period of January 1, 2010 to December 31, 2017. These water companies are listed in Shanghai Stock Exchange. It is noted that water companies' performance is the dependent variable, and gender diversity, board characteristics and control variables are independent variables.

Measurement of Variables

This section defines all related variables which is used in this study and measure of each variable. Water companies' performance is the dependent variable, gender diversity and board characteristics are independent variables and seven financial variables are control variables.

Dependent Variables

Following prior studies such as Adams and Mehran (2005), four alternative proxies of water companies' performance are selected to examine the relationship between gender diversification and board characteristics, and water companies' performance: Return on assets (ROA), Return on equity (ROE), Return on investment (ROI) and Stock returns (RET). ROA is computed as Net income divided by total asset (Reza and Tularam, 2017). Return on equity (ROE) is measured as net income divided by shareholders' equity (Reza, 2017). Return on investment capital (ROI) is measured as net income divided by the original capital cost of the investment in year (Zamfir et al., 2016). The daily stock return is computed as the ratio of logarithmic stock price (Reza, 2017).

Independent Variables

In this chapter, two proxies of gender diversity on the Chinese water companies' board are selected to show whether gender diversity have any impact on the Chinese water companies' financial performance. Thus, we use two measures of gender diversity on board –Number of women on board (WB) and % of women on board (%WB). WB is measured as the number of female directors on the water companies' board (Bloomberg, 2017; Li & Chen, 2018) whereas %WB, which is measured as the percentage of female directors on the water companies' board (Bloomberg; 2017; Li and Chen, 2016). We also include female executives in management measures, i.e., number of female Executives (FE) and % of female executives (%FE). FE are the total number of women executives in a water company (Bloomberg, 2017) whereas %FE are the percentage of women executives in a water company (Bloomberg, 2017).

Control Variables

This chapter has selected four board characteristics variables such as Board Sze (BS), Board Duration (BD) and #Board Meetings (BM) and seven financial variables for serve as controls. The financial control variables are - sales growth (GROWTH), financial leverage (LEV), asset turnover (TURNOVER), liquidity ratio (LIQUIDITY), firm size (SIZE), free cash flow (FCF) and dividend payout ratio (DIVIDEND).

BS measured as the total number of directors on the water companies board as at the end of each year (Al Farooque et al., 2020). BD is defined as the number of years on the board and BM are computed as the number of directors' meetings held in a fiscal year (Al Farooque., 2020). GROWTH is computed as annual growth rate of total sales (Dzingai & Fakoya, 2017). According to Kyere and Ausloos (2019), LEV is measured as total debt divided by shareholder's equity. TURNOVER is computed as revenue divided by Avg Assets (Nurlaela et al., 2019) and LIQUIDITY is defined as current assets divided by current liabilities (Nurlaela et al., 2019) SIZE is computed as the natural logarithm of total assets in a year (Conyon & He, 2017).). FCF is computed as net operating activities cash flow minus capital expenditures in the end of year. (Lin & Lin, 2016). DIVIDEND is defined as the ratio of total dividends to total net income in the end of year (Lueg & Lueg, 2020). Dependent independent and controls variables are summarised in Table 1.

METHODOLOGY

Ordinary Least Squares Regression

This study uses the following Ordinary least squares (OLS) regression model by the studies of Reza (2017), to examine the relationships between Women on Board, Women Executives, Corporate governance and the Chinese water company's performance over a period of eight years. A relationship model is:

$$\mathrm{PERFORMANCE}_{it} = \beta_0 + \beta_1 \mathrm{WB}_{it} + \beta_2 \%\mathrm{WB}_{it} + \beta_3 \mathrm{FE}_{it} + \beta_4 \%\mathrm{FE}_{it} + + \gamma \mathrm{Z}_{it} + \varepsilon_{it} \quad (1)$$

where $\mathrm{PERFORMANCE}_{it}$ = water companies' performance which is a dependent variable and is measured by various means. ROA, ROE, ROI and RET. gender diversity on board (WB and %WB) and female executives (FE and %FE) variables are taken to be the independent variables. Z_{it} represents the control variables (BS, BD, BM, GROWTH, LEV, TURNOVER, LIQUIDITY SIZE, FCF and DIVIDEND). The coefficients β_0 are the parameters to be estimated and so are $\beta_1, \beta_2, \beta_3, \beta_4$, and γ are the vector of coefficients. ε_{it} denotes a disturbance or error term. The subscripts denote the individual water companies (= 1,2, . . ., 19) and is the time period (= 2010, 2011, . . ., 2017).

Panel Regression Model

This study uses the following unbalanced panel (Random effects) regression model has been recently applied to this type of study (Binder, 1985). Using this powerful method, this study investigates the effect of gender diversification and board characteristics on the Chinese water companies' performance over a period of eight years, A relationship model is:

Table 1. Variable measurement

Variables	Notation	Measurement
Firm performance variables		
Return on assets	ROA	Net income divided by total asset
Return on equity	ROE	Net income divided by shareholders' equity
Return on investment capital	ROI	Net income divided by the original capital cost of the investment in year
Stock returns	RET	The ratio of logarithmic stock price
Gender diversity on boards variables		
Number of women on board	WB	The number of female directors on a water company board
% of women on board	%WB	The percentage of female directors in the water companies
Number of female executives	FE	Total number of women executives in a water company
% of female executives	%FE	The percentage of female executive in the water companies
Control variables		
Board size	BS	Total number of members on board of directors
Board duration	BD	The number of years on the board
#Board meetings	BM	The number of directors' meetings held e in a fiscal year
Sales growth	GROWTH	Annual growth rate of total sales
Financial leverage	LEV	Total debt divided by total equity
Asset turnover	TURNOVER	Revenue divided by Average Assets
Liquidity ratio	LIQUIDITY	Current assets divided by current liabilities
Firm size	SIZE	Natural logarithm of the total asset
Free cash flow	FCF	Net operating activities cash flow minus capital expenditures in the end of year.
Dividend payout ratio	DIVIDEND	Total dividends divided by total net income

Sources: Bloomberg and own calculation.

$$\mathrm{PERFORMANCE}_{it} = \beta_0 + \beta_1 \mathrm{WB}_{it} + \beta_2 \%\mathrm{WB}_{it} + \beta_3 \mathrm{FE}_{it} + \beta_4 \%\mathrm{FE}_{it} + \sum_{j=1}^{7} \gamma_j \mathrm{CONTRL}_{it}$$

$$+ \sum_{t=1}^{2010-2017} \delta_t \mathrm{YEAR}_{it} + \varepsilon_{it} \qquad (2)$$

where the subscripts denote individual water companies (= 1,2, . . ., 19) and is the time period (t = 2010, 2011, . . ., 2017) is used. The coefficients β_0 are the parameters to be estimated. $\beta_1, \beta_2, \beta_3, \beta_4$, γ_j and δ_t are the vector of coefficients. ε_{it} denotes a disturbance or error term. $\mathrm{PERFORMANCE}_{it}$ = water companies' performance which is a dependent variable and is measured by various means. ROA, ROE, ROI and RET. The gender diversity on board and female executives in management variables comprise two dimensions respectively, namely, WB and %WB, and FE and %FE. Control variables comprise BS, BD, BM, GROWTH, LEV, TURNOVER, LIQUIDITY SIZE, FCF and DIVIDEND.

EMPIRICAL RESULTS

Descriptive Statistics

Table 2 presents the descriptive statistics for the dependent, independent and control variables which are used in this study. From Table 2, it can be seen that all variables mean are positive except TURNOVER. Descriptive results show that the highest mean for LEV is 0.963, whereas TURNOVER has the lowest mean, which is -0.910. The mean results for the performance indicators ROA, ROE, ROI and RET are 1.141, 2.085, 0.661 and 1.919 respectively. These performance indicators- ROA, ROE, ROI and RET mean results are line with Khidmat et al. (2020), Lu and Bao (2018) and Loy and Rupertus (2020) respectively. Hence, these results indicate a positive return for the Chinese privatized water companies for the period of 2010-2017.

Table 2 also interprets the descriptive statistics for gender diversity on board, female executives and board characteristics to capture corporate governance on the board of the Chinese privatized water companies. Most of water companies' female director number was between 1 to 3. Only one company's female director number was 4 out of 19 Chinese water companies". WB and %WB are board gender diversity variables, with a mean of 0.104 and 0.829 and the maximum of 1.386 and 3.794, respectively. These results are line with Li and Chen (2018) who find that women directors on board and %women directors on board with the lowest value of zero, with a mean of 1.056 and 0.117 and the maximum of 5.0 and 0.6, respectively. The mean of number of #FE variable is 0.475 0.668, which reflects that nearly half of the water companies in the sample hire female executive. The mean of %FE is positive, i.e.,1.325 with the maximum of 4.199. These results are line with Lu and Bao (2018).

Control variables for board characteristics - the board size (BS) of the Chinese water companies mean value is 1.464, which indicates that most of the water companies have more than one director on their board. The mean value of BM is 1.510 which shows that on average, the board of directors of the Chinese water companies hold their board meetings every eight or nine months in a year. We have summarized Table 2 results as graphs for minimum, maximum, mean and standard deviation in Figure 1.

Table 2. Descriptive statistics

Variables	Obs	Min	Max	Mean	Std. Dev.
ROA	152	-1.166	3.043	1.141	0.794
ROE	152	-0.531	3.785	2.085	0.885
ROI	152	-0.841	1.638	0.661	0.372
RET	152	-102.996	110.588	1.919	29.111
WB	152	-0.284	1.386	0.104	0.294
%WB	152	0.000	3.794	0.829	1.213
FE	152	0.000	3.912	0.475	1.135
%FE	152	0.000	4.199	1.325	1.461
BS	152	0.000	3.305	1.464	1.134
BD	152	0.000	2.197	0.599	0.655
BM	152	0.000	4.605	1.510	1.330
GROWTH	152	-1.506	5.645	1.696	1.676
LEV	152	-0.440	3.135	0.963	0.709
TURNOVER	152	-2.685	2.654	-0.910	1.141
LIQUIDITY	152	-1.853	6.694	0.254	1.796
SIZE	152	-1.899	10.731	6.556	2.823
FCF	152	-6.032	5.675	0.645	2.056
DIVIDEND	152	0.000	7.556	2.607	1.930

Note: This table reports the descriptive statistics of dependent (ROA, ROE, ROI and RET), independent (WB, %WB, FE, %FE) and control (BS, BD BM, GROWTH, LEV, TURNOVER, LIQUIDITY, SIZE, FCF and DIVIDEND).

Correlation Matrix

Table 3 presents the correlation matrix between dependent, independent and control variables. The correlation results show a positive and negative, i.e., strong and weak relationship between the independent variables. The results provide the strong correlation between BD and BS, and BM and BS respectively. Bryman and Cramer's (1997), a correlation coefficient higher than 0.80 may be indicated a multicollinearity issue. Hence, we use these variables for the regression analysis.

It is important to note that dependent variables - ROA and ROE are positively related with gender diversity on boards (WB, %WB) and female executives (FE, %FE). However, only WB, and %FE are positively correlated with another dependent variable-ROI. On the contrary, %WB, and FE, are negatively correlated with ROI. Correlation matrix also provides the positive relationships between WB, FE, %FE, and dependent variable RET whereas negative relationships exist between %WB

Figure 1. Movements of minimum, maximum, mean and standard deviation
Notes: *Minimum, maximum, mean and standard deviation results are summarized as graphs here.*
Data Source: *Bloomberg.*

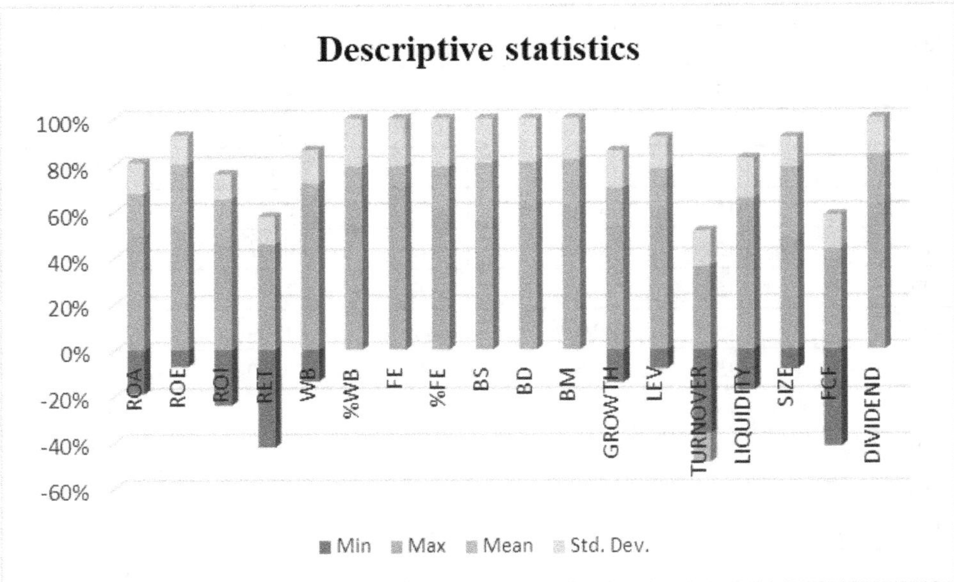

and RET. In this study, the maximum variance inflation factor (VIF) is 6.069. So, VIF does not greater than 10, which is consistent with Bryman and Cramer's (1997) observations. Hence, the multicollinearity between independent and control variables does not pose a serious problem in the regression model.

Ordinary Least Squares (OLS) Regression

A pooled ordinary least squares (OLS) regression model is used to investigate the association between gender diversity on boards, board characteristics and water companies' financial performance. Table 4 presents the results of OLS estimates of regression Eq. (1) when ROA, ROE, ROI and RET are the dependent variables. With regard to gender diversity on boards, WB and %WB do not affect the performance measures – ROA. these results support the Julizaerma and Zulkarnain (2012) results who find that total number of Board of Directors and %Women Directors of Malaysian public listed companies' do not affect the ROA. Similarly, WB and %WB are not linked with ROE and RET as well. ROE results are totally opposite from Vafaei et al. (2015) who find that presence of women on board and % of women on the board of directors of the Top 500 Australian firms affect ROE at 10% and 1% level respectively. Therefore, WB are positively and significantly related with

Table 3. Correlation matrix

	ROA	ROE	ROI	RET	WB	%WB	FE	%FE	BS	BD	BM	GROWTH	LEV	TURNOVER	LIQUIDITY	SIZE	FCF	DIVIDEND
ROA	1																	
ROE	0.772	1																
ROI	0.354	0.365	1															
RET	0.032	0.044	0.072	1														
WB	0.117	0.196	0.013	0.031	1													
%WB	0.103	0.129	-0.254	-0.023	0.620	1												
FE	0.225	0.079	-0.13	0.045	0.245	0.415	1											
%FE	0.199	0.214	0.017	0.071	0.326	0.463	0.343	1										
BS	0.218	0.328	-0.003	0.042	0.322	0.455	0.389	0.465	1									
BD	0.038	0.144	0.071	-0.035	0.093	0.282	0.416	0.294	0.749	1								
BM	0.181	0.294	-0.049	-0.016	0.123	0.370	0.148	0.487	0.777	0.497	1							
GROWTH	0.195	0.400	0.102	0.130	0.146	0.041	-0.041	0.119	0.237	0.103	0.281	1						
LEV	-0.171	0.151	-0.036	-0.043	0.216	0.188	0.205	-0.136	0.240	0.373	0.000	0.041	1					
TURNOVER	-0.133	0.061	0.353	0.071	-0.154	-0.246	0.200	-0.097	0.111	0.366	-0.004	0.036	0.139	1				
LIQUIDITY	-0.217	-0.089	-0.187	-0.000	0.143	-0.006	0.006	-0.125	-0.107	-0.115	-0.292	-0.092	0.214	-0.182	1			
SIZE	0.159	0.365	-0.128	-0.006	0.036	0.144	-0.444	-0.159	0.079	-0.242	0.384	0.314	-0.190	-0.498	-0.047	1		
FCF	0.114	0.088	0.017	0.081	0.039	0.030	0.004	-0.205	-0.024	-0.179	0.063	0.151	-0.039	-0.105	0.009	0.156	1	
DIVIDEND	0.223	0.298	0.037	-0.057	0.142	0.102	0.459	-0.023	0.273	0.373	0.031	0.061	-0.190	0.147	0.232	-0.164	0.047	1

Notes: This table reports correlation results among dependent (ROA, ROE, ROI and RET), independent (WB, %WB, FE, %FE) and control (BS, BD, BM GROWTH, LEV, TURNOVER, LIQUIDITY, SIZE, FCF and DIVIDEND) variables. The definition of variables is provided in Table 1. See Table 1 for variable definitions

Table 4. OLS results of dependents variables - ROA and ROE on independents and control variables

	ROA				ROE			
Variables	**Coefficient**	**St. Err**	**t**	**P> t**	**Coefficient**	**St. Err**	**t**	**P> t**
WB	0.169	0.278	0.61	0.545	0.246	0.282	0.87	0.384
%WB	-0.103	0.075	-1.36	0.176	-0.088	0.076	-1.15	0.254
FE	0.166**	0.081	2.04	0.043	0.064	0.082	0.78	0.436
%FE	0.023	0.054	0.43	0.666	0.093*	0.055	1.70	0.091
BS	0.283**	0.120	2.35	0.020	0.285**	0.122	2.33	0.021
BD	-0.211	0.169	-1.25	0.213	-0.267	0.171	-1.56	0.121
BM	-0.146	0.089	-1.64	0.103	-0.166*	0.090	-1.84	0.068
GROWTH	0.047	0.037	1.25	0.212	0.086**	0.038	2.25	0.026
LEV	-0.262***	0.097	-2.69	0.008	0.160	0.098	1.63	0.106
TURNOVER	-0.119*	0.064	-1.85	0.067	0.201**	0.065	3.07	0.003
LIQUIDITY	-0.134***	0.035	-3.81	0.000	-0.069**	0.035	-1.94	0.055
SIZE	0.046	0.034	1.33	0.184	0.171***	0.035	4.88	0.000
FCF	0.015	0.030	0.51	0.613	0.009	0.030	0.30	0.763
DIVIDEND	0.121***	0.038	3.14	0.002	0.122***	0.0392	3.11	0.002
Constant	0.499*	0.207	2.40	0.018	0.421	0.210	2.00	0.047
R-Squared	0.336	-	-	-	0.452	-	-	-
Year effect	Yes	-	-	-	Yes	-	-	-
Observations	152	-	-	-	152	-	-	-

Notes: This table reports the OLS regression of Equations (1) on the impact of gender diversity on boards and female executives on the financial performance. The independent variables are WB, %WB, FE, %FE and control variables are BS, BD BM GROWTH, LEV, TURNOVER, LIQUIDITY, SIZE FCF and DIVIDEND, and the dependent variable includes performance, which is defined as the ROA and ROE. See Table 1 for variables measurement.. t-value and p-value are given in parentheses.

*, ** and *** represent significance at 10%, 5% and 1% levels respectively.

financial performance measure ROI at the 5% level. whereas %WB negatively and significantly affect the financial performance measure ROI at the 5% level. These results support hypothesis H1a and H2b respectively.

From Table 4, we can see that FE positively affects ROA at the 5% level of significance. However, FE negatively and significantly related with ROI at 5% level. These results are in line with the hypothesis H3a and H3b respectively. With regard to another women executive variable - %FE positively and significantly linked with ROE and ROI at the 10% and 1% levels respectively. These findings support hypothesis H4a which show similar results to those of Shrader et al. (1997).

Table 5. OLS results of dependents variables – ROI and RET on independents and control variables

	ROI				RET			
Variables	**Coefficient**	**St. Err**	**t**	**P> t**	**Coefficient**	**St. Err**	**t**	**P> t**
WB	0.169**	0.133	2.28	0.024	0.303	12.034	-0.32	0.748
%WB	-0.103**	0.036	-2.53	0.012	-0.091	3.278038	-0.45	0.657
FE	0.166***	0.038	-2.92	0.004	-0.114	3.52684	0.55	0.582
%FE	0.023***	0.026	2.69	0.008	0.070	2.35309	1.1	0.272
BS	0.283	0.057	0.51	0.608	0.029	5.210161	1.72	0.088
BD	-0.211	0.080	0.31	0.758	0.024**	7.30688	-1.08	0.282
BM	-0.146	0.042	-1.25	0.215	-0.053	3.860588	-1.69	0.094
GROWTH	0.047	0.018	0.36	0.722	0.006	1.631474	1.27	0.208
LEV	-0.262	0.046	-0.43	0.667	-0.020	4.215142	-0.01	0.995
TURNOVER	-0.119***	0.030	3.17	0.002	0.097	2.795338	1.14	0.255
LIQUIDITY	-0.134**	0.016	-2.52	0.013	-0.042	1.529567	0.16	0.877
SIZE	0.046	0.016	-0.69	0.492	-0.011	1.498051	0.35	0.730
FCF	0.015	0.0143	1.65	0.101	0.023	1.298897	1.09	0.278
DIVIDEND	0.121*	0.018	1.69	0.093	0.031	1.674206	-1.1	0.272
Constant	0.499	0.099	7.82	0.000	0.775	8.976433	0.06	0.955
R-Squared	0.310	-	-	-	0.078	-	-	-
Year effect	Yes	-	-	-	Yes	-	-	-
Observations	152	-	-	-	152	-	-	-

Notes: This table reports the OLS regression of Equations (1) on the impact of gender diversity on boards and female executives on the financial performance. The independent variables are WB, %WB, FE, %FE and control variables are BS, BD BM GROWTH, LEV, TURNOVER, LIQUIDITY, SIZE FCF and DIVIDEND, and the dependent variable includes performance, which is defined as the ROI and RET. See Table 1 for variables measurement. t-value and p-value are given in parentheses.

*, ** and *** represent significance at 10%, 5% and 1% levels respectively.

These authors' show that percentage of women executives is an excellent predictor of firm profitability.

Hausman (1978) Test

Al-Tuwaijri *et al.* (2004) explore the appropriateness of using an OLS regression analysis to estimate this system of equations by employing a Hausman (1978) test. Then they claim that OLS estimators are potentially biased and inappropriate. Thus, to confirm the OLS regression analysis results, we tried to regress the unbalanced panel regression model to obtain unbiased results by addressing the presence of endogeneity. For unbalanced panel regression model, we estimated both the fixed

Table 6. Hausman test

Dependent Variables	chi2(12)	Prob>chi2	If Prob <0.05 use fixed effects	If Prob >0.05 use random effects	Prefer
ROA	8.97	0.705	-	0.705>0.05	Random effects
ROE	12.17	0.432	-	0.432>0.05	Random effects
ROI	8.84	0.716	-	0.716>0.05	Random effects
RET	2.75	0.997	-	0.997>0.05	Random effects

effect (FE) and random effect (RE) model. A question arises whether we should use the FE or RE model. For this question, we conducted the Hausman (1978) test to fix which specification affords more robust results. According to Hausman (1978) test, probability values are not significant, i.e., RE model is the best choice instead of FE model. So, in this study, we analysis the empirical results from the RE model. Hausman (1978) test results are shown in Table 6.

Random Effects Model

Table 7 presents the results of RE estimates of regression Eq. (2) when ROA, ROE, ROI and RET are the dependent variables. With regards to gender diversity on boards, asanticipated the coefficient estimations of WB is not significant with water companies' financial performance measure ROA and RET. ROA result totally opposite from Khan and Subhan (2019) those who find that number of females in bord are positively and significantly linked with ROA variables of listed firms in Pakistan at 1% level. In this study, WB has a positive and significant relationship with another financial performance measure – ROE and ROI at 10% and 5% levels respectively. ROE result is consistent with OLS regression result. Therefore, RE results show that %WB is negatively and statistically significant with ROA and ROI at 5% and 1% levels respectively. ROA and ROI results are not consistent with OLS regression results should be noted. This contrast in results addresses the importance for controlling for endogeneity. We also find from RE results that %WB is not correlated with ROE and market performance measure RET. These results are consistent with OLS regression result.

With regard to women executive variables, RE results show that #FE positively impact on ROA at the 1% level of significance. This result is consistent with OLS regression result. FE negatively and significantly related to ROI at the 5% level. However, ROI result is not consistent with OLS regression result. The contrast in results also addresses the importance for controlling for endogeneity. We find from

Table 7. RE effects results of dependents variables - ROA and ROE on independents and control variables

	ROA				ROE			
Variables	**Coefficient**	**Robust St. Err**	**z**	**P> z**	**Coefficient**	**Robust St. Err**	**z**	**P> z**
WB	0.169	0.107	1.57	0.117	0.246*	0.132	1.85	0.064
%WB	-0.103**	0.050	-2.03	0.042	-0.088	0.069	-1.27	0.204
FE	0.166***	0.055	2.99	0.003	0.064	0.073	0.88	0.381
%FE	0.023	0.061	0.38	0.702	0.093	0.057	1.64	0.102
BS	0.283***	0.053	5.26	0.000	0.285***	0.070	4.03	0.000
BD	-0.211	0.145	-1.46	0.144	-0.267**	0.121	-2.19	0.029
BM	-0.146***	0.052	-2.78	0.006	-0.166***	0.059	-2.78	0.005
GROWTH	0.047	0.053	0.89	0.375	0.086*	0.051	1.67	0.095
LEV	-0.262***	0.059	-4.41	0.000	0.160**	0.070	2.27	0.023
TURN	-0.119***	0.034	-3.5	0.000	0.201***	0.048	4.12	0.000
LIQ	-0.134***	0.019	-6.92	0.000	-0.069***	0.020	-3.35	0.001
SIZE	0.046	0.027	1.7	0.089	0.171***	0.037	4.61	0.000
FCF	0.015	0.038	0.4	0.692	0.009	0.039	0.24	0.814
DIVIDEND	0.121***	0.030	4.04	0.000	0.421*	0.245	1.72	0.086
Constant	0.499	0.215	2.32	0.020	0.817	0.000	-0.520	0.946
R-Squared (overall)	0.336	-	-	-	0.452	-	-	-
Year effect	Yes	-	-	-	Yes	-	-	-
Observations	152	-		-	152	-	-	-

Notes: This table reports unbalanced panel (RE effects) regression of Equations (2) on the impact of gender diversity on boards and female executives on the financial performance. The independent variables are WB, %WB, FE, %FE and control variables are BS, BD BM GROWTH, LEV, TURNOVER, LIQUIDITY, SIZE, FCF and DIVIDEND, and the dependent variable includes performance, which is defined as the ROA and ROE. See Table 1 for variables measurement. t-value and p-value are given in parentheses.

*, ** and *** represent significance at 10%, 5% and 1% levels respectively.

RE results that %FE only positively and significantly linked with ROI at 1% level. The relation result between %FE and ROI is supporting the OLS regression result.

CONCLUSION

This chapter examines the relationship between gender diversity, female executives, and the financial performance of 19 private Chinese water companies for the period of 2010-2017 using OLS and RE models. The empirical results show that WB,

Table 8. RE effects results of dependents variables – ROI and RET on independents and control variables

	ROI				RET			
Variables	**Coefficient**	**Robust St. Err**	**z**	**P> z**	**Coefficient**	**Robust St. Err**	**z**	**P> z**
WB	0.303**	0.154	1.96	0.050	-3.880	17.903	-0.22	0.828
%WB	-0.091**	0.036	-2.48	0.013	-1.460	4.207	-0.35	0.729
FE	-0.114**	0.056	-2.03	0.042	1.944	4.107	0.47	0.636
%FE	0.070***	0.021	3.30	0.001	2.594	2.714	0.96	0.339
BS	0.029	0.076	0.39	0.700	8.949	6.930	1.29	0.197
BD	0.024	0.071	0.35	0.729	-7.893	6.850	-1.15	0.249
BM	-0.053**	0.027	-1.96	0.050	-6.507	4.363	-1.49	0.136
GROWTH	0.006	0.021	0.30	0.762	2.064	1.490	1.39	0.166
LEV	-0.020	0.049	-0.41	0.684	-0.027	5.696	0.00	0.996
TURN	0.097***	0.028	3.40	0.001	3.192*	1.705	1.87	0.061
LIQ	-0.042***	0.013	-3.05	0.002	0.237	1.486	0.16	0.873
SIZE	-0.011	0.025	-0.45	0.655	0.519	1.042	0.50	0.619
FCF	0.023	0.018	1.30	0.195	1.413**	0.731	1.93	0.053
DIVIDEND	0.031*	0.018	1.66	0.096	-1.847	1.641	-1.13	0.260
Constant	0.775	0.116	6.67	0.000	0.506	6.787	0.07	0.941
R-Squared (overall)	0.310	-	-	-	0.078	-	-	-
Year effect	Yes	-	-	-	Yes	-	-	-
Observations	152	-	-	-	152	-	-	-

Notes: This table reports unbalanced panel (RE effects) regression of Equations (2) on the impact of gender diversity on boards and female executives on the financial performance. The independent variables are WB, %WB, FE, %FE and control variables are BS, BD BM GROWTH, LEV, TURNOVER, LIQUIDITY, SIZE, FCF and DIVIDEND, and the dependent variable includes performance, which is defined as the ROI and RET. See Table 1 for variables measurement. t-value and p-value are given in parentheses.

*, ** and *** represent significance at 10%, 5% and 1% levels respectively.

%WB, FE and %FE impact on the Chinese water companies' financial performance. Thus, gender diversity on board and female executives positively affect the Chinese private water companies to improve the performance more precisely and capability to control the managerial decisions. Hence, gender diversity on board and female executives can help to better board variety of the Chinese water industry and increase market share price, and improve the adequate water management as well as boost the water companies' financial performance. Thus, this chapter has implications for corporate governance research and its application to investment in the Chineese private water industry. Furthermore, the results of this chapter are important for researchers, regulators and policymakers for get benefit from policies that encourage board varieties in an individual water company level.

It is important to note that the limitation of this study is the unbalanced panel data. However, the limitations of data i.e., unbalanced panel regression model is well known for research. Furthermore, it would be beneficial, if this exercise can be repeated when balanced panel data becomes available for these 19 water companies. This study can be further extended along with a complementary investigation on the relationship between corporate governance (board of directors and ownership concentration) and investment performance, and risk-taking within the global water industry, especially following the GFC and COVID-19 pandemic.

REFERENCES

Abdullah, S. N., Ismail, K. N. I. K., & Nachum, L. (2016). Does having women on boards create value? The impact of societal perceptions and corporate governance in emerging markets. *Strategic Management Journal*, *37*(3), 466–476. doi:10.1002mj.2352

Adams, R. B., & Ferreira, D. (2009). Women in the boardroom and their impact on governance and performance. *Journal of Financial Economics*, *94*(2), 291–309. doi:10.1016/j.jfineco.2008.10.007

Adams, R. B., & Funk, P. (2012). Beyond the glass ceiling: Does gender matter? *Management Science*, *58*(2), 219–235. doi:10.1287/mnsc.1110.1452

Adams, R. B., & Mehran, H. (2005). *Corporate Performance, Board Structure and its Determinants in the Banking Industry*. Retrieved from https://papers.ssrn.com/sol3/papers.cfm?abstract_id=302593

Ahern, K. R., & Dittmar, A. K. (2012). The changing of the boards: The impact on firm valuation of mandated female board representation. *The Quarterly Journal of Economics*, *127*(1), 137–197. doi:10.1093/qje/qjr049

Al Farooque, O., Buachoom, W., & Sun, L. (2020). Board, audit committee, ownership and financial performance: Emerging trends from Thailand. *Pacific Accounting Review*, *32*(1), 54–81. doi:10.1108/PAR-10-2018-0079

Al-Tuwaijri, S. A., Christensen, T. E., & Hughes, H. E. II. (2004). The relations among environmental disclosure, environmental performance, and economic performance: A simultaneous equations approach. *Accounting, Organizations and Society*, *29*(5-6), 447–471. doi:10.1016/S0361-3682(03)00032-1

Allen, F., Qian, J., & Qian, M. J. (2005). Law, finance, and economic growth in China. *Journal of Financial Economics, 77*(1), 57–116. doi:10.1016/j.jfineco.2004.06.010

Ashforth, B. E., & Mael, F. (1989). Social identity theory and the organization. *Academy of Management Review, 14*(1), 20–39. doi:10.2307/258189

Asia Society Report. (2009). *Asia's Next challenge: Securing the region's water future.* A report by the Leadership group on water security in Asia. Retrieved from https://asiasociety.org/new-york/events/launch-asia-society-leadership-group-water-security-asia-report-asias-next-chall
enge

Bart, C., & McQueen, G. (2013). Why women make better decisions. *International Journal of Business Governance and Ethics, 8*(1), 93–99. doi:10.1504/IJBGE.2013.052743

Bloomberg. (2017). *Dataset.* Bloomberg Professional services.

Browder, G. J., Xie, S., Kim, Y., Gu, L., Fan, M., & Ehrhardt, D. (2008). *Improving the performance of China's urban water utilities.* The World Bank. Retrieved from https://documents1.worldbank.org/curated/zh/840621468016215926/pdf/409640P0704130Public.pdf

Bryman, A., & Cramer, D. (1997). *Quantitative data analysis with SPSS for windows.* Routledge.

Burgess, Z., & Tharenou, P. (2002). Women board directors: Characteristics of the few. *Journal of Business Ethics, 37*(1), 39–49. doi:10.1023/A:1014726001155

Carpenter, M. A. (2002). The implications of strategy and social context for the relationship between top management team heterogeneity and firm performance. *Strategic Management Journal, 23*(3), 275–284. doi:10.1002mj.226

Carter, D. A., D'Souza, F., Simkins, B. J., & Simpson, W. G. (2010). The gender and ethnic diversity of US boards and board committees and firm financial performance. *Corporate Governance, 18*(5), 396–414. doi:10.1111/j.1467-8683.2010.00809.x

Carter, D. A., Simkins, B. J., & Simpson, W. G. (2003). Corporate governance, board diversity, and firm value. *Financial Review, 38*(1), 33–53. doi:10.1111/1540-6288.00034

Chapple, L., & Humphrey, J. E. (2014). Does board gender diversity have a financial impact? Evidence using stock portfolio performance. *Journal of Business Ethics, 122*(4), 709–723. doi:10.100710551-013-1785-0

Conyon, M. J., & He, L. (2011). Executive compensation and corporate governance in China. *Journal of Corporate Finance, 17*(4), 1158–1175. doi:10.1016/j.jcorpfin.2011.04.006

Conyon, M. J., & He, L. (2017). Firm performance and boardroom gender diversity: A quantile regression approach. *Journal of Business Research, 79*, 198–211. doi:10.1016/j.jbusres.2017.02.006

Conyon, M. J., & Mallin, C. (1997). Women in the boardroom: Evidence from large UK companies. *Corporate Governance, 5*(3), 112–117. doi:10.1111/1467-8683.00051

Cox, T. H., & Blake, S. (1991). Managing cultural diversity: Implications for organizational competitiveness. *The Academy of Management Executive, 5*(3), 45–56.

Dwyer, S., Richard, O. C., & Chadwick, K. (2003). Gender diversity in management and firm performance: The influence of growth orientation and organizational culture. *Journal of Business Research, 56*(12), 1009–1019. doi:10.1016/S0148-2963(01)00329-0

Dzingai, I., & Fakoya, M. B. (2017). Effect of corporate governance structure on the financial performance of Johannesburg Stock Exchange (JSE)-listed mining firms. *Sustainability, 9*(6), 1–15. doi:10.3390u9060867

Fama, E., & Jensen, M. (1983). Separation of ownership and control. *The Journal of Law & Economics, 26*(2), 301–325. doi:10.1086/467037

Farrell, K. A., & Hersch, P. L. (2005). Additions to corporate boards: The effect of gender. *Journal of Corporate Finance, 11*(1-2), 85–106. doi:10.1016/j.jcorpfin.2003.12.001

Francoeur, C., Labelle, R., & Sinclair-Desgagné, B. (2008). Gender diversity in corporate governance and top management. *Journal of Business Ethics, 81*(1), 83–95. doi:10.100710551-007-9482-5

Groysberg, B., & Bell, D. (2013). Dysfunction in the boardroom. *Harvard Business Review, 91*(6), 89–97.

Hambrick, D. C. (2007). Upper echelons theory: An update. *Academy of Management Review, 32*(2), 334–343. doi:10.5465/amr.2007.24345254

Hambrick, D. C., & Mason, P. A. (1984). Upper echelons: The organization as a reflection of its top managers. *Academy of Management Review, 9*(2), 193–206. doi:10.2307/258434

Hausman, J. A. (1978). Specification tests in econometrics. *Econometrica*, *46*(6), 1251–1272. doi:10.2307/1913827

Hillman, A., Cannella, A., & Paetzold, R. (2000). The resource dependence role of corporate directors: Strategic adaptation of board composition in response to environmental change. *Journal of Management Studies*, *37*(2), 235–255. doi:10.1111/1467-6486.00179

Hillman, A. J. (2015). Board diversity: Beginning to unpeel the onion. *Corporate Governance*, *23*(2), 104–107. doi:10.1111/corg.12090

Hillman, A. J., Shropshire, C., & Cannella, A. A. Jr. (2007). Organizational predictors of women on corporate boards. *Academy of Management Journal*, *50*(4), 941–952. doi:10.5465/amj.2007.26279222

Horak, S., & Cui, J. (2017). Financial performance and risk behavior of gender-diversified boards in the Chinese automotive industry: Initial insights. *Personnel Review*, *46*(4), 847–866. doi:10.1108/PR-10-2015-0274

Hutterer, J. (2008). China's water market - Opportunities for foreign investors. *China Aktuell*, *2*, 157–177. http://www.grasshopperinvestments.com/downloads/67_Der_chine sische_Wassermarkt.pdf

Jalal, I. (2014). *Women, water, and leadership*. Asian Development Bank (ADB). ADB Briefs no. 24. Retrieved from https://www.adb.org/publications/women-water-and-leadership

Jensen, M. C., & Meckling, W. H. (1976). Theory of the firm: Managerial behavior, agency costs and ownership structure. *Journal of Financial Economics*, *3*(4), 305–360. doi:10.1016/0304-405X(76)90026-X

Jiang, F., & Kim, K. A. (2015). Corporate governance in China: A modern perspective. *Journal of Corporate Finance*, *32*, 190–216. doi:10.1016/j.jcorpfin.2014.10.010

Jiang, Y., & Zheng, X. (2014). Private sector participation and performance of urban water utilities in China. *Economic Development and Cultural Change*, *63*(1), 155–189. doi:10.1086/677739

Joecks, J., Pull, K., & Vetter, K. (2013). Gender diversity in the boardroom and firm performance: What exactly constitutes a "critical mass?". *Journal of Business Ethics*, *118*(1), 61–72. doi:10.100710551-012-1553-6

Julizaerma, M. K., & Zulkarnain, M. S. (2012). Gender diversity in the boardroom and firm performance of Malaysian public listed companies. *Procedia: Social and Behavioral Sciences*, *65*, 1077–1085. doi:10.1016/j.sbspro.2012.11.374

Jurkus, A. F., Park, J. C., & Woodard, L. S. (2011). Women in top management and agency costs. *Journal of Business Research*, *64*(2), 180–186. doi:10.1016/j.jbusres.2009.12.010

Khidmat, W. B., Khan, M. A., & Ullah, H. (2020). The effect of board diversity on firm performance: Evidence from Chinese listed companies. *Indian Journal of Corporate Governance*, *13*(1), 9–33. doi:10.1177/0974686220923793

Kyere, M., & Ausloos, M. (2019). Corporate governance and firms financial performance in the United Kingdom. *International Journal of Finance & Economics*, 1–15.

Lee, S. (2007). Private sector participation in the Shanghai water sector. *Water Policy*, *9*(4), 405–423. doi:10.2166/wp.2007.015

Li, H., & Chen, P. (2018). Board gender diversity and firm performance: The moderating role of firm size. *Business Ethics (Oxford, England)*, *27*(4), 294–308. doi:10.1111/beer.12188

Li, L. (2018). Private sector participation and performance of county water utilities in China. *China Economic Review*, *52*, 30–53. doi:10.1016/j.chieco.2018.06.001

Lin, D., & Lin, L. (2016). How does Corporate Governance Affect Free Cash Flow? *Journal of Applied Finance & Banking.*, *6*(3), 145–156.

Liu, Y., Wei, Z., & Xie, F. (2014). Do women directors improve firm performance in China? *Journal of Corporate Finance*, *28*(C), 169–184. doi:10.1016/j.jcorpfin.2013.11.016

Low, D. C., Roberts, H., & Whiting, R. H. (2015). Board gender diversity and firm performance: Empirical evidence from Hong Kong, South Korea, Malaysia and Singapore. *Pacific-Basin Finance Journal, 35*(A), 381-401.

Loy, T. R., & Rupertus, H. (2020). How Does the Stock Market Value Female Directors? International Evidence. *Business & Society*, *00*(0), 1–38.

Lu, D., & Bao, Y. (2018). *Board gender diversity and firm performance: Evidence from Chinese Firms*. Retrieved from https://www.semanticscholar.org/paper/Board-Gender-Diversity-and-Firm-Performance-%3A-from-Lu-Bao/f607cc4569ff4bc2dcdb978e4bba5a9338ed02f2

Lueg, K., & Lueg, R. (2020). Detecting green-washing or substantial organizational communication: A Model for testing two-way interaction between risk and sustainability reporting. *Sustainability*, *12*(6), 1–9. doi:10.3390u12062520

Miller, T., & del Carmen Triana, M. (2009). Demographic diversity in the boardroom: Mediators of the board diversity firm performance relationship. *Journal of Management Studies*, *46*(5), 755–786. doi:10.1111/j.1467-6486.2009.00839.x

Milliken, F. J., & Martins, L. L. (1996). Searching for common threads: Understanding the multiple effects of diversity in organizational groups. *Academy of Management Review*, *21*(2), 402–433. doi:10.2307/258667

Nguyen, T., Locke, S., & Reddy, K. (2015). Does boardroom gender diversity matter? Evidence from a transitional economy. *International Review of Economics & Finance*, *37*(C), 184–202. doi:10.1016/j.iref.2014.11.022

Nurlaela, S., Mursito, B., Kustiyah, E., Istiqomah, I., & Hartono, S. (2019). Asset turnover, capital structure and financial performance consumption industry company in Indonesia Stock Exchange. *International Journal of Economics and Financial Issues*, *9*(3), 297–301. doi:10.32479/ijefi.8185

Olstein, M., Jennings, J., & Geist, R. (2009). *Improving water utility capital efficiency*. Water Research Foundation.

Peda, P., Grossi, G., & Liik, M. (2013). Do ownership and size affect the performance of water utilities? Evidence from Estonian municipalities. *The Journal of Management and Governance*, *17*(2), 237–259. doi:10.100710997-011-9173-6

Perryman, A. A., Fernando, G. D., & Tripathy, A. (2016). Do gender differences persist? An examination of gender diversity on firm performance, risk, and executive compensation. *Journal of Business Research*, *69*(2), 579–586. doi:10.1016/j.jbusres.2015.05.013

Pfeffer, J., & Salancik, G. R. (1978). *The external control of organizations: A resource dependence perspective*. Harper & Row.

Post, C., & Byron, K. (2015). Women on boards and firm financial performance: A meta-analysis. *Academy of Management Journal*, *58*(5), 1546–1571. doi:10.5465/amj.2013.0319

Reza, R. (2017). *An Investigation of water investment performance: Analysis of the global water industry* [PhD Thesis]. Griffith University. Retrieved from https://research-repository.griffith.edu.au/handle/10072/371256

Romano, G., & Guerrini, A. (2014). The effects of ownership, board size and board composition on the performance of Italian water utilities. *Utilities Policy*, *31*, 18–28. doi:10.1016/j.jup.2014.06.002

Romano, G., Guerrini, A., & Leardini, C. (2015). Exploring the link between corporate governance and efficiency of Italian water utilities. *Agua y Territorio*, *6*(6), 123–132. doi:10.17561/at.v0i6.2815

Shrader, C. B., Blackburn, V. B., & Iles, P. (1997). Women in management and firm financial value: An exploratory study. *Journal of Managerial Issues*, *9*(3), 355–372.

Simpson, W. G., Carter, D., & D'Souza, F. P. (2010). What do we know about women on boards? *Journal of Applied Finance (JAF)*, *20*(2), 27–39.

Singh, V., & Vinnicombe, S. (2004). Why so few women directors in top UK boardrooms? Evidence and theoretical explanations. *Corporate Governance*, *12*(4), 479–488. doi:10.1111/j.1467-8683.2004.00388.x

Stiles, P., & Taylor, B. (2001). *Boards at work: how directors view their roles and responsibilities*. Oxford University Press.

Sullivan, C., Cohen, A., Jean-Marc Faurès, J., & Santini, G. (2008). *The rural water livelihoods index*. FAO Working Paper.

Tajfel, H. (1981). *Human groups and social categories*. Cambridge University Press.

Terjesen, S., Sealy, R., & Singh, V. (2009). Women directors on corporate boards: A review and research agenda. *Corporate Governance*, *17*(3), 320–337. doi:10.1111/j.1467-8683.2009.00742.x

Vafaei, A., Ahmed, K., & Mather, P. (2015). Board diversity and financial performance in the top 500 Australian firms'. *Australian Accounting Review*, *75*(25), 413–427. doi:10.1111/auar.12068

Wang, H., Wu, W., & Zheng, S. (2011). An econometric analysis of private sector participation in China's urban water supply. *Utilities Policy*, *19*(3), 134–14. doi:10.1016/j.jup.2011.01.004

World Economic Forum. (2016). *China has a water crisis - how can it be solved?* Retrieved from https://www.weforum.org/agenda/2016/04/china-has-a-water-cri sis-how-can-it-be-solved/

Yu, A. L., & Liu, D. L. (2006). *The privatization of water supply in China*. Retrieved from https://www.business-humanrights.org/en/latest-news/pdf-the-privatization-of-water-supply-in-china/

Zamfir, M., Manea, M. D., & Ionescu, L. (2016). Return on investment – Indicator for measuring the profitability of invested capital, *Valahian. Journal of Economic Studies (Glasgow, Scotland)*, *0*(21), 79–86.

UN. (2015). *Water and sustainable development*. Retrieved from https://www.un.org/waterforlifedecade/water_and_sustainable_development.shtml

ENDNOTES

1 http://factsanddetails.com/china/cat10/sub66/item390.html

2 https://www.davidthomas.asia/china-invest/china-is-the-second-largest-economy-in-the-world/#:~:text=China%E2%80%99s%20economy%20is%20the%20second%20largest%20in%20the,total%20GDP%20%28see%20chart%20below%20from%20Visual%20Capitalist%29.

Chapter 5
Corporate Response to Macroeconomic Shocks

Anitha Narayanan Nair
Modern College of Business and Science, Oman

ABSTRACT

COVID-19 has bought its fair share of troubles to the world when it came unannounced in late December 2019. Nobody was spared, and the corporate sectors bore the brunt of it along with the common man. Globally, almost all industries were affected by the pandemic due to lockdowns and restrictions which further intensified the problems of the corporate sectors. Many sectors faced shocks from both the demand side and the supply side. Unemployment, instabilities in the financial markets, and uncertainties prevailing in almost all sectors of the economy were predominant throughout the world. This chapter is an attempt to see how the demand shocks and supply shocks impacted the different industries and what measures were taken up by the governments and the corporate sectors to wade through this period of uncertainty and ambiguity.

INTRODUCTION

Shocks are an inevitable part of any economy. A macroeconomic shock can be comprehended as any unexpected event that can have a positive or a negative influence on the macroeconomic variables of an economy like unemployment, inflation, etc. Since the outbreak of Covid -19, most economies have been reeling under uncertainties. Shocks to a particular industry can be felt throughout the economy as firms and industries are interdependent on each other for the supply of inputs. This is primarily because of the reason that shocks in one industry can impact

DOI: 10.4018/978-1-6684-5342-1.ch005

other "downstream" industries that buy inputs from the affected industries (Daron Acemoğlu, 2016). Consequently, the entire economy becomes affected more than the actual harm that the economic shock could do on its own. This chapter aims to study the impact of these macroeconomic shocks on the corporate sectors and how they respond to these shocks. Many studies have been published on the impact of macroeconomic shocks on stock markets, labor markets, and consumer behavior (Sharma, Sha, & Sunila, 2020).

Due to the Pandemic, governments worldwide imposed stringent measures including social distancing and lockdowns which in turn affected firms- big and small in various ways (Iyke & Njindan, 2020). Restrictions imposed by the governments adversely affected businesses, which was reflected in the stock market indices, though it helped curb the spread of the disease (Ashraf, 2020). When a lockdown is imposed, it prevents the factors of production from being utilized to their full capacity (Bodnár, Roux, Lopez-Garcia, & Szörfi, 2020). This creates a gap between the maximum capacity that the economy can achieve; therefore, the amount of capacity utilization and the size of the output gap differ considerably from the levels depicted during normal times (Nelson, 1989). Countries around the world, adopted stringent economic policies to bridge this gap. However, policy measures alone, do not suffice in bringing the economy back into stability. The manner in which the firms proactively respond to the crisis act as a supplement to the government policies (Bhadra & Ray, 2021). Many firms around the world were quick to adapt to the changing scenario by adopting innovative methods so that businesses can continue operations (Han & Qian, 2020). In fact, many organizations, during the pandemic, opined that they could access new pools of talent without any locational restrictions, build a stronger work culture and reduce real estate costs to a great extent (Boland, Smet, Palter, & Sanghvi, 2020).

BACKGROUND

The emergence of covid-19 posed a serious threat not only to the people's health but also to business sectors, education sectors, health sectors, and all other allied sectors. To check the growing number of Covid-affected cases, governments all over the world took stringent measures that included social distancing, lockdowns, and quarantines. The entire world came to standstill when the lockdowns were imposed. It was the first time that many of us experienced what an actual lockdown is. All these measures took a drastic toll on the economies too. Many people lost their jobs since many firms were forced to close down as they could not keep themselves afloat during the lockdown periods. This was particularly the case for small-scale businesses, food, and hotel industries, the travel, and tourism sector, the entertainment industry, and the construction sector- to name a few. Many startups, the agriculture sector, gems/jewelry, textile, and tourism sectors reported huge losses during this time (G, 2020). There were major disruptions in the supply chains too. Entrepreneurs who were in the process of launching their businesses and those who had already just started their ventures, were, impacted significantly by the lockdowns and other government restrictions (Giones, et al., 2020)All these factors collectively paved the way for macroeconomic shocks.

MACROECONOMIC SHOCKS

Shocks are basically primitive exogenous forces that are not correlated with each other and they are economically meaningful (S.Bernanke, 1986). An exogenous shock can be understood as the occurrence of an unexpected event that is beyond the control of authorities and could have crucial negative impacts on the economy (Geithner, 2003). " Shocks also have indirect effects that reverberate throughout the economy and can affect output, investment, macroeconomic balances, debt, and poverty" (Geithner, 2003, p.9). Macroeconomic shocks take the form of aggregate demand shocks, aggregate supply shocks, and monetary and fiscal policy shocks.

When the SARS endemic emerged in 2003, the macroeconomic shocks were felt in different economies as stated by some research works (McKibbin, Fernando, & Roshen, 2020) and these macroeconomic shocks manifested themselves in the form of a significant decline in the overall consumption of goods and services by the consumers, a rise in the operating costs of the businesses, and a " re-evaluation of country risks reflected in increased risk premiums" (McKibbin, Fernando, & Roshen, 2020). Covid -19 was declared a pandemic and hence its effects on the economy were much more unprecedented. With the onset of the pandemic, almost all the sectors of the economy reeled under its impact. Most of the sectors, for instance, the travel and tourism industry, entertainment industry, automobile industry, etc were severely affected by the negative economic shocks.

Impact of Macroeconomic Shocks

An organization is said to be in crisis if there is "a low probability, a high impact situation that is perceived by critical stakeholders to threaten the viability of the organization and that is subjectively experienced by these individuals as personally and socially threatening" (Pearson, M., & Clair, 1998). In other words, any event that causes disruptions to a firm's normal functioning, if it impacts the firm's financial stability, or is a cause of loss of goodwill, then we can term the event to be an organizational crisis (Kunreuther, Howard, & Useem, 2018). Covid-19 happened to be one such event that caused an unexpected organizational crisis and uncertainties (Kunreuther, Howard, & Useem, 2018).

Many businesses which were involved in direct face-to-face contact with customers like the transport industry, entertainment, and recreation industry, were negatively impacted during this time. Micro, small, and medium-level enterprises along with women-led businesses also suffered during the pandemic as they lacked sufficient financial resources, and neither did they have enough Internet connectivity to shift towards online businesses. However, this was not the case with firms that were in the information technology sector, health sector, and the education sector (Rawdanowicz & Puy, 2021) as the transition to an online working system was more feasible for them.

When the pandemic struck, it was not only the aggregate demand and aggregate supply alone that were affected, but a mixture of "disaggregated shocks" that had an influence on different sectors in varying strengths and "in an asymmetric manner" (D & Farhi, 2020). These shocks were then transmitted to the entire economy from those sectors which had already been affected by health restrictions (Kightley & Jędrzejowicz, n.d). A supply shock can be understood as any unexpected change in the supply of goods and services, thereby, causing changes in the prices of these goods and services. Demand shocks on the other hand can be defined as any unexpected events causing a change in the demand for goods and services, thereby causing their' prices to change. Supply shocks are mostly previewed as shocks emerging from the labor side. Social distancing and lockdown measures which were devised to ensure the containment of the pandemic, actually, posed a challenge to workers of certain occupations. For instance, people who were involved in the transport sector, laundry services, beauty salons, manufacturing industry, construction industry, fisheries, etc would not be able to adopt "work from home" measures due to the nature of their work. On the contrary, people working in the financial sector, education sector, and IT sector could have a major portion of their work done from home. (Rio-Chanona, Mealy, Pichler, Lafond, & Farmer, 2020). Workers in the transport sector, agriculture, and fisheries sector are more prone to unemployment and the inherent risk of uncertainty for the workers in these sectors is more due to the pandemic. Consequently, they were more likely to reduce their consumption too. Coupled with this, many consumers also tended to reduce their overall consumption so as to reduce the risk of infections. Muellbauer (Muellbauer, 2020), in his article, has stated that lower income levels, increased job insecurity, and wealth effects (mainly due to declining asset prices) have attributed to reduced aggregate consumption, in addition to direct changes in consumption in specific sectors. Pilots, airline crew members, hotel managers, chefs, and other hotel staff faced less intensive supply shocks but strong demand shocks, owing to the fact that consumers had reduced their demand for travel and hotel accommodation. The aviation industry saw huge demand shocks due to international travel restrictions with very little impact on the supply side shocks. This was in sharp contrast to the grocery stores and hypermarkets which faced huge disruptions from the supply side (Ruch & Taskin, n.d). Another significant effect of the pandemic on the economy was the unusual increase in the levels of uncertainties pertaining to financial market tensions, which were distinctly higher during March 2020 (Kightley & Jędrzejowicz, n.d)

Certain sectors, specifically the aviation sector, oil industry, and the travel and tourism sector bore the brunt of the negative demand and supply shocks. Let us analyze the impacts on these sectors individually. To begin with, the aviation sector and airports all over the world experienced a huge decline in revenues due to the reduction in air traffic (Roy & Das, Economic Impact Of Covid 19 Pandemic, 2020). Globally, it was estimated that airport revenues dipped by more than $ 97 billion for the year 2020 (Gittens, 2020). International and domestic flight cancellations to curb the spread of the virus added to the woe. Airports, in general, face incredibly high fixed costs which are needed for the operation and maintenance of the airport infrastructure like runways and terminal buildings (Gittens, 2020). Added to this, we have lower revenues due to the loss of landing fees by airlines, loss of rent from terminal building stores, and loss of parking fees (Tomer & Kane, 2020). Eventually, the aviation industry may resort to laying off workers which include pilots, crew members, and baggage handlers leading to an increase in unemployment. This will lead to a decrease in the aggregate demand for other goods and services which will precipitate into a negative demand shock. However, with the onset of the extensive vaccination drive and the gradual easing of travel restrictions, a slow recovery can be seen in the aviation sector ("The impact, 2022). Several other measures like reducing the intake of new staff, postponing the delivery of new aircraft, and giving options for early retirement for employees were also adopted by the aviation sector to mitigate the losses faced by the industry (Roy & Das, Economic Impact Of Covid 19 Pandemic, 2020).

Another industry to be adversely impacted by the pandemic was the Oil Industry. Travel restrictions, lockdowns, and quarantines, all affected the demand for fuel. Many firms resorted to "work from home" which, in turn, reduced the need for air and road travel. The supply side was also affected negatively as the MENA region faced transport interruptions, which caused a decline in the availability of raw materials and capital (Nguyen & Arezki, 2020). The oil price collapse due to the unsuccessful negotiations between OPEC and its allies, coupled with the demand and supply shocks, makes it even more difficult for the oil-exporting countries to bounce back. The imbalance between the demand for oil and the supply of oil reflects itself in the falling prices of oil. The decline in oil prices leads to a reduction in export receipts and revenue to the government, which is definitely not a good indicator for oil-dependent countries.

The travel and tourism industry along with its allied sectors was another victim of the pandemic. The cancellation of domestic and international flights to curb the spread of the virus affected many people's travel plans. People around the world postponed their travel plans and staycations due to the fear of the virus. Hotels, travel agents, cruise travel, restaurants, and airlines suffered a major setback. The tourism sector had a multiplier effect on its allied sectors like agriculture, food and beverages, and the production of local handicrafts (ILO, 2020). Many firms in the travel and tourism sector faced persistent high costs with hardly any revenue due to the lockdowns and temporary closures of non-essential goods and services. As a result, these firms were forced to lay off workers and close operations. As per the World Travel and Tourism Council, more than 121 million jobs were affected in the travel and tourism industry worldwide, indicating a loss of $3.4 trillion in the global GDP (Wyman, 2020). Countries like Thailand and Vietnam reported that unemployment in the tourism sector was four times more than in the non-tourism sectors ((ILO), 2021). Spain and Italy which are popular travel destinations among tourists registered 14.3% and 13% contributions to the GDP respectively in 2019 (McCarthy, 2020) and these figures had considerably reduced in 2020.

Covid 19 played a major role in wreaking havoc in the financial sectors globally. By the end of February 2020, financial markets reported uncertainties and volatilities, and equity markets registered a rapid decline (Roy & Das, Economic Impact Of Covid 19 Pandemic, 2020). In March 2020, the U. S Treasury market which happened to be the most liquid market in the world started showing signals of reduced liquidity that created uncertainties in credit markets making it difficult for firms and governments to borrow funds for any period of time (COVID-19", 2020). Equity markets have recovered since March, though the recovery has been uneven. The financial and economic uncertainties prevailing in developing and emerging economies were also a cause of concern as these countries faced demand and supply shocks along with supply chain disruptions, the decline in international trade, and pandemic prevention measures (Roy & Das, Economic Impact Of Covid 19 Pandemic, 2020). One study conducted by Haddad, Moreira, and Muir, indicated that the main source of financial instabilities was the corporate bond market and this instability was visible as a decrease in liquidity. An interesting aspect here was that the greatest stress was seen on assets considered safe (Haddad, Moreira, & Muir, 2021). Another study conducted by Lei li, Marco Macchiavelli and Xing (Alex) Zhou indicated that the prime money market funds were also a source of financial turmoil (Li, Li, Macchiavelli, & Zhou, 2021).

Banks have also fallen prey to the pandemic. Many businesses were struggling to pay off their taxes, debts, and other operational costs. Under these circumstances, firms were left with no choice other than to reduce their workforce and cut costs ("Global", 2020). Many borrowers had lost their jobs due to covid 19 and banks suffered from losses due to the lack of repayment of loans. Business firms were reluctant to borrow money as most of the firms were trying to cut down costs or close down. Moreover, governments around the world advised people to go for "contactless payment" and to avoid handling currency notes as the currency notes could also be a source of contamination (Cevik, 2020). This was actually a challenge for banks, particularly in developing and emerging economies where the digitalization of banks was not available for all branches (Roy & Das, Economic Impact Of Covid 19 Pandemic, 2020). Apart from banks, stock markets also faced volatility due to the panic set by the pandemic. Government bond yields increased to a new high during the pandemic, as investors preferred to hold government bonds since they were perceived to be safe ("Impact", 2022). Over the year 2020, 10-year bond yields in the U.S. registered a higher increase than in Germany indicating that investors were more confident about the growth of U. S as compared to Germany ("Impact", 2022). The response of governments all over the world to the pandemic helped in bringing out an uneven recovery of the financial markets. Governments in different countries responded differently to the crisis. The extent of the vaccination drive and fiscal stimulus given by the Governments varied from country to country. For instance, though Germany and France had similar vaccination rates, there was a faster economic recovery in Germany than in France, due to a lower number of infections and a higher volume of fiscal spending ("Impact", 2022). A study conducted by Rebucci (Rebucci, Hartley, & Jiménez, 2022) showed that though the Federal Reserve System was crucial in stabilizing the bond prices globally, the quantitative easing measures adopted by the developing and emerging economies also contributed to stabilizing the local bond and exchange rate markets.

RESPONSE OF THE GOVERNMENT AND THE CORPORATE SECTORS

Governments around the world took up austere measures to keep the coronavirus from spreading. Health restrictions like lockdowns, social distancing, and curbing social gatherings, all resulted in severe repercussions for the corporate sectors. Firms in the travel and tourism industry were deeply impacted. To overcome all these disruptions, governments around the world started taking steps to promote recovery in this sector. Gradual easing of travel restrictions, following health protocols with private sectors, providing support through liquidity and fiscal policy measures, and promoting tourism (Wyman, 2020) were some of the measures taken to relieve the burden of these sectors. The Malaysian government delayed tax installments by 6 months for the travel and tourism sector. On the other hand, U. K reduced its VAT from 20% to 5% for the hospitality sector while, Hong Kong allocated $90.2 million to its tourism sector (OECD, 2020). Korea enabled tourism companies to receive support for "providing up to 90% leave allowance" for their workers for a period of 6 months (ILO, 2020). Countries like Singapore and Portugal went a step forward to provide training and improve the skills of tourism workers through free or subsidized courses (ILO, 2020). Portugal has adopted measures whereby full remuneration should be paid to workers if they were in quarantine or they were caring for a loved one who was in quarantine. In Thailand, travel vouchers were made available for local travelers so that domestic tourism could be motivated (ILO, 2020).

Different countries adopted different fiscal and monetary policies to combat the instabilities created by the pandemic. Countries like Chile introduced fiscal policy measures like deferred tax payments, increased subsidies, new tax measures to foster economic growth, and a one-time bonus for small SMEs. On the monetary side, The Financial Market Commission introduced provisions for deferred loans, and the use of mortgage guarantees to protect loans taken by SMEs ("Policy", 2021). Hong Kong introduced reduced interest rate loans to boost SMEs and also provided them with an extended time for repayment, while, Germany focused on providing grants to small and medium enterprises along with a temporary decrease in the VAT rate. The German government also introduced fiscal policy measures for supporting families and businesses affected by the pandemic ("Policy", 2021). The U.A.E government adopted measures like reduced government fees and taxes, increased the amount of subsidies made available for water and electricity, and simplified the business procedures to boost the economy. The central Bank of the U.A.E also reduced the required reserve ratio of commercial banks from 14% to 7%. Australia too had a set of fiscal and monetary measures in place. Low and middle-income receivers were given additional tax reliefs along with financial support for healthcare packages, the construction sector, and green investments. Additional expenditures on old age care and disability programs were also a part of the fiscal policies of Australia. Monetary easing in the form of policy rate reductions and government bond purchases was adopted by the reserve Bank of Australia. As far as the U.K. was concerned, several stringent fiscal and monetary policy measures were adopted by the country. Financial support to small-scale firms and other businesses affected by the pandemic, deferrals of VAT payments, and increased public expenditure on infrastructures were some of the prominent fiscal measures introduced. Speaking of monetary policies, the bank rate was cut to 0.1% and the UK countercyclical capital buffer rate was reduced to 0% ("Policy", 2021).

Several measures were taken at the right time by the central banks to reduce the tensions as pointed out by studies conducted by Rebucci (Rebucci A, J S Hartley and D Jiménez, 2021). In India, for instance, the Central Government along with the Reserve Bank of India announced various fiscal and monetary policy measures under the Atmanirbhar Bharat Abhiyan (Patnaik, 2022). This scheme was introduced in three phases. In the first phase, the Government decided to address the working capital needs, operational issues, and other problems faced by the Micro, Small, and Medium Enterprises (MSMEs) in India, due to the pandemic. For this purpose, the Government launched Rs. 200 million packages called the Emergency Credit Line Guarantee Scheme 1 (ECLGS 1). This scheme provided a 100 percent guarantee to member lending institutions for losses that were incurred by them due to the non-repayment of funds borrowed by MSMEs (Patnaik, 2022). The second phase, ECLGS 2 was aimed at providing a 100 percent guarantee to the member lending institutions for credit facilities extended by them to borrowers in its 26 sectors (identified by the Kamath Committee of RBI) (RBI, 2020) (Emergency Credit Line Guarantee Scheme (ECLGS), n.d.). The third phase, that is, ECLGS 3 supported the member lending institutions by providing a 100 percent guarantee to the member lending institutions for credit facilities given to firms in the hospitality industry, travel, and tourism sector, and aviation sector.

Firms in the private corporate sector that was financially more stable, could possibly stride over this crisis, though, it depends on the sector in which they are operating (Dev & Sengupta, 2020). Studies show that businesses were down, especially in the Mid-Atlantic area, where 54% of the firms closed down and employment levels were down at 47% (Bartik, et al., 2020). With increasing levels of unemployment, consumption also became restricted to essential goods which further deepened the already troubled aggregate supply. Many firms faced supply chain disruptions that led to a decline in production levels and an increase in production costs (Manuel & Herron, 2020). During the crisis period, the major concern for corporate firms was the payment of debts and salaries to employees (Donthu & Gustafsson, 2020). For many corporate sectors, this was a do-or-die situation as it was a question of survival for the firms and thus, they started "a new way of working based on technological usage" ("6 ways, n.d).

Many firms were quick to respond to lockdowns. In fact, several firms resorted to remote working for their employees so that the work would not be affected. But this sudden shift from on-site to online working created issues with many employees worldwide as many of them witnessed a skill gap (Agrawal, Smet, Lacroix, & Reich, 2020). Many firms, particularly in the U.S., adopted remote work and modified schedules for their employees (Covid-19", n.d.). A lot of firms emphasized paid sick leaves or the hiring of workers by large corporates like Walmart. Firms such as General Motors, GE, Ford, and 3M have refocused their skills on developing much-needed products like masks and ventilators (Cheema-Fox, LaPerla, Serafeim, & Wang, 2020). Giving employees paid sick leaves, avoiding employee layoffs, and providing employees with flexible working hours could help in improving the productivity of workers while alleviating costs by avoiding employee layoffs (Eccles, Ioannou, & Serafeim, 2014). It can also be expected that firms that are more positively inclined towards their employees, supply chain, and operational crisis response have a better tendency to enjoy better investor confidence and also earn fewer negative returns, specifically during the crisis (Lins, Servaes, & Tamayo, 2017).

According to a study conducted by Santanu Bhadra and Sougata Ray, 32.6% of the companies in the Indian scenario, continued their operations by resorting to working from home. 20.4 % of the firms also adopted cost restructuring through employee layoffs and salary cut-offs. About 19.9% of firms also explored new business opportunities by producing products that are more suited to the "new normal" (Bhadra & Ray, 2021)Another interesting prospect that surfaced was that of increased social responsibility by 11% of the firms, in the form of activities related to community services and the production of COVID- 19 related products. All these strategies actually helped the firms to rebound back (Bhadra & Ray, 2021). Companies like Amazon donated a large number of laptops in Seattle to families of children going to elementary school (Manuel & Herron, 2020). AT&T offered healthcare workers free service on FirstNet for a specific period of time, along with a donation of several chargers to hospitals so that patients, as well as healthcare workers, could stay in contact with their families and friends (Manuel & Herron, 2020). LVMH, a very popular brand name in the fashion and cosmetics industry, donated plenty of hand sanitizer to hospitals in Paris and has also increased its production facilities to raise the production of the sanitizers which will also be donated to the different health facilities ((DALL'ASEN & NICOLA, 2020). In the U. S., corporate sectors adopted both market and non-market measures to deal with the crisis (Zhang, 2021). Most of the firms listed in the Russell 1000 had adopted market strategies like work- from home policies along with health and safety policies for their workers and they also contributed to CSR and CPA (Zhang, 2021).

CONCLUSION

The pandemic disrupted the smooth functioning of all the economies around the world. Nobody can say with surety when the global economies will recover. However, countries around the world are adopting different policy measures to bring back their economies on track. Governments along with the Central banks and policymakers should ensure that financial stability is maintained. Increased vaccination rates in all the countries have helped to bring about a slow and gradual recovery.

Though many firms managed to buckle up, sectors like the tourism sector were severely impacted in all the countries. With lockdowns, social distancing, and quarantines, travel was dreaded by most people. Restrictions on social gatherings and suspension of flight operations around the globe had added to the already stressed tourism sector (Xiang, et al., 2021). Many firms in these popular tourist sites had to close down because of this. This led to a huge effect on countries that depended on the tourism industry as their mainstay. People working in these industries were more prone to unemployment and this also fuelled reduced aggregate demand from their sides.

Corporate sectors, for instance, in India, concentrated on operational continuity and innovation of goods and services apart from employee cost reduction (Bhadra & Ray, 2021). Corporations, around the world also started focusing on their corporate social responsibilities area. Many corporate firms were quick to respond to these macroeconomic shocks, while others struggled to cope with these shocks. Showing resilience to these macroeconomic shocks also depends on the industry in which the corporate firms operate.

REFERENCES

Adie Tomer, J. W. (2020). *We should bail out airlines during the coronavirus pandemic—but on taxpayers' terms.* Retrieved from https://www.brookings.edu/research/we-should-bail-out-airlines-during-the-coronavirus-pandemic-but-on-taxpayers-terms/

Agrawal, S., De Smet, A., Lacroix, S., & Reich, A. (2020, May 7). *Adapting employees' skills and roles to the post-pandemic ways of working will be crucial to building operating-model resilience.* Retrieved from https://www.mckinsey.com/business-functions/people-and-organizational-performance/our-insights/to-emerge-stronger-from-the-covid-19-crisis-companies-should-start-reskilling-their-workforces-now

Alexander, W., & Bartik, M. B. (2020, July 10). *The impact of COVID-19 on small business outcomes and expectations.* Retrieved from https://www.pnas.org/doi/10.1073/pnas.2006991117# doi:10.1073/pnas.2006991117

Ashraf, B. N. (2020, September). Economic Impact of Government Interventions During the COVID-19 Pandemic: International Evidence from Financial Markets. *Journal of Behavioral and Experimental Finance.* doi:10.1016/j.jbef.2020.100371

Baqaee, D., & Farhi, E. (2020). *Supply And Demand In Disaggregated Keynesian With An Application To The Covid-19 Crisis.* NBER Working Paper 27152.

Bernanke, B. S. (1986). *Alternative explanations of the money-income correlation.* Carnegie-Rochester Conference Series on Public Policy. Elsevier Science Publishers. doi:10.3386/w1842

Bhadra, S., & Ray, S. (2021, August 15). *Outbreak of COVID-19: Economic Shocks and Corporate Responses in India*. Retrieved from https://a-e-l.scholasticahq.com/

Boland, B., De Smet, A., Palter, R., & Sanghvi, A. (2020, June 8). *McKinsey and Company*. Retrieved from https://www.mckinsey.com/business-functions/people-and-organizational-performance/our-insights/reimagining-the-office-and-work-life-after-covid-19?cid=other-eml-alt-mip-mck&hlkid=8778afb0af6f4f938879e2846fe15066&hctky=11396825&hdpid=4256de30-f942-4b45-948

Cheema-Fox, LaPerla, Serafeim, & Wang. (2020, June 23). *Corporate Resilience and Response During Covid 19*. Retrieved from https://www.statestreet.com/: https://www.statestreet.com/content/dam/statestreet/documents/Articles/Corporate%20Resilience%20and%20Response%20During%20Covid19_3069576.3.2.GBL.pdf

Dall'asen, N. (2020, March 19). *LVMH Is Making Free Hand Sanitizer to Help French Hospitals Fight Coronavirus*. Retrieved from https://www.allure.com/story/lvmh-free-hand-sanitizer-france

Daron Acemoğlu, U. A. (2016, January 30). *Networks-and-macroeconomic-shocks*. Retrieved from voxeu.org: https://voxeu.org/article/networks-and-macroeconomic-shocks

del Rio-Chanona, R. P. M. (2020). Supply and demand shocks in the COVID-19 pandemic: an industry and occupation perspective. *Oxford Review of Economic Policy, 36*(Supplement_1), S94–S137. doi:10.1093/oxrep/graa033

Dev, S. M., & Sengupta, R. (2020, April). *Covid-19: Impact on the Indian Economy*. Retrieved from http://www.igidr.ac.in/pdf/publication/WP-2020-013.pdf

Donthu, N., & Gustafsson, A. (2020). Effects of COVID-19 on business and research. *Journal of Business Research, 117*, 284-289.

Eccles, R. G., Ioannou, I., & Serafeim, G. (2014). The impact of corporate sustainability on organizational processes and performance. *Management Science, 60*(11), 2835–2857. doi:10.1287/mnsc.2014.1984

Emergency Credit Line Guarantee Scheme (ECLGS). (n.d.). Retrieved from www.jatinverma.org: https://www.jatinverma.org/emergency-credit-line-guarantee-scheme-eclgs

Ferran Giones, a. A. (2020, November 14). Revising entrepreneurial action in response to exogenous shocks: Considering the COVID-19 pandemic. *Journal of Business Venturing Insights*. doi:10.1016/j.jbvi.2020.e00186

Franz Ulrich Ruch, T. T. (n.d.). *Demand and Supply Shocks Evidence from Corporate Earning Calls*. Retrieved from worldbank.org: https://openknowledge.worldbank.org/bitstream/handle/10986/36923/Demand-and-Supply-Shocks-Evidence-from-Corporate-Earning-Calls.pdf

Gaur, A., & Kumar, M. (2017). A systematic approach to conducting review studies: An assessment of content analysis in 25 years of IB research. *Journal of World Business*, *53*(2), 280–289. doi:10.1016/j.jwb.2017.11.003

Geithner. (2003). *Fund assistance for countries facing exogenous shocks*. Academic Press.

Gittens, A. (2020, May). Impacts of COVID-19 on aviation and the airport business. *International Airport Review*. Retrieved from https://www.internationalairportreview.com/article/117249/covid-19-airport-business-aci-world-recovery/

Ha Nguyen, R. A. (2020). *Coping with a dual shock: COVID-19 and oil prices*. Retrieved from https://cepr.org/voxeu/columns/coping-dual-shock-covid-19-and-oil-prices

Han, H., & Qian, Y. (2020). Did Enterprises' Innovation Ability Increase During the COVID-19 Pandemic? Evidence From Chinese Listed Companies. *Asian Economic Letters*, 1-5.

ILO. (2020). *The impact of COVID-19 on the tourism sector*. Retrieved from https://www.ilo.org/wcmsp5/groups/public/---ed_dialogue/---sector/documents/briefingnote/wcms_741468.pdf

International, A.C. (2022). *The impact of COVID-19 on airports—and the path to recovery*. Retrieved from https://aci.aero/2022/06/28/the-impact-of-covid-19-on-airportsand-the-path-to-recovery/

Iyke, B. N. (2020, October 26). *economic-policy-uncertainty-in-times-of-covid-19-pandemic*. Retrieved from https://a-e-l.scholasticahq.com/article/17665-economic-policy-uncertainty-in-times-of-covid-19-pandemic justcapital.com. (n.d.). *The COVID-19 Corporate Response Tracker: How America's Largest Employers Are Treating Stakeholders Amid the Coronavirus Crisis*. Retrieved from https://justcapital.com/reports/the-covid-19-corporate-response-tracker-how-americas-largest-employers-are-treating-stak e/reports/the-covid-19-corporate-response-tracker-how-americ as-largest-employers-are-treating-stakeholders-amid-the-coro navirus-crisis/

Katalin Bodnár, J. L.-G. (2020). RError! Hyperlink reference not valid. etrieved from https://www.ecb.europa.eu/pub/economic-bulletin/articles/2020/html/ecb.ebart202007_01~ef0a77a516.en.html

Kightley & Jędrzejowicz. (n.d.). *Macroeconomic policy response to the Covid-19*. Retrieved from https://www.bis.org/publ/bppdf/bispap122_r.pdf

Kunreuther, H. a. (2018). *Mastering Catastrophic Risk: How Companies Are Coping with disruption*. Oxford University Press.

Lins, K. V., Servaes, H., & Tamayo, A. (2017). Social capital, trust, and firm performance: The value of corporate social responsibility during the financial crisis. *The Journal of Finance*, 1785–1824.

Lukasz RawdanowiczD. P. (2021, June 22). Retrieved from https://cepr.org/voxeu/columns/covid-19-and-corporate-sector -where-we-stand

Luo, A. (2019, July 18). *Content Analysis: A Step-by-Step Guide with Examples*. Retrieved from https://www.scribbr.com/methodology/content-analysis/

Manuel, T., & Herron, T. L. (2020). An ethical perspective of business CSR and the COVID-19 pandemic. *Society and Business Review, 15*(3), 235-253.

McCarthy, N. (2020). COVID-19's Impact On Tourism: Which Countries Are The Most Vulnerable? *Forbes*. Retrieved from https://www.forbes.com/sites/niallmccarthy/2020/05/05/covid-19s-impact-on-tourism-which-countries-are-the-most-vulnerabl e-infographic/?sh=641bfa6d1906

McKibbin & Fernando. (2020, March 2). *The Global Macroeconomic Impacts of COVID-19: Seven scenarios*. Retrieved from https://www.brookings.edu/wp-content/uploads/2020/03/20200302_covid19.pdf

Mercy Ogunnusi, T. O.-A. (2021). Lessons learned from the impact of COVID-19 on the global construction industry. *Journal of Engineering, Design and Technology.*

Muellbauer, J. (2020, April). *The coronavirus pandemic and US consumption.* Retrieved from VoxEU.org: https://voxeu.org/article/coronavirus-pandemic-and-us-consumption

https://ssbr-edu.ch/. (n.d.). *6WaysThatCovid19HasHadAPositiveImpactOnBusinesses.* Retrieved from https://ssbr-edu.ch/6-ways-that-covid19-has-had-a-positive-impact-on-businesses/

Nelson, R. A. (1989). On the Measurement of Capacity Utilization. *The Journal of Industrial Economics*, 273–286.

OECD. (2020). *Tourism Policy Responses to the Coronavirus (Covid 19).* Retrieved from https://www.oecd.org/coronavirus/policy-responses/tourism-policy-responses-to-the-coronavirus-covid-19-6466aa20/

Patnaik, A. (2022). Measuring Demand and Supply Shocks From COVID-19: An Industry-Level Analysis for India. *Margin: The Journal of Applied Economic Research*, 76-105. doi:10.1177/09738010211067392

Pearson, C. M. (1998). Reframing Crisis Management. *Academy of Management Review*, *23*(1), 59–76. doi:10.5465/amr.1998.192960

RBI. (2020). *Report of the expert committee on resolution framework for COVID-19 related stress.* Retrieved from https://rbidocs.rbi.org.in/rdocs/PublicationReport/Pdfs/EXPERTCOMMITTEED58A96778C5E4799AE0E3FCC13DC67F2.PDF

Rebucci, A., Hartley, J. S., & Jiménez, D. (2021). *An event study of COVID-19 central bank quantitative easing in advanced and emerging economies.* NBER Working Paper 27339.

Roy, S. (2020). *Economic impact of Covid 19.* Academic Press.

Seetharaman, G. (2020, March 14). How different sectors of the economy are bearing the brunt of the coronavirus outbreak. *The Economic Times.*

Sha, S. S. (2020). Part A: Special Section on COVID-19 Research. *Emerging Markets Finance & Trade*, *56*(15), 3551–3553.

Sharma, Y. S. (2020, July 25). Research on Pandemics Special Issue of the Journal Emerging Markets Finance and Trade. *Emerging Markets Finance & Trade*, 2133–2137. https://www.tandfonline.com/

Shohini Roy, D. D. (2020). *Economic Impact of Covid 19 Pandemic*. Retrieved from https://www.researchgate.net/publication/343222400_ECONOMIC_IMPACT_OF_COVID-19_PANDEMIC

Soni, P. (2021, January 6). *Effects of COVID-19 lockdown phases in India: an atmospheric perspective*. Retrieved from https://www.ncbi.nlm.nih.gov/pmc/articles/PMC7785398/

The COVID-19 Corporate Response Tracker: How America's Largest Employers Are Treating Stakeholders Amid the Coronavirus Crisis. (n.d.). Retrieved from https://justcapital.com/reports/the-covid-19-corporate-response-tracker-how-americas-largest-employers-are-treating-stakeholders-amid-the-coronavirus-crisis/

weforum. (2020). *Impact of COVID-19 on the Global Financial System*. Retrieved from https://www3.weforum.org/docs/WEF_Impact_of_COVID_19_on_the_Global_Financial_System_2020.pdf

Wyman, O. (2020). *To Recovery and Beyond the future of travel & tourism in the wake of COVID 19*. Retrieved from https://wttc.org/Portals/0/Documents/Reports/2020/To%20Recovery%20and%20Beyond-The%20Future%20of%20Travel%20Tourism%20in%20the%20Wake%20of%20COVID-19.pdf?ver=2021-02-25-183120-543

Xiang, Rasoo, Hang, Javid, Javed, & Artene. (2021, May 6). *The Effect of COVID-19 Pandemic on Service Sector Sustainability and Growth*. Retrieved from https://www.frontiersin.org/articles/10.3389/fpsyg.2021.633597/full

Zhang, Y. (2021). Corporate Responses to COVID-19: A Nonmarket Strategy Approach. *Sociological Perspectives*, *64*(5), 1032–1057.

Chapter 6 Corporate Financial Management Decisions During COVID-19

Rengarajan Veerasamy
Arab Open University, Oman

Kabaly Subramanian
Arab Open University, Oman

Subrahmaninan Muthuraman
Arab Open University, Oman

ABSTRACT

Financial decisions such as investment and financing will have to be made in accordance with the environmental conditions prevailing in a particular time. This chapter will focus on the corporate financial decisions during the current pandemic situation. In financing decisions, cost of capital is the determining factor, and accordingly, financing modes are preferred by the organizations. Financial decisions made in a difficult time are resulting in negative cash profits in most of the cases. With the ongoing COVID-19 crisis, the stock markets suffered a severe shock resulting in negative returns, and the stock market crash risk has become higher than normal. COVID-19 has made the financing and investment markets more challenging. Financing decisions are the hardest decisions that companies could make during COVID-19 times as the cost of capital might skyrocketed and the companies themselves would find their profits declining significantly. Corporates must now be thinking seriously about alternative sources of funding for their business requirements.

DOI: 10.4018/978-1-6684-5342-1.ch006

INTRODUCTION

Financial decisions made in a difficult time result in negative cash profits in most cases, as these decisions are not supported by the environmental forces like demand for a product, raising price level, reduced disposable income etc. Joseph et al. (2020) present that any global crisis makes a firm cashless but at the same time makes companies with high level of cash more competitive in the long run. Investment decisions such as expanding the existing business, replacing old assets with new ones, modernizing the existing state of factory and office etc. are made after carefully estimating the return on investment and payback period of those projects. Thus, the present value of cash inflows is compared with present value of cash outflows and if the result of this comparison is positive, such investment are favored by the finance team of an organization. In Financing decisions, cost of capital is the determining factor and accordingly financing modes are preferred by the organizations. At the same time, financial decisions must be made at the right time to attain maximum returns. For example, if the market is moving downwards and the supply side is greater than the demand side, then the returns are not maximized, rather revenues are focused on covering the costs.

Schoemaker & Russo (2016) presents that decision making is the process of choosing the best alternative among the alternatives within the purview of limited resource availability. Financial decisions such as investment and financing decisions are crucial for an organization as these decisions are the hopes of an organization in achieving target revenue and profit. Lie et al. (2021) argues that due to this ongoing COVID-19 crisis, the stock markets suffered a severe shock as it resulted in negative returns and the stock market crash risk has become higher than normal. Thus, financing decisions are the hardest decisions that companies could make during COVID -19 times as the cost of capital might have skyrocketed and the companies themselves would have found their profits declining significantly. With declining profits, and higher cost of capital, companies must have felt the difficulties associated with funding their investment projects through debt or equity financing modes. Yun Ke (2022) argues that cost of capital of organizations' during COVID times had increased to a greater extent. Thus, COVID-19 has made the financing and investment markets more challenging. Corporate must now be thinking seriously about alternative sources of funding and be using them for funding their investment projects.

Financial Management Decisions during Crisis Times

Every crisis is a lesson for an organization and to come out from that crisis, companies will be forced to experiment with certain innovative and unused means of financing to explore the business opportunities. This has been quite normal as the crisis makes every organization think beyond the conventional ways of making certain decisions that include financing and investment decisions too. Organizations use a variety of methods to evaluate long-term capital investment projects such as payback period, Net Present Value, Internal Rate of Return, Profitability Index etc. All these methods are useful for any organization to make an investment decision. Payback period gives an estimate of period that a project would take in returning the capital invested, Net present value calculates the present of value of benefits that a company would receive from investment decisions, internal rate of return provides an estimate of a rate at which present value of cash inflows could be same as present value of cash outflows. Thus, all these methods are helping organizations in choosing the right investment decision. At the same, during crisis times, companies must use other sophisticated methods to evaluate long-term investment decisions as crisis times are quite different from normal times in terms of challenges that an organization would face.

The approach of an organization gets changed during crisis times. Shareholders' wealth is the core objective that organizations attempt to maximize during normal times, but during unfavorable economic times, organizations simply look for covering their costs in full so, it can sustain its competitive position in the market.

OBJECTIVES OF THE CHAPTER

Following are the objectives of this chapter:

(i) To present the differences that usually exist between financial management decisions during normal and crisis times
(ii) To present some of the presumptions that financial management decisions have been made must be having as some of the characteristics of hard time decisions.
(iii) To recommend risk adjusted cost of capital as one of the superior methods for estimating the cost of capital in financing decisions
(iv) To present the importance of NPV, ENPV and Discounted payback period techniques in evaluating capital investment decisions to be made in crisis times

Financial Management - Approaches – Normal Times Vs Crisis Times

Financial management decisions usually include making financing decisions, making investment decisions, and preparing reports for aiding the decision-making process.

Organizations will have to determine the rate of return that should be earned from an investment decision. The expected rate of return estimated has close connection with the rate at which money had been borrowed by an organization, which is termed as cost of capital. Cost of capital becomes the yardstick for evaluating various capital investment decisions. During crisis times like COVID, organizations mostly show interest in investing in projects that fetch minimal returns or just covering the cost of capital from investments. Financial Management Approaches to be followed during normal and crisis times been presented below:

It is evident from the above analysis that normal times and crisis times must be viewed separately by the organizations, so that objectives like shareholders wealth maximization can be achieved. Shareholders' wealth is the core of an organization during normal times, but during crisis times, there has been loss of earnings for all, so there should be adjustments in the shareholders wealth maximization. Those adjustments in shareholders' wealth could be shared with everyone, stakeholders' benefits could be enhanced. Corporates are working to maximize the wealth of shareholders. It must always be the core objective. During crisis time, risk perceived by an organization would be reduced to a certain extent. This approach could bring down the earnings of an organization to a little extent. So, shareholders maximization approach is not sacrificed here, at the same time, risk perceived is little reduced. To make all stakeholders equally important in profit sharing, an equally shared benefit approach could have been considered as priority as there has been crisis affecting everyone in that company.

NORMAL TIMES VS CRISIS TIMES

The focus of an organization is two-fold:

Normal Times

Net Present Value = Present value of Cash inflows – Present value of Cash outflows

Crisis Times

Sustainable worth of Business Continuity = Minimum Expected Rate of Return * Total Value of Assets

Organizations must be working hard to thrive business during crisis times. During such periods, even though higher profits are not desired, but minimum profits must be earned by them, so they can continue to perform in the market and look for reviving the situation towards better. Sustainable worth of Business Continuity

Table 1. Presenting the approaches adopted in financial management during normal and crisis times

	Normal Times	Crisis Times
Debt Financing	Organizations mostly prefer borrowing during normal times, as interest is fully tax deductible and certain tax advantages could be claimed by a company	Organizations must think about minimizing the risk associated. Debt Financing can be used as the last resort since it makes companies to pay interest annually irrespective of financial performance and assets are getting mortgaged.
Shareholders Wealth Maximization	Organizations must be focusing on shareholders maximization and making decisions that aim at providing maximum benefits to shareholders. Thus, shareholders' wealth is the ultimate objective of an organization in financial management decisions.	Organizations must think of providing an equal number of benefits for all related stakeholders like employees, creditors, bankers, shareholders, customers etc. As the crisis is affecting everyone widely, the shared benefits approach must likely be the core objective of an organization. Shared benefits must be the approach to be followed all times. During normal times, it is given due importance and at the same time, during crisis this approach must be given due priority, so that organizations can ensure everyone is taken care of equally.
Investment Decisions	Organizations are looking for actions that give maximum benefits. Investment decisions are made based on Net Present Value to be derived from that action.	During crisis, additional care must be taken in addition to loss of money value. Organizations must estimate all possible risk factors affecting the return of an investment. An advanced NPV method like Expected Net Present Value can be used for evaluating investment decisions.
What if Analysis	During normal times, companies do perform what if analysis in estimating cash inflows. Variations expected in all important variables such revenue and expenses are all considered and accordingly estimates are made.	Extended what if analysis is required here since all variables includes fixed components are subject to change. So, organizations must be carefully examining all possible changes that would affect the return.
Risk Adjusted Incremental Benefits Analysis for making decisions.	Normally, companies make decisions based on incremental benefits that they would receive from a course of action. Normal approach for making decision is Incremental Revenues must be higher than incremental relevant costs, so that the proposed action would offer additional benefits to an organization in terms of revenue and ROI	Organizations must think about determining the risk adjusted incremental benefits and costs. Accordingly, risk adjusted incremental benefits would be calculated and decisions could be made. Incremental revenues and cost must be discounted at risk premium rate and a comparison could be made for making decisions

can be defined as the state of performance at which businesses need to operate to achieve corporate goals during crisis times. As business continuity would become one of the major concerns for an organization in crisis times, minimal return that an organization needs to sustain so that there would be no compromise in achievement of corporate goals. So, sustainable value of business continuity can be regarded as the state of profit of an organization, which is very much needed for them to continue to perform its operations successfully and move towards achieving corporate goals including shareholders wealth maximization.

Literature Review Supporting Viewing Financial Management during Crisis Separately

Zubair et al. (2020) argue that a financial crisis is the root cause for facing lower growth opportunities and higher financial constraints. They also argue that theories predict declines in investment during a financial crisis. During financial crisis times, companies can think of using liquid sources. Companies can make use of additional support provided by government agencies to meet out their liquidity crunch or additional financial requirements. During crisis times, growth rate of a company is gradually declining, and they will also face challenges in getting the required amount of funds for completing their long-term growth-oriented investments. Secondly, internal resources whatever available must be used well by the company and if required, they must be using external sources. This must be the approach during crisis times for funding companies' financial needs.

Hanwool oh et al. (2002) argue that during crisis times like pandemic, good public financial management is very much important to ensure efficiency and transparency in resources like finance and materials management. The government must try to reduce the use of public revenues so that there could be savings which can be saved for meeting pandemic needs. Though this approach is applicable for governments, still companies can think of implementing this during crisis times like COVID. Organization must make use of existing resources well without much borrowing, so that existing obligations only must be met. Companies must think of using internal resources well so that it can avoid borrowing during pandemic times.

Duchin et al. (2010) observed that credit crisis had affected the publicly listed companies in negatively. They observed that any crisis is affecting the performance of organizations negatively. So, COVID crisis must also have produced negative consequences on the performance of various organizations. Companies must be carefully choosing the financing and investment options in crisis times, so that they can survive meeting their financial obligations even during crisis times.

Companies must evaluate and choose the ideal source of financing to meet their requirements as each of the financing options has its own advantages and disadvantages. Companies can make use of internal sources of funds such retained earnings during crisis times so that the hazards of any external financing could be minimised. (Wang, 2010, Yang et al., 2009). They argue that choosing the right financing options for making any kind of investment decision is the key to survive in crisis times. Companies must be thinking seriously about the sources of finance to fund their investment options. During crisis times, financing options must be very carefully chosen so that companies do not get trapped in higher cost of financing modes.

Behavioural finance in general and in crisis times, shows that people are more of loss averse rather than being risk averse. This means, people want to avoid having losses on their investment. Investors do not want to lose their investment normally and during crisis investors are more loss averse. Similarly, corporate organizations during crisis times, they try to avoid risks as much as possible and they do not want to incur losses as well. This is the usual tendency of general investors and corporate investors too. During crisis times, investors follow investment strategies that aim at reducing losses.

Characteristics of Financial Decisions Made During Crisis Times

Organizations are looking for certain benefits in any financial decision made by them. In investment decisions, they are looking for higher rates of return and in financing decisions they are looking for the lowest possible cost of capital with lesser administrative procedures. Financing and investment decisions are made under certain assumptions.

Financial decisions made in crisis times should be having the following characteristics:

1. Decisions having the ability to cover cost and produce minimal expected rate of return
2. Decisions must focus on sustainability and continuity of the operations rather than maximum profits
3. Decisions must yield positive Expected Net Present Value for the organization to cover the impacts of all controllable risk factors that are internal and specific for an organization.
4. Business Continuity and resilience should be the focal point and shareholders wealth maximization must be revisited to include continuity and resilience.
5. The risk adjusted rate of return can be regarded as the yardstick for examining and evaluating the investment and financing decisions of an organization.

Financial Decisions in Crisis Times like COVID- 19

Organizations must be making financial decisions under certain assumptions. When those assumptions become variable forces, then companies will need to operate in complex environment situations wherein everything becomes an unpredictable variable. In those situations, an organization must be looking for certain KPIs or decision criteria that would help them in making financial and investment decisions.

Figure 1. Those KPIs been summarized and given in the figure below

Financing Decisions during COVID-19 Times

Memon et al. (2017) presents that financing decisions involve deciding about the right mix of debt and equity in the corporate capital structure that provides the maximum value of the firm, considering ROE and ROA as bases. Organizations are trying to maximize the total value of the firm by keeping the right mix in debt/ equity combination. Usually, cost of capital is the criteria for making financing decisions as companies do not want to spend so much amount of spare so much of profits as interest and dividends since they want to retain profits for future expansion. Retained earnings must be maximized so that they will have enough sum of amount for future expansion purpose and the total value of equity is also getting enhanced.

Secondly, excessive debt dependence is also a major threat for an organization as it poses a greater risk in terms of reduced capacity in repayments.

Companies need to examine the cost of capital of different funding options and the risk factors that the company is exposed to. Organizations must set a nominal rate as the expected rate of return, as it includes the expected inflation rate as well. Organization can determine the risk adjusted cost of capital and that can become the yardstick for examining financing options and the investment options.

Risk Adjusted Cost of Capital = Nominal Cost of Capital + Specific Project Based Risk element + Unexpected Risk element.

To illustrate this concept, let us say a company is examining two options whether equity or debt can be used for funding a project. The estimates are given below:

Table 2. Debt vs. Equity

Project	Debt			Equity		
	Nominal Rate of Interest/Dividends	Specific Project based return (%)	Unexpected Return	Nominal Rate of Interest/Dividends	Specific Project based return (%)	Unexpected Return
A	8%	4% with probability of 0.6	1% with a probability of 0.5	12%	4% with probability of 0.6	1% with a probability of 0.5

Now the risk adjusted cost of capital can be calculated as

Risk Adjusted Cost of Capital = Nominal Cost of Capital + Specific Project Based Risk element + Unexpected Risk element.

Project A

Cost of Debt = 8% + (4*0.6) + (1 * 0.5) = 8 + 2.4 + 0.5 = 10.9%

Cost of Equity = 12% + (4*0.6) + (1*0.5) = 12 + 2.4 + 0.5 = 14.9%

As the cost of debt is cheaper than the cost of equity, the company can be advised to employ debt source of financing. This risk adjusted cost of capital can also be used as an expected rate to examine and evaluate the investment projects.

In addition, companies should also seriously examine keeping the assets for longer duration, even beyond the life, to minimize the chances of having a loan. Sale of old assets can also be regarded as one of the sources of funding, as crisis like COVID-19 is affecting corporate revenue streams so badly, companies' profits get affected negatively.

INVESTMENT DECISIONS DURING COVID-19 TIMES

Investment decisions must be carefully made by an organization as it needs huge amounts of money to make investments and the return expected from such investments are subject to various risks including pandemic-based risk. Organizations normally consider Net Present Value (NPV) for evaluating the investment projects. Žižlavský (2014) presents that NPV method consists of discounting all future cash flows (both in- and out-flow) emanating from the project at a given discount rate and then summing them together.

Techniques That Can Be Used for Evaluating Investment Projects during Crisis Like COVID Times

Some of the methods, companies can make sure for evaluating capital investment projects are discussed below:

(i) **NPV** = Present value of cash inflows expected from a Project – Present value of Cash outlay required for implementing the project.

To illustrate these points, let us consider the following example:

Table 3. Techniques

	Project A	Project B	Project C
Present Value of Cash inflows	120,000	140,000	138,000
Present value of Cash outflows	120,000	130,000	141,000
NPV	**0**	**10,000**	**(3,000)**

(ii) Expected Net Present Value

Peymankar et al. (2021) explains that ENPV is the best tool to be used when maximizing the of a project is expected to yield cash flows whose occurrence is uncertain, which are characterised with different scenarios. In ENPV calculations, NPV of a project under varied circumstances can be calculated. Later, that NPV can be multiplied with a probability to ascertain the ENPV

To illustrate this, let us consider the following example.

As per the ENPV calculations, project B is ideal for the company as it gives maximum returns after incorporating all risk factors.

Table 4. Techniques

	Project A	Project B	Project C
NPV considering varied scenario	1,000	2,000	2,500
Probability of occurrence	0.8	0.5	0.2
ENPV (NPV * P(x))	**$ 800**	**$ 1,000**	**$ 500**

Table 5. A project requires $ 10,000 initial investment is expected to yield cash inflows like

Year	Cash inflows
1	4,000
2	5,000
3	4,000

(iii) Discounted Payback Period

Financetrain (2022) presents that the discounted payback period is the number of years that a project will take to recover the cost of initial investment in terms of the present value of cash inflows. Usually, payback is calculated based on cash inflows and outflow of a project to determine the number of years that an investment project would take to recover the initial investment. This calculation is not considering the time value of money. So, discounted cash flows are usually calculated for the future cash inflows. After calculating the present value of each year's cash inflows, payback period can be calculated, so the issue of having not considered time value of money in payback period is duly removed. This method is illustrated as below:

Normal Payback period for this project is

2 + 1,000/4,000 = 2 + 0.25 = 2.25 years

Discounted payback is = 2 + (10,000 – 7766) /4130

Table 6. The discounted payback can be calculated like (assuming discount rate as 10%)

Year	Cash inflows	Present Value Table value	Present Value	Cumulative cash inflows
1	4,000	0.909	3,636	3.636
2	5,000	0.826	4,130	7,766
3	4,000	0.751	3,004	10,770

= 2 + 2,234 / 4,130
= 2 + 0.54
= 2.54 years

This method estimates cash inflows and the present value of cash inflows reasonably after considering all relevant risk factors. The payback period calculated based on discounted cash flow is more realistic since the time value of money on cash inflows is duly recognized and considered.

SUMMARY OF FINDINGS AND DISCUSSION

Financial management is crucial for the success of an organization. Organizations will have to see different environmental situations ranging from good to moderate to bad. With good financial management strategies, organizations can achieve their core objectives such as Profit maximization and shareholders wealth maximization. Organizations' financial must be stronger enough so that wealth of shareholders can be maximized. Organizations must be carefully examining financing and investment options so that appropriate cost of capital can be determined and that can become the yardstick for evaluating various capital investment projects.

In estimating cost of capital, the risk elements such as pandemic risk and other non-controllable risk factors must be duly included so that it becomes an appropriate rate that could be considered duly in financing and investment decisions. Risk elements must be duly examined, and those risk elements must be duly incorporated in cost of capital estimations so that it becomes an acceptable rate for normal times and crisis times.

Investment decisions are normally made considering the Net Present Value of a project. If NPV is positive, then that project is given due consideration for acceptance. Since risks like pandemic risks and other non-controllable risks are not duly incorporated in the discounting process, an advanced methodology in NPV could be used for evaluating an investment project. In this regard, Expected Net Present Value (ENPV) can be regarded as one of the appropriate methods for evaluating investment projects. Secondly, discounted payback can be calculated in place of normal payback and decisions can be made accordingly.

Advancement in methods to be used for evaluating financing and investment decisions are required since pandemic risks have put companies' upside down recently. Organizations will have to be extremely careful in making financing and investment decisions during pandemic times and even before pandemic. The issue of non-controllable risk factors such as pandemic risk must be incorporated in cost of capital estimation process and in long term investment evaluation processes, so that the loss that might arise due to such pandemic risks would be well managed.

CONCLUSION

Financial management involves making investment and financing decisions wisely to achieve the corporate objectives. Finance Managers will have to examine financing and investment options carefully, so that shareholders' wealth maximization principle/ goal is not compromised. The techniques to be used for examining financing and investment options must be carefully chosen during crisis times like COVID-19 since challenges in this period are more enormous than the normal period. Organizations must be employing some sophisticated techniques to evaluate financing and investment decisions so that corporate remain intact, and the company can keep continuing its business in the market and achieve resilience to the market needs.

Organizations must be able to design techniques innovatively as the times they are in is so complex and highly risky. The management must think of using such sophisticated techniques in their financial management decisions, so shareholders' wealth becomes undisturbed. Risk adjusted cost of capital and ENPV can be used by the finance managers for examining the projects for investments and financing options and accordingly decisions could be made. During crisis times, the techniques used for evaluating options should also be innovative, so that corporate goals can be intact for the organization.

FUTURE RESEARCH PERSPECTIVES

Financial management is crucial for the success of an organization. Companies must be giving good importance to these financial management decisions since those decisions determine companies profit and loss-making capacities. When companies are in trouble due to any crisis, then strategies to be adopted to escape from the consequences of such crisis must be carefully learnt by them, so that each of the challenges can be very well addressed by an organization. Thus, financial management during crisis times has always been a big research topic to be studied by researchers in detail. The behavioral finance theory and the relevant application of this theory during crisis times can also be studied well in order to develop a pattern of investment and financing decisions of corporates made in crisis times.

REFERENCES

Duchin, R., Ozbas, O., & Sensoy, B. (2010). Costly external finance, corporate investment, and the subprime mortgage credit crisis. *Journal of Financial Economics*, *97*(3), 418–435. doi:10.1016/j.jfineco.2009.12.008

Eact. (2022). *Cash and Working Capital Management in the Corona crisis*. EACT.

Joseph. (2020). *Cash in the time of corona*. CEPR.

Ke. (2022). The impact of COVID-19 on firms' cost of equity capital: Early evidence from U.S. public firms. *Finance Research Letters*.

Khan, A., Shaikh, M., Shah, A. B., Zahid, I., & Shaikh, F. M. (2017). Impact of Financing Decisions on Firm's Performance: An Empirical Study of Pakistani Listed Firm's in KSE. *International Journal of Management and Information Technology, 12*(1).

Liu, Z., Huynh, T. L. D., & Dai, P. F. (2021). The impact of COVID-19 on the stock market crash risk in China. *Research in International Business and Finance*, *57*, 101419. doi:10.1016/j.ribaf.2021.101419 PMID:34744246

Oh. (2020). *Financial management operations under the COVID-19 pandemic: The Korean Experience*. iadb.org

Peymankar, M., Davari, M., & Ranjbar, M. (2021). Maximizing the expected net present value in a project with uncertain cash flows. *European Journal of Operational Research*, *294*(2), 442–452. doi:10.1016/j.ejor.2021.01.039

Schoemaker, P. J., & Russo, J. E. (2016). *Decision Making*. The Palgrave Encyclopaedia of Strategic Management. doi:10.1057/978-1-349-94848-2

Wang, D. (2010). Corporate investment, financing, and dividend policies in the high-tech industry. *Journal of Business Research*, *63*(5), 486–489. doi:10.1016/j.jbusres.2009.04.006

Žižlavský, O. (2014). Net present value approach: Method for economic assessment of innovation projects. *Procedia: Social and Behavioral Sciences*, *156*, 506–512. doi:10.1016/j.sbspro.2014.11.230

Zubair, S., Kabir, R., & Huang, X. (2020). Does the financial crisis change the effect of financing on investment? Evidence from private SMEs. *Journal of Business Research, 110*, 456-463. doi:10.1016/j.jbusres.2020.01.063

Chapter 7
Does Financial Attitude Impact Trading Activity of Retail Investors During the COVID-19 Pandemic in the Sultanate of Oman?

Shanmuga Pria
https://orcid.org/0000-0003-1117-3831
University of Technology and Applied Sciencce, Oman

VenkataVara Prasad
University of Technology and Applied Science, Oman

ABSTRACT

The purpose of this research is to find out whether retail investor trading activity was influenced by their financial attitude during the COVID-19 pandemic. The research follows the descriptive and causal research design on a sample size of 87 retail investors obtained through snowball sampling method in which respondents were first identified with the help of financial advisors from five brokerage companies in Oman. The identified respondents were requested to forward the Google survey form to other participants. The study results reveal that the majority of the respondents were in agreement that they can be optimistic regardless of the current COVID-19 situation. There was found to be no difference in the mean rating given by Omanis and non-Omanis towards financial anxiety, optimism, financial security, precautionary savings, financial literacy, financial satisfaction, and risk involvement. Nationality matters only for investor confidence as the mean ratings given for it differ between Omanis and non-Omanis.

DOI: 10.4018/978-1-6684-5342-1.ch007

INTRODUCTION

Behavior finance is the attempt to understand the reasoning pattern. This includes the emotional process involved and how much it influences the investor's decision-making process. It is -in general terms- the what, why and how of finance. The concept of behavior finance is also associated with psychology, since it is a study of reactions that are based on a given situation, that explains the reasons behind such behavior. As such, the decisions made as a result of utilizing the understanding of finance. In addition to that, behavioural finance refers to the application of psychology to finance. According to behavioural finance, individuals' views and conduct influence their financial decisions and financial markets. This will help to examine the impact of psychology on financial practitioners' behaviour and how that affects stock markets (Kapoor. S., et al, 2017).

Any news or information that is available for the investor can play a major role in influencing investment markets. Investment behaviour is the reaction that is based on the uncertainty about the future. Risk involvement is also a major concept that contributes to explaining investment behaviour. It is only natural for every investor to have a different perspective depending on who they are as a person, therefore, some investors are willing to take risk for better returns whereas others prefer to reduce the risk with minimal return. Information availability is also a major part of how investors react or behave during trading periods in the market (Paisarn et al., 2021).

Financial attitude is a subject that is related closely with investors behaviour, knowledge, and financial literacy (understand how finance work). Therefore, it is the state of mind that is made from the individual investors experience. (Ameliawati, and Setiyani, 2018). Personal tendency toward financial matters can be defined as financial attitude. Financial attitudes are the result of a decision-maker's behaviour, and they can be entrenched through economic and non-economic factors (Rai et al, 2019).

COVID-19 is a contagious disease that causes fever, cough, and shortness of breath in people who are infected. It spreads mostly through person-to-person contact, with infected people coughing, sneezing, or speaking, releasing respiratory droplets into the air. The COVID-19 pandemic has halted years of progress in the fight against poverty and put a generation of children's lives in jeopardy (WorldVision .org). COVID-19 caused a big drop of activities in the investment market; however, it did not stop the retail investors to take the risk of investing during such times which could possibly yield much greater returns. Also, in the aftermath of the coronavirus, the OECD predicted an increase in FDI inflows in 2012. Supply and demand shocks, combined with reduced investor price decreases, are projected to cause a further dip in direct investment in the Middle East and Africa region.

The entire planet had a global impact which suddenly caused people worldwide to get affected by this pandemic of COVID-19. The efforts to maintain stability during such difficult times were a questionable matter. Thus, we chose to tackle such problems in our research and explore what others couldn't understand yet.The coronavirus 2019 (COVID-19) has created a public fitness disaster and a financial disaster. The fast spread of the virus has had a significant influence on global financial markets. It produced an unprecedented amount of risk and resulted in huge losses for investors in a short period. (Dayong, Z. et al., 2020)

One of the costliest pandemics in recent memory will be caused by the new coronavirus (COVID-19), which is not just a human and health catastrophe on an unprecedented scale. According to the most current statistics, the COVID-19 pandemic has a big effect on the economy and financial markets. Several financial markets across the globe have suffered significant losses since the outbreak of the epidemic. Covid-19 had a short-term detrimental influence on GCC stock markets. According to the findings of this research, the stock markets of GCC nations are less affected than the global stock markets. Finally, the data verified the two-way spillover impact on the GCC stock markets due to Chinese stock market movements (Salman, A., 2021). Research into Covid-19's effects on worldwide financial markets and a reference to estimate future patterns in the global stock market once the pandemic fades have benefited from the results. (Salman, 2021). In addition, GCC stock markets are influenced favorably by crude oil (WTI) price, while the global oil market and stock market implied volatility are negatively affected (Bahrini, 2020). Daily returns on the Muscat stock market indexes decreased as confirmed fatalities increased during the COVID-19 outbreak. (www.msx.om)

These the chart showing from Oct-2018 to Oct 2021 trading activity between three different industries in Oman to see the impact of before Pandemic and after Pandemic.

Despite the widespread belief that Covid-19's impact should be the same throughout stock markets worldwide, actual research on this topic is scarce. Therefore, it is critical to understand the effects of a new coronavirus pandemic on Muscat stock markets, including the impact on daily trading activity of the investors. Retail investors are not necessarily professional individuals who invest in the market in small quantities. They could be called small investors since they trade in smaller amounts but in large quantities, enough to impact the market. COVID-19 caused a big drop in activities in the investment market; however, it did not stop the retail investors from taking the risk of investing during such times, which could yield much greater returns. Since retail investors are a major part of the market, our research can potentially make new findings progress and possibly raise new questions that can be answered in future research.

LITERATURE REVIEW AND HYPOTHESES

The current study offers eight characteristics of financial attitude as antecedents of retail investors' financial conduct, which is assessed by their trading activity during the COVID-19 epidemic. We chose our dependent and independent variables based on a thorough examination of the literature, which has postulated that financial attitude impacts financial behavior (Kadoya and Khan, 2017) and that this behavior may be represented by trading activity (Lewis and Mackenzie, 2000). Additionally, our suggested model is congruent with the financial management framework developed by Parrotta and Johnson (1998) based on the Deacon and Firebaugh Family Resource Management Model. According to Parrotta, J., et al. (1998), increasing income contributed to improved satisfaction, and suggested financial behaviors contributed to better financial management.

Furthermore, the Theory of Planned Behavior (TPB; Ajzen, 2020) conducted a study on the in which he explains how much behavior is influenced by experience with finance, as well as how planning influences behavior at both conscious and sub-conscious levels. Scholars have claimed that attitudes have more predictive ability in instances when conduct is documented through particular acts (Ajzen and Fishbein, 2000). Jorgenson (1967), investigated the theory of investment behavior in order to provide a concept of investment behavior in a modern context with reference to previous studies on the subject. The study goes on to show, with data, that conduct is driven by market norms, which are likewise

The following table illustrates the details:

Research Gap: Covid-19 pandemic caused a big drop of activities in the investment market (Bahrini, R., et al., 2020.) The analysis of the literature of the area of behavioral finance is necessitated to study the application of psychology to influence in the financial decisions during such unexpected Covid times. Based on the above exhaustive examination of the literature found that there is insufficient study on retail investors' financial attitudes and the characteristics that may influence their financial behavior even in the setting of a typical scenario (e.g., one without any special pressures). In reality, when it comes to financial judgments in everyday scenarios, the existing literature has mostly concentrated on cognitive components such as financial literacy and quantitative abilities (Fernandes et al., 2014). In comparison, the impact of characteristics such as deliberative thinking and optimism on financial behavior has largely gone unstudied (Stromback et al., 2017). Notably, despite its relevance in affecting financial objectives, only a few research have explored the influence of financial attitude on retail investors' behavior (Yong et al., 2018). As a result, there are considerable study gaps in (a) the effect of financial attitude on retail investors' behavior during an extrinsic event such as the COVID-19 pandemic. No study has addressed this gap in financial literature in Oman. To fill these gaps, this

Table 1. Details of chapter

Scholar	Year	Theme of study	Findings / conclusion
Odera, E. O.	2011	Impact financial decision making	Factors like overconfidence, cognitive dissonance, regret theory, and prospect theory. provide strategies to assist individuals to resolve these mental errors and emotional pitfalls and suggest important investment approach.
Ameliawati, M., & Setiyani, R.	2018	influence of financial attitude	The results indicate positive influence of financial experience to financial management behavior through financial literacy
Archuleta, K., et al	2020	Financial goal setting therapy	The study proved that Solution Focused Financial Therapy, did indeed help reduce financial anxiety.
Archuleta, K., et al	2013	Mental health effect on financial distress	The research found that financial satisfaction, student loans, and gender are associated with financial anxiety.
Dawson, C.	2015	financial optimism and entrepreneurial satisfaction	The results of the study found that optimism reduces employee pay satisfaction.
Remund, D.L	2010	Definition for financial literacy in a complex economy	Australia, Canada and the United Kingdom use conceptual definitions of financial literacy similar to the definition in the United States
Ashraf, B.N.	2020	unprecedented effect on economic activity	Study found important policy implications, primarily by showing that government social distancing measures have both positive and negative economic impact.
Kyrolainen, P. J., & Perttunen, J.	2003	momentum trading and herding of active vs. passive investors	Results reveal that active trading might not have solely positive effects on the efficiency of asset.
Anand, P., & Cowton, C. J	1993	investment portfolios on non-financial' dimensions of utility functions	The results indicate that Finance theory conventionally focuses on risk and return for evidence of a growing number of investors.
Wilaiporn et.al	2021	influence of investor decisions	The level of overconfidence bias they exhibit for characteristics and behavioural patterns that lead to investor bias.
Talwar.m., et al	2021	investors' behavior in the face of a health crisis	Interest in financial issues exerted the strongest influence, followed by deliberative thinking on trading activity.
Yuesti,A,et al	2020	financial literacy effect on the depression condition of the COVID-19	financial literacy helps in the depression condition of the COVID-19 pandemic
Bobzien, L., & Kalleitner, F	2020	the health crisis and subsequent economic crisis	Perceiving economic threats and preferring central crisis management also explain attitude dynamics within individuals over time.
Bhargava et al	2021	impact of retail investors on stock liquidity	The results indicate increased access to financial markets facilitated by fintech innovations to trading platforms, along with ample free time.
Gurbaxani, A., & Gupte, R	2021	impact of investment and financial decisions of individuals	The finding indicate that measures taken to prevent the spread of COVID-19 (such as lockdown and travel restrictions) affected individual income.
Al-Awadhi et al	2020	impact of the COVID-19 virus on stock market returns	The results indicate that both the daily growth in total confirmed cases and in total cases of death caused by COVID-19 have significant negative effects on stock returns.
Bir, J. S.	2014	Knowledge, Attitude and their Effect on the Recently Graduated Employees' Financial Management Practices	Financial knowledge possessed by them was found to be insignificant in predicting their financial management practices.
Baker, H.K., et al	2019	financial literacy and demographic variables relate to behavioral biases	The results support the view that individual investors do not always act rationally
Skagerlund,et Al	2018	Financial literacy and the role of numeracy	The results indicate that individuals are financially illiterate while interventions to increase the level of financial literacy are ineffective.
Ekayana et.al	2020	The influence of investment motivation and financial literacy on investment interest	Interest as well as, financial literacy did have a positive impact in the Indonesian capital market.
Kulkarni, M. S., & Srinivas, V.	2021	The attitude of the average investor about the share market post-pandemic.	In spite of the pandemic there is optimism among the investors and general public about the economy as well as the share markets
Kumthakar, S., & Nerlekar, V	2020	Analyze the impact of COVID 19 on the investment preferences of retail investors and also on the investment industry in India.	majority of the respondents changed their portfolio post COVID 19. This indicates the impact of market volatility on the investments. People are not willing to take any short term risks and want to shift their investments into less volatile and less risky avenues.
Singh, B	2021	To understand the shift in the investment preference and choice in the post- Covid scenario.	Even then we have the negativity and the fear of lockdown; the investors' find multiple avenues and options for making an investment. However there, investment preferences choice and pattern has taken a paradigm shift during the lockdown.
Seraj AHA et.al.,	2022	Examines the influence of financial literacy on investment decisions with the moderating effect of the overconfidence behavioural bias.	Financial literacy positively and significantly influenced investment decisions.

study was carried out on the main impact of financial attitude on the trading activity of retail investors during the Covid-19 pandemic in sultanate of Oman in order to identify the scope of this impact to make new findings progress and possibly which help to raise new questions that can be answered in future research. The aims of this study are to examine the influence of retail investors financial attitude on their trading activity during the Covid-19 pandemic and measure financial attitude of retail investors according to specific dimensions drawn from literature. The conceptual model drawn from extant review of literature is presented below.

THE CONCEPTUAL MODEL

Figure 1. The hypothesized relation examined in this investigation

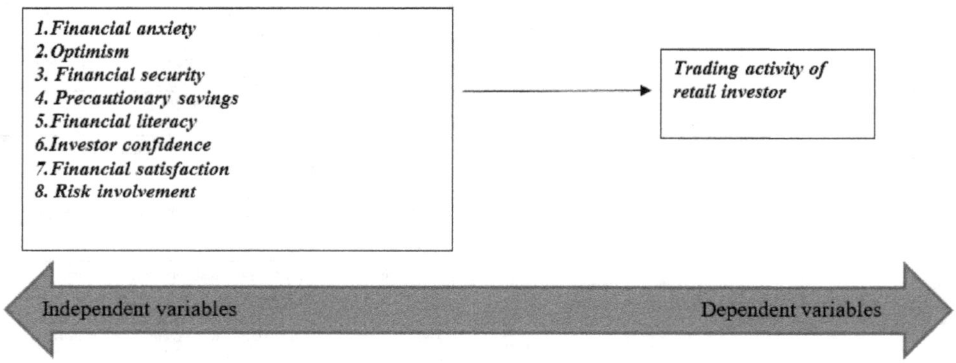

RESEARCH HYPOTHESES

Figure 1 depicts the hypothesized relation examined in this investigation. Most of the measurements that have been utilized in this current study were adapted from past-established instruments contextualizing the topic to Omani equity Industry. The instruments further contextualized to traders in Muscat stock exchange.

Based on the above model, the following hypothesis are derived:

H1: There is association between Financial Anxiety (FA)and trading activity.
H2: There is relationship between Optimism (Op) and trading activity
H3: There is relationship between Financial Security (FS)and trading activity
H4: There is relationship between Precautionary savings (PS)and trading activity.
H5: There is relationship between Financial literacy (FL and trading activity

Table 2. Summary of variable definitions

Sl.No	Variables	Variable Definition	Description
01.	**Financial Anxiety**	Financial Anxiety is defined as the obsessive fear and unsettledness over your own finance which could have risen from individuals' personal financial problems. It raises the chances to cause an individual to make unnecessary decisions for the individual own well-being. (Archuleta, K., et al. 2013)	FINANX
02.	**Optimism**	Optimism is when the investors believe in their ability to confront challenges face on and improve their finance regardless. Optimists will always overestimate their likelihood of positive events only to be disappointed in the outcome in most cases. (Dawson, C., 2015)	OPT
03.	**Financial Security**	Financial security is defined as a balanced state of finances. It is an appropriate level of liquidity of assets and availability of irreplaceable financial reserves, as well as the resistance to negative influences of the internal and external environment and the ability of the enterprise to independently improve also, implement a strategy for conducting its own financial activity in the future. (Archuleta, K., et al. 2013)	FINSEC
04.	**Precautionary savings**	Precautionary saving occurs due to the unresponsiveness of certainty about future income and precautionary motives to delay consumption and saving may rise in the present. Savings are closely related to people's thought processes in putting off what is currently being consumed in order to save for the future Carroll & Kimball (2008)	PRSAV
05.	**Financial literacy**	According to, Financial Literacy is the possession of skills and knowledge that helps in making the right decisions regarding financial resources. This includes understanding savings, debts and investment which achieves a sense of one's financial security(Remund, D.L., 2010)	FINLIT
06.	**Investors confidence (IC)**	Refers to investors' willingness to engage in the investment opportunities and associated intermediation channels available to them based on their perception of risk and return. Strengthening and enhancing the confidence of investors is of paramount importance to reach sustainable development and to ensure the stability of the capital market. To reach this level of stability, there must be a clear or semi-compulsory policy regarding the payment of dividends, which enhances the confidence of investors and attracts a lot of investors, especially those who have fear of getting involved in the stock market.(Barber, B. M., & Odean, T, 2002).	INVCNF
07.	**Financial Satisfaction**	Financial satisfaction use the terms "financial happiness" and "financial well-being" and "financial wellness" interchangeably, while others keep them independent concepts. Furthermore, the majority of studies are inconsistent in how they define and quantify the notion. Financial well-being as satisfaction with one's present financial situation and debt level using both subjective and objective criteria. Others describe financial well-being as being content with one's financial status overall (Archuleta et al, 2011).	FINSAT
08.	**Risk Involvement**	Risk involvement is risk bearing capacity and interest of the investors. There many factors which affect the risk involve are Risk capacity, Company name, Credibility of sponsors, Peer group, Tolerance, Risk adjusted return and Fund objectives. There is a importance relationship among the age and the risk behaviour and on this bases we can sum up by saying that as people grow their risk appetite becomes at a low level and instead of being risk takers they are more prone to avoid risk. (Sharma, P. D. P., & Rao, D. N. (2014)	RISINV

H6: There is relationship between Investors' confidence (IC) and trading activity
H7: There is relationship between Financial Satisfaction (FS)and trading activity
H8: There is relationship between Risk Involvement (RI)and trading activity.

METHODOLOGY

Listed brokerage firms in Muscat securities market such as Ubhar Capital, Global Finance International, Capital Company, U Capital, FINCORP and Horizon Capital were approached. The questionnaire was prepared electronically using google forms and sent to the research wing head of the brokerage firm who then forwarded the google survey form to their clients. The responses of the survey were also collected by researchers from referrals of known investors who are actively trading. This snowballing sampling method enabled the researcher to get 38 with filled questionnaires. Hence the sample size stands at 38 for our research. For the study, a survey questionnaire was constructed and developed to provide a baseline for financial attitude on trading activity. It consisted of two parts viz. (i) Demographic information and (ii) Financial attitude and Trading activity. All measurement items (24 items) coming from each construct and its Cronbach alpha level 0.72 passes the minimum requirement (Nunnally, 1960).

EMPIRICAL FINDINGS

The frequency and percentage of responses received for Financial Attitude on the Trading Activity of Retail Investors during the Covid-19 pandemic in Sultanate of Oman are presented below.

Gender and Financial Attitude

Table 5 depicts that the independent sample t-test shows that the result is insignificant for all eight constructs as the p-value is greater than 0.05 except for Optimism i.e., there is a difference in the Financial attitude towards trading activity vs. gender. Hence it is inferred that males and females perceived optimism towards trading activity differently. Males show a greater optimism than females at the time of trading during Covid-19 (9.47 >.7.25) In FINANX construct, females show greater anxiety compared to males (10 > 9.74), in FINSEC males show greater security compared to females (9.26 > 9.00), in PRSAV, females show greater Precautionary savings compared to males (10.5 > 9.44). In FINLIT, hence males intend to be Financial literate more than females (8.91 > 6) In INVCNF again males show more Investor confidence than females (9.71 >8.50). In construct FINSAT, males are more financial satisfied on the rerturns obtained from stock than females (8.82 > 7.25). Moreover, Construct RISINV shows that Risk involvement is higher for males than females (9.38 > 8.75).

Table 3. Demographic Profile

	Category	Frequency	Percent
Age	18-25 years	5	13.16%
	25-35 years	3	7.89%
	36-45 years	23	60.53%
	46-55 years	7	18.42%
Gender	Male	34	89.47%
	Female	4	10.53%
Educational Qualification	Secondary school	3	7.89%
	Diploma	8	21.05%
	Bachelor	1	2.63%
	B.Tech	10	26.32%
	Masters	13	34.21%
	Ph.D	3	7.89%
Nationality	Omani	21	55.26%
	Non-Omani	17	44.74%
Occupation	Students	8	21.05%
	Employed	29	76.32%
	Business	1	2.63%
Period of trading	Less than 1 year	11	28.9%
	1-2 years	10	26.3%
	2-3 years	4	10.5%
	3-4 years	5	13.2%
	4-5 years	2	5.3%
	more than 5 years	6	15.8%
Financial education	Yes	21	27.6%
	No	12	15.8%
	Maybe	5	6.6%
Understanding of Investment	Yes	25	32.9%
	No	8	10.5%
	Maybe	5	6.6%
Optimist person	Yes	19	50.0%
	No	19	50.0%
Decision to trade in Covid	Yes	17	22.4%
	No	15	19.7%
	Maybe	6	7.9%

Source: Primary data

Table 4. Trading activity during Covid 19

	Category	Frequency	Percent
Postponement Of Decision durign Covid- 19	Strongly Agree	2	5.26%
	Agree	3	7.89%
	Neither Agree nor Disagree	14	36.84%
	Disagree	14	36.84%
	Strongly Disagree	5	13.16%
False decisions during investing	Strongly Agree	5	13.16%
	Agree	13	34.21%
	Neither Agree nor Disagree	9	23.68%
	Disagree	8	21.05%
	Strongly Disagree	3	7.89%
Planning irrespective of Covid-19 conditions	Strongly Agree	11	28.9%
	Agree	10	26.3%
	Neither Agree nor Disagree	4	10.5%
	Disagree	5	13.2%
	Strongly Disagree	2	5.3%
Nothing can go wrong during pre or post Covid 19	Strongly Agree	4	10.53%
	Agree	7	18.42%
	Neither Agree nor Disagree	8	21.05%
	Disagree	5	13.16%
	Strongly Disagree	14	36.84%
Secure to trade even during Covid -19 conditions	Strongly Agree	3	7.89%
	Agree	10	26.32%
	Neither Agree nor Disagree	12	31.58%
	Disagree	8	21.05%
	Strongly Disagree	5	13.16%
Financial future irrespective of the pandemic conditions	Strongly Agree	2	5.26%
	Agree	10	26.32%
	Neither Agree nor Disagree	11	28.95%
	Disagree	11	28.95%
	Strongly Disagree	4	10.53%
Confident of financial future	Strongly Agree	4	10.53%
	Agree	7	18.42%
	Neither Agree nor Disagree	13	34.21%
	Disagree	11	28.95%
	Strongly Disagree	3	7.89%
Hard to save money	Strongly Agree	2	5.26%
	Agree	11	28.95%
	Neither Agree nor Disagree	10	26.32%
	Disagree	10	26.32%
	Strongly Disagree	5	13.16%
Pandemic has led to reduced spending	Strongly Agree	4	10.53%
	Agree	8	21.05%
	Neither Agree nor Disagree	6	15.79%
	Disagree	15	39.47%
	Strongly Disagree	5	13.16%
To care for future is essential for me	Strongly Agree	2	5.26%
	Agree	7	18.42%
	Neither Agree nor Disagree	13	34.21%
	Disagree	14	36.84%
	Strongly Disagree	2	5.26%
Learning about finance	Strongly Agree	7	18.42%
	Agree	11	28.95%
	Neither Agree nor Disagree	13	34.21%
	Disagree	7	18.42%
	Strongly Disagree	0	0.00%

continued on following page

Table 4. Continued

New experience from investing during pandemic condition	Strongly Agree	6	15.79%
	Agree	8	21.05%
	Neither Agree nor Disagree	12	31.58%
	Disagree	7	18.42%
	Strongly Disagree	5	13.16%
Confident of making profits out of my investments during pandemic	Strongly Agree	2	5.26%
	Agree	10	26.32%
	Neither Agree nor Disagree	17	44.74%
	Disagree	7	18.42%
	Strongly Disagree	2	5.26%
Investor confidence in the Muscat Securities Market	Strongly Agree	3	7.89%
	Agree	9	23.68%
	Neither Agree nor Disagree	11	28.95%
	Disagree	9	23.68%
	Strongly Disagree	6	15.79%
Quit trading because of Covid-19	Strongly Agree	1	2.63%
	Agree	7	18.42%
	Neither Agree nor Disagree	12	31.58%
	Disagree	8	21.05%
	Strongly Disagree	10	26.32%
Satisfied with my portfolio	Strongly Agree	3	7.89%
	Agree	10	26.32%
	Neither Agree nor Disagree	14	36.84%
	Disagree	10	26.32%
	Strongly Disagree	1	2.63%
Satisfied with my meticulous planning of my investment	Strongly Agree	3	7.89%
	Agree	10	26.32%
	Neither Agree nor Disagree	18	47.37%
	Disagree	7	18.42%
	Strongly Disagree	0	0.00%
Satisfied with the returns	Strongly Agree	5	13.16%
	Agree	7	18.42%
	Neither Agree nor Disagree	14	36.84%
	Disagree	7	18.42%
	Strongly Disagree	5	13.16%
Willing to take additional risk	Strongly Agree	4	10.53%
	Agree	8	21.05%
	Neither Agree nor Disagree	13	34.21%
	Disagree	9	23.68%
	Strongly Disagree	4	10.53%
Avoid taking risks	Strongly Agree	2	5.26%
	Agree	8	21.05%
	Neither Agree nor Disagree	13	34.21%
	Disagree	7	18.42%
	Strongly Disagree	8	21.05%
Interested in insurance products	Strongly Agree	5	13.16%
	Agree	9	23.68%
	Neither Agree nor Disagree	10	26.32%
	Disagree	9	23.68%
	Strongly Disagree	5	13.16%

Table 6. Independent sample T-test

Independent samples t test					
	Nationality	**N**	**Mean**	**Std. Deviation**	**Sig.**
FINANX	Omani	17	9.65	2.029	.470
	Non-Omani	21	9.86	2.535	
OPT	Omani	17	8.94	3.152	.622
	Non-Omani	21	9.48	2.804	
FINSEC	Omani	17	8.59	1.970	.695
	Non-Omani	21	9.76	2.022	
PRSAV	Omani	17	9.47	2.322	.663
	Non-Omani	21	9.62	2.559	
FINLIT	Omani	17	8.71	2.173	.039
	Non-Omani	21	8.52	3.326	
INVCNF	Omani	17	9.65	2.621	.023
	Non-Omani	21	9.52	1.537	
FINSAT	Omani	17	8.88	1.900	.357
	Non-Omani	21	8.48	2.400	
RISINV	Omani	17	9.35	2.999	.049
	Non-Omani	21	9.29	1.765	

Nationality and Financial Attitude

Table 6 depicts that the independent sample t-test shows that the result is in significant for all five constructs as the p-value is greater than 0.05 For the constructs, Financial literacy, Investor confidence and Risk involvement, the results show a significant difference between Omani and non – Omnai respondents with p value less than 0.05. Hence it is inferred that Omanis and Non- Omanis perceived show similar attitude towards trading with respect to constructs FINANX, OPT, FINSEC, PRSAV and FINSAT. Omanis show a greater investor confidence than non- omanis at the time of trading during Covid-19 (9.65 >9.52) and are also financially satisfied than Non Omanis (8.88> 8.48) With respect to Risk involvement, Omanis are willing to take higher risk than Non - Omanis with a mean of 9.35>9.29 and mean difference is significant too with p value less than 0.05

Table 5. Independent sample T-test

Independent samples t test					
	Gender	**N**	**Mean**	**Std. Deviation**	**Sig.**
FINANX	Male	34	9.74	2.340	.592
	Female	4	10.00	2.160	
OPT	Male	34	9.47	2.608	.007
	Female	4	7.25	5.058	
FINSEC	Male	34	9.26	2.035	.506
	Female	4	9.00	2.582	
PRSAV	Male	34	9.44	2.259	.217
	Female	4	10.50	3.873	
FINLIT	Male	34	8.91	2.633	.269
	Female	4	6.00	3.559	
INVCNF	Male	34	9.71	2.023	.524
	Female	4	8.50	2.380	
FINSAT	Male	34	8.82	1.992	.073
	Female	4	7.25	3.403	
RISINV	Male	34	9.38	2.400	.984
	Female	4	8.75	2.217	

FINANCIAL ATTITUDE AND TRADING ACTIVITY

Table 7 depicts that the ANOVA f-test results that shows that there are few significant effect of financial attitude constructs on the trading activity of investors. For FINANX, P value is 0.27 which is less than 0.05, there is no effect in average rating given by financial anxiety towards trading activities. FOR OPT construct, optimism is having an influence on trading activity (P value is less than 0.05). FOR FINSEC the F statistic is 0.50, while P value is 0.61 which is more than 0.05, hence proving that financial security has no effect on trading activity. For PRSAV, when tested with ANOVA, the F statistic is 0.57, while P value is 0.57 which is more than 0.05 that precautionary savings has no effect on trading activity. With regard to RISKINV, INVCNF, FINSAT, p value being more than 0.05 signifies insignificant effect.

Table 7. ANOVA F test between average rating of respondents towards trading activity and financial attitude constructs

		Sum of Squares	Mean Square	F	Sig.
FINANX	Between Groups	20.168	5.042	1.38	0.27
	Within Groups	174.700	5.294		
	Total	194.868			
OPT	Between Groups	23.131	5.783	4.50	0.02
	Within Groups	295.738	8.962		
	Total	318.868			
FINSEC	Between Groups	2.818	.705	0.50	0.61
	Within Groups	154.050	4.668		
	Total	156.868			
PRSAV	Between Groups	52.695	13.174	0.57	0.57
	Within Groups	164.700	4.991		
	Total	217.395			
FINLIT	Between Groups	31.529	7.882	2.32	0.11
	Within Groups	265.550	8.047		
	Total	297.079			
INVCNF	Between Groups	19.251	4.813	0.52	0.82
	Within Groups	138.013	4.182		
	Total	157.263			
FINSAT	Between Groups	10.228	2.557	.51	.72
	Within Groups	164.325	4.980		
	Total	174.553			
RISINV	Between Groups	.723	.181	0.50	0.61
	Within Groups	205.488	6.227		
	Total	206.211			

DISCUSSION AND CONCLUSION

Financial literacy was found to be the important factor for the success of respondents in their trading activities. It is possible that from the results the respondents think that the covid-19 pandemic did help them understand finance better. This is in consistent with results of Seraj et.al., (2022). Fear of loss does not hinder their decisions during Covid-19 for majority of the respondents. As far as the process of making the final decision regarding “my investment puts investors under stress” takes a neutral side. It is notable to mention that majority of the respondents (64%) were in agreement that they can be optimistic regardless of the current Covid-19 situation. Also, getting good returns does not seem to cause prompt actions by the respondents. The majority of the respondents (36 percent) seem to strongly disagree to the assumption of nothing could go wrong during the pre-covid-19 and post covid-19 period. Also, getting good returns does not seem to cause prompt actions by the respondents (62 percent). The assumption of nothing could go wrong during the pre-covid-19 and post covid-19 period was cited by 52 percent. The variable financial security appears to have the least effect on the respondents as 62 percent disagree that covid-19 is not a threat for their trading activities. As far as the investors' confidence toward their financial security irrespective of the pandemic conditions, the respondents are indifferent about the financial future of their investment (56 percent). The respondents seem to have a neutral opinion towards precautionary savings. (46 percent). As far as the respondents confidence toward how confident are they in making profits in their investments during the pandemic, (44 percent) seem to be again neutral. The respondents also show that their confidence toward the Muscat Securities Market during the corona pandemic had not changed regardless of the situation, (53 percent) In addition to that, the respondents seem to disagree that covid-19 caused them to quit trading, with (57 percent). The majority of the responses seem to have equal opinions on the financial satisfaction variable, and satisfaction towards their returns. The variable risk involvement shows that the respondents are willing to take some risk in their investments (34 percent) and 23 percent are not willing to take additional risk during the covid-19 situation. The respondents are not willing to avoid all risks (21 percent strongly disagreeing). The interest of the respondents on insurance products after the covid-19 period seems to have an equal opinion that insurance products can be of benefit for some investors and not for others.

As per the finding of t test it is concluded that there is no difference in the mean rating given by males and females except for optimism, where in males are optimist in trading activity during Covid -19 period than females. Moreover, when tested with t test it is further concluded that there is no difference in the mean rating given by Omanis and Non-Omanis towards, financial anxiety, optimism, financial security, precautionary savings, financial literacy financial satisfaction and risk involvement. Nationality matter only for Financial literacy, Investor confidence and Risk involvement as the mean ratings given for it differs between Omanis and non-Omanis.ANOVA test results reveals that the two variables optimism "Dawson, C., 2015" and financial satisfaction "Parrotta, J.L. and Johnson, P.J., 1998" have an effect on the trading activity of the investors during pandemic. While other independent variables such as financial anxiety, financial security, precautionary savings, financial literacy, investor confidence and risk involvement fail to significantly explain their effect on trading activity of the investors. The covid-19 risk doesn't cause financial anxiety among investors. Since it is treated as a potential real-life risk, investors don't see the covid-19 as a financial risk.It is possible to overcome the problem of the investors confidence by giving financial advice to the investors to help them gain confidence in their investment such as, provide a suggestion to make an investment in low-risk shares.Since investors are not concerned with their savings, giving them advice on possible saving plans might help them start saving.The covid-19 does not seem to cause any effect on the investors optimism. Therefore, it is possible to advise them into making more investments regardless of the situation.Risk management is an issue with some investors while others know how to manage it, so it is suggested to provide counseling with the investors who wish to learn how to manage the risk of their investments. Also, it was found that the majority of the respondents were in agreement that they can be optimistic regardless of the current Covid-19 situation. Thus, this study shows that the retail investors can still actively perform regardless of the panic situation with the pandemic as they do not see this as a financial threat for their investment.

Hence based on the study results it is inferred that the covid-19 risk doesn't cause financial anxiety among investors. Since it is treated as a potential real-life risk, investors don't see the covid-19 as a financial risk. It is possible to overcome the problem of the investors confidence by giving financial advice to the investors to help them gain confidence in their investment such as, provide a suggestion to make an investment in low-risk shares. Since investors are not concerned with their savings, giving them advice on possible saving plans might help them start saving. The covid-19 does not seem to cause any effect on the investors optimism. Therefore, it is possible to advise them into making more investments regardless of the situation. Risk management is an issue with some investors while others know how to manage it, so it is suggested to provide counseling with the investors who wish to learn how to manage the risk of their investments.

ACKNOWLEDGMENT

We are grateful to Ubhar Capital, Global Finance International, Capital Company, U Capital, FINCORP, Horizon Capital for the support and the co-operation of the firms that helped us obtain our research data and allow us to reach their clients for information.

REFERENCES

Ajzen, I. (2020). The theory of planned behavior: Frequently asked questions. *Human Behavior and Emerging Technologies*, *2*(4), 314–324. doi:10.1002/hbe2.195

Ajzen, I., & Fishbein, M. (2000). Attitudes and the attitude-behavior relation: Reasoned and automatic processes. *European Review of Social Psychology*, *11*(1), 1–33. doi:10.1080/14792779943000116

Al-Awadhi, A. M., Alsaifi, K., Al-Awadhi, A., & Alhammadi, S. (2020). Death and contagious infectious diseases: Impact of the COVID-19 virus on stock market returns. *Journal of Behavioral and Experimental Finance*, *27*, 100326. doi:10.1016/j.jbef.2020.100326 PMID:32292707

Ameliawati, M., & Setiyani, R. (2018). The influence of financial attitude, financial socialization, and financial experience to financial management behavior with financial literacy as the mediation variable. *KnE Social Sciences*, 811-832.

Anand, P., & Cowton, C. J. (1993). The ethical investor: Exploring dimensions of investment behaviour. *Journal of Economic Psychology*, *14*(2), 377–385. doi:10.1016/0167-4870(93)90007-8

Archuleta, K. L., Britt, S. L., Tonn, T. J., & Grable, J. E. (2011). Financial satisfaction and financial stressors in marital satisfaction. *Psychological Reports*, *108*(2), 563–576. doi:10.2466/07.21.PR0.108.2.563-576 PMID:21675570

Archuleta, K. L., Dale, A., & Spann, S. M. (2013). College students and financial distress: Exploring debt, financial satisfaction, and financial anxiety. *Financial Counseling and Planning*, *24*(2), 50–62.

Archuleta, K. L., Mielitz, K. S., Jayne, D., & Le, V. (2020). Financial goal setting, financial anxiety, and solution-focused financial therapy (SFFT): A quasi-experimental outcome study. *Contemporary Family Therapy*, *42*(1), 68–76. doi:10.100710591-019-09501-0

Ashraf, B. N. (2020). Economic impact of government interventions during the COVID-19 pandemic: International evidence from financial markets. *Journal of Behavioral and Experimental Finance*, *27*, 100371. doi:10.1016/j.jbef.2020.100371 PMID:32835011

Bahrini, R., & Filfilan, A. (2020). Impact of the novel coronavirus on stock market returns: Evidence from GCC countries. *Quantitative Finance and Economics*, *4*(4), 640–652. doi:10.3934/QFE.2020029

Baker, H. K., Kumar, S., & Goyal, N. (2019). Personality traits and investor sentiment. *Review of Behavioral Finance*.

Barber, B. M., & Odean, T. (2002). Online investors: Do the slow die first? *Review of Financial Studies*, *15*(2), 455–488. doi:10.1093/rfs/15.2.455

BhargavaR.LouX.OzikG.SadkaR.WhitmoreT. (2022). Quantifying Narratives and their Impact on Financial Markets. *Available at* SSRN 4166640. doi:10.2139/ssrn.4166640

Bir, J. S. (2014). Knowledge, attitude and their effect on the recently graduated employees' financial management practices and satisfaction. *Economic Literature*, *12*, 69–81.

Bobzien, L., & Kalleitner, F. (2021). Attitudes towards European financial solidarity during the Covid-19 pandemic: evidence from a net-contributor country. *European Societies, 23*(sup1), S791-S804.

Dawson, C. (2017). Financial optimism and entrepreneurial satisfaction. *Strategic Entrepreneurship Journal*, *11*(2), 171–194. doi:10.1002ej.1244

Ekayana Sangkasari Paranita, E., & Mahardika Agustinus, M. (2020). The Influence of Investment Motivation and Financial Literacy on Interest in Investing During the COVID-19 Pandemic. In *Proceeding of the 3rd International Conference of Banking, Accounting, Management adn Economic* (Vol. 169). Atlantis Press.

Fernandes, D., Lynch, J. G. Jr, & Netemeyer, R. G. (2014). Financial literacy, financial education, and downstream financial behaviors. *Management Science*, *60*(8), 1861–1883. doi:10.1287/mnsc.2013.1849

Gurbaxani, A., & Gupte, R. (2021). A study on the impact of COVID-19 on investor behaviour of individuals in a small town in the state of Madhya Pradesh, India. *Australasian Accounting. Business and Finance Journal*, *15*(1), 70–92.

Jorgenson, D. (1967). The theory of investment behavior. In *Determinants of investment behavior* (pp. 129–175). NBER.

Kadoya, Y., & Khan, M. S. R. (2017). Explaining financial literacy in Japan: New evidence using financial knowledge, behavior, and attitude. *Behaviorand Attitude*.

Kapoor, S., & Prosad, J. M. (2017). Behavioural finance: A review. *Procedia Computer Science*, *122*, 50–54. doi:10.1016/j.procs.2017.11.340

Kulkarni, M. S., & Srinivas, V. (n.d.). Investor Attitude Towards Share Markets Post Covid 19 Pandemic. *Journal of Management & Entrepreneurship*, 171.

Kumthakar, S., & Nerlekar, V. (2020). Analytical Study of Investment Patterns and Investment Preferences of Retail Investors Post COVID 19. *Journal of Seybold Report*, (1533), 9211.

KyrolainenP. J.PerttunenJ. (2003). Investors' activity and trading behavior. *Available at* SSRN 302685.

Lewis, A., & Mackenzie, C. (2000). Morals, money, ethical investing and economic psychology. *Human Relations*, *53*(2), 179–191. doi:10.1177/a010699

Nunnally, J. (1960). The place of statistics in psychology. *Educational and Psychological Measurement*, *20*(4), 641–650. doi:10.1177/001316446002000401

Odera, E. O. (2011). *The behaviour and financial performance of individual investors in Kenya* [Doctoral dissertation]. University of Nairobi.

Paisarn, W., Chancharat, N., & Chancharat, S. (2021). Factors Influencing Retail Investors' Trading Behaviour in the Thai Stock Market. *Australasian Accounting, Business and Finance Journal*, *15*(2), 26–37. doi:10.14453/aabfj.v15i2.3

Parrotta, J. L., & Johnson, P. J. (1998). The impact of financial attitudes and knowledge on financial management and satisfaction of recently married individuals. *Financial Counseling and Planning*, *9*(2), 59.

Rai, K., Dua, S., & Yadav, M. (2019). Association of financial attitude, financial behaviour and financial knowledge towards financial literacy: A structural equation modeling approach. *FIIB Business Review*, *8*(1), 51–60. doi:10.1177/2319714519826651

Remund, D. L. (2010). Financial literacy explicated: The case for a clearer definition in an increasingly complex economy. *The Journal of Consumer Affairs*, *44*(2), 276–295. doi:10.1111/j.1745-6606.2010.01169.x

Salman, A., & Ali, Q. (2021). Covid-19 and its impact on the stock market in GCC. *Journal of Sustainable Finance & Investment*, 1-17.

Seraj, A. H. A., Alzain, E., & Alshebami, A. S. (2022, September 30). The roles of financial literacy and overconfidence in investment decisions in Saudi Arabia. *Frontiers in Psychology*, *13*, 1005075. doi:10.3389/fpsyg.2022.1005075 PMID:36248580

Sharma, P. D. P., & Rao, D. N. (2014). A Study of Risk Orientation of Retail Investors in Indian Mutual Fund Industry with Special Reference to Rajasthan, India. India.

Skagerlund, K., Lind, T., Strömbäck, C., Tinghög, G., & Västfjäll, D. (2018). Financial literacy and the role of numeracy–How individuals' attitude and affinity with numbers influence financial literacy. *Journal of Behavioral and Experimental Economics, 74*, 18–25. doi:10.1016/j.socec.2018.03.004

Strömbäck, C., Lind, T., Skagerlund, K., Västfjäll, D., & Tinghög, G. (2017). Does self-control predict financial behavior and financial well-being? *Journal of Behavioral and Experimental Finance, 14*, 30–38. doi:10.1016/j.jbef.2017.04.002

Talwar, M., Talwar, S., Kaur, P., Tripathy, N., & Dhir, A. (2021). Has financial attitude impacted the trading activity of retail investors during the COVID-19 pandemic? *Journal of Retailing and Consumer Services, 58*, 102341. doi:10.1016/j.jretconser.2020.102341

Wilaiporn, P., Nongnit, C., & Surachai, C. (2021). *Factors Influencing Retail Investors' Trading Behaviour in the Thai Stock Market*. Academic Press.

Yong, C. C., Yew, S. Y., & Wee, C. K. (2018). Financial knowledge, attitude and behaviour of young working adults in Malaysia. *Institutions and Economies, 10*(4).

Yuesti, A., Ni, W. R., & Suryandari, N. N. A. (2020). Financial literacy in the COVID-19 pandemic: Pressure conditions in Indonesia. *Entrepreneurship and Sustainability Issues, 8*(1), 884–898. doi:10.9770/jesi.2020.8.1(59)

Zhang, D., Hu, M., & Ji, Q. (2020, October). Financial markets under the global pandemic of COVID-19. *Finance Research Letters, 36*, 101528. doi:10.1016/j.frl.2020.101528 PMID:32837360

Chapter 8
Corporate Governance Practices During COVID-19

Kavitha Govindaraj
PSGR Krishnammal College for Women, India

Bala Thripurasundari Venkatesh
PSGR Krishnammal College for Women, India

ABSTRACT

The novel coronavirus (COVID-19) that emerged in December 2019 did not only cause health problem to people but also disrupted the entire global economic condition. COVID-19 is one of the most prominent issues in the 21st century. The COVID-19 pandemic has brought unusual challenges to corporates and their boards. COVID-19 raised the sphere of corporate governance practices. All listed companies look for effective and qualitative corporate governance practices by conscientiously integrating transparency, accountability, responsibility, and control. Distancing, travel restrictions, forbidding events for controlling the spread of COVID-19 have had bad impacts on economic conditions in the world. The crises occurred in corporates as well. The corporates where at risk in the time of pandemic, and it raised serious apprehension to corporate governance practices. The objective of this study is to assess the effect of corporate governance practices during COVID-19 and provide insight regarding the opportunities and challenges faced by corporates during the COVID-19 pandemic.

INTRODUCTION

The novel Coronavirus (COVID – 19) which emerged in December 2019 did not

DOI: 10.4018/978-1-6684-5342-1.ch008

only cause health problem to people but also disrupted the entire global economic condition. The COVID-19 is one of the most prominent issues in the 21st century. The COVID -19 epidemics has brought unusual challenges to corporates and their boards. This COVID – 19 raised the sphere of Corporate Governance Practices. All Listed Companies look for effective and qualitative Corporate Governance Practices by conscientiously integrating transparency, accountability, responsibility and control (Khalil Jebran, Shihua Chen, 2021).

Crises can be of two classes, that is where the management has the control over the event or there is no control over the event. The crises in the management can occur where there is loss in the production, sale or investment. The management of the corporation can act to crises by changing the reforms and making effect to introduce new reforms that suits the crises that occurred. The new practices should have long-term effectiveness and not only manage day-to-day crises but also to act on uncertain crises.

The Governments from all over the world enforce various measures like lockdown, social distancing, travel restrictions, forbidding events for controlling the spread of COVID -19 which has bad impact on economic conditions in the world. The Governments from all parts of the world initiated economic policies and other policies to reduce the impact of economic crises due to COVID -19. The Crises occurred in corporates as well. The Corporates where at risk in the time of pandemic and it raised serious apprehension to Corporate Governance Practices. The objective of this study is to assess the effect of Corporate Governance Practices during COVID -19 and provides insights regarding the opportunities and challenges faced by corporates during COVID -19 pandemic.

The Indian Corporate Governance Framework

- Protection of minority shareholders

The protection of minority shareholders is an important aspect of corporate governance in India. Minority shareholders are those who hold shares in a company but do not have control over its management. They rely on the company's board of directors to act in their best interests and to ensure that their rights are respected.

- Accountability of the top management of the company

The top management of a company, including the board of directors and the senior executives, is accountable for the overall direction and performance of the company. They are responsible for making strategic decisions, setting policies, and ensuring that the company complies with relevant laws and regulations.

- Timely reporting and adequate disclosures to shareholders

Timely reporting and adequate disclosures to shareholders are important aspects of corporate governance in India. Shareholders have a right to receive accurate and timely information about the company's financial performance, business operations, and other matters that may affect their investment. This helps shareholders to make informed decisions and to hold the company accountable for its actions.

- Corporate Social Responsibility

There is a growing recognition that CSR is closely linked to corporate governance, as it involves the management of a company's social, environmental, and economic impacts and the accountability of the company to its stakeholders. Effective CSR can contribute to a company's reputation, customer loyalty, and long-term financial performance. It can also enhance the trust and confidence of stakeholders in the company (Sheeja Sivaprasad, Sudha Mathew, 2021).

Corporate Governance in India

Corporate governance in India refers to the system of rules, practices, and processes by which a company is directed and controlled. The aim of corporate governance is to ensure that the company is run in the best interests of its stakeholders, which include shareholders, management, customers, suppliers, financiers, government, and the community.

In India, corporate governance is regulated by the Companies Act, 2013, which lays down the rules and regulations governing the formation, financing, and operation of companies in India. The Act also establishes the rights and responsibilities of shareholders, directors, and management, and provides for the appointment of independent directors and auditors.

In addition to the Companies Act, there are also several other laws and regulations that impact corporate governance in India, including the Securities and Exchange Board of India (SEBI) Listing Regulations, the SEBI Takeover Regulations, and the SEBI Corporate Governance Regulations.

There are also several best practices and codes of corporate governance that have been developed by industry associations and other organizations, such as the Confederation of Indian Industry (CII) and the Institute of Chartered Accountants of India (ICAI). These codes provide guidance on issues such as board composition, executive compensation, and disclosure and transparency. (https://ecgi.global/content/corporate-governance-india)

7 Pillars of Corporate Governance

1. **Transparency:** This involves disclosing all relevant information about the company's operations and financial performance to shareholders and the public.
2. **Responsibility:** This means that the company's management and board of directors are responsible for the company's actions and decisions.
3. **Independence:** This means that the board of directors should be independent of the company's management, and should not be subject to any conflicts of interest.
4. **Fairness:** This involves treating all shareholders fairly and equitably, and not engaging in any actions that would benefit one group of shareholders at the expense of others.
5. **Accountability:** This means that the company's management and board of directors are accountable to the shareholders for the company's performance and actions.
6. **Integrity:** This involves acting with honesty and integrity, and upholding the company's values and ethical standards.
7. **Stewardship:** This means that the company's management and board of directors have a duty to protect and enhance the long-term value of the company for the benefit of all shareholders. (https://www.pwc.ie/services/human-resource-services/insights /the-eight-key-effective-corporate-governance-practices.html)

National Committees on Corporate Governance (India)

In India, there are several committees, organizations, and regulatory bodies that have been established to promote and enforce good corporate governance practices.

1. **SEBI (Securities and Exchange Board of India):** SEBI is the regulator responsible for overseeing the capital markets in India. It has issued several guidelines and regulations on corporate governance, including the SEBI Listing Regulations and the SEBI Corporate Governance Regulations.
2. **Ministry of Corporate Affairs (MCA):** The MCA is the government ministry responsible for overseeing the regulation of companies in India. It is responsible for implementing the Companies Act, 2013, which sets out the rules and regulations governing corporate governance in India.
3. **CII (Confederation of Indian Industry):** The CII is a national business association that has developed a set of best practices on corporate governance for Indian companies. These best practices are known as the CII Code of Corporate Governance.

4. **ICAI (Institute of Chartered Accountants of India):** The ICAI is a professional organization that sets standards and guidelines for the accounting profession in India. It has developed a set of corporate governance guidelines for listed companies in India.
5. **NSE (National Stock Exchange of India):** The NSE is one of the leading stock exchanges in India. It has developed a set of corporate governance guidelines for listed companies, known as the NSE Corporate Governance Guidelines.

Committees across the Globe on Corporate Governance

There are several committees, organizations, and regulatory bodies around the world that have been established to promote and enforce good corporate governance practices.

1. **OECD (Organisation for Economic Co-operation and Development) Principles of Corporate Governance:** These principles, which were revised in 2020, provide a framework for good corporate governance practices and are widely adopted by governments, regulators, and listed companies around the world.
2. **UK Corporate Governance Code:** The UK Corporate Governance Code, which is issued by the Financial Reporting Council, sets out the principles and best practices of corporate governance for listed companies in the UK.
3. **King Code of Governance Principles for South Africa:** The King Code is a set of principles and practices that provide guidance on corporate governance for South African companies. It was first published in 1994 and has been revised several times since then.
4. **Sarbanes-Oxley Act (SOX):** This legislation, which was passed in the United States in 2002, introduced a number of reforms to improve corporate governance in the wake of a number of corporate scandals. SOX requires companies to implement internal controls, certify the accuracy of their financial statements, and disclose any material changes in their financial condition.
5. **Corporate Governance Council of the Tokyo Stock Exchange:** This council was established in 2003 to promote good corporate governance practices among listed companies in Japan. It issues guidelines and best practices on corporate governance, and also operates a corporate governance rating system.

Sustainable Corporate Governance Practices

Sustainable corporate governance refers to the practices and processes that a company uses to ensure that it is run in an ethical and responsible manner, with a focus on long-term value creation for all stakeholders. This can include a wide range of practices, such as implementing effective risk management processes, promoting transparency and accountability, and ensuring that the rights and interests of all stakeholders, including shareholders, employees, customers, and the wider community, are taken into account.

One important aspect of sustainable corporate governance is ensuring that the company is able to manage and mitigate risks effectively. This can include financial risks, such as those associated with market fluctuations or changes in interest rates, as well as non-financial risks, such as those related to environmental impact or social and governance issues. To effectively manage and mitigate risks, companies may implement a range of processes and procedures, such as risk assessments, scenario planning, and regular reviews of risk management policies and practices.

To support this kind of governance, different framework, such as GRI framework, UN Global Compact, or SASB (Sustainability Accounting Standards Board) are used to measure and report sustainable performance. (Alsayegh, Maha Faisal, et al. (2020))

During Covid 19 pandemic, sustainable corporate governance practices have taken on even greater importance. The pandemic has brought to the fore a number of issues that companies need to address in order to continue operating in an ethical and responsible manner. Some of the key sustainable corporate governance practices that companies have focused on during the pandemic include:

1. Risk Management
2. Stakeholder Engagement
3. Health and Safety
4. Financing
5. Social and Community Responsibility
6. Financing
7. Investment on Technology

Additionally, companies have had to be more agile and adaptable, responding quickly to the rapidly changing situation and making decisions that balance short-term operational needs with long-term sustainability goals.

Board's Role in the Crises

Effective corporate governance is one which allows the Board to effectively control the management of the company and be accountable to the shareholders. One of the major duties of the Corporate Governance is to disclose the shareholders and the public the true state of affairs in the Annual Report and Balance Sheet.

Boards have to make sure that management has the ability to act accordingly by prioritizing the safety and well – being of the employees of the company's and those who are dependent on the company.

The necessity for corporate is to have a practical board to overcome the health and financial challenges. The importance for Board of Directors in COVID – 19 crises are as follow:

1. Revamp the reporting and diligence of a company and inform the risks that lay ahead.
2. The company should be informed about the specific industry related risk and the business risk that the company has to face due to pandemic.
3. A committee has to be formed in the company to assess the impact of COVID – 19 on issues and operations of the company.
4. Company COVID – 19 committee should monitor the strategic decisions relating to the company.
5. Succession planning is important in the event of top-level directors falling ill.
6. The scope of the management to raise funds from the company at times of crises when the medical expenses in excess of the insurance cover for the employee and the knowledge of insurance cover is important.
7. Companies conduct their commercial operations remotely where digital governance has come. All Listed Companies conduct their Annual General Meeting (AGM) and Extra Ordinary General Meeting (EGM) through virtual platforms which has brought in transparency and shareholder activism. The pandemic has made it difficult for companies to hold in-person meetings, including board meetings and general meetings. As a result, many companies have had to hold virtual meetings using video conferencing or other digital platforms. This has presented new challenges in terms of ensuring the effectiveness and fairness of virtual meetings, as well as the security and confidentiality of the information discussed. (Khalil Jebran, Shihua Chen (2021))

Relaxations from Compliance with Certain Provisions of The SEBI (Listing Obligations and Disclosure Requirements) Regulations, 2015 (LODR) Due to The COVID -19 Virus Pandemic

These relaxations are intended to provide relief to companies affected by the pandemic, while maintaining the integrity and transparency of the markets.

The following are some of the key relaxations provided by SEBI:

- Extension of time for holding AGM: SEBI has allowed companies to hold their Annual General Meetings (AGMs) by September 30, 2020, instead of the earlier deadline of June 30, 2020.
- Electronic voting: SEBI has permitted companies to conduct AGMs and other shareholder meetings using electronic means, such as video conferencing or other audio-visual means, in order to enable social distancing.
- Extension of time for submission of financial results: SEBI has extended the time for submission of financial results for the financial year ended March 31, 2020, to June 30, 2020.
- Disclosure of impact of COVID-19: SEBI has asked companies to disclose the impact of the COVID-19 pandemic on their financial and operational performance in their financial results for the financial year ended March 31, 2020.
- Extension of time for submission of annual report: SEBI has extended the time for submission of the annual report for the financial year ended March 31, 2020, to June 30, 2020.

Practical Issues and Implications regarding Corporate Governance for decision making during COVID -19

- Dividend Management
- Risk Management
- Corporate Social Responsibility
- Disclosure
- Business Continuity and Recovery
- Company's Annual General Meeting
- Remote Work
- Quorum Provision
- Capital Allocation and Maintenance
- Executive Pay and Incentives
- Internal Control

Dividend Management

In the event of COVID – 19 Declaration of Dividend is one of the key issues that corporates faced. Dividend means the share of profits or the retained earnings that is paid to the shareholders of the company. In the company the dividend is declared by the Board of Directors. Company that declared dividend at time of COVID -19 outbreaks did not issue dividend keeping in mind the uncertainty and conflicting market condition.

Risk Management

Managing risk is an important managerial responsibility. Corporate Governance includes Risk Management. The role of key professional is to ensure that the risk is not diversified to the objective of the corporate. The Board must monitor the changes and if necessary, the board should introduce alternate controls that strengthen and support the cause of an effective control environment.

1. Identify your risk.
2. Be agile.
3. Think people.
4. Consider Business Continuity.

The pandemic has brought new risks and uncertainties for companies, including supply chain disruptions, financial risks, and health and safety risks. Companies have had to review and update their risk management policies and procedures to address these new challenges. (Patel, CS Divyesh and Patel, Dr. Naresh, (2020))

Corporate Social Responsibility

Corporate Social Responsibility is a way of showing the commitment and concern that the company has towards the society. CSR is an ethical behaviour. The expenditure that the company has to spend at least 2% of its average net profit of the company during the three immediately preceding years.

Any contribution made by the company to CSR funds for COVID – 19 is acceptable CSR activity according to Ministry of Corporate Affairs. Further according to Companies Act 2013, any contribution made to PM CARES FUND shall be eligible as CSR contribution by the corporate.

CSR COVID – 19 INITIATIVES BY VARIOUS CORPORATES

- Supporting Small Businesses
- Supporting remote learning
- Providing food and other essential supplies
- Donating medical supplies
- Providing financial assistance to healthcare organizations and individuals
- Philanthropic donations
- Production of essential goods
- Financial assistance

- Volunteering
- Information & awareness
- Supporting the healthcare system
- Helping the vulnerable communities

Disclosure

COVID -19 is a period of uncertainty, it is important for business to communicate to their shareholders and investors, including employees of the company, customers regarding their responses to the crises.

The pandemic has led to significant changes in the business and economic environment, and companies have had to communicate these changes to their shareholders and other stakeholders. This has required companies to make timely and accurate disclosures about the impacts of the pandemic on their operations, financial performance, and future prospects.

Ministry of Corporate Affairs w.e.f 23rd March, 2020 developed a simple web-based form mainly focusing on the confidence disclosure and building measure to determine the readiness of the company to deal with COVID -19. Disclosure is a key role in Corporate Governance. All listed entities which aim at securing investor protection should disclose without any delay is the top priority. Proactive board of such companies must make sure if the disclosures are made and continue assessing the situation, communicating with the regulators and publishing public disclosures where ever necessary.

Business Continuity and Recovery

Business Continuity is the major stress that the corporates are facing during COVID -19. Maintaining the business is difficult at times of crises. Financial Distress or Business Distress happens when the company is not able to meet its regular production or provision of services. At times of extreme crises like this the directors of the company has to take reasonable care which involves assessing and minimizing the risk in similar crises.

Priorities to ensure business continuity:

1. Ensuring Security and Employee Welfare
2. Assessment of Liquidity
3. Communication with Stockholders
4. Using the Government Support

Company's Annual General Meeting

Pursuant to the provisions of Companies Act 2013, it is required that every company other than One Person Company to hold an Annual General Meeting. AGM should be held in the business hours and (9.00 AM – 5.00 PM). AGM can be held at any day other than national holiday. The meeting can be held in the registered office of the company or at some other place in the same city, town or village where the registered office of the company is situated.

Generally Annual General Meetings will be conducted by in-person but which is not possible due to pandemic. Multiple AGMs were cancelled. Ministry of Corporate Affairs gave an opportunity to the corporates, which are unable to conduct Annual General Meeting may file an application to the Registrar of Companies via form GNL -1 for extending AGM of the companies. Later AGMs were conducted through hybrid-mode (part physical, part virtual). When AGM is cancelled payment of dividend and capital raising which require AGM approval will be delayed. (Bhasin, M., (2012))

Ministry of Corporate Affairs (MCA)

The Ministry of Corporate Affairs have taken steps during COVID -19

- The Ministry of Corporate Affairs (MCA) (vide Circular No.14/ 2020 dated 8 April 2020) on clarification on passing of ordinary and special resolutions by companies under The Companies Act, 2017 and rules made thereunder on account of the threat posed by COVID-19.

Securities Exchange Board of India (SEBI)

As per the SEBI (Listing Obligations and Disclosure Requirements) Regulations, 2015 ("LODR"), the top 100 listed entities by market capitalization have to hold their Annual General Meetings (AGM) within five months from date of closing of the financial year. Given the COVID-19 pandemic, SEBI has permitted these entities to delay their AGM by one month. Moreover, listed entities whose financial year ended on December 31, 2019, are allowed to conduct their AGMs till September 30, 2020.

Remote Work

The shift to remote work has challenged traditional models of corporate governance, particularly in terms of board meetings and decision-making processes. Companies have had to adapt to virtual meetings and find ways to ensure that all stakeholders can participate and have their voices heard.

Quorum Provision

Quorum is the minimum number of members that must be present at a meeting for the meeting to be considered valid and for any decisions to be made. The quorum provision is generally specified in a company's articles of association or bylaws.

During the COVID-19 pandemic, the quorum requirement for meetings may be challenging to meet due to social distancing and travel restrictions. To address this issue, some companies have adopted alternative methods for holding meetings, such as virtual meetings, which allow members to participate remotely.

SEBI (Securities and Exchange Board of India) also provides guidance on e-voting and remote meetings during the Covid-19 outbreak. Companies have been permitted to use e-voting as a mode of voting in the general meetings, provided that the members are able to cast their votes electronically and are able to access the explanatory statement and the resolutions remotely.

Capital Allocation and Maintenance

The COVID-19 pandemic has had a significant impact on the global economy, and companies have had to adjust their capital allocation and maintenance strategies to respond to the crisis.

During times of economic uncertainty, companies may need to focus on maintaining their liquidity in order to ensure their ability to continue operating and to meet their financial obligations. This may involve reducing or postponing capital expenditures, increasing cash reserves, and seeking additional financing through debt or equity markets. It's also important for companies to assess their risk profile, by identifying and evaluating potential sources of risk such as supply chain disruptions, workforce shortages, and changes in consumer demand. This can help companies to make informed decisions on capital allocation and maintenance.

In addition, companies may need to prioritize the preservation of their cash reserves over the return on capital. This might mean postponing or cancelling projects or investments, reducing dividends, and/or retaining earnings.

Another important consideration is the ability to continue to invest in growth, as the pandemic and its aftermath will eventually come to an end, companies that can keep investing in growth during the downturn can emerge stronger when the recovery comes. This can include continued investment in research and development, and strategic investments that may be more difficult for competitors to replicate.

Executive Pay and Incentives

1. Alignment with performance: Many companies have had to adjust their financial performance expectations for the year due to the pandemic. As a result, companies may need to adjust their executive pay and incentives to align with the new performance expectations.
2. Fairness and equity: Companies should consider how their executive pay and incentive programs will be perceived by employees, shareholders, and other stakeholders. They may need to adjust their programs to ensure they are perceived as fair and equitable.
3. Long-term sustainability: Companies should focus on creating executive pay and incentives that are aligned with long-term sustainability, rather than short-term gains. This will help to ensure that their companies are well-positioned for success in the long term.
4. Flexibility: Companies should consider the potential for future disruptions and uncertainty when designing executive pay and incentives programs. Providing flexibility to make adjustments as needed in response to unforeseen events can be beneficial.
5. Transparency: Companies should be transparent with stakeholders about how they are approaching executive pay and incentives during the pandemic, and explain the rationale behind any changes that are made.
6. Balance: Companies should ensure that their executive pay and incentives are balanced with other financial and operational considerations, such as maintaining liquidity, and ensuring the long-term viability of the company.

Internal Control

Internal controls are a critical component of corporate governance, and they play a crucial role in ensuring the integrity and reliability of a company's financial reporting, as well as protecting against fraud, waste, and abuse. The COVID-19 pandemic has presented a number of challenges for companies in terms of maintaining effective internal controls under corporate governance.

A. Board oversight: The Board of Directors have a critical role in overseeing the company's internal controls. They should ensure that the company's internal controls are regularly reviewed, evaluated, and updated as necessary, in light of the new challenges posed by the pandemic. This includes ensuring that the company's risk management systems are adequate and that they are able to identify, assess, and manage new risks in a timely manner.

B. Auditing and monitoring: Companies may need to increase the frequency and scope of monitoring and auditing, to ensure that their internal controls are functioning effectively in the new remote work environment. This includes, but not limited to financial controls, compliance, and internal audit functions.

C. Third-party vendors and partners: The pandemic have also brought attention to the importance of monitoring and managing risks associated with third-party vendors and partners, especially those that are critical to the company's operations. Companies should review and update their due-diligence and risk-mitigation practices to ensure that they are adequate to address the challenges posed by the pandemic.

CORPORATE GOVERNANCE OF TATA MOTORS DURING COVID-19

Tata Motors, one of India's leading automobile companies, has implemented a number of measures to ensure good corporate governance during the COVID-19 pandemic.

- Philosophy

As a Tata Company, the Company's philosophy on Corporate Governance is founded upon a rich legacy of honest, just and clear governance practices, many of which were in place even before they were mandated by adopting the highest standards of professionalism, honesty, integrity and ethical behaviour. As a worldwide organisation, the Corporate Governance practices followed by the Company and its subsidiaries are harmonious with international standards and best practices. Through the Governance mechanism in the Company, the Board along with its committees undertakes its custodian responsibilities to all its stakeholders by ensuring transparency, fair play and independence in its decision making.

- Board of Directors

The Board currently comprises of 6 Directors, out of which 5 Directors (83.33%) are Non-executive Directors, including 2 Women Directors. The Company has a Non-Executive Chairman and 3 Independent directors ('IDs'), including 2 women Independent Directors, comprise half of the total strength of the Board.

- Code of Conduct

Whilst the Tata Code of Conduct is applicable to all Whole-time Directors and employees of the Company, the Board has also adopted the Tata Code of Conduct for NINEDs and IDs as specified under Schedule IV of the Act and Regulation 26(3) of the SEBI Listing Regulations. Pursuant to Regulation 26(5) of the SEBI Listing Regulations, all members of senior management have confirmed that there is no material, financial and commercial transactions wherein they have a personal interest that may have a potential conflict with the interest of the Company at large. Pursuant to Regulation 26(3) of the SEBI Listing Regulations, all the Board members and senior management of the Company as on March 31, 2021 have affirmed compliance with their respective Codes of Conduct. A Declaration to this effect, duly signed by the CEO & MD is reproduced at the end of this Report. Furthermore, pursuant to the provisions of Regulations 8 and 9 under the SEBI (Prohibition of Insider Trading) Regulations, 2015 the Company has adopted and endeavours adherence to the Tata Code of Conduct for Prevention of Insider Trading and the Code of Corporate Disclosure Practices.

- Annual General Meeting

In view of COVID-19 pandemic, the Ministry of Corporate Affairs ('MCA') has vide its circular dated May 5, 2020 read with circulars dated April 8, 2020, April 13, 2020, and January 13, 2021 (collectively referred to as 'MCA Circulars') and SEBI Circular dated May 12, 2020 and January 15, 2021 (collectively referred to as 'SEBI Circulars') permitted the holding of the Annual General Meeting through video-conferencing / other audio visual means ('VC / OAVM'), without the physical presence of the Members at a common venue. In compliance with the provisions of the Act, MCA Circulars and SEBI Circulars, the AGM of the Company is being held through VC / OAVM.

- Corporate Social Responsibility

a. Donated to the PM Cares fund and various state governments to support the fight against COVID-19
b. Providing support to local communities through distribution of essential goods such as food and medical supplies, as well as through financial aid to organizations working on the frontlines of the pandemic.
c. Supporting employees and their families, through financial assistance and programs to address mental and emotional well-being.
d. Supporting the production of medical equipment such as ventilators and personal protective equipment (PPE).

e. Supporting the production of oxygen concentrators and other medical devices to support COVID-19 treatment.
f. Implementing strict safety protocols and measures in its manufacturing plants to protect its employees and continue operations. (https://investors.tatamotors.com/financials/75-ar-html/pdf/report-corporate-governance.pdf)

CORPORATE GOVERNANCE OF INDIAN OIL DURING COVID-19

Indian Oil Corporation Limited (IOCL) is India's largest oil and gas company. During the COVID-19 pandemic, IOCL has implemented a number of measures to ensure good corporate governance and address the impacts of the pandemic.

- Philosophy

Indian Oil strongly believes that good Corporate Governance practices ensure ethical and efficient conduct of the affairs of the Company in a transparent manner and also help in maximising value for all the stakeholders like shareholders, customers, employees, contractors, vendors and the society at large. Good Corporate Governance practices help in building an environment of trust and confidence among all the constituents. The Company attempts to sustain the principles and practices of Corporate Governance to set the seal on transparency, integrity and accountability in its functioning, which are key to achieve its vision of being the 'Energy of India' and a broadly esteemed Company.

- Board of Directors

As on March 31, 2021, the Board of the Company comprised 10 Directors, including six Executive Directors (Whole-time Directors including the Chairman), two Government Nominee Directors and two Independent Directors.

- Code of Conduct

The Company has set high standards of ethical and responsible conduct of business to create value for all its stakeholders. The Code of Conduct for Board Members and Senior Management Personnel of the Company has been laid down by the Board, which is circulated to all concerned and is also hosted on the website of the Company. The Directors and Senior Management Personnel of the Company have affirmed compliance with the provisions of the Code of Conduct for the year ended March 31, 2021 under Regulation 26(3) of SEBI (LODR) and no material financial or commercial transactions, which may have a potential conflict with the interest of the Company, were reported by them.

- Annual General Meeting

In view of the Covid pandemic, the company's Annual General Meeting (AGM) was held through Online through Video Conferencing (VC) / Other Audio-Visual Means (OAVM).

- Corporate Social Responsibility

    a. It has also been implementing several programs and initiatives to promote community health and hygiene, and has been providing safe drinking water to the surrounding communities through its water supply schemes.
    b. Indian Oil has provided primary and secondary healthcare facilities to the surrounding communities through its hospitals, mobile medical units, health camps and dispensaries.

It's also likely that Indian Oil has continued to support these activities and adapted them to the changing circumstances brought about by the COVID-19 pandemic. Additionally, Indian Oil also has a wide range of CSR activities that can be seen on its annual report, like environment protection, women empowerment, skill development, and others.

It's worth noting that, Indian Oil's CSR activities are guided by the company's commitment to making a positive impact on the communities in which it operates, and align with the national priorities and sustainable development goals set by the Government of India. (https://iocl.com/download/IndianOil_IR_02_08_2021_double_pg_view.pdf)

CORPORATE GOVERNANCE OF INFOSYS DURING COVID-19

As for Infosys, a global leader in consulting, technology, and outsourcing services, it has emphasized its strong corporate governance structure and practices that have been implemented in the company, that help it to better prepare for and respond to crisis such as COVID-19.

- Philosophy

Infosys corporate governance is a reflection of its value system embrace its culture, policies, and relationships with its stakeholders. Integrity and transparency are its key to corporate governance practices and performance and ensure that they withhold and gain the trust of our stakeholders at all times. Infosys is committed in defining, following and practicing the top-level corporate governance across all business functions. A strong independent and distinctive Board leadership ensures the deployment of effective corporate governance throughout the corporation. Independent Board Committees engage through the year to envisage industry-leading governance practices.

- Board of Directors

The size and composition of the board comprises of 66.67% of Independent Directors and 33.33% of Non-Executive and Non-Independent Director and Executive Directors. In which 77.78% are men and 22.22% are women. The board comprises of 66.67% of Indians and 33.33% Foreign National.

- Code of Conduct

All employees and governance body members are trained on the Code of Conduct and Ethics. They have a Smart Awareness Quiz, which includes training modules that employees are mandatorily required to take up every year to renew their commitment to the Code of Conduct and Ethics.

- Annual General Meeting

Pursuant to the General Circular numbers 20/2020, 14/2020,17/2020, 39/2020 and 02/2021 issued by the Ministry of Corporate Affairs and Circular number SEBI/HO/CFD/CMD1/CIR/P/2020/79 and SEBI/HO/CFD/CMD2/CIR/P/2021/11 issued by SEBI, the 40th AGM of the Company will be held through video-conferencing and other audio-visual means.

- Corporate Social Responsibility

    1. Donating to organizations working to combat the spread of COVID-19 and to provide aid to those affected by the pandemic.
    2. Providing support to local communities in the form of food and medical aid, as well as to frontline healthcare workers.

3. Partnering with organizations to provide education and training to individuals and communities affected by the pandemic, as well as to support economic recovery efforts.
4. Implementing internal programs to support the mental and emotional well-being of its employees, as well as to provide support for those who have been impacted by the pandemic.
5. Investing in technology and innovation to create solutions that can help address the challenges posed by the pandemic. (https://www.infosys.com/)

COVID 19 and the Evolution of Comparative Corporate Governance

One way in which the pandemic may have influenced the evolution of comparative corporate governance is by highlighting the importance of good governance in enabling companies to navigate crisis situations and emerge stronger.

Companies with strong governance practices may have been better able to adapt to the challenges posed by the pandemic, such as supply chain disruptions, financial risks, and health and safety risks.

By promoting the adoption of new technologies and digital platforms for communication and decision-making. The widespread shift to remote work and the need for virtual meetings have led many companies to adopt new technologies and platforms for communication and collaboration. This may have implications for the way in which corporate governance is practiced in the future.

Greater focus on stakeholder engagement and sustainability in corporate governance. The crisis has highlighted the importance of engaging with stakeholders, including shareholders, employees, customers, and communities, and of considering the social and environmental impacts of business operations. This may lead to a greater emphasis on stakeholder engagement and sustainability in comparative corporate governance.

Recent Developments in Corporate Governance

1. **Increased focus on sustainability and ESG (environmental, social, and governance) issues:** There is a growing awareness of the need for companies to be more socially and environmentally responsible, and to consider the long-term impacts of their actions. This has led to an increased focus on sustainability and ESG issues in corporate governance.
2. **Increased use of technology:** The rise of technology has led to the use of digital platforms and tools to facilitate communication and decision-making

within companies. This has also made it easier for shareholders to participate in the governance of companies and for companies to disclose information to shareholders.

3. **Greater emphasis on stakeholder engagement:** There is a growing recognition that companies have a responsibility to a wider group of stakeholders, including employees, customers, suppliers, and the community, in addition to shareholders. This has led to an increased emphasis on stakeholder engagement in corporate governance.
4. **Increased regulation:** In response to corporate scandals and other issues, governments around the world have introduced stricter regulations to improve corporate governance. These regulations often require companies to disclose more information and to adopt higher standards of governance.
5. **Growing importance of diversity and inclusion:** There is a growing recognition that diversity and inclusion are important for good corporate governance. This has led to an increased focus on diversity and inclusion in the composition of boards of directors and other decision-making bodies.Top of Form (Sheeja Sivaprasad, Sudha Mathew. (2021))

CONCLUSION

COVID – 19 is a human tragedy. The country's economy depends on the corporate undertaking in the country. The financial strength of the corporate depends on the good governance exercised by its corporate personnel. The Boardroom efficacy is the important topic these days. It is more necessary to understand the new board rules on transparency and integrity. The board has to constantly address the gap in the compliance, changes in the legislative, the risks that are emerging and at the same time the leader's accountability for all these are wanted for the board to be more effective. With all the measures introduced by the Government, few rules introduce the possibility of conducting the meetings through virtual mode without any presence of members physically. COVID – 19 has made the corporates to build their technology. Boards are seeking to avoid cyber-attacks and data leaks that has negative impact on the financial health of the company. In short, companies, investors and stakeholders will have to work together in order to cross through the crises that occurred due to COVID -19. Martin Hirt, Sven Smit, Chris Bardley, Robert Uhlaner, Mihir Mysore, Yuval Atsom, and Nicholas Northcote (2020) said that Corporate has to act according to five horizons namely "Resolve, Resilience, Return, Reform and Reimagination" to battle against COVID – 19. Corporate governance is not merely a company's administration. It refers to honest, structured and clear functioning of the corporate management system. Corporate governance refers to a code of conduct to which the top management must stand while running the corporate enterprise. Corporate governance refers to a set of systems, regulation and rules which ensure that the company is managed in the best interest of all corporate stakeholders.

Overall, the COVID-19 pandemic has highlighted the need for effective corporate governance practices that are flexible, responsive, and transparent.

REFERENCES

Alsayegh, M. F. (2020). Corporate Economic, Environmental, and Social Sustainability Performance Transformation through ESG Disclosure. *Sustainability*, *12*(9).

Bargon, D., & Wong, S.C. (2004). *Asia's Governance Challenge*. Academic Press.

Bhasin, M. (2012). 'Voluntary' Corporate Governance Disclosures Made in the Annual Reports: An Empirical Study. *International Journal of Management & Innovation*, *4*(1).

Jebran & Chen. (2021). COVID – 19 Crises and Corporate Governance Responses. *International Journal of Finance & Economics*.

Mehran, H., Morrison, A.D., & Shapiro, J.D. (2011). *Corporate governance and banks: What have we learned from the financial crisis?* FRB of New York Staff Report, (502).

Pagach, D., & Wieczorek, M. (2020). The Challenges and Opportunities for ERM Post COVID 19: Agenda for future research. *Journal of Risk and Financial Management*.

Patel & Divyesh. (2020). *COVID-19 and Corporate Governance (India): Practical Issues, Implications and New Relief Measures*. Academic Press.

Sivaprasad & Mathew. (2021). Corporate Governance. *The International Journal of Business in Society*.

Chapter 9 The Impact of Corporate Social Responsibility (CSR) on Firm Performance During the COVID-19 Pandemic: Evidence From Oman

Essia Ries Ahmed
Faculty of Business, Karabük University, Turkey

Jawaher Hamdan Al-Alawi
University of Nizwa, Oman

Hajar Saeed Al-Rissi
University of Nizwa, Oman

ABSTRACT

This study investigates the impact of corporate social responsibility's features as predictor variables of firm performance with a sample of firms belonging to financial and industrial sectors in the Muscat Stock Exchange (MSX) in the Sultanate of Oman. This study analysed data for 75 financial and industrial firms. It used annual reports for the physical years 2019 and 2020 to analyze the impact of CSR features on firm performance during COVID-19 pandemic. The present study tested the hypotheses and utilised variables via utilizing the Smart-PLS for data analysis. The results found that CSR has a positive impact on firm performance in the financial and industrial sectors in the Sultanate of Oman.

DOI: 10.4018/978-1-6684-5342-1.ch009

INTRODUCTION

The connection between CSR and corporation performance has moved so interest between researchers (Habaragoda, 2018). Some studies detect a positive relation amidst the two constructs, while some others point to a negative connection (Mishra, & Suar, 2010). The analyses of CSR as moved to treatise the effect of CSR on its financial significance for the institution instead of discussing its effect on the broader community (Kong, Antwi-Adjei, & Bawuah, 2020). CSR is a common practice that must be promoted by governments, NGOs, and consumers, as well CSR is the voluntary participation in social and environmental programs (Blasi, Caporin, & Fontini, 2018). The notion of CSR is so aware and the execution of CSR is an irreplaceable action for maintaining the environment for sustained development, which is decent for the community, business, the milieu, and investors (Thanh, Huan, & Hong, 2021).

According to Ying, Tikuye, and Shan, (2021) Corporate Social Responsibility is defined as an "*Approach to minimizing the negative effects of company output and operations and guarantee the welfare of the community and the merciful practices of corporations beneath compression by owners and shareholders to improve profitability instead of the institutions' mason or upkeep*".

CSR is the training of works that integrates social, environmental, and economic issues into its interactions with stakeholders and business operations. CSR emphatically affects the presentation of companies working in CSR, while companies' irresponsibility activities social decrease their performance (Wei, Peng, Huang, & Yeh, 2020). CSR is getting more and more attention from companies themselves, but it is also getting more and more attention from society as a whole (Li, Cheng, & Xu, 2021). CSR positively and significantly affects corporate performance indicators, specifically Returns to (ROE), (EPS), and (ROA) (Yang, Bento, & Akbar, 2019). CSR has important and positively correlated with corporate performance, while the mediating influence of CEO (CEO) and ownership is positively correlated with corporate performance and ownership with CSR (Javeed, & Lefen, 2019). Corporate Social Responsibility (CSR) for an organization is critical as the organization is possible to fulfill certain obligations towards its investors and the culture in which it operates (Carroll, 2021). The timely operation of CSR is very essential to promote corporation sustainability and corporation value (Leszkiewicz, Hormann, & Krafft, 2021). Corporate CSR performance is a key aspect of increasing corporate financial performance agents through the (ROE), and (ROA) (Buallay, El Khoury, & Hamdan, 2021). The problem of CSR and performance is the lack of a study on CSR in Oman and poor performance (Magd, & Karyamsetty, 2021). Thus, the main objective to study the relationship between CSR and firm performance.

LITERATURE REVIEW

In this area, emphasis will be placed on previous research in the last five years. The majority of the research has determined that CSR and firms' performance, for example, Ho, Lu, and Lucianetti, (2021) the reason for this study is to study whether and how two company-wide factors temperate the relationship among CSR activities and company performance: the "alignment" of CSR activities, hazard preferences, (PMS). Using review responses from senior supervisors of special Italian corporations and archival data matching on the pecuniary performance of these corporations, the writers explain that the favorable impact of CSR actions on company performance depends on the alignment of CSR with risks, which makes competitive advantages, and the range to which the performance management system is supported to the company for its strategical initiatives. The results indicate that to extractor economic avails from CSR activity, companies' essential alignment of CSR activity with hazard preferences and depend on a performance management system to beat the causal vagueness among CSR activities and competitive advantage.

Al-Shammari, Banerjee, and Rasheed, (2021) study the target to improve and exam the theory of dual responsibility to clarify the link between (CSR) and company showing. They study whether companies that fulfill their economic and social responsibilities at the same time do better than companies that fail to do so. They also study the moderating effects of the company's position on this relationship. The writers used a longitudinal plate sample from 137 S&P 500 companies and years data among 2013 and 2004 collected of several data sources. The writers use randomly bound analyses to measurement a company's capacities in the regions of development and research, marketing, and operations. These measurements of ability are then used in conjunction with measurements of CSR and the measurement of the state of the company to test hypotheses for this study. The writers as well performed multiple different durability checks and complementary analyzes using different econometric techniques and various running of the main variants of interest. The outcomes appear that CSR is positively correlated with company performance and that the impact of CSR on performance is more powerful for companies with high levels of research and operational possibility and development. The authors also discovered support for 3-way interaction among CSR, economic responsibility, corporate situation, this indicates that companies with high gregarious and economic responsibilities and economic situations would relish the highest levels of performance.

Thanh, Huan, and Hong, (2021) The study goals to assess the impact of CSR on company profitability through exploration of the function mediator of variables like (CR) and (CPI). They utilize the quantitative technicality of minimum square structured equation modeling (PLS-SEM) technicalities for studying SMEs enterprises data from South Vietnam in 2020. The results indicate a positive and important effect of CSR on company performance through the role of mediator in the registry business and consumer price index.

Lan, Chen, Li, Guo, and Huang, (2021) study that CSR is a catalyst for company performance, not a forthright driving force. By using the specimen of US companies, they tested the empowerment hypothesis and found that CSR positively modifies the link between marketing investments and the company's financial profitability, that is, the empowerment hypothesis is corroborative. Úbeda-García, Claver-Cortés, Marco-Lajara, and Zaragoza-Sáez, (2021) study the objectives of analyzing the link among CSR and company profitability. Covariance-based structural neutralization modeling (partial least squares) has been applied to a specimen from Spanish hotel companies. The finding obtained showed a forthright and positive link between CSR and profitability. Muñoz, Fernández, and Salinero, (2021) A (CSR) analysis of a specimen of wineries in Spain and their impact on corporate performance. They used a questionnaire it was formed with a certified measure that contains social and environmental dimensions. The end example consisted of 127 companies that engaged in the National Wine Exhibition (FENAVIN) in 2019, and this was analyzed using mass and mean-variance analysis to check the existence of a CSR profitability link. Profitability was indicated by using the medium (ROA) for the previous 3 years. The finding acquired backing the common view that companies participating in CSR achieve top results. Conversely, they find wineries that are further environmentally responsible are lower profitable and that those with extra socially responsible behavior have no important link with CSR profitability.

Galdeano, Ahmed, Fati, Rehan, and Ahmed, (2019) are studying the understand how the financial performance in the financial sector could be improved. Here, the study worked to find out how CSR and regulatory engagement can be used to predict financial performance. Likewise, the study also examined the mediating role of organizational participation in the link between corporate social responsibility and financial performance. Employees at the administrative level were sampled from seven retail banks in Bahrain for this survey. Structural equation design results reported an important impact of CSR on financial performance. Accordingly, the research also indicated a statistically significant link between organizational engagement and financial performance. Above all, the research also indicated a considerable moderation of organizational engagement in the relationship of CSR and financial performance. The research presents notable implications for hypothesis and practice followed by the field of future research.

RESEARCH HYPOTHESIS

The Link between CSR and Firm Performance

Ho, Lu, and Lucianetti, (2021) the results indicate that to extract benefits of economic from CSR activities, companies need to align CSR activities with risk preferences and depend on a performance management system to beat the causal opacity between corporate social responsibility activities and competitive features. Al-Shammari, Banerjee, and Rasheed, (2021) the outcomes display that CSR is positively correlated with company profitability and that the impact of corporate social responsibility on performance is significant for corporates with higher levels of research and operational ability and development. The authors also catch support for the three ways interaction among CSR, corporate status, and economic responsibility, suggesting that companies with high economic and social tasks and economic situations would interest the highest performance levels. Thanh, Huan, and Hong, (2021) outcomes suggest a positive and important influence of corporate social responsibility on companies' performance Via mediating role of CSR and CPI. Lan, Chen, Li, Guo, and Huang, (2021) The upshot is that employee's mistreatment dampens the moderating impact of CSR because it may cause clients to view CSR activities as self-interest cosmetic procedures rather than purely charitable actions in nature. Úbeda-García, Claver-Cortés, Marco-Lajara, and Zaragoza-Sáez, (2021) the outcomes obtained showed a directly and positively link between CSR and performance. Muñoz, Fernández, and Salinero, (2021) The outcomes obtained don't support the public opinion that companies participating in CSR achieve better results. Conversely, they set up that wineries that are more environmentally accountable are the least profitable and that those with extra socially accountable performance have no important relationship with CSR performance. Galdeano, Ahmed, Fati, Rehan, and Ahmed, (2019) structural equation modeling results reported a significant influence of CSR on financial performance. Accordingly, the survey also indicated a statistically significant relationship between organizational engagement and financial performance. Notably, the research also indicated a significant moderation of organizational engagement in the Relation of CSR and financial performance. The research presents notable implications for theory and practice followed by the field of future research. Thus, the hypothesis will be:

H1: A positive relationship between CSR and firm performance.

METHODOLOGY

This section presents the study that was used in that research. This includes the most important points of research, study design, population, and sampling method, measurement of variables, unit of analysis, measurements, data analysis methods.

Study Design

This is a descriptive study using quantitative methods, in which qualitative data is collected through secondary data. The dependent variable (DV) in this report is firm performance. The factors affecting corporate social responsibility are independent variables.

Population and Sampling Method

For this research, the population of this study will be financial and industrial companies that are currently in Oman. In this search, the sample size of the research is 39. This study examines the link between CSR and corporate performance and uses secondary data for analysis.

Table 1. Population of research

Sector	Companies
Financial	35
Industrial	40
Total	75

In this research, the sample size will be 39 companies from one sector (financial and industrial -2019 &2020). We choose this sector since it's very significant in the sultanate of Oman

Table 2. Sample size of research

Sector	No. of Companies	Sample
Financial	35	20
Industrial	40	19
Total	75	39

Table 3. Measurement variables

Dependent Variable	Acronym	Measurement
Return On Assets	ROA	Net-Income after-tax/Total Assets
Return On Equity	ROE	Net-Income after-tax/Total Equity

Measurement of Variables

The present researcher utilized a set different of measurements in request to measure its chosen variables that are in the firm social responsibility (energy, Employee health, and safety, Employee Training, Employee assistance/benefits, Employee remuneration, Industrial relations, Product or services development, Product Safety, Product or services quality, community involvement) and company Performance (ROA & ROE).

Table 4. Measurement of independent variables

<table>
<tr><th></th><th>CSR Items</th><th>Discloser</th><th>No. Discloser</th><th>Index</th></tr>
<tr><td>1</td><td>Energy</td><td>ü</td><td rowspan="10">xxx</td><td rowspan="10">xxx</td></tr>
<tr><td>2</td><td>Employee health and safety</td><td>ü</td></tr>
<tr><td>3</td><td>Employee Training</td><td>ü</td></tr>
<tr><td>4</td><td>Employee assistance/benefits</td><td>ü</td></tr>
<tr><td>5</td><td>Employee remuneration</td><td>ü</td></tr>
<tr><td>6</td><td>Industrial relations</td><td>ü</td></tr>
<tr><td>7</td><td>Product or service development</td><td>ü</td></tr>
<tr><td>8</td><td>Product safety</td><td>ü</td></tr>
<tr><td>9</td><td>Product or service quality</td><td>ü</td></tr>
<tr><td>10</td><td>Community involvement</td><td>ü</td></tr>
</table>

Table 5. Descriptive statistics of variables

	Mean	Minimum	Maximum	Standard-D
ROA	0.032	-0.254	0.287	0.079
ROE	0.065	-0.367	0.460	0.127
CSR	0.475	0.500	0.800	-0.568

Units of Analysis

The analysis units for this study, where the secondary data was used for the firms of the financial sector (20 companies) and industrial sector (19 companies) in MSX for 2019 and 2020. In this study, information collected is examined with (SEM) with (PLS) approach.

RESULTS

Descriptive Statistics (2019)

The outcomes of the descriptive statistics, the dependent variable, the company's performance, showed that the company's performance level was 0.475 showing the average performance of the company, with a standard deviation of -0.568. Moreover, the maximum and minimum values pointed that the CSR is 0.500 and 0.800, respectively. In count, the descriptive analysis of the determinants shows that the return on assets is a mean of 0.032 with a standard deviation of 0.079; The mean return on equity is 0.065 with a standard deviation of 0.127.

Table 6. Discriminant validity constructs

	CSR	ROA	ROE
CSR	1.000		
ROA	0.259	1.000	
ROE	0.318	0.745	1.000

Discriminant Validity

In PLS to test discriminatory validity, there are criteria employed. The square root of each AVE of each construct must have a high relationship level as well as the corresponding constructs. Thus, to manage discriminant validity, the square root of each construct in its AVE must be assessed against the relationships of the constructs for all the different structures.

The structural model analysis was performed once the measurement model had been analyzed and had passed all criteria. The associated check for the coefficient of determination (R^2) has been completed. During this work, the return on assets is internal to show a value of R^2 0.067, 0.042. and an internal ROE to show the value of R^2 0.101, 0.077. Company performance (intrinsic) indicating that (ROA) 8%, 4% and (ROE) 10% and 8% of the variance in company performance will be explained by the two forecasters: (Return on Assets, Return on Equity). So, the current work meets the performance significantly.

Table 7. Explanation of the variance

Matrix	R Square	R Square A
ROA	0.067	0.042
ROE	0.101	0.077

Hypothesis Testing

Table 1.6 analyses the outcomes linked to the hypothesis testing and finds that most of the hypotheses are not rejected (supporting only one hypothesis) and the result revealed that ROE is positively significant with the company's performance where $P < 0.001$, $t = 3.343$. This result indicates that the return on equity has an important impact on the company's performance. The outcomes showed that the return on assets was negative with the significant performance of the company where it was $P < 0.012$, $t = 2.514$. This outcome shows that the return on assets does not have an important effect on the firm's performance.

Table 8. Path coefficients

	Original Sample	Sample Mean (M)	Standard Deviation	T Statistics (O/STDEV)	P Values
CSR - > ROA	0.259	0.266	0.103	2.514	0.012
CSR - > ROE	0.318	0.329	0.095	3.343	0.001

Note: Significance levels: *** P < 0. 001 (t >3.33), **p < 0. 01 (t >2.33), *p < 0.05 (t >1.605)

Figure 1. Results of industrial sector

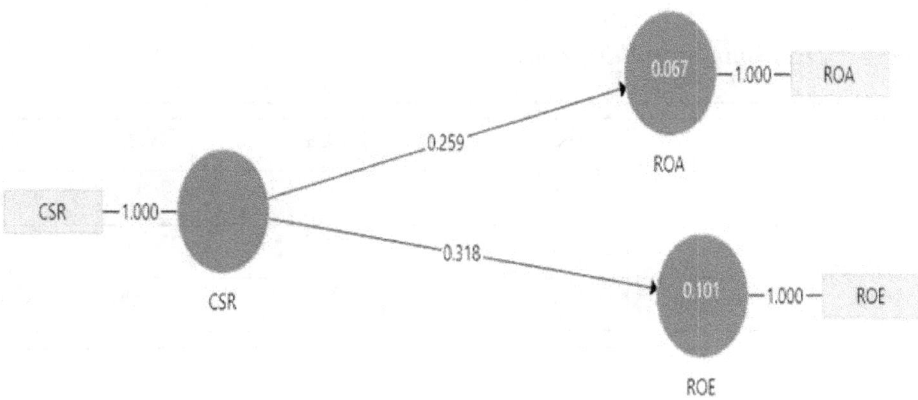

Descriptive Statistics (2020)

The outcomes of the descriptive statistics, the dependent variable, the company's performance, showed that the company's profitability level was 0.467% representing the average company's performance, with a standard deviation of 0.197. Furthermore,

Table 9. Descriptive statistics of variables

	Mean	Min	Max	Standard-D
ROA	0.037	-0.264	0.714	0.138
ROE	0.061	-0.349	0.472	0.146
CSR	0.467	0.000	0.800	0.197

the minimum and maximum values show that the company's performance is 0.000% and 0.800%, respectively. In addition, the descriptive analysis of the determinants shows that the return on assets is an average of 0.037% with a standard deviation of 0.138; The return on equity is 0.061% with a standard deviation of 0.146.

Discriminant Validity

In PLS to test discriminatory validity, there are criteria used. The square root of each AVE of each construct must have a great relationship level as well as the corresponding constructs. Thus, to manage discriminant validity, the square root of each structure in its AVE must be compared against the relationships of the constructs for all the different structures.

Table 10. Discriminant validity constructs

	CSR	ROA	ROE
CSR	1.000		
ROA	0.260	1.000	
ROE	0.326	0.755	1.000

The structural model was evaluated after the measurement model was analyzed and passed all the criteria. The coefficient of determination (R^2) is checked. In this paper, the variable (ROA) is the endogenous variable whose value R^2 was found to be 0.067, 0.042. The variable (ROE) which is the internal width has an R^2 value of 0.106 and 0.082 Company performance (substantial) indicating that (ROA) 7%, 4%, and (ROE) 11% and 8% of the variance in company performance can be explained

Table 11. Explanation of the variance

Matrix	R Square	R Square A
ROA	0.067	0.042
ROE	0.106	0.082

Table 12. Path coefficients

	Original Sample	Sample Mean (M)	Standard Deviation	T Statistics (O/STDEV)	P Values
CSR - > ROA	0.260	0.270	0.089	2.925	0.004
CSR - > ROE	0.326	0.326	0.085	3.835	0.000

Note: Significance levels: *** P < 0. 001 (t >3.33), **p < 0. 01 (t >2.33), *p < 0.05 (t >1.605)

by the predictors: (return on assets, return on equity). So, the current business largely meets the performance of the company.

Hypothesis Testing

Table 1.10 studies the results of hypothesis analysis and found that most of the hypotheses are not supported (supporting only one hypothesis), and the results showed that corporate social responsibility positively affects the return on equity (ROE) where P < 0.000, t = 3.835. This result indicates that corporate social responsibility has a positive impact on firm performance. The results showed that corporate social responsibility positively affects the return on assets (ROA) where

Figure 2. Results of Service Sector

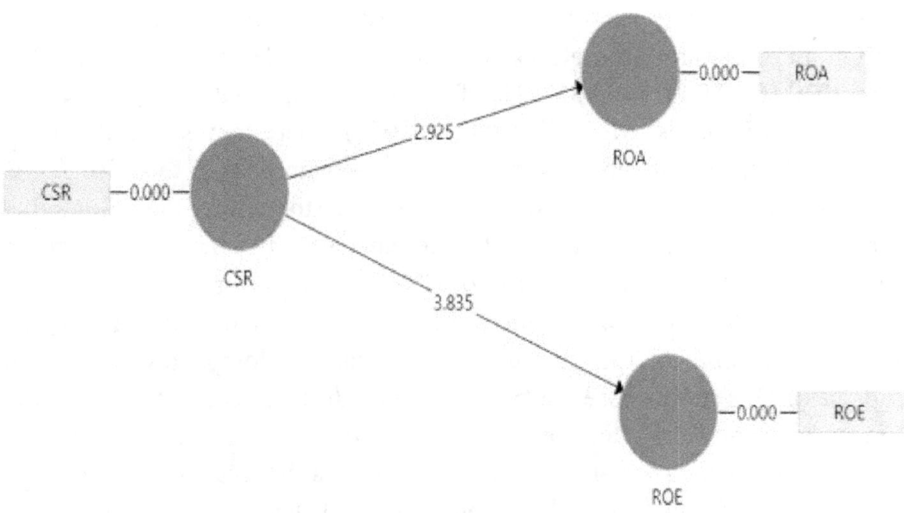

$P < 0.004$, $t = 2.925$. This result indicates that corporate social responsibility has a significant impact on firm performance.

DISCUSSION AND CONCLUSION

The basic key of this research is to determine the link between CSR and company profitability in the Muscat Stock Exchange in the Sultanate of Oman. Subsequently, the study aims to analyze and perceive the impact of CSR and corporate profitability during COVID-19 (Salam, & Bajaba, 2021). Within the review of the previous literature, this analysis identifies 2 variables that affect the firm performance were the freelance variables that are unit on corporate social responsibilities (ROA and ROE). From all freelance variables that area unit is known, hypotheses were fashioned to inquire regarding the target. The analysis used quantitative knowledge to be obtained from two sectors. A total of 39 out of 75 corporations (financial sector and industrial sector) were with success collected during this research.

Return on assets is one of the independent variables associated with CSR about the performance of the company. The results in 2019 showed a positive association between corporate social responsibility and ROA ($P < 0.004$, $t = 2.925$). In addition, 2020 also shows a significant positive correlation between corporate social responsibility and return on assets ($P < 0.012$, $t = 2.514$), the hypothesis is supported in both years. This fact indicates that the increase in return on assets will affect the greater control over firm performance in the Omani-listed companies. This result is related to the previous study of (Yang, Bento, & Akbar, 2019) where they found that CSR positively and important affects corporate performance measurements, specifically return on assets (ROA).

The outcomes show a positive relationship between corporate social responsibility and ROE. In 2019 were corporate social responsibility and ROE ($P<0.001$, $t=3.343$) and in 2020 ($P<0.000$, $t=3.835$). This finding correlates with the previous study (Broadstock, Matousek, Meyer, Tzeremes, 2020) where they stated that there is a positive effect of CSR policies on (ROE). The main goal of this research is to examine the link between CSR and firm performance to improve the profitability of companies in the Sultanate of Oman. This research used two independent variables (ROA and ROE) to measure the effect of CSR on firm performance.

The data in this report were collected from financial and industrial companies whose sample size was 39 companies (20 financial companies, 19 industrial companies). This study chose the financial and industrial sectors because they are the most secure and exploited compared to other companies, where we merged the two companies, which are among the strong options that play an exceptional and important role, and give remarkable progress, and therefore the companies can compete strongly in the State of Oman and other countries, and analysis studies were followed up corporations listed on the Muscat Stock Exchange and the use for profits on industrial and financial companies.

The results and statistics of the companies were viewed by searching for results (Return on Asset and Return on Equity) the validity between companies was tested, the criteria applied and a high correlation level was built in the companies to deal with the distinct validity. Also, hypotheses and results emerged to us, positive and negative for the firm performance of the companies. Positive results have a great impact on the company, and negative results have done not affect the possibility of the company only slightly.

This study found that the CSR has shown a positive effect on firm performance in sectors (Financial and Industrial) that listed companies Sultanate of Oman. The research provides an understanding of Firms may be affected differently in terms of content, and the responsibility of the company may increase with an increase in focus on (ROA and ROE) which becomes of great impact in terms of its relevance (firm performance) and which appear positively and represent standards resulting in high positive results in responsibility. Performance has a foundation and effectiveness on distinguishing companies, and studies may have a radical change by extracting models of important interest off responsibility and being independent.

RECOMMENDATION

This study contains many recommendations for future studies. First, this study examined the connection between (CSR) and corporation performance. This research deals with the connection between (CSR) and corporation performance. There is a lack of previous research that studies the influence of other variables on the link between (CSR) and corporation performance that would help in improving company performance. Second, this study recommends Studying CSR is a common practice that governments, NGOs, and consumers must promote. CSR is voluntary participation in social and environmental programmers. Third, future researchers should test the connection between (CSR) and corporation performance in Corporate Governance. CSR is receiving rising interest from firms themselves, but also rising interest from the community as a whole. Fourthly, Study of the CSR positively and important impacts a companies' performance indexes, specifically on (ROE), earnings per share ratios, and (ROA). Fifth, the authors use random boundary analysis to measure a company's abilities in the areas of research, development, marketing, and operations. These measures of ability are then used in conjunction with CSR measures and the measure of the state of the company to investigate the hypotheses of this research. Sixth, CSR has an important and positive association with company performance, whereas the mediating impact of (CEO) and royal-ism positively correlate to companies' performance and royal-ism with CSR.

REFERENCES

Al-Shammari, M. A., Banerjee, S. N., & Rasheed, A. A. (2021). Corporate social responsibility and firm performance: A theory of dual responsibility. *Management Decision*.

Blasi, S., Caporin, M., & Fontini, F. (2018). A multidimensional analysis of the relationship between corporate social responsibility and firms' economic performance. *Ecological Economics*, *147*, 218–229. doi:10.1016/j.ecolecon.2018.01.014

Broadstock, D. C., Matousek, R., Meyer, M., & Tzeremes, N. G. (2020). Does corporate social responsibility impact firms' innovation capacity? The indirect link between environmental & social governance implementation and innovation performance. *Journal of Business Research*, *119*, 99–110. doi:10.1016/j.jbusres.2019.07.014

Buallay, A., El Khoury, R., & Hamdan, A. (2021). Sustainability reporting in smart cities: A multidimensional performance measures. *Cities (London, England)*, *119*, 103397. doi:10.1016/j.cities.2021.103397

Carroll, A. B. (2021). Corporate social responsibility (CSR) and the COVID-19 pandemic: Organizational and managerial implications. *Journal of Strategy and Management*.

Galdeano, D., Ahmed, U., Fati, M., Rehan, R., & Ahmed, A. J. M. S. L. (2019). Financial performance and corporate social responsibility in the banking sector of Bahrain: Can engagement moderate? *Management Science Letters*, *9*(10), 1529–1542. doi:10.5267/j.msl.2019.5.032

Habaragoda, B. S. (2018). Corporate social responsibility (CSR) and firm performance: Impact of internal and external CSR on financial performance. *Business and Management*, *10*(3), 284.

Ho, J., Lu, C., & Lucianetti, L. (2021). Does engaging in corporate social responsibility activities influence firm performance? The moderating effects of risk preferences and performance measurement systems. *Management Decision*, *59*(13), 15–37. doi:10.1108/MD-07-2020-0925

Javeed, S. A., & Lefen, L. (2019). An analysis of corporate social responsibility and firm performance with moderating effects of CEO power and ownership structure: A case study of the manufacturing sector of Pakistan. *Sustainability, 11*(1), 248. doi:10.3390u11010248

Kong, Y., Antwi-Adjei, A., & Bawuah, J. (2020). A systematic review of the business case for corporate social responsibility and firm performance. *Corporate Social Responsibility and Environmental Management, 27*(2), 444–454. doi:10.1002/csr.1838

Lan, T., Chen, Y., Li, H., Guo, L., & Huang, J. (2021). From driver to enabler: The moderating effect of corporate social responsibility on firm performance. *Economic Research-Ekonomska Istraživanja, 34*(1), 2240–2262. doi:10.1080/1331677X.2020.1862686

Leszkiewicz, A., Hormann, T., & Krafft, M. (2021). Smart Business and the Social Value of AI. In *Smart Business and Better Management*. Emerald Group Publishing Ltd.

Li, X., Cheng, B., & Xu, H. (2021). Time-Based Corporate-Social-Responsibility Evaluation Model Taking Chinese Listed Forestry Companies as an Example. *Sustainability, 13*(14), 7971. doi:10.3390u13147971

Magd, H., & Karyamsetty, H. (2021). Assessing the Significance of Corporate Social Responsibility Actions to Achieve Sustainable Business and Organizational Performance during the COVID-19 Pandemic in Oman. *Global Business and Management Research, 13*(3).

Mishra, S., & Suar, D. (2010). Does corporate social responsibiliinfluencethe e the firm performance of Indian companies? *Journal of Business Ethics, 95*(4), 571–601. doi:10.100710551-010-0441-1

Muñoz, R. M., Fernández, M. V., & Salinero, Y. (2021). Sustainability, Corporate Social Responsibility, and Performance in the Spanish Wine Sector. *Sustainability, 13*(1), 7. doi:10.3390u13010007

Salam, M. A., & Bajaba, S. (2021). Corporate social responsibility during the COVID-19 pandemic: A sequential mediation analysis. *Social Responsibility Journal.*

Thanh, T. L., Huan, N. Q., & Hong, T. T. T. (2021). Effects of corporate social responsibility on SMEs' performance in an emerging market. *Cogent Business & Management, 8*(1), 1878978. doi:10.1080/23311975.2021.1878978

Úbeda-García, M., Claver-Cortés, E., Marco-Lajara, B., & Zaragoza-Sáez, P. (2021). Corporate social responsibility and firm performance in the hotel industry. The mediating role of green human resource management and environmental outcomes. *Journal of Business Research*, *123*(C), 57–69. doi:10.1016/j.jbusres.2020.09.055

Wei, A. P., Peng, C. L., Huang, H. C., & Yeh, S. P. (2020). Effects of corporate social responsibility on firm performance: Does customer satisfaction matter? *Sustainability*, *12*(18), 7545. doi:10.3390u12187545

Yang, M., Bento, P., & Akbar, A. (2019). Does CSR influence firm performance indicators? Evidence from Chinese pharmaceutical enterprises. *Sustainability*, *11*(20), 5656. doi:10.3390u11205656

Ying, M., Tikuye, G. A., & Shan, H. (2021). Impacts of firm performance on Corporate Social Responsibility Practices: The mediation role of Corporate Governance in Ethiopia corporate business. *Sustainability*, *13*(17), 9717. doi:10.3390u13179717

Chapter 10
COVID-19 Pandemic Jolt:
Qualitative Research on Investor Behavior Toward Mutual Funds Investment With Special Reference to Tamilnadu

Radhamani K.
https://orcid.org/0000-0001-6621-9847
P.K.R. Arts College for Women, Gobichettipalayam, India

ABSTRACT

Due to high instability in the markets and a situation similar to the year 2008, investors are worried about their investments and want to make quick decisions regarding the investments. Due to COVID-19, financial health has recessed. Investors are finding it difficult to decide whether they should continue their investment or redeem all and keep the cash aside for an emergency because life is unpredictable. In this context, secure monitoring and evaluation of mutual funds has become essential.

INTRODUCTION

The purpose of investment is to earnings of income and wealth through various approaches. In this present scenario, the fear of unknown is emerging and many businesses are facing financial crisis. So, the investments depend on current earnings, professional and business background, dependent members in the family, social status and future prospects. Already people are reeling under pressure on account of pay-cuts and job-losses. While the discretionary expenses may be down because of the lockdown, managing household expenses with limited resources is a matter

DOI: 10.4018/978-1-6684-5342-1.ch010

for concern. However, one also needs to keep an eye on the financial goals and try to ensure that they are on track. People normally have three main objectives:

- Safety
- Return
- Liquidity

CONCEPTS AND REVIEWS

Concepts of the Study

Mutual funds are funds which have been pooled together and invested in specific investment goals by investors. Mutual funds are pools of cash that are managed by experts and placed in portfolios to maximise returns at specific risk levels. It is a capital raising strategy for investing in securities and issuing units to investors in accordance with the objectives of the proposal report. To spread risk, securities investments are spread across multiple businesses. Diversifications decrease risk because no two stocks can move in the same direction at the same time. Unit holders are well-known to mutual fund investors. Investors are entitled to a portion of the profits or losses generated by their investment. Mutual funds are regulated by the Securities and Exchange Board of India (SEBI).

MUTUAL FUNDS SCHEMES

According to the Maturity Plan

On maturity plan separated into open and closed schemes. Mutual funds are one of the most ample, simple, and adaptable ways to build a diversified investing portfolio. There are various sorts of mutual funds, each with its own set of possibilities to meet investors' varying risk tolerances. Let's look at the many types of mutual funds on the market now to assist you make an informed investment selection. Any mutual fund will, in general, invest in equities, debt, or a combination of the two. They can also be either open-ended or closed-ended mutual fund schemes.

Open-Ended Funds

This scheme allows investors to purchase or sell units at any time. It has no set maturity date. For investments and redemptions, you deal directly with the Mutual

Fund. The major characteristic is liquidity. You can immediately buy or sell your units at net asset value ("NAV") based pricing. The majority of mutual funds, roughly 59%, are open-end funds.

Close-Ended Funds

This form of scheme has a defined maturity period and investors can only invest in the New Fund Offer during the initial launch period (NFO). No new investments are allowed until the bid ends. Because of the demand and supply situation, the expectations of the unit holder and other market factors, the market price at the stock exchange could vary from the scheme's net asset value (NAV). It's possible to sell your units directly to the mutual funds at NAV-related pricing through periodic repurchases in some closed ended schemes as well. The SEBI Regulations ensure that the investors are provided with at least one of the two exit routes.

Interval Funds

It functions as a mixture of open and closed-ended schemes, allowing investors to exchange units at predefined intervals. They can be listed on the stock exchange, or they can be sold or redeemed at NAV-related rates at pre - determined intervals. One should look for personalized guidance when it comes to choosing a scheme to invest in. Choose the scheme that gives the best combination of growth, stability, and income while keeping your risk tolerance in mind. Let's look at the various types of equities and debt mutual funds that are accessible in India

Equity or Growth Schemes

These are among the most common schemes for mutual funds. They encourage investors to take part in stock markets. These schemes, while classified as high risk, often have a high return potential in the long run. In their prime earning stage, they are perfect for investors looking to create a portfolio that gives them superior returns over the long term. Usually an equity fund or diversified equity fund as it is commonly called invests over a range of sectors to distribute the risk.

EQUITY FUNDS ARE FURTHER CLASSIFIED INTO THREE TYPES

Sector-Specific Funds

These are mutual funds that invest in a particular industry or sector. Infrastructure, banking, mining, and other sectors, as well as specific segments such as mid-cap, small cap, and large-cap segments, are examples. They are appropriate for investors with a high risk tolerance and the potential to generate high returns.

Index Funds

Investors who plan to invest in equities mutual funds but don't want to rely on the fund manager should look into index funds. The strategy of an index mutual fund is the same as the index it is based on. Index funds promise to measure the quality of the index they are tracking. They also limit losses to the proportional loss of the index they follow, making them appropriate for investors with a moderate risk appetite.

Tax Saving Funds

Investors can receive tax advantages by investing in these funds. They are also known as Equity Linked Saving Schemes since they invest in shares (ELSS). The lock-in period for these types of schemes is three years. The scheme's investments are tax deductible under Section 80C of the Income Tax Act of 1961.

Money Market Funds or Liquid Funds

These funds invest in short-term debt securities, intending to deliver an acceptable return to investors over a short period of time. These funds are suited for investors with a low risk appetite who are seeking to park their surplus funds over a short-term. These can be used instead of saving money in a bank account.

Fixed Income or Debt Mutual Funds

These funds put the majority of their money into fixed income investments, such as government securities, bonds, debentures, and other fixed-income mechanisms. They offer a low-risk, low-return perspective, making them excellent for conservative investors looking for a consistent income. They are, nevertheless, under risk of default.

Balanced Funds

These are mutual fund schemes that invest in both equities and debt, as the name implies. The allocation may change in response to market risks. They are better suited to investors searching for a combination of moderate returns and low risk.

Hybrid / Monthly Income Plans (MIP)

These funds are comparable to balanced funds but the share of equity assets is reduced compared to balanced funds. As a result, they're also known as marginal equity funds. They are especially ideal for investors who are retired and desire a steady income with comparatively low risk.

Gilt Funds

Only government securities are held by these funds. They're favoured by risk averse investors who don't want to take any credit risks. They are, nevertheless, vulnerable to a high risk of interest rate fluctuations.

REVIEW OF LITERATURE

Mitalbhayani (2017) found that, while the mutual fund business in India appears to be growing, the increase is concentrated both in terms of investors category and geographical location. Institutional investors, T-15 cities, and debt-oriented schemes dominate the market, leaving plenty of room for expansion. However, a sizable number of investors remain outside the industry's purview. The fund houses' ability to contact various sectors of investors remains a major concern. One possible answer is to increase financial education and awareness in order to support investors to invest in mutual funds. This will entice investors to invest in mutual funds. The restricted distribution network and investors service can be expanded to reach outside of major cities.

Shivangi Agarwal & Nawazish Mishra (2017) a study of the risk-adjusted performance of the Indian mutual fund industry. It was discovered that 90% of the strategies outperform their benchmark. It implies that the funds performed better at the time of research; so, investors seeking consistent returns may consider investing in these schemes.

Anil and Kumar (2018) examined the service quality features of mutual funds in their research. According to the findings of the study, the trustworthiness of mutual fund investment businesses is a crucial element in determining the level of satisfaction of mutual fund investors

O.V.A.M Sridevi (2018) demonstrated that, of the two schemes, both mid cap and small cap funds outperformed the benchmark return. Not all of the funds have shown a positive return. The performance of the Axis Balanced Fund in the Mid Cap Fund is minor, however the performance of the HSBC Balanced Fund in the Small Cap Fund is regarded as desirable. However, based on the findings of the preceding study, it is possible to conclude that the schemes provide a wide range of results.

Dr. Megha Mehta (2020) concluded that, during this scenario of covid 19 and recession, middle class investors were quite aversive towards investment because of already committed responsibilities. Still today, India's middle class is more optimistic, confident, and globalized. Thus, from above analysis we found that middle class investors highly wanted to invest in fixed deposits and insurance and very less in gold, real estate, and shares & bonds. They wanted to keep cash & cash equivalents as alternative for contingencies.

Reshma Raju Mini (2020) the goal of investment is to achieve a risk-free, consistent return. However, it is dependent on the investor's investment, taking into account his or her income level and risk-taking capabilities. When compared to other nations, our residents' understanding of mutual funds is quite low, which contributes to a lack of interest in such types of investment. As a result, in order to make mutual funds more familiar, the industry should implement awareness campaigns, novel financial instruments, ads, and other means that can support the country's individual as well as economic goals.

Research Gap

The researcher discovered a gap in the prior investigations after examining the above literature. Most of the contributions were made on performance analysis of mutual fund schemes, perception of investors, Mutual fund performance evaluation based on a benchmark index, performance analysis of debt and equity mutual fund schemes, risk analysis of mutual funds, return & risk analysis of selected specific mutual funds in India. There is less contribution on investor's behaviour towards mutual funds investment. Hence this was identified as the research gap. In order to fulfill the research gap, the researcher has chosen this topic as her research work. Hence the study.

Research Question

- What is the investment behavior or portfolio choice of the investors in generating regular income for present life time?

- Why are people hesitant to invest into mutual fund investment?

Objectives of the Study

- To identify the investor behavior towards various mutual fund schemes in this present scenario.
- To explore the behavioural intent of investors towards mutual fund investment

Research Methodology

The qualitative study in views to get the objectives, factors, opinion, attitude, experience and challenges of the investors in investing mutual funds. A convenient sampling technique has been used. The study was carried out by the face to face interview of 41 respondents and a further qualitative analysis was carried out with the opinion of those 41 respondents. The overall time for each individual interview is in the range of 15 to 25 minutes. Records are taken during the interviews, and the researcher listens to the recorded interview data and transliterated in a written form. The data is arranged by questions to look at all applicants and their responses. Nvivo software used to analysis the qualitative data analysis of the respondents. The tools used for analysis are thematic analysis, mind map with thematic analysis, cluster analysis, tree map of nodes of coded qualitative data.

ANALYSIS AND INTERPRETATION

The behaviours of individual investors may be studied in the theory of planned behaviour as an addition to the theory of reasoned action. This theory's action that purpose is the immediate falling of their behaviour. This theory suggests that the behaviour of an individual, which is the responsibility of the attitude to an active and subjective standard, should be governed by investors' behaviour intention. In recent years the mutual funds are an increasingly favoured investment mode and growing number of AMC funds. The performance and growth of overall asset management companies are increase from 2018 onwards. The newly launched funds are another development that reflects the boom in the mutual funds market and rapid growth. In developed countries, the tremendous number of mutual funds investors worldwide indicates the behaviour of the investors and option of investment. Investors' behaviour or perception is based on two dimensions: risk and return. The investors invest based on different investment criteria. It consists of different parameters for evaluating the acquisition goal valued by financial and strategy of investors.

The qualitative study focuses on the behavioural intent of the investors. 41 respondents were analysed through face to face interviews. During face to face interview researcher received the feelings, expression, attitude and experience of the investors. The recording was made during the interview session. The audio has been converted into transcript and finally made analysis using Nvivo software for qualitative analysis. The tools used for analysis are thematic analysis, mind map with thematic analysis, cluster analysis, tree map of nodes of coded qualitative data. The following questions were asked during the interview session.

- Demographic profile of the investors.
- What is the objective of your investment?
- What are the most important factors to consider before choosing mutual funds?
- How are investors priorities before selecting a company for investment?
- What Types of advice sought before making a decision?
- What are the Challenges faced by mutual funds investors?
- How to overcome these challenges?
- How many years of mutual fund experience do the participants have and their prospect to remain active in mutual funds?

RESPONDENTS PROFILE

A total of 20 mutual fund investors were interviewed about the investment decision behaviour of mutual funds investors in Erode and their background profile are presented in table. Most of the investors are educated with undergraduate degree, postgraduates and professional degree holders. Majority of the respondents are male. None of these investors have less than one years of investment experience. All the respondents are current investors. All the respondents have more than enough experience and knowledge to know how investment decisions are formed. Most of the respondents invested their funds into more than two assets, with a minimum age of 22.

WHAT IS THE OBJECTIVE OF YOUR INVESTMENT?

As an investor, decision making is a complex process. When to invest, Where to invest, how to invest and which scheme is most suitable to the financial need of an individual. The primary objectives of the investors are the safety of the capital, income and growth. Most of the investors preferred to invest only on the safety funds.

Table 1. Interviewees background information

Interviewees	Experience	Gender	Age	Investment status	Education level	Investment in more than two assets
R1	21	Male	56	Current investor	B.Tech	Yes
R2	03	Male	30	Current investor	B.E	Yes
R3	08	Male	38	Current investor	MBA	Yes
R4	02	Male	25	Current investor	B.Sc CT	Yes
R5	03	Male	32	Current investor	MBA	Yes
R6	15	Male	36	Current investor	B.E	Yes
R7	02	Male	38	Current investor	B.Sc CS	Yes
R8	05	Male	36	Current investor	MBBS	Yes
R9	03	Female	36	Current investor	M.Com	Yes
R10	20	Male	41	Current investor	MCA	Yes
R11	24	Male	52	Current Investor	12th	Yes
R12	02	Female	27	Current investor	M.Sc Cs	Yes
R13	02	Female	31	Current investor	MBA	Yes
R 14	03	Male	28	Current investor	BE	Yes
R 15	07	Male	30	Current investor	B.Sc	No
R 16	01	Male	22	Current investor	BE	No
R 17	10	Female	38	Current investor	M.Com	Yes
R 18	05	Male	26	Current investor	MBA	Yes
R 19	15	Male	56	Current investor	M.Com, BBL	Yes
R 20	03	Male	26	Current investor	BE	No

As an investor, you must have a specific goal in mind. Investments are categorised into three primary objectives: safety, growth, and income. These are investments that help you to determine what type of investments to make and help prepare for what lies ahead. Therefore, before you begin to invest, it is essential to understand the investment and its goals to pick the right mix and make informed investments that best suit your needs. **(R1)**

A mutual fund is a platform to invest our money and gain profit to earn better returns compared to bank deposits. **(R2).**

Investment is to make a stable growth in our current position and it's based on the profit motive and safety of investing assets. **(R3)**

Capital growth and safety. **(R4)**

Mutual funds investment gives economic growth, when it is long term investment and not short term investment. **(R5)**

The primary objective of mutual fund investment is to earn profit and safety for the investment fund. Focus on income may buy some of the schemes that give fixed income assets. **(R19)**

Long term returns, safety and security. **(R20)**

WHAT ARE THE MOST IMPORTANT FACTORS TO CONSIDER BEFORE CHOOSING MUTUAL FUNDS?

Chart shows the thematic analysis of factors. The factors can be classified into three categories: personal factors, organisationalfactors and marketing factors. 20 responses linked with personal factors that influence the investor's decision, market factors related to external factors influencing the investors' decisions and organisational factors that influence the investors' decisions.

HOW INVESTORS PRIORITIES BEFORE SELECTING A COMPANY FOR INVESTMENT?

As an investors first priorities their investment objectives based on their needs. To analyse the schemes based on certain categories like profile of the company, economic and market conditions, financial roadmap, evaluation of risk tolerance, volatility and asset allocation.

WHAT TYPES OF ADVICE SOUGHT BEFORE MAKING A DECISION?

As investors before investing into mutual get some helps or advice have to take from fund managers or friends or family, otherwise do some researches or collect information from different sources like newspapers, AMFI website based on the categories and schemes. It found that majority of the investors option is based on their own plans and planning, market risk and risk return analysis in addition to this do research and collect information from different online and offline sources.

In addition to the priorities, this section describes whether interviewees seek any additional information from third parties before making investment decisions. It was found that the majority of the interviewees relied so much on their findings from fundamental analysis, reading about the company, finding the general trend

Figure 1. Factors – coding

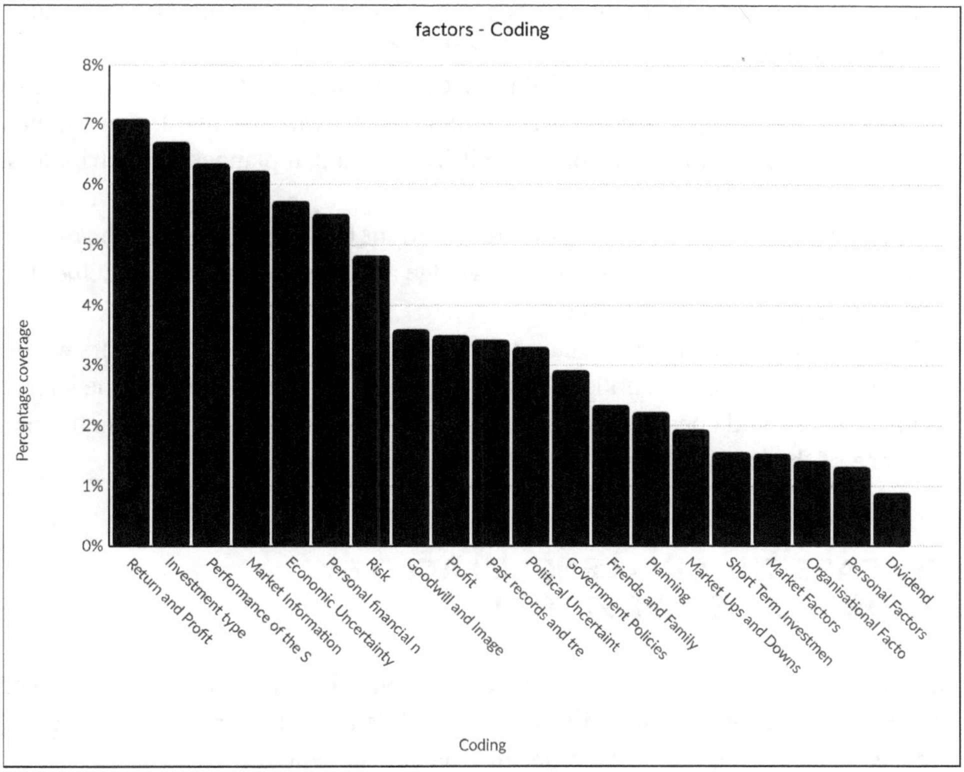

of the company from online search, newspapers, magazines and journals. They do not rely solely on third parties because they believe that it is difficult to trust third parties fully because everyone is similar when making decisions.

Figure 2. Mind map diagram with thematic analysis

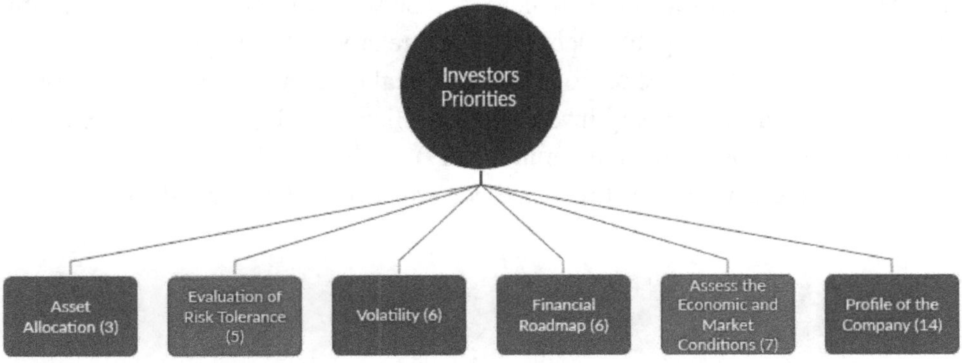

Before making a decision you should know a few things. First is to plan it out: Investing in mutual funds through a systematic plan or SIP is an important financial decision. Then the timing factor: you should know when is the best time to invest in mutual funds. Once I have decided to invest in mutual funds and planned things out, it is now time to put it in action. There are many ways to invest, you can buy it directly from fund houses, or purchase it from financial planners or distributors, or through banks. **(R1)**

We want to read about their terms and conditions before entering into the mutual fund company, then we should have knowledge about schemes, check whether the website is legal or illegal etc. **(R2)**

Before making a decision, we have to select the goals like how many years we are going to invest. We should notice the purpose of investing and to select the source of funds. We should consider the age and profile of the investors. Based on the risk tolerance of the investors we should provide the suitable funds. **(R3)**

WHAT ARE THE CHALLENGES FACED BY MUTUAL FUNDS INVESTORS?

All the investors have their own challenges while invest in mutual funds. The challenges are categories into different themes like lack of awareness, confidence, knowledge, transparency, risk factors and market challenges.

Mutual funds have certain risk factors; Mutual fund Schemes are not guaranteed or assured return products. Investment in mutual funds units involves investment risk such as trading volumes, Settlement risk, liquidity risk, default risk including the possible loss of principal. As the price/value/interest rates of the securities in which the Scheme invests Fluctuates, the value of investment in a mutual Fund Scheme may go up or down. Past performance does not guarantee future performance of any mutual fund scheme. **(R1)**

We cannot expect profit sometimes in mutual funds; most investment schemes may be high. Mutual funds are challenging one we take risk we will gain profit. High taxes, record-high public debt levels and relatively low tax rates. **(R2)**

The challenges for investors to invest in mutual funds are market fluctuations at the national level.The primary investment for a lien period is the net asset value or increased or decreased the mutual fund. **(R19)**

Lumpsum long term investment and performance of the fund. **(R20)**

HOW TO OVERCOME THESE CHALLENGES?

Investors have a lot of challenges in market while investing their funds. As investors has to be ready to face the challenges. To overcome the challenges to gain more knowledge and confidence.

Figure 3. Overcome these challenges – coding

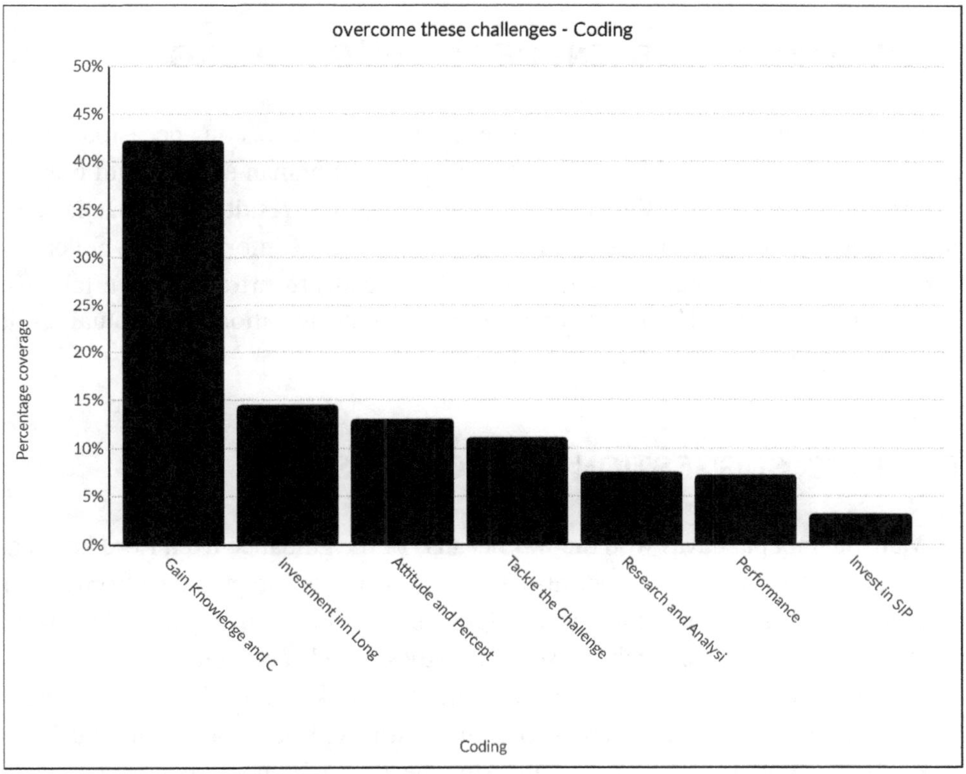

HOW MANY YEARS OF MUTUAL FUND EXPERIENCE DO THE PARTICIPANTS HAVE AND THEIR PROSPECT TO REMAIN ACTIVE IN MUTUAL FUNDS?

The respondents experience as investors and whether they would like to remain active as investors in the mutual funds. It is essential to know the impact of them remaining active in mutual funds. It is essential to know the impact of their prior investment experience on the subsequent purchase of mutual funds because it has been documented that investors' previous experiences influence their participation in the mutual funds. The experience of the investors is very good. They described that when compared to short term investment long term and SIP are better. Investors know where to invest, when to invest, what funds to invest and which company funds give more profit. Investors invest their funds for a minimum of 5 years and longer than 10 years to gain more return, knowledge, information, need to create more confidence, watch market ups and downs, be ready to take risk to earn high return and be ready to face the challenges and obstacles.

WHAT MAKE INVESTMENT DECISIONS GO WRONG?

This section outlines why the interviewees' investment decisions occasionally go wrong. As advocated by behavioural finance, several human errors could prevent the intended outcomes. With regard to this construct, result show that lack of understanding of financial behaviour because some of the information is not easily accessible and rumours going on in the market, especially from traders, uncertainties, lack of information and human error, is the cause of the deviation of the actual result from the expected result of investment decisions.

FINDINGS, SUGGESTION AND CONCLUSION

In Mahabharata pandavas won the war because of the guidance from Lord krishna. Same can be true in mutual funds also. Get proper advice and guidance from senior investors, friends or family members and fund managers. As investors get help from the trustworthy and dependable investment advisor and stay focused on the goals. Ready to face challenges like market challenges and risk factors. There are different risk factors like market risk, credit risk, interest risk, financial risk and business risk. To overcome these challenges investors need to gain more knowledge, create confidence level, do research and analysis, attend more seminar and awareness programme which is organised by AMFI and other recognised bodies, focus on long term rather than short term, change the attitude and perception of the investors mind and tackle the challenges and hardships in investment. Occasionally the investment decisions may go wrong because of human errors but stick on your goals and focus on long term investment.

Investors gain complete knowledge of market information, economic uncertainty, market ups and downs, government and political policies. Investors do proper research and analysis based on their investment objectives and select the schemes accordingly. Sometime the investors decision may go wrong but they have to be ready to face the challenges and gain more knowledge towards market risk. Proper fundamental analysis can be done to check the background of the company and technical analysis to forecast the schemes performance.

REFERENCES

Agarwal & Mishra. (2017). A Study of the Risk Adjusted Performance of Mutual Funds Industry in India. *Review of Innovation and Competitiveness.*

Anil & Kumar. (2018). The service quality attributes of mutual funds. *International Journal of Pure and Applied Mathematics, 118*(5).

Mehta & Shah. (2012). Preference of Investors for Indian Mutual Funds and its performance evaluation. *Pacific Business Review International*, *5*(3), 62–76.

Mini. (2020). A study on the awareness of mutual funds investment in India. *International Journal of Scientific & Technology Research, 9*(1).

Mitalbhayani. (2017). A study of recent trends in Indian Mutual Fund Industry. *International Research Journal of Engineering and Technology, 4*(4).

Sridevi. (2018). Performance Analysis of Mutual Funds- A Study On Selected Mid Cap And Small Cap Funds. *International Journal of Business And Management Invention, 7*(7).

ADDITIONAL READING

A., B., & S., F. (2001). A Data Envelopment Analysis Approach to Measure the Mutual Fund Performance. *European Journal of Operational Research, 135*, 477-492.

B., M. (1995). Returns from Investing in Equity Mutual Funds 1971 to 1991. *Journal of Finance, 50*, 49-72.

Danila, N. (2012). Estimating the Risk of Mutual Funds in Indonesia by Employing Value at Risk (VaR). *Asian Journal of Business and Accounting*, *5*(2), 99–118.

Hentatia, R., Kaffelb, A., & Prigentc, J.-L. (2010). Dynamic Versus Static Optimization of Hedge Fund Portfolios: The Relevance of Performance Measures. *International Journal of Business*, *15*(1).

Hsieh, H.-H., & Hodne, K. (2013). A Review of Performance Evaluation Measures for Actively-Managed Portfolios. *Journal of Economics and Behavioral Studies, 5*(12), 815-824.2122.

Hsu, P., & Chang, Y.-M. (2008). Performance of Risk Measures in China's Stock Markets. *Journal of International Management Studies*, *3*(2), 98–102.

J, E. E., J., G. M., & R, B. C. (1996). The Persistence of Risk-Adjusted Mutual Fund Performance. *Journal of Business, 69*, 133-157.

Singh, P. (2006). *Study of performance of mutual funds in India*. Galgotia Publications.

Chapter 11
Impact of COVID-19 on the Financial Management of MSMEs:
An Analytical Review

Abhijit Sharad Kelkar
University of Fujairah, UAE

Nithya Ramachandran
https://orcid.org/0000-0002-5061-4591
University of Technology and Applied Sciences, Oman

ABSTRACT

With the advent of advanced information technology and related tools in late 1990s, the scope, nature, and avenues of the business opportunities and its financial perspectives changed. Stabilization and equating of the demand and supply for the sources of inflows and outflows of funds remained the challenges across the industry. The struggling players during this time remained MSMEs due to their limited scale and more importantly limited cushioning capacity to absorb the shocks of financial downs. The micro, small, and medium enterprise (MSME) sector has emerged as a highly vibrant and dynamic sector of the Indian economy over the last five decades. It contributes significantly to the economic and social development of the country by fostering entrepreneurship and generating many employment opportunities at comparatively lower capital cost, next only to agriculture. MSMEs are complementary to large industries as ancillary units, and this sector contributes significantly to the inclusive industrial development of the country.

DOI: 10.4018/978-1-6684-5342-1.ch011

BACKGROUND

The MSMEs are widening their domain across sectors of the economy, producing diverse range of products and services to meet demands of domestic as well as global market. In India, the enterprises have been classified broadly into Manufacturing and Services. While adjusting to the emerging and consistently emerging business environment, MSMEs started playing considerably quantifiable role in the GDP of India. The position of India's Micro, Small and medium enterprises (MSME) is the largest in world after china. MSME plays a significant role to accelerate the growth of Indian economy.

However, with the entry and long lasting impact of the uncertainty in the form of pandemic like Covid-19, the entire picture got changed.

The ongoing COVID-19 pandemic has caused unprecedented disruptions to economic activities across countries, and India is no exception. The pandemic has severely affected and still affects the operational aspects of Value Chains, Network of Products, Trade, Services, Supply Chain and Logistics, Channel Financing and overall International Business globally. With the movement of the material from demand as well as supply side getting affected badly, the impact of the same does not get only on the MSMEs but on overall economy.

To what extent to have a debt-ridden operational economy of the organization remains to be the independent choice of every organization. The reason being, it entirely depends on the reasons for which funds are required, the sources to which they will be applied and more importantly, the duration within which they will get recovered while creating the returns on investments as well.

To quote, 'The Hindu' published a report wherein the survey conducted by All India Manufacturers Organization clearly showed that with more than 6 Crore MSMEs in India, more than 30% will face the forced closure for non-ability to sustain condition by the end of 2021. Same survey has observed that more than 71% of the Organizations have disturbed and infrequent salary schedule.

As per the Confederation of All India Traders (CAIT) Report in 2021, more than 30 Crores of Traders will face the Covid-19 and related lockdown loss estimating to more than INR 400 Lakh.

Not only the restrictions on the new capacity to invest and borrow, the maintenance of the operational status of the organization itself is a big challenge to the MSMEs in India. In addition to the existing operational expenses, the pending finance costs and cash outflows for long future periods will add certain fuel to the fire.

Even though Government of India has been keen enough to boost the MSMEs with the Long Term Repo Operations (LTRO) through RBI, it will act as a temporary measure and that too creation of another financial burden on the already troubled MSMEs. To repay the previous loan, opting for a new loan prove to be the wise strategy provided the flow of goods and services observe consistency in terms of quantum, speed and increase. However, in the current scenario, rather than external strengthening of the MSMEs, internal boosting and drastic strategy change are more crucial.

In this context, with the perspectives and perceptions of the MSMEs about the current and expected situation portray the real essence of the Covid-19 and its impact on the financial management and financial performance of the MSMEs.

INTRODUCTION

Small and medium-sized enterprises (MSMEs) have developed into a vibrant and active segment of the Indian economy, according to Gade (2018). It has been discovered to be a determinant in a person's growth and development. MSMEs contribute significantly to the creation of jobs at a low cost of capital, to the establishment of enterprises in less developed regions, to the reduction of regional inequalities, and to the equitable distribution of the country's income and wealth. MSMEs act as support groups for a wide variety of businesses, increasing chances for vertical integration in rural and distant locations and so providing a significant contribution to the country's budget. MSME, as well as the agriculture business, offer several prospects for both personal and paid employment. MSME is associated with higher economic growth rates, inclusive and long-term populations, and low-cost non-agricultural livelihoods in a variety of ways, including promoting gender equality in society, ecologically sustainable growth, and, most importantly, protection against deflation, as MSME has always demonstrated.

In India, there is a Ministry of Micro, Small, and Medium Enterprises. It is the primary executive authority in India for developing and implementing rules, regulations, and laws pertaining to small and medium-sized companies. It is a government entity in India. The Ministry of Small-Scale Industries and Agro-Rural Industries was established in October 1999. Many people were delighted when Shelly et al. (2020) discussed the Make-in-India concept, believing it would benefit the industrial sector. The project's objective is to reduce the enormous gap between the Chinese and Indian markets. It is critical for the entire country to participate in the "Make in India" initiative. The development of skills in providing input assistance as a factor service is vital to the success of the Indian government's massive initiative, which is ensured at the grassroots level through the engagement of MSMEs.

Following the COVID-19 epidemic, governments began providing financial assistance and other forms of assistance to small firms and their employees, Sonobe et al. (2021) report. This is because smaller firms are more susceptible than bigger enterprises to changes in their supply chain, labour supply, and final demand for goods and services. However, because MSMEs are so diverse, the severity of the pandemic's impact varies significantly according to the characteristics of each. Businesses with a large workforce, revenue, and cash flow are significantly impacted by the epidemic. During this trying period, we're attempting to determine which businesses have begun conducting business online and how their usage of internet commerce and their jobs are related. The quantity of assistance provided by the government to MSMEs and the extent to which it satisfied their demands.

MSMEs IN INDIA

Small enterprises are estimated to account for around 8% of India's GDP. Additionally, they account for around 45 percent of industrial production and more than 40 percent of exports. They might be dubbed the "Backbone of the Country" due to their significance. MSMED, or Micro, Small, and Medium Enterprises, is a 2006 law in India. MSME stands for Micro, Small, and Medium Enterprises, and was established by the Indian government. These firms are specialised in the creation, manufacture, processing, and storage of items and goods. MSMEs are a significant element of the Indian economy and have contributed significantly to the country's social and economic development (Lending Kart, 2021). It not only creates jobs, but also aids in the development of the country's backward and rural areas. According to the government's 2018-19 annual report, India has around 6,08,41,245 small companies. The Micro, Small, and Medium Enterprises Development (Amendment) Bill, 2018, proposes to redefine MSMEs by categorising them according to their yearly revenue as manufacturing or service firms. There would be no need for additional inspections to determine how much money was spent on plant and machinery under the new or amended classification. Additionally, MSMEs' actions will be transparent, non-discriminatory, and objective.

Since its inception, the Indian economy's small business sector has seen a great deal of activity. MSMEs manufacture and sell a diverse range of products for both domestic and international markets. They aided in the establishment and growth of the khadi, village, and coir industries. They have collaborated with the appropriate ministries, state governments, and individuals to assist rural regions in growing. MSMEs have been critical in rural regions in terms of employment creation (Lending Kart, 2021). In comparison to large firms, they have contributed significantly to the industrialization of these areas at a relatively minimal cost to the local populace. Because small firms assist large enterprises, they have made a significant contribution to the country's socioeconomic growth. Small firms contribute to the growth of the country in a variety of ways, including minimal investment, operational flexibility, and relocation to a new site, low import rates, and a significant contribution to local production (Lending Kart, 2021). With the capability and capacity to develop appropriate indigenous technology, fierce competition in domestic and international markets, technologically advanced industries, and defence materials, the country can provide knowledge, training, and skill upgradation through specialised training centres. Additionally, it may generate new firms by giving information, training, and skill development.

IMPACT OF COVID 19 ON MSMEs

According to Anand et al., the government considered it prior to the commencement of the COVID-19 epidemic (2020). Small firms were stated to be opposed to it because they believed it would harm their operations since larger enterprises would receive more funding from the government as a result of their size. The present economic crisis provided the ideal opportunity to implement changes without facing opposition from certain groups. Current MSMEs criteria, which focused only on investment, were largely believed to have impeded small business development. Micro units must invest one crore rupees (about US$133,000 at current exchange rates) and generate a revenue of INR Rs.5 crores (approximately US$667,000 at current market prices). Two criteria must be satisfied in order for an industrial or service firm to be classified as small, medium, or large under the new composite definition. If a business's revenue is less than 250 crores (about US$33 million at current exchange rates), it is classified as an MSME. If a firm exceeds the investment and revenue thresholds for its category, it gets demoted.

The higher threshold was implemented to aid small firms in growing by encouraging them to invest more and benefit from economies of scale and reduced expenses. At the moment, it's difficult to estimate the number of enterprises and employees in the MSME sector. The most current study of unincorporated enterprises, conducted in 2015 and 2016, is an excellent source of information (Indrakumar, 2020). The results of the 2015-16 survey may be used to estimate the number of MSME enterprises and workers infected with the COVID-19 virus. There were 63.4 million enterprises in 2015-16, with 19.6 million engaged in manufacturing, 20.6 million engaged in services, and the remainder engaged in retail and wholesale trade. In retail and wholesale commerce, there were 23 million establishments. MSMEs employed a total of 101 million people, including owner-managers and employees (Own Account Enterprises). Manufacturers and other enterprises each owned 36% of the corporation, with retail and wholesale trade accounting for the remaining 38%. The majority of work carried out by small companies in India is carried out by small firms. Additionally, they account for around 30% of the country's GDP.

According to Saturwa et al. (2021), the Covid-19 outbreak, which began in early 2020, has had a significant economic impact, particularly on the wealthy. Micro, small, and medium-sized companies (MSMEs) are more susceptible to get the Covid-19 virus due to their limited financial resources.

GOVERNMENT RESPONSES TO SUPPORT MSMEs

People in India and throughout the world are having a lot of difficulties with small enterprises at the moment, since both the global and local economy are uncertain about the future. Cash flow issues, a decline in demand and profitability are just a few of the issues facing small businesses. All of these factors jeopardise their long-term sustainability and growth (MSMEs). The Indian government has established a slew of new programmes in the last year or two to assist small firms with COVID-19 issues (SMB, 2021).

This plan provides small firms with an additional loan of up to Rs 3 lakh crore at a low interest rate during a pandemic, allowing them to cover their working capital needs and resume operations. The Guaranteed Emergency Credit Line (GECL), which is supported by the ECLGS plan, ensures SMB owners that they will receive funds in the event of a financial emergency (SMB, 2021). SCBs, financial institutions, and non-bank financial companies (NBFCs) would make this loan available to individuals who qualify for an additional working capital term credit facility. On the other hand, the emergency credit line is not available to everyone. Small enterprises must have debt or loans on their balance sheet to be considered.

MSMEs will have to compete with enterprises from other nations as soon as a global tender for government procurement is published. To assist its domestic firms, it has suspended overseas bidding on purchases up to Rs 200 million. As a result, SMEs in the United States will be able to compete on an equal level. The Fund of Funds can assist high-growth MSMEs with long-term viability and development potential in obtaining the capital they require (SMB, 2021). The government has allocated Rs 50,000 crore for this initiative, which aims to encourage small firms to expand and become more transparent.

The MSME ministry classified enterprises last year according to how much money they spent on equipment and machinery and how much money they earned. This has resulted in the inclusion of a large number of small and medium-sized firms in the MSME category, which entitles them to a variety of special programmes. However, there is a disadvantage to this. The gains will go to larger MSMEs at the cost of small firms. They account for 30% of GDP and employ more than 100 million people. In the aftermath of the COVID-19 virus, these figures demonstrate the critical role of small enterprises in the economy and government.

RESEARCH PROBLEM

MSME is believed to account for a sizable portion of our country's GDP. It has bolstered the economy by expanding employment rates and manufacturing output to fulfil domestic and international demand. Micro-enterprises account for the lion's share of the MSME sector. Manufacturing MSMEs had difficulties obtaining loans during the height of Covid-19. There are several simple options for small enterprises in India to obtain bank loans (Kadam & Pandey, 2020). They are less interested in industrial expansion and long-term progress currently. Additionally, the COVID 19 virus has had a significant influence on manufacturing SME manufacturing. Their present resources have been depleted by the virus, leaving them unable to do tasks. As a result, the majority of enterprises lack sufficient employees. This signifies that the MSME is currently experiencing financial difficulties. This is one of the most challenging issues it faces.

RESEARCH SIGNIFICANCE

According to Singh et al. (2020), MSMEs account for a sizable portion of the Indian economy and have contributed significantly to the country's social and economic success. It not only creates jobs, but also aids in the development of the country's backward and rural areas. They employ more people than any other industry, with the exception of agriculture. In India, small and medium-sized firms manufacture 90% of industrial units (SMEs). As a result, they account for a sizable portion of India's GDP growth. Small firms sell or manufacture finished items.

Small and medium-sized enterprises (SMEs) are a significant part of India's manufacturing sector and have evolved into the country's economic development engine, which means they contribute to the country's growth. Due to their significant influence on output, exports, and employment, small and medium-sized firms increasingly play a critical role in the Indian economy. Small firms account for 40% of industrial value added and 50% of manufacturing exports. In the next decade, SMEs are estimated to account for more than 90% of industrial units and 40% of value added in India's manufacturing sector.

The MSME sector encompasses a diverse range of sectors, the majority of which are manufacturing-based. As India nears self-sufficiency, small industrial enterprises are investing heavily in modernization, technology, and infrastructure. This tendency is expected to continue in 2021. (Tata Capital, 2021). All of these items cost a lot of money. As long as small and medium-sized firms can obtain government loans now, they will be able to sustain this sector in the years to come.

RESEARCH OBJECTIVES

- To Calculate overall MSMEs sector's contribution toward the Indian economy in terms of output, employment, income, investment, or export.
- To look at the issues that the MSMEs segment faced challenges during the prior to and during the COVID-19 outbreak.
- To investigations the government's policy measures to revitalize the MSMEs sector.
- To gain a deeper grasp of the financial management of MSMEs during Covid times.

RESEARCH METHODOLOGY

Literature Review

Impact On MSMES Before Covid-19

According to a new analysis, micro, small, and medium-sized enterprises (MSMEs), which include service, packaging, infrastructure and manufacturing, information technology, and chemicals, have been the fastest-growing sectors of the Indian economy over the previous two decades. Over the last several years, a growing number of small firms have shifted their focus to the industrial sector in search of development and expansion. Job creation occurs as a result of introducing core industries to rural and backward areas, as well as allowing individuals to work remotely. India's MSME population is estimated to be over 6.3 million, accounting for around 29% of GDP growth through local and foreign commerce. It accounts for almost half of what the country sells.

Additionally, MSMEs employ 11.10 million workers in core manufacturing, 3.6 million in commerce, and 3.7 million in other industries, which is a sizable workforce. India is on pace to achieve its objective of becoming a $5 trillion economy by 2025, as well as the development of SMEs, based on the facts. There is a strategy to increase the efficiency of small enterprises in India and to raise the country's Ease of Doing Business (EoDB) score. The Ministry of Micro, Small, and Medium-Sized Enterprises unveiled the initiative (MSMEs). The strategy provides several proposals including technological innovation, talent development, knowledge management, expanded financing alternatives, improved interdepartmental policy and programme coordination, and adjustments to India's regulatory structure for small and medium-sized firms (Atlantic Council, 2022). Although the modifications in the seventy-page document are beneficial, they fall short of our expectations. In

Figure 1. Firm characteristics

	(1) Mean and (SD) Whole Sample	(2) Highest Country Mean	(3) Lowest Country Mean
Agriculture	0.032	0.072	0.01
	(0.18)	IND	MSY
Hard-hit manufacturing	0.194	0.446	0.059
	(0.40)	IDN	MNG
Other manufacturing	0.378	0.799	0.157
	(0.49)	BGD	IDN
Hard-hit service	0.065	0.094	0.004
	(0.25)	MNG	BGD
Other service	0.328	0.563	0.046
	(0.47)	MNG	BGD
Microenterprise	0.494	0.814	0.276
	(0.50)	LAO	BGD
Small enterprise	0.268	0.456	0.137
	(0.43)	BGD	IDN
Medium enterprise	0.238	0.467	0.046
	(0.41)	VNM	LAO
Female-headed	0.298	0.590	0.090
	(0.46)	LAO	IND
Firm age (years)	13.4	20.2	8.9
	(12.4)	IND	IDN
Export-oriented	0.194	0.519	0.064
	(0.40)	PAK	IDN
Selling online	0.590	0.836	0.257
	(0.49)	VNM	MNG
Online sales 2019	0.210	0.352	0.087
	(0.292)	VNM	BGD

summary, it offers a lengthy list of high-level suggestions on how to transform the MSME sector, but it lacks operational strategies or concrete methods for putting those suggestions into practise. India has a large number of small enterprises, which the government wishes to strengthen as it competes with China. There are still issues with the government's efforts to increase China's MSMEs' global competitiveness.

There is nothing comparable in India, where over a long period of time, there have been several clusters for things that are hardly recognised outside of India. Rather than that, Amazon and Walmart-owned Flipkart are the industry's dominant players. This is not to say, however, that India cannot emulate Alibaba. Policymakers have recognised this and have proposed "one district, one product" initiatives aimed at boosting cluster-based industrial growth and transforming districts into export hubs. If India is to succeed China as the world's industrial centre, these activities must be viewed as combative. Traditional companies must educate themselves about e-commerce, and e-commerce enterprises must be provided with incentives and infrastructure to accelerate the growth of the country's e-commerce exports. To expand, it is necessary to promote local B2B platforms similar to Alibaba's (Atlantic Council, 2022). To effect these changes, policies and efforts in addition to those advocated by the MSME or the National E-Commerce Policy must be implemented. India must address these issues if it wants to modernise its small business policy. Otherwise, these measures will remain only concepts with limited impact. For multinational corporations, India's quest for MSMEs is an untapped source of business that has the potential to generate significant revenue.

Impact On MSMES During Covid-19

Covid-19's spread is the most significant economic event of our time. The pandemic that hindered social and economic activity in the spring and summer of 2020 has impacted countries and people worldwide, and it will continue to do so. According to the International Labour Organization, there has already been an economic and labour market shock. It has an effect on both supply (the production of products and services) and demand (the people who desire them) (consumption and investment). Business has changed, and it may be impossible to revert to the previous state. The most significant shift has occurred in terms of individuals and their lifestyles (Mint, 2020).

MSMEs, which form the bedrock of India's inclusive economic story, have been particularly hard struck by the coronavirus, which has disrupted their cash cycles. MSMEs are critical components of both local and global value chains, and hence their condition is critical. However, the economic crisis has necessitated a new strategy that needs small firms, as well as larger ones, to be more efficient and contemporary. In some respects, Covid-19 represents a watershed moment for India's massive MSME sector, since it has the potential to accelerate the country's economic transformation. Firms have been compelled to consider all possible outcomes in order to adapt and prosper in this environment, despite the absence of a silver lining. It is past time for India to accelerate its transformation and prosperity (Mint, 2020). Businesses must be prepared for this journey, but the rate of digital adoption in many areas cannot be exaggerated. It's not uncommon for firms to consider their future operations. The sector of Micro, Small, and Medium-Sized Enterprises (MSMEs) is no exception. MSMEs have risen in recent years as a result of digitization. According to several experts, many small firms have shifted their focus away from traditional platforms and into digital infrastructure, which is more critical than ever. However, some of them have fallen behind the expected growth curve of digital adoption because they did not believe in the importance of digital way of working adoption and adaption. As a result of the lockout, many small firms have realised the need of digitization. They've either launched a website or expanded their service offerings to include e-commerce.

Numerous small companies may benefit from digital technology in a variety of ways, not simply via the sale of their products and services on digital platforms. For them, this is an excellent opportunity to transform the way they conduct business. They may modernise and expand their firms by using new business methods.

Post Covid-19 Impact on MSMES

Small companies, or "MSMEs," were one of the most susceptible sectors during the outbreak due to their size and lack of financial resources. According to research and polls, the nationwide lockdown that began in April 2020 had a detrimental effect on roughly 95% of enterprises, with 70% of firms closing their doors until August 2020. As of February 2021, around 40% of enterprises remained affected, despite minimal attempts done to restore normalcy. As a small company owner, MSMEs confront three significant challenges: market entry, expansion, and cash flow. For Indian MSMEs, the 2021 lockdown resulted in an average 11% decrease in business volume. This is in comparison to a 46% decline in business volume throughout the country in 2020. The Times of Israel, 2021, reports as follows: Between March and May 2020, apparel makers in the export industry lost around Rs. 150 million. India's leather sector is projected to have lost Rs. 11,210 crore in the global market. Self-employed MSME units, which account for 35% of the MSME sector, are unlikely to recover and have already begun to close.

FACTORS RESPONSIBLE FOR VULNERABILITY OF MSMES

Crunch of Capital – In India, small businesses are usually much unstructured. Most of their transactions are done in cash, and they don't record them well in accounting records. Because there isn't enough precise transaction data, these businesses don't get the credit score they need to get formal business loans from the government (TOI, 2021).

High Cost of Transaction – In both offline and online forms of payment, MSMEs have low transaction volumes. This means that transaction costs are high, both for offline and online payment forms. In the long run, this has a big impact on the company's profit margin, which is how much money the company makes.

Risk Perceptions by Banks & Financial Institutions – When small businesses don't have a good credit score or a lot of money as collateral, most banks see them as risky. When the customer is a start-up, this problem gets worse. Even if banks agree to give out loans, the interest rate will still be higher than normal (TOI, 2021). According to the size of the business, the cash flow pattern, and the types of vendors they work with, different MSMEs have different financial needs. People need personalised services and goods for all of this.

Cybercrime – SMEs are thought to be more vulnerable to cybercrime and phishing because they don't know how to handle digital banking and transactions properly.

MANAGING THE CRISIS

It is critical for small firms to do an immediate audit of their finances and security. To assist small companies in the event of a pandemic, the government may provide them with soft loans with longer repayment periods and increased credit levels. MSMEs must rethink their complete value offer, which includes enhancing product quality, expanding distribution networks, and using innovative marketing tactics. To make it simpler for individuals and firms in the market to connect, they require a robust digital ecosystem.

The Indian government established an e-marketplace to encourage small enterprises to purchase from the government (GeM). Individuals who operate in a digitally engaged market environment have the potential to save money, increase productivity, develop new goods, and be safer. Collaboration with research institutes, technology start-ups, and firms in other countries may be an advantageous strategy for small businesses seeking to manufacture low-cost items and enter the Indian market. ECLGS, a low repo rate, e-market connectivity, PF and EPF support for enterprises and their staff, as well as other government programmes for small businesses, are beginning to bear fruit.

FINDINGS AND CONCLUSION

MSMEs struggled to keep their finances afloat during the shutdown due to reduced or non-existent business, poor demand, and low customer confidence. The MSME sector has been critical to India's economy since it has facilitated economic and social growth by fostering entrepreneurship and providing a large number of employment. MSMEs are small firms that assist larger businesses, which significantly contributes to the country's inclusive industrial growth.

The COVID-19 virus wreaked havoc on small enterprises. MSMEs lacked a well-balanced flow of company activities and lacked a long-term strategy (Business World, 2022). The majority of MSMEs struggled to keep their financial wheels going during the shutdown due to reduced or non-existent business, poor demand, and low customer confidence. Since the lock-down began, almost all migrant workers have returned to their homes. Migrant employees were also unable to reach their employment due to a lack of buses and trains. This made it hard to fully restart previously shuttered firms. Along with these issues, the prolonged COVID shutdown has had a significant impact on the country's supply chain.

The revised definition of MSMEs would benefit the manufacturing sector, boost its contribution to GDP, and provide millions of employment for India's rapidly rising youthful population. MSMEs having an annual turnover of Rs 250 crore and capital

Figure 2. Segment-Wise Non-Performing Asset

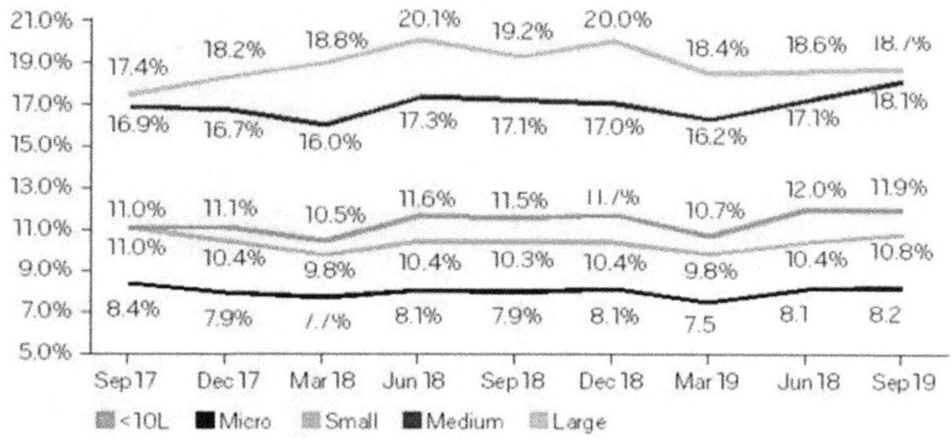

expenditure of Rs 50 crore on equipment and machinery will be included to the list. There will be more opportunities for small enterprises to manufacture goods. They will be more competitive, enabling them to seize new possibilities in both domestic and foreign markets. It states that a business must achieve specific investment and revenue standards in order to be classified as an MSME. If an organisation want to be classified as an MSME, it must choose whether it must fulfil both the investment and revenue standards and only one of them.

It is critical to highlight that if both criteria are used simultaneously, the aims of MSMEs that are redefining themselves will not be realised. An MSME must fulfil at least one of the standards, if not all of them (Business World, 2022). MSMEs should improve their cost competitiveness in the future, and a fair playing field for all should be established. Our exporters would be more competitive if business expenses were reduced and a level playing field existed throughout the country. Imports of commodities that India might manufacture domestically would be reduced as well.

The SME sector, which is at the core of the Indian economy, has a substantial influence on the GDP and labour market of the country.

It has demonstrated via fresh ideas and adaptability that it is capable of being adaptable and long-lasting, particularly throughout the recent year of economic turbulence (Tata Capital, 2021). It is critical to remember that in many small firms, the source of raw materials and the workers' home region are frequently separated, which makes obtaining raw materials more difficult and increases the cost of acquiring them. Individuals who reside in large cities also have far more economic power and activity than people who live in small towns (Business World, 2022).

Figure 3. Employment

	(1)	(2)	(3)	(4)
Variables	**Permanent Employees**		**Non-permanent Employees**	
Agri-business	-0.113	-0.123	-0.157	-0.172
	(0.259)	(0.259)	(0.239)	(0.238)
Hard-hit manufacturing	-0.424***	-0.419***	-0.325***	-0.333***
	(0.124)	(0.124)	(0.123)	(0.123)
Hard-hit service	-0.832***	-0.830***	-0.656***	-0.658***
	(0.177)	(0.179)	(0.184)	(0.184)
Other service	-0.051	-0.069	0.052	0.040
	(0.110)	(0.111)	(0.109)	(0.109)
Female-headed	0.186*	0.198*	0.159	0.162
	(0.101)	(0.102)	(0.101)	(0.102)
Firm age (years)	0.003	0.004	0.001	0.001
	(0.004)	(0.004)	(0.004)	(0.004)
Small enterprise	0.334***	0.327***	0.054	0.042
	(0.110)	(0.110)	(0.107)	(0.107)
Medium enterprise	0.334***	0.312**	-0.003	-0.025
	(0.122)	(0.121)	(0.119)	(0.119)
Export-oriented	-0.249**	-0.283**	-0.152	-0.179
	(0.113)	(0.114)	(0.113)	(0.113)
Selling online	-0.307***		-0.295***	
	(0.098)		(0.098)	
Online sales 2019		-2.209***		-1.281**
		(0.511)		(0.504)
Online sales 2019 squared		2.916***		1.547***
		(0.583)		(0.565)
India	-0.694***	-0.814***	-0.706***	-0.785***
	(0.201)	(0.200)	(0.193)	(0.192)
Indonesia	-0.298	-0.431**	-0.138	-0.243
	(0.211)	(0.211)	(0.206)	(0.205)
Lao PDR	-0.573***	-0.622***	-0.367*	-0.444**
	(0.201)	(0.198)	(0.195)	(0.191)
Malaysia	-0.312*	-0.387**	-2.192***	-2.272***
	(0.173)	(0.171)	(0.173)	(0.171)
Mongolia	0.129	0.099	0.203	0.190
	(0.185)	(0.186)	(0.177)	(0.178)
Pakistan	-0.883***	-0.962***	-0.823***	-0.914***
	(0.200)	(0.197)	(0.192)	(0.189)
Viet Nam	-1.088***	-1.156***	-1.805***	-1.885***
	(0.184)	(0.183)	(0.181)	(0.181)
Pseudo R-squared	0.0333	0.0364	0.0828	0.0826
Log-likelihood	-2,827	-2,818	-2,863	-2,864

As a result, the government should enact new or clarify existing laws to disperse economic power and make it easier for small firms to establish themselves near the source of raw materials and labour, but with some limitations to ensure that this provision is not overused. To assist MSMEs in remaining safe from the pandemic COVID-19, they will require significant assistance from the public. It is advised that small enterprises' value chains be improved further. This will strengthen their

Figure 4. No. of MSMEs in 2019
Source: Lal, et al. (2020)

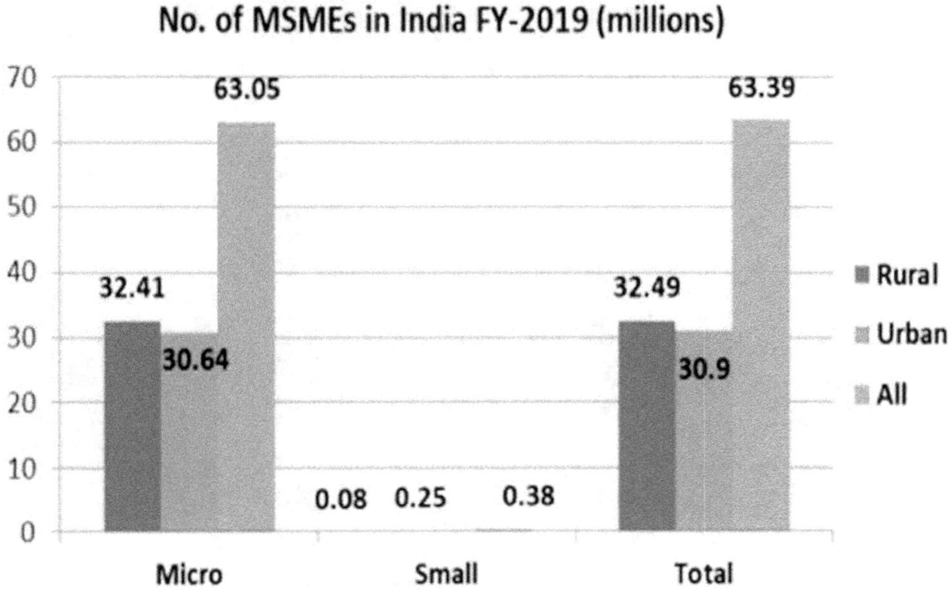

structural capabilities, increasing their efficiency and, as a result, the country's overall export growth pace.

In view of the global supply chain disruptions caused by the COVID-19 pandemic, India should expand its production capacity to mitigate the impact on import demand and fulfil domestic demands. Capacity expansion in the United States at this time will not only assist in mitigating the impact of COVID-19, but will also enable us to expand our worldwide export footprint, particularly to our top export markets. This would enable the country to develop into a manufacturing hub for the global supply chain and a significant exporter globally in the future.

RECOMMENDATIONS AND SUGGESTIONS

Small and medium-sized company owners (MSMEs) have never been recognised for their critical role in accomplishing the Sustainable Development Goals (SDGs). Every day is MSME day, as we work around the clock to assist small businesses in growing through international commerce. MSMEs should follow the following guidelines:

Figure 5. Sales

	(1)	(2)	(3)	(4)
Variables	**Sales in First Half of 2020**		**Expectation of Sales Growth in 2020**	
Agri-business	0.120	0.125	0.399	0.404
	(0.258)	(0.257)	(0.250)	(0.250)
Hard-hit manufacturing	–0.257*	–0.246	–0.027	–0.025
	(0.150)	(0.151)	(0.123)	(0.123)
Hard-hit service	–1.175***	–1.171***	–1.114***	–1.120***
	(0.226)	(0.225)	(0.184)	(0.185)
Other service	0.130	0.123	0.144	0.147
	(0.139)	(0.140)	(0.104)	(0.104)
Female-headed	–0.144	–0.135	0.086	0.084
	(0.122)	(0.122)	(0.099)	(0.099)
Firm age (years)	–0.004	–0.005	–0.001	–0.001
	(0.004)	(0.004)	(0.004)	(0.004)
Small enterprise	0.324**	0.327**	0.181*	0.183*
	(0.129)	(0.129)	(0.105)	(0.105)
Medium enterprise	0.172	0.184	0.186	0.192*
	(0.153)	(0.152)	(0.117)	(0.117)
Export-oriented	0.230*	0.260*	0.042	0.031
	(0.139)	(0.139)	(0.110)	(0.110)
Selling online	0.079		0.059	
	(0.117)		(0.094)	
Online sales 2019		0.022		0.079
		(0.641)		(0.500)
Online sales 2019 squared		–0.188		0.164
		(0.728)		(0.570)
India	–0.057	–0.022	1.212***	1.207***
	(0.193)	(0.191)	(0.194)	(0.193)
Indonesia	0.010	0.072	4.319***	4.304***
	(0.208)	(0.206)	(0.227)	(0.226)
Lao PDR	0.634***	0.691***	2.216***	2.226***
	(0.199)	(0.194)	(0.197)	(0.194)
Malaysia			0.404**	0.406***
			(0.159)	(0.157)
Mongolia	0.433**	0.439**	1.475***	1.473***
	(0.175)	(0.175)	(0.171)	(0.171)
Pakistan	–0.017	0.020	1.116***	1.134***
	(0.194)	(0.189)	(0.190)	(0.187)
Viet Nam			3.107***	3.094***
			(0.183)	(0.182)
	(0.198)	(0.197)	(0.169)	(0.169)
Observations	1,344	1,344	2,051	2,051
Pseudo R-squared	0.0156	0.0157	0.124	0.124
Log-likelihood	–2,100	–2,100	–3,114	–3,113

- Small firms that leverage e-commerce platforms are five times as likely to export as those who do not.
- Even while e-commerce has the potential to help small businesses thrive, many small firms still struggle to navigate the many rules and regulations that apply in each nation.
- Many small firms struggle to obtain cost-effective bank funding that enables them to do international commerce.
- Every day, millions of small companies rely on our rules and standards to facilitate and expedite cross-border commerce.

Figure 6. The Percentage Proportion of MSMEs in India
Source: Lal, et al. (2020)

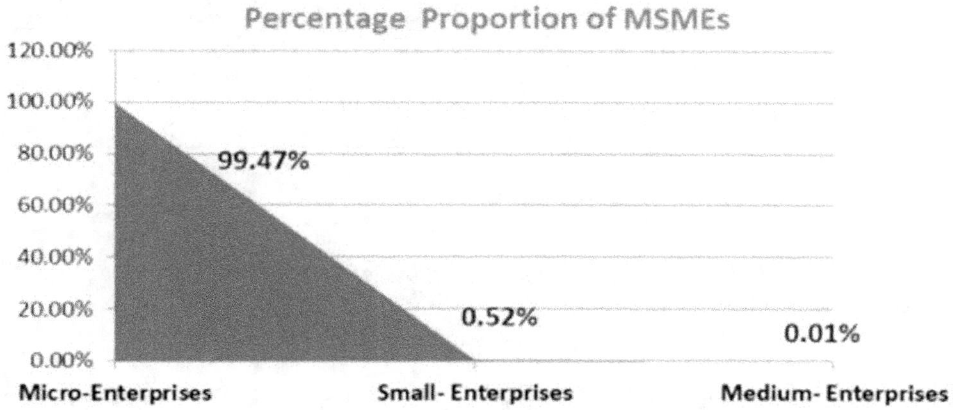

Figure 7. Cash Shortage

Variables	(1) Coefficient	(2) ME	(3) Coefficient	(4) ME
Agri-business	0.244	0.054	0.215	0.045
	(0.274)	(0.060)	(0.280)	(0.059)
Hard-hit manufacturing	−0.303**	−0.067**	−0.405***	−0.085***
	(0.141)	(0.031)	(0.147)	(0.031)
Hard-hit service	−0.066	−0.014	−0.288	−0.060
	(0.201)	(0.044)	(0.208)	(0.044)
Other service	−0.509***	−0.112***	−0.533***	−0.112***
	(0.122)	(0.026)	(0.126)	(0.026)
Female-headed	−0.318***	−0.070***	−0.282**	−0.059**
	(0.113)	(0.025)	(0.116)	(0.024)
Firm age (years)	−0.005	−0.001	−0.004	−0.001
	(0.004)	(0.001)	(0.004)	(0.001)
Small enterprise	−0.209*	−0.046*	−0.140	−0.029
	(0.123)	(0.027)	(0.126)	(0.026)
Medium enterprise	−0.159	−0.035	−0.097	−0.020
	(0.137)	(0.030)	(0.142)	(0.030)
Export-oriented	0.234*	0.052*	0.177	0.037
	(0.130)	(0.028)	(0.133)	(0.028)
Online sales 2019	0.761	0.075	0.308	0.032
	(0.567)	(0.069)	(0.586)	(0.068)
Online sales 2019 squared	−0.965		−0.364	
	(0.638)		(0.658)	
> 60% decrease in permanent employment			1.167***	0.248***
			(0.189)	(0.037)
41–60% decrease in permanent employment			1.154***	0.246***
			(0.207)	(0.041)
21–40% decrease in permanent employment			0.987***	0.212***
			(0.174)	(0.036)
Up to 20% decrease in permanent employment			0.547***	0.119***
			(0.134)	(0.029)
Increase in permanent employment			−0.252	−0.053
			(0.233)	(0.048)
Pseudo R-squared	0.0910		0.123	
Log-likelihood	−1,292		−1,247	

Figure 8. Digitization

	(1) Mean and (SD) Whole Sample	(2) Highest Country Mean	(3) Lowest Country Mean	(4) No. of Observations
Online sales 2019	0.210 (0.292)	0.352 VNM	0.087 BGD	2,140
Digital payment dummy	0.385 (0.487)	0.681 LAO	0.071 BGD	1,425
Plan to increase online sales dummy	0.695 (0.461)	0.847 IDN	0.388 MNG	2,140

Figure 9. Five Most Critical Problems Faced by MSMEs
Source: Lal, et al. (2020)

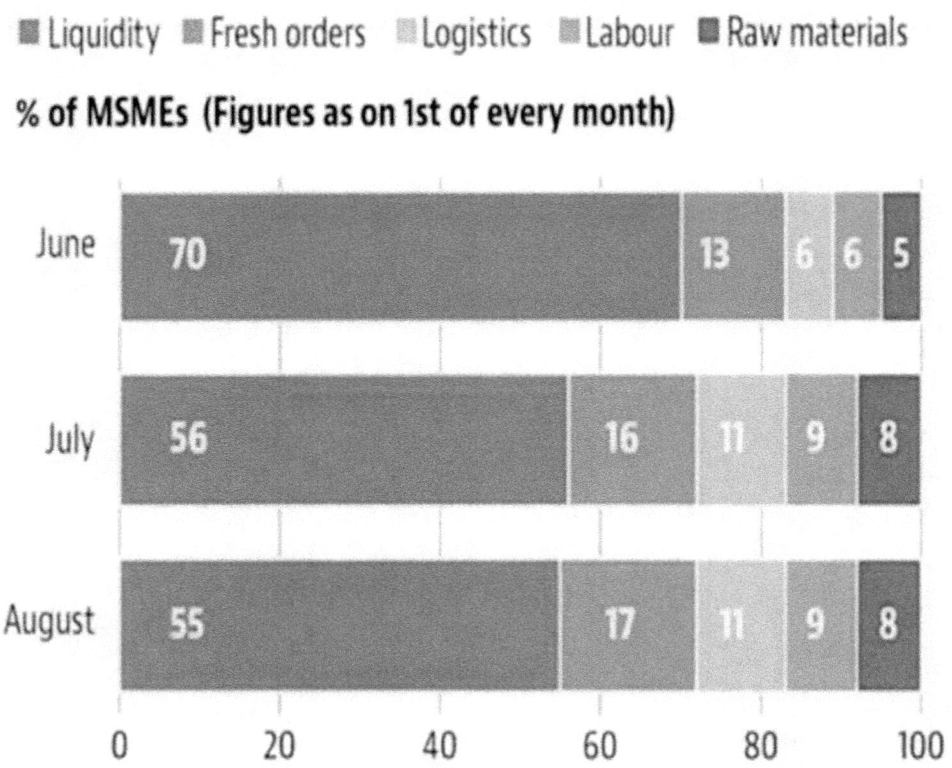

Figure 10. Government support needs

	(1) Mean and (SD) Whole Sample	(2) Highest Country Mean	(3) Lowest Country Mean	(4) No. of Observations
Support received in March–April				
Any support	0.59 (0.49)	0.82 MSY	0.21 IDN	2,237
Tax support	0.31 (0.46)	0.59 MNG	0.05 BGD	2,237
Loan support	0.25 (0.44)	0.70 BGD	0.07 IDN	2,237
Support received in May–June				
Any support	0.56 (0.50)	0.71 MNG	0.25 IDN	1,475
Tax support	0.31 (0.46)	0.67 MNG	0.06 PAK	1,475
Loan support	0.20 (0.40)	0.41 BGD	0.11 MNG	1,475
Support needed at the time of survey				
Tax support needs	0.53 (0.50)	0.73 MNG	0.08 BGD	2,237
Loan support needs	0.48 (0.50)	0.69 MSY	0.27 IDN	2,237

Figure 11. Half of the Indian Startups in Serious Danger Due to COvid-19

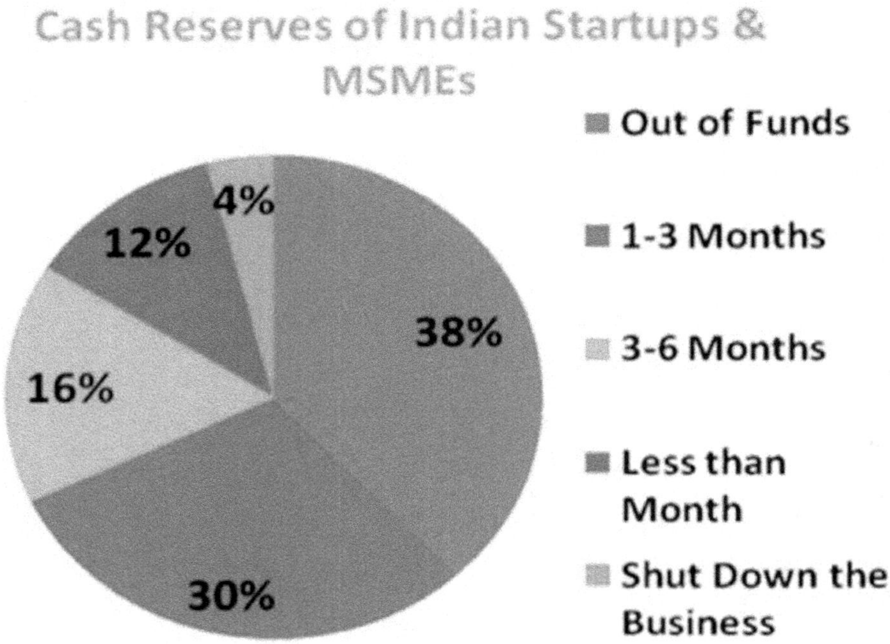

REFERENCES

Anand, A., Gayatri, M. N., Narain, N., Mishra, S., & Sood, S. (2020). *Impact of COVID-19 pandemic on micro, small, and medium enterprises (MSMEs): India report*. Academic Press.

Atlantic Council. (2022). *India must transform its micro, small, and medium enterprises*. Available at https://www.atlanticcouncil.org/blogs/southasiasource/india-must-transform-its-micro-small-and-medium-enterprises/

Business World. (2022). *MSMEs Participating In The Post COVID Recovery*. Available at https://www.businessworld.in/article/MSMEs-Participating-In-The-Post-COVID-Recovery/27-03-2021-385041/

Gade, S. (2018). MSMEs' role in economic growth–a study on India's perspective. *International Journal of Pure and Applied Mathematics*, *118*(18), 1727–1741.

Indrakumar, D. (2020). COVID-19 and its impact on Micro, Small and Medium Enterprises in India. *Manpower Journal*, *54*(3&4), 75–88.

Kadam, S. A., & Pandey, D. (2020). Post COVID-19 opportunities and challenges formicro small medium enterprises (MSMEs) development in India. *Asian Journal of Advances in Research*, 1-4.

Lal, B.S., Sachdeva, P., & Simran, M.T., 2020. Impact of Covid-19 on micro small and medium enterprises (MSMEs): An overview. *International Journal of Multidisciplinary Research and Development.*

Mint. (2020). *Covid impact on MSMEs.* Available at https://www.livemint.com/opinion/online-views/opinion-covid-and-its-impact-on-economy-and-msmes-11603604611652.html

Saturwa, H. N., Suharno, S., & Ahmad, A. A. (2021). The impact of Covid-19 pandemic on MSMEs. *Jurnal Ekonomi Dan Bisnis*, *24*(1), 65–82. doi:10.24914/jeb.v24i1.3905

Sethi, A., & Verma, P. (2018). Role of MSME's In Economic Growth Of India. *Journal of Ravishankar University*, *24*(1), 19–26. doi:10.52228/JRUA.2018-24-1-4

Shelly, R., Sharma, T., & Bawa, S. S. (2020). Role of micro, small and medium enterprises in Indian economy. *International Journal of Economics and Financial Issues*, *10*(5), 84–91. doi:10.32479/ijefi.10459

Singh, L. B., Mondal, S. R., & Das, S. (2020). Human resource practices & their observed significance for Indian SMEs. *Revista ESPACIOS, 41*(7).

SMB. (2021). *Government schemes to help MSMEs tide over COVID-19 woes.* Available at https://yourstory.com/smbstory/government-schemes-help-msmes-tide-over-covid-lockdown/amp

Sonobe, T., Takeda, A., Yoshida, S., & Truong, H. T. (2021). *The impacts of the Covid-19 pandemic on micro, small, and medium enterprises in Asia and their digitalization responses*. Academic Press.

Tata Capital. (2021). *What Would Be the Role of SMEs in Changing India's Economic*. Author.

Chapter 12
Impact of COVID-19 on Capital Structure Towards Maruti Suzuki India Limited

Janaki P.
Vellalar College for Women (Autonomous), India

Mounaarthi K.
Vellalar College for Women (Autonomous), India

ABSTRACT

The purpose of the study is to analyse the change in capital structure of Maruti Suzuki India Limited during the time of COVID-19. The main objective of the study is to analyse the key determinants of capital structure of a company before and during pandemic period. In order to analyse the capital structure of Maruti Suzuki India Limited, the ratio analysis has been used. The ratio includes capital gearing ratio, leverage, debt equity ratio, total investment to long-term liabilities, ratio of fixed assets to funded debt, ratio of current liabilities to proprietors' funds, ratio of reserve to equity capital, and interest coverage ratio. The study covers the period of five years, and it is based on secondary data obtained from the published annual report of Maruti Suzuki India Limited. From the analysis, it shows that the overall capital structure of the company is satisfactory during the study period. However, the company performance in the pandemic period is good.

INTRODUCTION

The finance is considered as a lifeline of every business enterprise. It is important for

DOI: 10.4018/978-1-6684-5342-1.ch012

a business man to manage the finance efficiently. The capital acts as the substance for starting up a new business. The major types of capital sources are debt capital, equity capital and retained earnings. The capital structure has been defined as the combination of debt and equity used by the company in order to finance the overall operations and growth of the company. The capital structure of the company is helpful in understanding the current financial health, risk profile and compatibility with specific investment.

In December 2019, the number of unidentified pneumonia cases were reported in the Wuhan, China. The centers for disease control has declared the unknown pneumonia as novel coronavirus pneumonia on 7th January 2020. The international committee on taxonomy of viruses later changed the name of novel coronavirus pneumonia to severe acute respiratory syndrome coronavirus 2. On 11th February 2020, the disease was declared as COVID 19 by the world health organization. More than 220 countries have been affected by the coronavirus and every country has been gone to a lockdown in the year 2020.In India, first COVID 19 cases filed on 27th January 2020 in Kerala. The coronavirus has not only affected the standard of living but also affected many industrial sectors in the country. The industrial sectors like automobiles, educations, electronics, travel, tourism, transportation and agriculture are affected by the coronavirus. In this pandemic situation, many sectors have been shut down their business and know many companies has been trying to overcome their losses. In this regard, the purpose of the study has been an attempt to analyse the capital structure of Maruti Suzuki India Limited before and during the pandemic period.

The Maruti Suzuki India Limited (MSIL) is formerly known as Maruti Udyog Limited. The company is a subsidiary of Suzuki Motor Corporation of Japan. The Maruti Suzuki India Limited company is the largest car passenger company in India. During the year 2020, the company has registered an overall sales volume decline of 16.1% in both the domestic and export markets because of pandemic situation. Therefore, the main purpose of the study is to find out the impact on capital structure during the pandemic situation.

REVIEW OF LITERATURE

For purpose of the study the researcher has reviewed many national and international research articles relating to capital structure of the company. It has been presented as follows:

Aishwarya, Sudharani R., and Dr. N. Suresh (2020) made a study on the impact of capital structure on profitability of companies listed on the Indian stock exchange with respect to the automobile industry. The research helped in understanding both the positive and negative impact of capital structure on profits of Indian automobile companies by using variables like return on capital employed, return on long-term funds, return on net worth, gross profit margin, operating profit, and return on asset. The study hypothesis showed that ROCE, ROLT, and RONW had a positive effect and GP, OP, and ROA had a negative impact on debt equity and interest coverage ratios, and the study also proved that the relationship between profitability and capital structure variables was strongly significant. Fixed effect and random effect models were used to evaluate the hypothesis using data from 17 automobile companies covering 10 years (2010 – 2019). The result of the study was recommended that the firms improve their performance by using an optimal capital structure. Similarly, a fair mix of debt and equity should be established to ensure that the firm maintains capital adequacy.

K. Jnaneswar, J. S. Aishwarya and D. Bhagath Soorya (2021) studied the impact of capital structure on the financial performance of hotel industry and automobile industry. The study had made an attempt to solve how capital structure influences the company's profitability. In this research the researcher has considered the hotel industry and the automobile industry were the fastest growing industries of the Indian economy and account for about 8% and 9% of the country's GDP respectively. In the study, five major hotel and automobile companies' capital structures and profitability during the previous ten years were taken into consideration. The regression analysis was used to determine whether there was a relationship between profitability variables and capital structure variables. The Karl Pearson's correlation analysis was used to determine if the dependent variables impacted the independent variables. The findings of this study revealed that the capital structure variable had an influence on the profitability of both the industries. According to the regression analysis, there was a relationship between the capital structure variable and the profitability variable. The capital structure and profitability variable had a negative correlation, which indicated that the value of debt equity and debt asset ratios increases, the value of profitability decreases.

Dharmendr Mistry and Pallavi Vysa (2021) analysed the factors affecting capital structure decision: empirical evidence from Indian oil and gas sector. The independent variable as profitability(ROA), liquidity (current ratio) and tangibility (fixed assets to total assets ratio), on the dependent variable as capital structure (debt - equity ratio) of the oil and gas public sector in India during the period of five years has been analysed through the statistical model. The study found that the independent variable like ratio of assets and current ratio had shown a negative impact on capital structure decision, while on the other hand independent variable fixed assets to total assets was found to had a positive impact on capital structure decision.

Maha Shehadeh et al., (2022), studied on the impact of ownership structure and corporate governance on capital structure of Jordanian industrial companies. The study investigated the impact of ownership structure and corporate governance (CG) on the capital structure using 798 firm-year observations of listed companies in the amman stock exchange (2005- 2018). The ordinary least squares were utilized to examine the relationships between the dependent variable and a set of independent variables, including ownership concentration factors and CG factors. The study was revealed that a strong negative relationship between largest shareholder and capital structure. Regarding the CG factors, the regression results had shown that the board size, composition and number of meetings were the factors correlated significantly positive with capital structure.

Agnes Mudamakin et al., (2022) examined the capital structure analysis of manufacturing firms listed on the Indonesia stock exchange in the covid-19 pandemic era. The study on capital structure was measured with the leverage ratio by calculating the debt ratio, the debt to equity ratio and the long-term debt to equity ratio. The study was utilised the quantitative method by conducting a mean difference test. The samples of the study were based on the manufacturing firms listed on the Indonesia stock exchange. The study found that there was no significant difference between the leverage ratio before the covid-19 pandemic and during the Covid-19 pandemic.

From the above overview of the studies reviewed shows that, the present study differs from other earlier studies in the aspect of the period of the study, methodology, scope and objectives. Hence, the research gap is filled and the present study has been undertaken.

STATEMENT OF THE PROBLEM

The financial achievement of every business is depends on its capital structure. A worthy capital structure of the company is leads to stable profit and high earnings of the shareholder. The risk and return of the shareholder are influences by the choice of debt and equity of the firm's capital structure. The Maruti Suzuki India Limited is one of the leading passenger car company in India. The operations of Maruti Suzuki were suspended in the final part of March 2020 due to unprecedented COVID-19 outbreak which lead to a nationwide shutdown of economic activities.

In this regard, an attempt is made to analyse the impact of COVID 19 in the capital structure of Maruti Suzuki India Limited. The comparison is made on capital structure of the company before and after COVID 19 period. The present study has find the answer for the following questions:

- What are the key determining factors of capital structure?
- What is the position of capital structure before and after the pandemic period?

SCOPE OF THE STUDY

The study aimed to find the impact on capital structure during the pandemic period of Maruti Suzuki India Limited. The study covers the period of 2016-2017 to 2020-2021. The scope of the study mainly involves in the comparison of capital structure before and during the pandemic period.

OBJECTIVES OF THE STUDY

The main objective of the study is to examine the impact of capital structure in pandemic period on Maruti Suzuki India Limited. The main objectives are:

- To determine the key factors of capital structure of the company.
- To made the comparative analysis on the components of capital structure before and during the pandemic period.

RESEARCH METHODOLOGY

Research methodology denotes the systematic way to the research work by the researcher. The methodology adopted for the study is given below:

Sampling Design

The simple random sampling technique is used to select the company for the present study.

Period of the Study

The study covers a period of five years from 2016-2017 to 2020-2021. In 2016-2017 to 2018 -2019 is considered as normal period and remaining two years are measured as pandemic period. The accounting year commences from 1st April to 31st March.

Sources of Data

The study is based on secondary data obtained from the published annual reports of Maruti Suzuki India Limited from 2016-2017 to 2020-2021 and certain information is collected through the official website of the company.

Tools of Analysis

The capital structure of Maruti Suzuki India Limited is analysed with the help of financial ratios. Ratios were calculated and interpreted by comparing them with standard norms.

LIMITATIONS OF THE STUDY

Some of the limitations of the study are given as follows:

- Almost the entire analysis made in the study is based on the financial statements given in the annual reports of the company and it is subjected to inherent defects of the financial statements.
- The study is confined to a period of 5 years only from 2016-2017 to 2020-2021. An analysis of 5 years' data may not show the real performance of the company.

FINDINGS

Analysis of Capital Structure

The term 'capital structure' refers to the relationship between various long term forms of financing such as debentures (long-term), preference share capital and equity share capital including reserves and surplus. Capital structure ratios are calculated to test the long-term financial position of a firm. Following ratios are generally calculated to analyse the capital structure of the firm.

- Capital gearing ratio
- Leverage
- Debt equity ratio
- Total investment to long-term liabilities
- Ratio of fixed assets to funded debt
- Ratio of current liabilities to proprietors' fund
- Ratio of reserve to equity capital
- Interest coverage ratio

Capital Gearing Ratio

The term 'capital gearing' is used to describe the relationship between equity share capital including reserves and surpluses to preference share capital and fixed interest-bearing loans. The Table 1 shows the calculated value of capital gearing ratio of the concern during the study period.

Table 1. Capital gearing (Rs. in Crores)

Year	Fixed income bearing funds	Equity shareholders' funds	Capital gearing ratio
2016-2017	14819.5	36431.10	0.41
2017-2018	17612.8	41757.30	0.42
2018-2019	16790.3	46141.50	0.36
2019-2020	14115.1	48437	0.29
2020-2021	18700.6	51366.80	0.36

Source: Annual report of Maruti Suzuki India Limited

- During the study period, the capital gearing ratio of the company is low gear that means the debt of company is low than its equity. It also shows a fluctuating trend. The highest capital gearing ratio is 0.42 in the year 2017 - 2018.
- In the comparison of normal period with pandemic period, the capital gearing ratio is decreasing trend during the study period. Hence, it shows a satisfactory position in pandemic period.

Leverage

Leverage ratio are used to determine the relative level of debt load that a business has incurred. These ratios compare the total debt obligation to either the assets or equity of a business. Leverage ratio includes financial leverage, operating leverage and combined leverage. The Table 2 shows the calculated value of leverage of the firm during the study period.

Financial Leverage

- During the study period, the financial leverage ratio of the company is equal to 1. It indicates that the company's debt and equity are equal. It also shows

Table 2. Calculated value of leverage of the firm during the study period

Year	Financial leverage	Operating leverage	Combined leverage
2016-2017	1.01	2.92	2.98
2017-2018	1.03	2.42	2.46
2018-2019	1.01	2.08	2.09
2019-2020	1.02	1.96	2.02
2020-2021	1.02	1.90	1.92

Source: Annual report of Maruti Suzuki India Limited

a fluctuating trend. The highest financial leverage is 1.03 in the year 2017 - 2018.

- In the comparison of normal period with pandemic period, the financial leverage ratio shows an equal trend during the study period.

Operating Leverage

- The operating leverage ratios are in decreasing trend. This implies lower fixed costs and higher variable cost. In this situation, the company has to achieve minimum sales for covering its fixed cost. The highest operating leverage is 2.92 in the year 2016-2017.
- In the comparison of normal period with pandemic period, the normal period leverage ratios are higher than pandemic period operating leverage. It shows the company is earn low profit in pandemic period than the normal period.

Combined Leverage

- During the study period, the combined leverage of the company is in decreasing tend. The highest combined leverage is 2.98 in the year 2016-2017.
- In the comparison of normal period with pandemic period, the combined leverage ratio shows a decreasing trend during the pandemic period.

Debt Equity Ratio

Debt equity ratio is also known as external – internal equity. It is calculated to measure the relative claims of outsiders and the owners against the firm's assets. The Table 3 shows the calculated value of debt equity ratio of the concern during the study period.

Table 3. The calculated value of debt equity ratio of the concern during the study period (Rs. in Crores)

Year	Outsiders funds	Shareholders' funds	Debt equity ratio
2016-2017	13865	36431.10	0.38
2017-2018	166915.50	41757.30	0.41
2018-2019	15976.80	46141.50	0.35
2019-2020	13277.60	48437	0.27
2020-2021	17425.50	51366.80	0.34

Source: Annual report of Maruti Suzuki India Limited

- During the study period, the debt equity ratio of the company is in fluctuating trend. The highest debt equity ratio is 0.41 in the year 2017 – 2018. In general, a lower debt equity ratio is preferred as it indicates less debt on a company's balance sheet. However, this will also vary depending on the stage of the company's growth and its industry sector. Hence, there was no general norm for debt equity ratio but most of company prefer 1:1 as satisfactory norm.
- In the comparison of normal period with pandemic period, there is a fluctuating trend in debt equity ratio during the pandemic period.

Total Investment to Long- Term Liabilities

The ratio is calculated by dividing the total of long-term fund by the long- term liabilities of the company. The Table 4 shows the calculated value of total investment to long-term liabilities of the concern during the study period.

- The total investment to long-term liabilities of the company is fluctuating trend during the study period. The highest total investment to long-term liabilities is 23.77 in the year 2016 - 2017.
- In the comparison of normal period with pandemic period, the total investment to long-term liabilities of the firm has decreased in the year 2019-2020 and increased to 20.80 in the year 2020-2021.

Ratio of the Fixed Assets to Funded Debts

The ratio is used to measure the relationship between the fixed asset and funded debts of the firm. The Table 5 shows the calculated value of fixed assets to funded debts of the concern during the study period.

Table 4. Shows the calculated value of total investment to long-term liabilities of the concern during the study period (Rs. in Crores)

Year	Total investment	Long term liabilities	Total investment to Long-term liabilities
2016-2017	37873.2	1593.10	23.77
2017-2018	43777	2170.70	20.17
2018-2019	48630.5	2640	18.42
2019-2020	51109.3	2820.30	18.12
2020-2021	53960.7	2593.90	20.80

Source: Annual report of Maruti Suzuki India Limited

Table 5. The calculated value of fixed assets to funded debts of the concern during the study period (Rs. in Crores)

Year	Fixed assets	Funded debts	Ratio of Fixed assets to Funded debts
2016-2017	14545.00	1442.1	10.09
2017-2018	15484.90	2019.7	7.67
2018-2019	17007.90	2125	8.00
2019-2020	17118.60	2669.3	6.41
2020-2021	16446.80	2442.9	6.73

Source: Annual report of Maruti Suzuki India Limited

- The ratio of fixed assets to funded debts of the company shows a fluctuating trend during study period. The highest ratio of fixed assets to funded debts is 10.09 in the year 2016 - 2017.
- In the comparison of normal period with pandemic period the ratio of fixed assets to funded debts of the firm has decreased in the year 2019-2020 and increased in the year 2020-2021.

Ratio of Current Liabilities to Proprietors' Fund

The ratio specify the amount of long-term funds raised by the proprietors as against short-term borrowings. The Table 6 shows the calculated value of current liabilities to proprietors' fund of the concern during the study period.

Table 6. The calculated value of current liabilities to proprietors' fund of the concern during the study period (Rs. in Crores)

Year	Current liabilities	Proprietors' fund	Ratio of current liabilities to proprietors' fund
2016-2017	13226.40	36431.10	0.36
2017-2018	15442.10	41757.30	0.37
2018-2019	14150.30	46141.50	0.31
2019-2020	11294.80	48437	0.23
2020-2021	16106.70	51336.80	0.31

Source: Annual report of Maruti Suzuki India Limited

- The ratio of current liabilities to proprietors' fund of the company shows a fluctuating trend during the study period. The highest ratio of current liabilities to proprietors' fund is 0.37 in the year 2016 - 2017.
- In the comparison of normal period with pandemic period, the current liabilities to proprietors' fund of the firm has decreased to 0.23 in the year 2019-2020 and increased to 0.31 in the year 2020-2021.

Ratio of Reserve to Equity Capital

The ratio indicates the general retained profit of a firm for its future growth. The Table 7 shows the calculated value of reserve to equity capital of the concern during the study period.

- The ratio of reserve to equity capital of the company shows a fluctuating trend during the study period. The highest ratio of reserve to equity capital is 339.17 in the year 2020 - 2021.
- In the comparison of normal period with pandemic period, the ratio of reserve to equity capital of the firm has shown an increasing trend during the pandemic period.

Interest Coverage Ratio

The interest coverage ratio measures the ability of a company to pay the interest on its outstanding debt. The Table 8 shows the calculated value of interest coverage ratio of the concern during the study period.

Table 7. The calculated value of reserve to equity capital of the concern during the study period (Rs. in Crores)

Year	Reserve	Equity capital	Ratio of reserve to equity capital
2016-2017	36280.10	151	240. 26
2017-2018	41606.30	151	80.78
2018-2019	45990.50	151	304.57
2019-2020	48286	151	319.77
2020-2021	51215.80	151	339.17

Source: Annual report of Maruti Suzuki India Limited

Table 8. The calculated value of interest coverage ratio of the concern during the study period (Rs. in Crores)

Year	Earning before interest & tax	Interest	Interest coverage ratio
2016-2017	10049.7	89.40	112.41
2017-2018	11349.1	345.70	32.83
2018-2019	10541.4	75.80	139.07
2019-2020	7197.7	132.90	54.16
2020-2021	5260.2	100.80	52.18

Source: Annual report of Maruti Suzuki India Limited

- The interest coverage ratio of the company shows a fluctuating trend during the study period. The highest interest coverage ratio is 139.07 in the year 2018 - 2019.
- In the comparison of normal period with pandemic period, the interest coverage ratio of the company has decreasing trend during the pandemic period.

DISCUSSION

- In the comparison of normal period with pandemic period, the interest coverage ratio, combined leverage and financial leverage are showing a decreasing trend during the study period. As a result, the company's interest coverage ratio indicates a satisfactory position during the pandemic period.

- In the comparison of normal period with pandemic period, the ratio of reserve to equity capital shows an increasing trend during the study period
- In the comparison of normal period with pandemic period, the financial leverage shows an equal trend during the study period.
- In the comparison of normal period with pandemic period, the capital gearing ratio, debt equity ratio, total investment to long-term liabilities, ratio of fixed assets to funded debt, ratio of current liabilities to proprietors' fund are showing a fluctuating trend during the study period. Hence, the company has a low debt-equity ratio, which is good for the company.
- The findings of the present research are not consistent with any of the earlier studies.

SUGGESTIONS

Based on the findings of the present study, the following suggestions have been made:

- The capital gearing ratio of the company is satisfactory. Hence, it is suggested that in order to reduce the unpredicted risk in future, the firm can increase its fund through equity capital.
- The leverage ratio of the company shows a decreasing trend during the study period. Therefore, the ratio is not satisfactory. Hence, it is suggested that the company should concentrate on reduce the cost to earn more profit in future.
- The debt equity ratio of the Maruti Suzuki India Limited is satisfactory. Hence, it is suggested that the company should quite increase the debt components in their capital structure to take advantage of trading on equity.

CONCLUSION

The present study has been conducted in Maruti Suzuki India Limited for the period of (2016-2017 to 2020-2021), to find out the capital structure of the company using ratio analysis. From the analysis, it is concluded that the overall capital structure of the company is satisfactory during the study period. However, the company performance in the pandemic period is good. The results of the research may be useful for its future capital structure decision of the company. Hence, if Maruti Suzuki India Limited adopts the suggestion offered, it could have a best capital structure in future.

REFERENCES

Aishwarya & Suresh. (2020). A Study on Impact of Capital Structure on Profitability of Companies Listed in Indian Stock Exchange with respect to Automobile Industry. *Journal of Seybold Report, 15*(7), 1560 – 1574.

Cuevas-Vargas, Cortes-Palacios, & Lozano-Garcia. (2022). Impact of capital structure and innovatin on firm performance. Direct and indirect effects of capital structure. *Procedia Computer Science, 199*, 1082-1089.

Google Scholar. (n.d.). https://scholar.google.co.in/

Gupta, Sharma, & Gupta. (2014). Management Accounting. Kalyani Publishers.

Jnaneswar, K., Aishwarya, J. S., & Bhagath Soorya, D. (2021). The Impact of Capital Structure on the Financial Performance of Hotel Industry and Automobile Industry. *Asian Journal of Economics, Finance and Management, 4*(3), 21 – 31. Retrieved from https://www.globalpresshub.com/index.php/AJEFM/article/view/1102

Maruti Suzuki India Limited. (n.d.). https://www.marutisuzuki.com/

Mistry & Vyas. (2021). Factors Affecting Capital structure decision: Empirical evidence from Indian oil and gas sector. *International Journal of Financial Management, 11*(2), 13-18.

Money Control. (n.d.). www.moneycontrol.com

Moore, S. (n.d.). *News-Medical.net – An AZonetwork site.* https://www.news-medical.net/amp/health/History-of-COVID-19.aspx

Mudamakin, A. K. B., Wulandari, A. A., & Poeh, M. M. (2022). Capital Structure Analysis of Manufacturing Firms Listed on the Indonesia Stock Exchange (Idx) in the Covid-19 Pandemic Era. *International Conference on Applied Science and Technology on Social Science 2021, 647*, 256-259.

The Investopedia Team. (2022, May 17). *Investopedia.* https://www.investopedia.com/ask/answers/03/062003.asp

World Health Organisation. (2020, April 27). https://www.who.int/news/item/27-04-2020-who-timeline---covid-19

Compilation of References

Abdullah, A. A. B. (2018). Factors Influencing Islamic Banks' Capital Structure in Developing Economies. *Journal of Islamic Accounting and Business Research.*

Abdullah, S. N., Ismail, K. N. I. K., & Nachum, L. (2016). Does having women on boards create value? The impact of societal perceptions and corporate governance in emerging markets. *Strategic Management Journal, 37*(3), 466–476. doi:10.1002mj.2352

Abuzayed, B., Bouri, E., Al-Fayoumi, N., & Jalkh, N. (2021). Systemic risk spillover across global and country stock markets during the COVID-19 pandemic. *Economic Analysis and Policy, 71*, 180–197. doi:10.1016/j.eap.2021.04.010

Acciarini, C., Boccardelli, P., & Votale, M. (2021). Resilient companies in the time of Covid-19 pandemic: a case study approach. *Journal of Entrepreneurship and Public Policy, 10*(3), 336-351. doi:10.1108/JEPP-03-2021-0021

Acharya, V., & Steffen, S. (2020). The risk of being a fallen angel and the corporate dash for cash in the midst of COVID. *Review of Corporate Finance Studies, 9*(9), 430–471. doi:10.1093/rcfs/cfaa013

Adams, R. B., & Mehran, H. (2005). *Corporate Performance, Board Structure and its Determinants in the Banking Industry*. Retrieved from https://papers.ssrn.com/sol3/papers.cfm?abstract_id=302593

Adams, R. B., & Ferreira, D. (2009). Women in the boardroom and their impact on governance and performance. *Journal of Financial Economics, 94*(2), 291–309. doi:10.1016/j.jfineco.2008.10.007

Adams, R. B., & Funk, P. (2012). Beyond the glass ceiling: Does gender matter? *Management Science, 58*(2), 219–235. doi:10.1287/mnsc.1110.1452

Adekoya, O. B., & Oliyide, J. A. (2020). How COVID-19 drives connectedness among commodity and financial markets: Evidence from TVP-VAR and causality-in-quantiles techniques. *Resources Policy*, 101898. PMID:34173426

Adie Tomer, J. W. (2020). *We should bail out airlines during the coronavirus pandemic—but on taxpayers' terms.* Retrieved from https://www.brookings.edu/research/we-should-bail-out-airlines-during-the-coronavirus-pandemic-but-on-taxpayers-terms/

Agarwal & Mishra. (2017). A Study of the Risk Adjusted Performance of Mutual Funds Industry in India. *Review of Innovation and Competitiveness.*

Agarwal, A., Chandra, K., Maloney, M., & Tam, M. (2020). *Planning for uncertainity: Performance management under COVID-19.* Strategy and Corporate Finance McKinsey & Company. Retrieved from https://www.mckinsey.com/business-functions/strategy-and-corporate-finance/our-insights/planning-for-uncertainty-performance-management-under-covid-19

Agrawal, S., De Smet, A., Lacroix, S., & Reich, A. (2020, May 7). *Adapting employees' skills and roles to the post-pandemic ways of working will be crucial to building operating-model resilience.* Retrieved from https://www.mckinsey.com/business-functions/people-and-organizational-performance/our-insights/to-emerge-stronger-from-the-covid-19-crisis-companies-should-start-reskilling-their-workforces-now

Ahern, K. R., & Dittmar, A. K. (2012). The changing of the boards: The impact on firm valuation of mandated female board representation. *The Quarterly Journal of Economics*, *127*(1), 137–197. doi:10.1093/qje/qjr049

Ahood & Nobanee. (2021). Main Functions of Financial Management. Academic Press.

Aishwarya & Suresh. (2020). A Study on Impact of Capital Structure on Profitability of Companies Listed in Indian Stock Exchange with respect to Automobile Industry. *Journal of Seybold Report, 15*(7), 1560 – 1574.

Ajzen, I. (2020). The theory of planned behavior: Frequently asked questions. *Human Behavior and Emerging Technologies*, *2*(4), 314–324. doi:10.1002/hbe2.195

Ajzen, I., & Fishbein, M. (2000). Attitudes and the attitude-behavior relation: Reasoned and automatic processes. *European Review of Social Psychology*, *11*(1), 1–33. doi:10.1080/14792779943000116

Akbar, S., Rehman, S., Liu, J., & Ali Shah, S. Z. (2017). Credit supply constraints and financial policies of listed companies during the 2007–2009 financial crisis. *Research in International Business and Finance*, *42*, 559–571. doi:10.1016/j.ribaf.2017.07.001

Akers, H. (2014). *Key macroeconomic variables*. EHow Contributor.

Al Farooque, O., Buachoom, W., & Sun, L. (2020). Board, audit committee, ownership and financial performance: Emerging trends from Thailand. *Pacific Accounting Review*, *32*(1), 54–81. doi:10.1108/PAR-10-2018-0079

Al-Awadhi, A. M., Alsaifi, K., Al-Awadhi, A., & Alhammadi, S. (2020). Death and contagious infectious diseases: Impact of the COVID-19 virus on stock market returns. *Journal of Behavioral and Experimental Finance*, *27*, 100326. doi:10.1016/j.jbef.2020.100326 PMID:32292707

Al-Azzam, B. A.-D. (2022). *Factors influencing the capital structure of Industrial Firms during the Covid 19: Evidence from Jordanian firms*. Academic Press.

Albulescu, C. T. (2021). COVID-19 and the United States financial markets' volatility. *Finance Research Letters, 38*, 101699. doi:10.1016/j.frl.2020.101699 PMID:32837380

Alexander, W., & Bartik, M. B. (2020, July 10). *The impact of COVID-19 on small business outcomes and expectations*. Retrieved from https://www.pnas.org/doi/10.1073/pnas.2006991117# doi:10.1073/pnas.2006991117

Ali, H. (2022). Corporate dividend policy in the time of COVID-19: Evidence from the G-12 countries. *Finance Research Letters, 46*, 1–9. doi:10.1016/j.frl.2021.102493 PMID:34658678

Allen, F., Qian, J., & Qian, M. J. (2005). Law, finance, and economic growth in China. *Journal of Financial Economics, 77*(1), 57–116. doi:10.1016/j.jfineco.2004.06.010

Alpaslanoğlu, A. (2021). The Effects of COVID-19 Pandemic on Business Areas and Post COVID-19 Management Trends. *Turkish Studies - Social Sciences, 16*(1), 131–156. doi:10.47356/TurkishStudies.47192

Alsayegh, M. F. (2020). Corporate Economic, Environmental, and Social Sustainability Performance Transformation through ESG Disclosure. *Sustainability, 12*(9).

Alshammari, M. M., & Alwan, A. A. (2016). *IT disaster recovery and business continuity based on VMware SRM solution for Kuwait Oil Company (KOC)*. IEEE.

Al-Shammari, M. A., Banerjee, S. N., & Rasheed, A. A. (2021). Corporate social responsibility and firm performance: A theory of dual responsibility. *Management Decision*.

Altavilla, C., Barbiero, F., Boucinha, M., & Burlon, L. (2020). *The great lockdown: pandemic response policies and bank lending conditions*. European Central Bank (No. 2465).

Al-Tuwaijri, S. A., Christensen, T. E., & Hughes, H. E. II. (2004). The relations among environmental disclosure, environmental performance, and economic performance: A simultaneous equations approach. *Accounting, Organizations and Society, 29*(5-6), 447–471. doi:10.1016/S0361-3682(03)00032-1

Ameliawati, M., & Setiyani, R. (2018). The influence of financial attitude, financial socialization, and financial experience to financial management behavior with financial literacy as the mediation variable. *KnE Social Sciences*, 811-832.

an Bhaird, C. M. (2013). Demand for debt and equity before and after the financial crisis. *Research in International Business and Finance, 28*, 105–117. doi:10.1016/j.ribaf.2012.10.001

Anand, A., Gayatri, M. N., Narain, N., Mishra, S., & Sood, S. (2020). *Impact of COVID-19 pandemic on micro, small, and medium enterprises (MSMEs): India report*. Academic Press.

Anand, P., & Cowton, C. J. (1993). The ethical investor: Exploring dimensions of investment behaviour. *Journal of Economic Psychology, 14*(2), 377–385. doi:10.1016/0167-4870(93)90007-8

Andrew Ellul, I. E. (2020). The COVID-19 Pandemic Crisis and Corporate Finance. *The Review of Corporate Finance Studies, 9*(3), 421–429. doi:10.1093/rcfs/cfaa016

Angelopoulou, E., Balfoussia, H., & Gibson, H. D. (2014). Building a financial conditions index for the euro area and selected euro area countries: What does it tell us about the crisis? *Economic Modelling*, *38*, 392–403. doi:10.1016/j.econmod.2014.01.013

Anil & Kumar. (2018). The service quality attributes of mutual funds. *International Journal of Pure and Applied Mathematics, 118*(5).

Arbor, J. (2005). The effect of capital structure on profitability: An empirical analysis of listed firms in Ghana. *The Journal of Risk Finance*, *6*(5), 438–444. doi:10.1108/15265940510633505

Archuleta, K. L., Britt, S. L., Tonn, T. J., & Grable, J. E. (2011). Financial satisfaction and financial stressors in marital satisfaction. *Psychological Reports*, *108*(2), 563–576. doi:10.2466/07.21.PR0.108.2.563-576 PMID:21675570

Archuleta, K. L., Dale, A., & Spann, S. M. (2013). College students and financial distress: Exploring debt, financial satisfaction, and financial anxiety. *Financial Counseling and Planning*, *24*(2), 50–62.

Archuleta, K. L., Mielitz, K. S., Jayne, D., & Le, V. (2020). Financial goal setting, financial anxiety, and solution-focused financial therapy (SFFT): A quasi-experimental outcome study. *Contemporary Family Therapy*, *42*(1), 68–76. doi:10.100710591-019-09501-0

Ashforth, B. E., & Mael, F. (1989). Social identity theory and the organization. *Academy of Management Review*, *14*(1), 20–39. doi:10.2307/258189

Ashraf, B. N. (2020, September). Economic Impact of Government Interventions During the COVID-19 Pandemic: International Evidence from Financial Markets. *Journal of Behavioral and Experimental Finance*. doi:10.1016/j.jbef.2020.100371

Asia Society Report. (2009). *Asia's Next challenge: Securing the region's water future*. A report by the Leadership group on water security in Asia. Retrieved from https://asiasociety.org/new-york/events/launch-asia-society-leadership-group-water-security-asia-report-asias-next-chall
enge

Asif, A. &. (2016). *Impact of Capital Structure on Firm Value Creation-Evidence from the Cement Sector of Pakistan*. Academic Press.

Aslanidis, N., Bariviera, A. F., & Perez-Laborda, A. (2021). Are cryptocurrencies becoming more interconnected? *Economics Letters*, *199*, 109725. doi:10.1016/j.econlet.2021.109725

Atlantic Council. (2022). *India must transform its micro, small, and medium enterprises*. Available at https://www.atlanticcouncil.org/blogs/southasiasource/india-must-transform-its-micro-small-and-medium-enterprises/

Audil Rashid Khaki, A. A. (2020, March). Factors affecting the capital structure: New evidence from GCC countries. *Journal of International Students*, *13*(1), 9–27. doi:10.14254/2071-8330.2020/13-1/1

Badran, O. (2021). Business analysis in post-pandemic era. *Academy of Strategic Management Journal.*, *20*, 2021.

Bahrini, R., & Filfilan, A. (2020). Impact of the novel coronavirus on stock market returns: Evidence from GCC countries. *Quantitative Finance and Economics*, *4*(4), 640–652. doi:10.3934/QFE.2020029

Baig, T., & Goldfajn, I. (1999). Financial market contagion in the Asian crisis. *IMF Staff Papers*, *46*(2), 167–195.

Baker, H. K., Kumar, S., & Goyal, N. (2019). Personality traits and investor sentiment. *Review of Behavioral Finance*.

Baker, S. R., Bloom, N., Davis, S. D., Kost, K. J., Sammon, M. C., & Viratyosin, T. (2020). *The unprecedented impact of stock market impact of COVID-19.* NBER Working Paper No. 26945. Retrieved from https://www.nber.org/system/files/working_papers/w26945/w26945.pdf

Balakrishnan, R., Danninger, S., Elekdag, S., & Tytell, I. (2011). The transmission of financial stress from advanced to emerging economies. *Emerging Markets Finance and Trade, 47*(sup2), 40-68.

Balli, F., de Bruin, A., Chowdhury, M. I. H., & Naeem, M. A. (2020). Connectedness of cryptocurrencies and prevailing uncertainties. *Applied Economics Letters*, *27*(16), 1316–1322. doi:10.1080/13504851.2019.1678724

Baqaee, D., & Farhi, E. (2020). *Supply And Demand In Disaggregated Keynesian With An Application To The Covid-19 Crisis.* NBER Working Paper 27152.

Barber, B. M., & Odean, T. (2002). Online investors: Do the slow die first? *Review of Financial Studies*, *15*(2), 455–488. doi:10.1093/rfs/15.2.455

Bargon, D., & Wong, S.C. (2004). *Asia's Governance Challenge*. Academic Press.

Barigozzi, M., Hallin, M., Soccorsi, S., & von Sachs, R. (2021). Time-varying general dynamic factor models and the measurement of financial connectedness. *Journal of Econometrics*, *222*(1), 324–343. doi:10.1016/j.jeconom.2020.07.004

Bart, C., & McQueen, G. (2013). Why women make better decisions. *International Journal of Business Governance and Ethics*, *8*(1), 93–99. doi:10.1504/IJBGE.2013.052743

Baruník, J., Kočenda, E., & Vácha, L. (2017). Asymmetric volatility connectedness on the forex market. *Journal of International Money and Finance*, *77*, 39–56. doi:10.1016/j.jimonfin.2017.06.003

Baruník, J., & Křehlík, T. (2018). Measuring the frequency dynamics of financial connectedness and systemic risk. *Journal of Financial Econometrics*, *16*(2), 271–296. doi:10.1093/jjfinec/nby001

Baur, D. (2003). Testing for contagion—Mean and volatility contagion. *Journal of Multinational Financial Management*, *13*(4-5), 405–422. doi:10.1016/S1042-444X(03)00018-5

Beirne, J., Caporale, G. M., Schulze-Ghattas, M., & Spagnolo, N. (2013). Volatility spillovers and contagion from mature to emerging stock markets. *Review of International Economics, 21*(5), 1060–1075. doi:10.1111/roie.12091

Bernanke, B. S. (1983). *Non-monetary effects of the financial crisis in the propagation of the Great Depression.* National Bureau of Economic Research (No. W1054).

Bernanke, B. S. (1986). *Alternative explanations of the money-income correlation.* Carnegie-Rochester Conference Series on Public Policy. Elsevier Science Publishers. doi:10.3386/w1842

Bhabra, H. L., Liu, T., & Tirtiroglu, D. (2008). Capital structure choice in a nascent market: Evidence from listed firms in China. *Journal of Financial Management, 37*(2), 341–364. doi:10.1111/j.1755-053X.2008.00015.x

Bhadra, S., & Ray, S. (2021, August 15). *Outbreak of COVID-19: Economic Shocks and Corporate Responses in India*. Retrieved from https://a-e-l.scholasticahq.com/

BhargavaR.LouX.OzikG.SadkaR.WhitmoreT. (2022). Quantifying Narratives and their Impact on Financial Markets. *Available at* SSRN 4166640. doi:10.2139/ssrn.4166640

Bhasin, M. (2012). 'Voluntary' Corporate Governance Disclosures Made in the Annual Reports: An Empirical Study. *International Journal of Management & Innovation, 4*(1).

Bir, J. S. (2014). Knowledge, attitude and their effect on the recently graduated employees' financial management practices and satisfaction. *Economic Literature, 12*, 69–81.

BIS. (2009). *The international financial crisis: Timeline, impact and policy responses in Asia and the Pacific. BIS Papers No 52.* Bank for International Settlements.

Blasi, S., Caporin, M., & Fontini, F. (2018). A multidimensional analysis of the relationship between corporate social responsibility and firms' economic performance. *Ecological Economics, 147*, 218–229. doi:10.1016/j.ecolecon.2018.01.014

Bloomberg. (2017). *Dataset.* Bloomberg Professional services.

Bobzien, L., & Kalleitner, F. (2021). Attitudes towards European financial solidarity during the Covid-19 pandemic: evidence from a net-contributor country. *European Societies, 23*(sup1), S791-S804.

Bodea, N. B.-M.-F. (2014). The Role of Capital Structure in Company's Financing. *Economics and Applied Informatics.*

Boland, B., De Smet, A., Palter, R., & Sanghvi, A. (2020, June 8). *McKinsey and Company*. Retrieved from https://www.mckinsey.com/business-functions/people-and-organ izational-performance/our-insights/reimagining-the-office-an
d-work-life-after-covid-19?cid=other-eml-alt-mip-mck&hlkid=8
778afb0af6f4f938879e2846fe15066&hctky=11396825&hdpid=4256de3
0-f942-4b45-948

Borgards, O., Czudaj, R. L., & Van Hoang, T. H. (2021). Price overreactions in the commodity futures market: An intraday analysis of the Covid-19 pandemic impact. *Resources Policy, 71*, 101966. doi:10.1016/j.resourpol.2020.101966 PMID:36569184

Bouri, E., Cepni, O., Gabauer, D., & Gupta, R. (2021). Return connectedness across asset classes around the COVID-19 outbreak. *International Review of Financial Analysis, 73*, 101646. doi:10.1016/j.irfa.2020.101646

Brave, S. A., & Butters, R. A. (2011). Monitoring financial stability: A financial conditions index approach. *Economic Perspectives, 35*(1), 22.

Broadstock, D. C., Matousek, R., Meyer, M., & Tzeremes, N. G. (2020). Does corporate social responsibility impact firms' innovation capacity? The indirect link between environmental & social governance implementation and innovation performance. *Journal of Business Research, 119*, 99–110. doi:10.1016/j.jbusres.2019.07.014

Browder, G. J., Xie, S., Kim, Y., Gu, L., Fan, M., & Ehrhardt, D. (2008). *Improving the performance of China's urban water utilities.* The World Bank. Retrieved from https://documents1.worldbank.org/curated/zh/840621468016215926/pdf/409640P0704130Public.pdf

Bryman, A., & Cramer, D. (1997). *Quantitative data analysis with SPSS for windows.* Routledge.

Buallay, A., El Khoury, R., & Hamdan, A. (2021). Sustainability reporting in smart cities: A multidimensional performance measures. *Cities (London, England), 119*, 103397. doi:10.1016/j.cities.2021.103397

Bui, T. (2022). The determinants and evolution of corporate ownership structure: Evidence from spinoffs. *Scenarios Not Adequately Addressed by Economic Theories, 1*, 10.

Burgess, Z., & Tharenou, P. (2002). Women board directors: Characteristics of the few. *Journal of Business Ethics, 37*(1), 39–49. doi:10.1023/A:1014726001155

Business World. (2022). *MSMEs Participating In The Post COVID Recovery.* Available at https://www.businessworld.in/article/MSMEs-Participating-In-The-Post-COVID-Recovery/27-03-2021-385041/

Calvo, S., & Reinhart, C. (1996). *Capital Flows to Latin America: Is there Evidence of Contagion Effects?* World Bank Policy Research Working Paper Series 1619.

Cambón, M. I., & Estévez, L. (2016). A Spanish financial market stress index (FMSI). *The Spanish Review of Financial Economics, 14*(1), 23–41. doi:10.1016/j.srfe.2016.01.002

Çamlıca, F. (2016). Responsiveness of monetary policy to financial stress in Turkey. *Central Bank Review, 16*(4), 143–150. doi:10.1016/j.cbrev.2016.11.003

Carpenter, M. A. (2002). The implications of strategy and social context for the relationship between top management team heterogeneity and firm performance. *Strategic Management Journal, 23*(3), 275–284. doi:10.1002mj.226

Carroll, A. B. (2021). Corporate social responsibility (CSR) and the COVID-19 pandemic: Organizational and managerial implications. *Journal of Strategy and Management*.

Carter, D. A., D'Souza, F., Simkins, B. J., & Simpson, W. G. (2010). The gender and ethnic diversity of US boards and board committees and firm financial performance. *Corporate Governance*, *18*(5), 396–414. doi:10.1111/j.1467-8683.2010.00809.x

Carter, D. A., Simkins, B. J., & Simpson, W. G. (2003). Corporate governance, board diversity, and firm value. *Financial Review*, *38*(1), 33–53. doi:10.1111/1540-6288.00034

Casado, M. G., Glennon, B., Lane, J., McQuown, D., Rich, D., & Weinberg, B. A. (2020). *The Effect of Fiscal Stimulus: Evidence from COVID-19 (No. w27576)*. National Bureau of Economic Research.

Castillo, C. (2004). Disaster preparedness and Business Continuity Planning at Boeing: An integrated model. *Journal of Facilities Management*, *3*(1), 8–26. doi:10.1108/14725960510808365

Cevik, E. I., Dibooglu, S., & Kenc, T. (2013). Measuring financial stress in Turkey. *Journal of Policy Modeling*, *35*(2), 370–383. doi:10.1016/j.jpolmod.2012.06.003

Chadwick, M. G., & Ozturk, H. (2019). Measuring financial systemic stress for Turkey: A search for the best composite indicator. *Economic Systems*, *43*(1), 151–172. doi:10.1016/j.ecosys.2018.09.004

Chancharoenchai, K., & Dibooglu, S. (2006). Volatility spillovers and contagion during the Asian crisis: Evidence from six Southeast Asian stock markets. *Emerging Markets Finance & Trade*, *42*(2), 4–17. doi:10.2753/REE1540-496X420201

Chandy, L., Gertz, G., & Linn, J. (2009). *Tracking the global financial crisis: An analysis of the IMF's world economic outlook*. Wolfensohn Center for Development at Brookings. http://www. brookings. edu/reports/2009/05_financial_crisis _linn. aspx.

Chapple, L., & Humphrey, J. E. (2014). Does board gender diversity have a financial impact? Evidence using stock portfolio performance. *Journal of Business Ethics*, *122*(4), 709–723. doi:10.100710551-013-1785-0

Chatzoglou, P. C., Chatzoudes, D., Sarigiannidis, L., & Theriou, G. (2018). The role of firm-specific factors in the strategy-performance relationship: Revisiting the resource-based view of the firm and the VRIO framework. *Management Research Review*, *41*(1), 46–73. doi:10.1108/MRR-10-2016-0243

Cheema-Fox, LaPerla, Serafeim, & Wang. (2020, June 23). *Corporate Resilience and Response During Covid 19*. Retrieved from https://www.statestreet.com/: https://www.statestreet.com/content/dam/statestreet/documents/Articles/Corporate%20Resilience%20and%20Response%20During%20Covid19_3069576.3.2.GBL.pdf

Chen, X., Wang, Z., Li, X., Liu, Z., & Li, K. (2021). The impact of COVID-19 on the Securities Market: Evidence from Chinese Stock and Bond Markets. *Procedia Computer Science*, *187*, 294–299. doi:10.1016/j.procs.2021.04.065

Chirella. (1992). The interaction of the financing and investment decisions: Preliminary results in the Australian context. *Asia Pacific Journal of Management.*

Choi, S. Y. (2022). Volatility spillovers among Northeast Asia and the US: Evidence from the global financial crisis and the COVID-19 pandemic. *Economic Analysis and Policy*, *73*, 179–193. doi:10.1016/j.eap.2021.11.014

Choudhry, T., & Jayasekera, R. (2014). Returns and volatility spillover in the European banking industry during global financial crisis: Flight to perceived quality or contagion? *International Review of Financial Analysis*, *36*, 36–45. doi:10.1016/j.irfa.2014.05.003

Chou, R., Ng, V., & Pi, L. (1994). Cointegration of International Stock Market Indices. *IMF Working Paper*, *94*(94), i. doi:10.5089/9781451950700.001

Cipollini, A., & Mikaliunaite, I. (2020). Macro-uncertainty and financial stress spillovers in the Eurozone. *Economic Modelling*, *89*, 546–558. doi:10.1016/j.econmod.2019.11.017

Conyon, M. J., & He, L. (2011). Executive compensation and corporate governance in China. *Journal of Corporate Finance*, *17*(4), 1158–1175. doi:10.1016/j.jcorpfin.2011.04.006

Conyon, M. J., & He, L. (2017). Firm performance and boardroom gender diversity: A quantile regression approach. *Journal of Business Research*, *79*, 198–211. doi:10.1016/j.jbusres.2017.02.006

Conyon, M. J., & Mallin, C. (1997). Women in the boardroom: Evidence from large UK companies. *Corporate Governance*, *5*(3), 112–117. doi:10.1111/1467-8683.00051

Corbet, S., Larkin, C., & Lucey, B. (2020). The contagion effects of the COVID-19 pandemic: Evidence from gold and cryptocurrencies. *Finance Research Letters*, *35*, 101554. doi:10.1016/j.frl.2020.101554

Corbet, S., Meegan, A., Larkin, C., Lucey, B., & Yarovaya, L. (2018). Exploring the dynamic relationships between cryptocurrencies and other financial assets. *Economics Letters*, *165*, 28–34. doi:10.1016/j.econlet.2018.01.004

Cox, T. H., & Blake, S. (1991). Managing cultural diversity: Implications for organizational competitiveness. *The Academy of Management Executive*, *5*(3), 45–56.

Cronin, D., & Dunne, P. G. (2019). How effective are sovereign bond-backed securities as a spillover prevention device? *Journal of International Money and Finance*, *96*, 49–66. doi:10.1016/j.jimonfin.2019.05.001

Cuevas-Vargas, Cortes-Palacios, & Lozano-Garcia. (2022). Impact of capital structure and innovatin on firm performance. Direct and indirect effects of capital structure. *Procedia Computer Science, 199*, 1082-1089.

Dall'asen, N. (2020, March 19). *LVMH Is Making Free Hand Sanitizer to Help French Hospitals Fight Coronavirus*. Retrieved from https://www.allure.com/story/lvmh-free-hand-sanitizer-france

Dao, T. T., & Ta, T. D. N. (2020). A meta-analysis: Capital structure and firm performance. *Journal of Economic Development, 22*(1), 111–129. doi:10.1108/JED-12-2019-0072

Daron Acemoğlu, U. A. (2016, January 30). *Networks-and-macroeconomic-shocks*. Retrieved from voxeu.org: https://voxeu.org/article/networks-and-macroeconomic-shocks

Dawson, C. (2017). Financial optimism and entrepreneurial satisfaction. *Strategic Entrepreneurship Journal, 11*(2), 171–194. doi:10.1002ej.1244

de le Torre, A., Martinez Peria, M., & Schmulker, S. (2010). Bank involvement with SMEs: Beyond relationship lending. *Journal of Banking & Finance, 34*(9), 2280–2293. doi:10.1016/j.jbankfin.2010.02.014

Deghi, A. D. (2021). *IMF Working Paper, WP/21/86*. IMF.

Deghi, A., Seneviratne, D., Tsuruga, T., & Vandenbussche, J. (2021). *Corporate funding and the COVID-19 crisis*. IMF Working Paper, WP/21/86, 1-36.

del Rio-Chanona, R. P. M. (2020). Supply and demand shocks in the COVID-19 pandemic: an industry and occupation perspective. *Oxford Review of Economic Policy, 36*(Supplement_1), S94–S137. doi:10.1093/oxrep/graa033

Demary & Hüther. (2020). *Why the COVID-19 Pandemic Could Increase the Corporate Saving Trend in the Long Run*. Academic Press.

Demirer, M., Diebold, F. X., Liu, L., & Yilmaz, K. (2018). Estimating global bank network connectedness. *Journal of Applied Econometrics, 33*(1), 1–15. doi:10.1002/jae.2585

Dev, S. M., & Sengupta, R. (2020, April). *Covid-19: Impact on the Indian Economy*. Retrieved from http://www.igidr.ac.in/pdf/publication/WP-2020-013.pdf

Dick, C. S., Schmeling, M., & Schrimpf, A. (2013). Macro-expectations, aggregate uncertainty, and expected term premia. *European Economic Review, 58*, 58–80. doi:10.1016/j.euroecorev.2012.11.005

Diebold, F. X., Liu, L., & Yilmaz, K. (2017). *Commodity connectedness (No. w23685)*. National Bureau of Economic Research. doi:10.3386/w23685

Diebold, F. X., & Yilmaz, K. (2009). Measuring financial asset return and volatility spillovers, with application to global equity markets. *Economic Journal (London), 119*(534), 158–171. doi:10.1111/j.1468-0297.2008.02208.x

Diebold, F. X., & Yilmaz, K. (2012). Better to give than to receive: Predictive directional measurement of volatility spillovers. *International Journal of Forecasting, 28*(1), 57–66. doi:10.1016/j.ijforecast.2011.02.006

Diebold, F. X., & Yılmaz, K. (2014). On the network topology of variance decompositions: Measuring the connectedness of financial firms. *Journal of Econometrics*, *182*(1), 119–134. doi:10.1016/j.jeconom.2014.04.012

Diebold, F. X., & Yilmaz, K. (2015). Trans-Atlantic equity volatility connectedness: US and European financial institutions, 2004–2014. *Journal of Financial Econometrics*, *14*(1), 81–127.

Dimson, J. M. (2020). *COVID-19 and European small and medium-size enterprises: How they are weathering the storm.* https://www.mckinsey.com/industries/public-and-social-sector/our-insights

Ding, W. e., Levine, R., Lin, C., & Xie, W. (2021). Corporate immunity to the COVID-19 pandemic. *Journal of Financial Economics*, *141*(2), 802–830. doi:10.1016/j.jfineco.2021.03.005 PMID:34580557

Dinh. (2020). The Effect of Capital Structure on Financial Performance of Vietnamese Listing Pharmaceutical Enterprises. *Journal of Asian Finance, Economics and Business*, *7*(9), 329–340.

Donthu, N., & Gustafsson, A. (2020). Effects of COVID-19 on business and research. *Journal of Business Research, 117*, 284-289.

Driffield, N. L., Mahambare, V., & Pal, S. (2007). How does ownership structure affect capital structure and firm value? Recent evidence from East Asia. *Economics of Transition*, *15*(3), 535–573. doi:10.1111/j.1468-0351.2007.00291.x

Duchin, R., Ozbas, O., & Sensoy, B. (2010). Costly external finance, corporate investment, and the subprime mortgage credit crisis. *Journal of Financial Economics*, *97*(3), 418–435. doi:10.1016/j.jfineco.2009.12.008

Dungey, M., & Gajurel, D. (2014). Equity market contagion during the global financial crisis: Evidence from the world's eight largest economies. *Economic Systems*, *38*(2), 161–177. doi:10.1016/j.ecosys.2013.10.003

Duprey, T., Klaus, B., & Peltonen, T. (2017). Dating systemic financial stress episodes in the EU countries. *Journal of Financial Stability*, *32*, 30–56. doi:10.1016/j.jfs.2017.07.004

Dwyer, S., Richard, O. C., & Chadwick, K. (2003). Gender diversity in management and firm performance: The influence of growth orientation and organizational culture. *Journal of Business Research*, *56*(12), 1009–1019. doi:10.1016/S0148-2963(01)00329-0

Dzingai, I., & Fakoya, M. B. (2017). Effect of corporate governance structure on the financial performance of Johannesburg Stock Exchange (JSE)-listed mining firms. *Sustainability*, *9*(6), 1–15. doi:10.3390u9060867

Eact. (2022). *Cash and Working Capital Management in the Corona crisis*. EACT.

Eccles, R. G., Ioannou, I., & Serafeim, G. (2014). The impact of corporate sustainability on organizational processes and performance. *Management Science*, *60*(11), 2835–2857. doi:10.1287/mnsc.2014.1984

Edwards, S. (1998). *Interest rate volatility, capital controls, and contagion* (No. w6756). National Bureau of Economic Research.

Edwards, S., & Susmel, R. (2001). Volatility dependence and contagion in emerging equity markets. *Journal of Development Economics*, *66*(2), 505–532. doi:10.1016/S0304-3878(01)00172-9

Egbunike, C. F. (2018). *Macroeconomic factors firm characteristics and financial performance*. Emerald. doi:10.1108/AJAR-09-2018-0029

Eggers, F. (2020). Masters of disasters? Challenges and opportunities for SMEs in times of crisis. *Journal of Business Research*, *116*, 199–208. doi:10.1016/j.jbusres.2020.05.025 PMID:32501306

Ekayana Sangkasari Paranita, E., & Mahardika Agustinus, M. (2020). The Influence of Investment Motivation and Financial Literacy on Interest in Investing During the COVID-19 Pandemic. In *Proceeding of the 3rd International Conference of Banking, Accounting, Management adn Economic* (Vol. 169). Atlantis Press.

Emergency Credit Line Guarantee Scheme (ECLGS). (n.d.). Retrieved from www.jatinverma.org: https://www.jatinverma.org/emergency-credit-line-guarantee-scheme-eclgs

Engidaw, A. E. (2022). Small businesses and their challenges during COVID-19 pandemic in developing countries: in the case of Ethiopia. *Journal of Innovation and Entrepreneurship*.

Fairlie, R. (2020). The impact of COVID-19 on small business owners. *Journal of Economics & Management Strategy*. PMID:32904856

Fama, E., & Jensen, M. (1983). Separation of ownership and control. *The Journal of Law & Economics*, *26*(2), 301–325. doi:10.1086/467037

Fani, S. V., & Subriadi, A. P. (2019). Business continuity plan: Examining of multi-usable framework. *Procedia Computer Science*, *161*, 275–282. doi:10.1016/j.procs.2019.11.124

Farrell, K. A., & Hersch, P. L. (2005). Additions to corporate boards: The effect of gender. *Journal of Corporate Finance*, *11*(1-2), 85–106. doi:10.1016/j.jcorpfin.2003.12.001

Fasanya, I. O., Oyewole, O., Adekoya, O. B., & Odei-Mensah, J. (2020). Dynamic spillovers and connectedness between COVID-19 pandemic and global foreign exchange markets. *Economic Research-Ekonomska Istraživanja,* 1-26.

Fernandes, D., Lynch, J. G. Jr, & Netemeyer, R. G. (2014). Financial literacy, financial education, and downstream financial behaviors. *Management Science*, *60*(8), 1861–1883. doi:10.1287/mnsc.2013.1849

Ferran Giones, a. A. (2020, November 14). Revising entrepreneurial action in response to exogenous shocks: Considering the COVID-19 pandemic. *Journal of Business Venturing Insights*. doi:10.1016/j.jbvi.2020.e00186

Financial Stability Board. (2020). *Holistic Review of the March Market Turmoil*. Financial Stabilility Board. Retrieved from https://www.fsb.org/wp-content/uploads/P171120-2.pdf

Francoeur, C., Labelle, R., & Sinclair-Desgagné, B. (2008). Gender diversity in corporate governance and top management. *Journal of Business Ethics*, *81*(1), 83–95. doi:10.100710551-007-9482-5

Frank, M., & Goyal, V. K. (2009). Capital structure decisions: Which factors are reliably important? *Financial Management*, *38*(1), 1–37. doi:10.1111/j.1755-053X.2009.01026.x

Franz Ulrich Ruch, T. T. (n.d.). *Demand and Supply Shocks Evidence from Corporate Earning Calls*. Retrieved from worldbank.org: https://openknowledge.worldbank.org/bitstream/handle/10986/36923/Demand-and-Supply-Shocks-Evidence-from-Corporate-Earning-Calls.pdf

Freeman, R. E. (2010). *Strategic Management: A Stakeholder Approach*. Cambridge University Press. doi:10.1017/CBO9781139192675

Furceri, D., Ganslmeier, M., Ostry, J. D., & Yang, N. (2021). *Initial Output Losses from the Covid- 19 Pandemic: Robust Determinants (No. 2021/018)*. International Monetary Fund.

Gade, S. (2018). MSMEs' role in economic growth–a study on India's perspective. *International Journal of Pure and Applied Mathematics*, *118*(18), 1727–1741.

Galdeano, D., Ahmed, U., Fati, M., Rehan, R., & Ahmed, A. J. M. S. L. (2019). Financial performance and corporate social responsibility in the banking sector of Bahrain: Can engagement moderate? *Management Science Letters*, *9*(10), 1529–1542. doi:10.5267/j.msl.2019.5.032

Gasbarro, D., Le, K. S., Schwebach, R. G., & Zumwalt, J. K. (2017). An analysis of syndicated loan announcements during the global financial crisis. *Journal of Financial Research*, *40*(4), 535–565. doi:10.1111/jfir.12134

Gaur, A., & Kumar, M. (2017). A systematic approach to conducting review studies: An assessment of content analysis in 25 years of IB research. *Journal of World Business*, *53*(2), 280–289. doi:10.1016/j.jwb.2017.11.003

Geithner. (2003). *Fund assistance for countries facing exogenous shocks*. Academic Press.

Ghimire, A. M. (2021). Analysis of the Impact of Capital Structure in the Innovation of a Firm Using the Techniques of Financial Engineering. *Proceedings of the International Conference on Industrial Engineering and Operations Management*.

Gittens, A. (2020, May). Impacts of COVID-19 on aviation and the airport business. *International Airport Review*. Retrieved from https://www.internationalairportreview.com/article/117249/covid-19-airport-business-aci-world-recovery/

Goel, T., & Serena, J. M. (2020). Bonds and syndicated loans during the Covid-19 crisis: decoupled again? *BIS Bulletin*, *29*(1). Retrieved from https://www.bis.org/publ/bisbull29.pdf

Golubeva, O. (2021). Firm performance during the COVID-19 outbreak: International evidence from 13 countries. *Corporate Governance*, *21*(6), 1011–1027. doi:10.1108/CG-09-2020-0405

Goodell, J. W. (2020). COVID-19 and finance: Agendas for future research. *Finance Research Letters*, *35*, 101512. doi:10.1016/j.frl.2020.101512 PMID:32562472

Google Scholar. (n.d.). https://scholar.google.co.in/

Graham, J. R., Leary, T. M., & Roberts, M. R. (2014). *A century of capital structure; the leveraging of corproate America.* NBER Working Paper Series 19910.

Gropp, R., & Heider, F. (2010). The Determinants of bank capital structure. *Review of Finance*, *14*(4), 587–622. doi:10.1093/rof/rfp030

Groysberg, B., & Bell, D. (2013). Dysfunction in the boardroom. *Harvard Business Review*, *91*(6), 89–97.

Guiso, L. P., Sapienza, P., & Zingales, L. (2018). Time varying risk aversion. *Journal of Financial Economics*, *128*(3), 403–421. doi:10.1016/j.jfineco.2018.02.007

Gul, S. (2019). Capital Structure and Default Risk: Evidence from Korean Stock Market. *Journal of Asian Finance, Economics and Business*, *6*(2), 15–24.

Gunay, S. (2021). Comparing COVID-19 with the GFC: A shockwave analysis of currency markets. *Research in International Business and Finance*, *56*, 101377. doi:10.1016/j.ribaf.2020.101377 PMID:36540770

Gupta, Sharma, & Gupta. (2014). Management Accounting. Kalyani Publishers.

Gurbaxani, A., & Gupte, R. (2021). A study on the impact of COVID-19 on investor behaviour of individuals in a small town in the state of Madhya Pradesh, India. *Australasian Accounting. Business and Finance Journal*, *15*(1), 70–92.

Ha Nguyen, R. A. (2020). *Coping with a dual shock: COVID-19 and oil prices.* Retrieved from https://cepr.org/voxeu/columns/coping-dual-shock-covid-19-and-oil-prices

Habaragoda, B. S. (2018). Corporate social responsibility (CSR) and firm performance: Impact of internal and external CSR on financial performance. *Business and Management*, *10*(3), 284.

Hakkio, C. S., & Keeton, W. R. (2009). Financial stress: What is it, how can it be measured, and why does it matter? *Economic Review (Kansas City, Mo.)*, *94*(2), 5–50.

Halling, M., Yu, J., & Zechner, J. (2020). How did COVID-19 affect firms access to public capital markets? *Review of Corporate Finance Studies*, *9*(9), 501–533. doi:10.1093/rcfs/cfaa008

Hamao, Y., Masulis, R. W., & Ng, V. (1990). Correlations in price changes and volatility across international stock markets. *Review of Financial Studies*, *3*(2), 281–307. doi:10.1093/rfs/3.2.281

Hambrick, D. C. (2007). Upper echelons theory: An update. *Academy of Management Review*, *32*(2), 334–343. doi:10.5465/amr.2007.24345254

Hambrick, D. C., & Mason, P. A. (1984). Upper echelons: The organization as a reflection of its top managers. *Academy of Management Review*, *9*(2), 193–206. doi:10.2307/258434

Han, H., & Qian, Y. (2020). Did Enterprises' Innovation Ability Increase During the COVID-19 Pandemic? Evidence From Chinese Listed Companies. *Asian Economic Letters,* 1-5.

Hassan, I., Politsidis, P. N., & Sharma, Z. (2020). Global syndicated lending during the COVID-19 pandemic. *Journal of Banking & Finance*. Advance online publication. doi:10.1016/j.jbankfin.2021.106121

Hausman, J. A. (1978). Specification tests in econometrics. *Econometrica*, *46*(6), 1251–1272. doi:10.2307/1913827

He Huang, Y. Y. (2021). Rethinking capital structure decision and corporatesocial responsibility in response to COVID-19. *Accounting and Finance*, *61*(3), 4757–4788. doi:10.1111/acfi.12740

Helfert, E. (2006). *Tehnici de analiză financiară*. BMT.

Herbane, B., Elliott, D., & Swartz, E. (2004). Business Continuity Management: Time for a Strategic Role? *Long Range Planning (Long Range Plan), 37*(6), 386-386. . doi:10.1016/j.lrp.2004.07.010

Hernandez, J. A., Kang, S. H., Shahzad, S. J. H., & Yoon, S. M. (2020). Spillovers and diversification potential of bank equity returns from developed and emerging America. *The North American Journal of Economics and Finance*, *54*, 101219. doi:10.1016/j.najef.2020.101219

Hillman, A. J. (2015). Board diversity: Beginning to unpeel the onion. *Corporate Governance*, *23*(2), 104–107. doi:10.1111/corg.12090

Hillman, A. J., Shropshire, C., & Cannella, A. A. Jr. (2007). Organizational predictors of women on corporate boards. *Academy of Management Journal*, *50*(4), 941–952. doi:10.5465/amj.2007.26279222

Hillman, A., Cannella, A., & Paetzold, R. (2000). The resource dependence role of corporate directors: Strategic adaptation of board composition in response to environmental change. *Journal of Management Studies*, *37*(2), 235–255. doi:10.1111/1467-6486.00179

Hirsch, J., & Walz, U. (2009). *Financing decisions along a firm's life cycle: Debit as a commitment device.* German Research Foundation.

Hoanţă, N. (2003). *Finanţele firmei*. Economica.

Ho, J., Lu, C., & Lucianetti, L. (2021). Does engaging in corporate social responsibility activities influence firm performance? The moderating effects of risk preferences and performance measurement systems. *Management Decision*, *59*(13), 15–37. doi:10.1108/MD-07-2020-0925

Holló, D., Kremer, M., & Lo Duca, M. (2012). *CISS-a composite indicator of systemic stress in the financial system* (No. 1426). ECB Working Paper.

Horak, S., & Cui, J. (2017). Financial performance and risk behavior of gender-diversified boards in the Chinese automotive industry: Initial insights. *Personnel Review*, *46*(4), 847–866. doi:10.1108/PR-10-2015-0274

HotchkissE. S. (2020). *Corporate Capital Raising During the COVID Crisis*. doi:10.2139/ssrn.3723001

Hourvouliades, N. L. (2022). Financing Small Businesses: The Agony of Securing Funding. In K. Biginas, S. Sindakis, A. Koumproglou, V. Sarantinos, & P. Wyer (Eds.), Small Business Management and Control of the Uncertain External Environment (pp. 229-258). Emerald Publishing Limited.

https://ssbr-edu.ch/. (n.d.). *6 Ways That Covid 19 Has Had A Positive Impact On Businesses*. Retrieved from https://ssbr-edu.ch/6-ways-that-covid19-has-had-a-positive-impact-on-businesses/

Huang, R., & Ritter, J. R. (2021). Corporate cash shortfalls and financing decisiosn. *Review of Financial Studies*, *34*(4), 1789–1833. doi:10.1093/rfs/hhaa099

Huotari, J. (2015). *Measuring financial stress–A country specific stress index for Finland*. Bank of Finland Research Discussion Paper, (7).

Hutterer, J. (2008). China's water market - Opportunities for foreign investors. *China Aktuell*, *2*, 157–177. http://www.grasshopperinvestments.com/downloads/67_Der_chinesische_Wassermarkt.pdf

Huynh, T. L. D., Nasir, M. A., & Nguyen, D. K. (2020). Spillovers and connectedness in foreign exchange markets: The role of trade policy uncertainty. *The Quarterly Review of Economics and Finance*, *79*, 1–14. doi:10.1016/j.qref.2020.09.001 PMID:33052186

Illing, M., & Liu, Y. (2006). Measuring financial stress in a developed country: An application to Canada. *Journal of Financial Stability*, *2*(3), 243–265. doi:10.1016/j.jfs.2006.06.002

ILO. (2020). *The impact of COVID-19 on the tourism sector*. Retrieved from https://www.ilo.org/wcmsp5/groups/public/---ed_dialogue/---sector/documents/briefingnote/wcms_741468.pdf

IMF. (2020). *Assessing the impact of COVID-19 pandemic on the corporate and banking sectors in Latin America*. International Monetary Fund. Retrieved from https://www.imf.org/-/media/Files/Publications/REO/WHD/2020/Oct/English/CorporateFinancial.ashx

Indrakumar, D. (2020). COVID-19 and its impact on Micro, Small and Medium Enterprises in India. *Manpower Journal*, *54*(3&4), 75–88.

International, A. C. (2022). *The impact of COVID-19 on airports—and the path to recovery*. Retrieved from https://aci.aero/2022/06/28/the-impact-of-covid-19-on-airportsand-the-path-to-recovery/

Iqbal, A., & Kume, O. (2014). Impact of financial crisis n firms' capital structure in the UK, France and Germany. *Multinational Finance Journal, 18*(3/4), 1–33. doi:10.17578/18-3/4-3

Islami, M., & Kurz-Kim, J. R. (2014). A single composite financial stress indicator and its real impact in the euro area. *International Journal of Finance & Economics, 19*(3), 204–211. doi:10.1002/ijfe.1483

Ismail, W. A. (2007). *Islamic bank performance and capital structure.* MPRA Paper No. 6012.

Iyke, B. N. (2020, October 26). *economic-policy-uncertainty-in-times-of-covid-19-pandemic.* Retrieved from https://a-e-l.scholasticahq.com/article/17665-economic-policy-uncertainty-in-times-of-covid-19-pandemic

Jalal, I. (2014). *Women, water, and leadership.* Asian Development Bank (ADB). ADB Briefs no. 24. Retrieved from https://www.adb.org/publications/women-water-and-leadership

Javeed, S. A., & Lefen, L. (2019). An analysis of corporate social responsibility and firm performance with moderating effects of CEO power and ownership structure: A case study of the manufacturing sector of Pakistan. *Sustainability, 11*(1), 248. doi:10.3390u11010248

Jebran & Chen. (2021). COVID – 19 Crises and Corporate Governance Responses. *International Journal of Finance & Economics.*

Jensen, M. C. (1976). Theory of the Firm: Managerial Behaviour, Agency Costs and Ownership Structure. *Journal of Financial Economics, 3*(4), 305–360.

Jensen, M. C., & Meckling, W. H. (1976). Theory of the firm: Managerial behavior, agency costs and ownership structure. *Journal of Financial Economics, 3*(4), 305–360. doi:10.1016/0304-405X(76)90026-X

Jess Benhabib, X. L. (2016). Sentiments, financial markets, and macroeconomic fluctuations. *Journal of Financial Economics*, 420–443.

Jiang, F., & Kim, K. A. (2015). Corporate governance in China: A modern perspective. *Journal of Corporate Finance, 32*, 190–216. doi:10.1016/j.jcorpfin.2014.10.010

Jiang, Y., & Zheng, X. (2014). Private sector participation and performance of urban water utilities in China. *Economic Development and Cultural Change, 63*(1), 155–189. doi:10.1086/677739

Ji, Q., Bouri, E., Lau, C. K. M., & Roubaud, D. (2019). Dynamic connectedness and integration in cryptocurrency markets. *International Review of Financial Analysis, 63*, 257–272. doi:10.1016/j.irfa.2018.12.002

Jnaneswar, K., Aishwarya, J. S., & Bhagath Soorya, D. (2021). The Impact of Capital Structure on the Financial Performance of Hotel Industry and Automobile Industry. *Asian Journal of Economics, Finance and Management, 4*(3), 21 – 31. Retrieved from https://www.globalpresshub.com/index.php/AJEFM/article/view/1102

Joecks, J., Pull, K., & Vetter, K. (2013). Gender diversity in the boardroom and firm performance: What exactly constitutes a "critical mass?". *Journal of Business Ethics, 118*(1), 61–72. doi:10.100710551-012-1553-6

Jorgenson, D. (1967). The theory of investment behavior. In *Determinants of investment behavior* (pp. 129–175). NBER.

Joseph. (2020). *Cash in the time of corona.* CEPR.

Julizaerma, M. K., & Zulkarnain, M. S. (2012). Gender diversity in the boardroom and firm performance of Malaysian public listed companies. *Procedia: Social and Behavioral Sciences, 65*, 1077–1085. doi:10.1016/j.sbspro.2012.11.374

Jurkus, A. F., Park, J. C., & Woodard, L. S. (2011). Women in top management and agency costs. *Journal of Business Research, 64*(2), 180–186. doi:10.1016/j.jbusres.2009.12.010

justcapital.com. (n.d.). *The COVID-19 Corporate Response Tracker: How America's Largest Employers Are Treating Stakeholders Amid the Coronavirus Crisis.* Retrieved from https://justcapital.com/reports/the-covid-19-corporate-response-tracker-how-americas-largest-employers-are-treating-stake/reports/the-covid-19-corporate-response-tracker-how-americas-largest-employers-are-treating-stakeholders-amid-the-coronavirus-crisis/

Kadam, S. A., & Pandey, D. (2020). Post COVID-19 opportunities and challenges formicro small medium enterprises (MSMEs) development in India. *Asian Journal of Advances in Research*, 1-4.

Kadoya, Y., & Khan, M. S. R. (2017). Explaining financial literacy in Japan: New evidence using financial knowledge, behavior, and attitude. *Behaviorand Attitude.*

Kahle, K. M., & Stulz, R. M. (2013). Access to capital, investment, and the financial crisis. *Journal of Financial Economics, 110*(2), 280–299.

Kapoor, S., & Prosad, J. M. (2017). Behavioural finance: A review. *Procedia Computer Science, 122*, 50–54. doi:10.1016/j.procs.2017.11.340

Karger, M., Lester, B., Lindsay, D., Liu, S., Weill, P. O., & Zuniga, D. (2020). *Corporate bond liquidity during the COVID-19 crisis (Paper No. 27355).* National Bureau of Economic Research.

Karkowska, R., & Urjasz, S. (2021). Connectedness structures of sovereign bond markets in Central and Eastern Europe. *International Review of Financial Analysis, 74*, 101644. doi:10.1016/j.irfa.2020.101644

Karolyi, G. A., & Stulz, R. M. (1996). Why do markets move together? An investigation of US-Japan stock return comovements. *The Journal of Finance, 51*(3), 951–986. doi:10.1111/j.1540-6261.1996.tb02713.x

Katalin Bodnár, J. L.-G. (2020). RError! Hyperlink reference not valid.etrieved from https://www.ecb.europa.eu/pub/economic-bulletin/articles/2020/html/ecb.ebart202007_01~ef0a77a516.en.html

Kaushik, M. (2020). The Impact of Pandemic COVID -19 in Workplace. *European Journal of Business Management and Research.*, *12*, 10. doi:10.7176/EJBM/12-15-02

Ke. (2022). The impact of COVID-19 on firms' cost of equity capital: Early evidence from U.S. public firms. *Finance Research Letters*.

Kennickell, A. B., Kwast, M. L., & Pogach, J. (2015). Small Businesses and Small Business finance during the financial crisis and the great depression: New evidence from the survey of consumer finances. Federal Research Organization - Center for Financial Research.

Khalfan, T., & Sturluson, J. P. (2018). Corporate finance approaches of Icelandic private firms after the financial crisis. *Managerial Finance*, *44*(11), 1274–1291. doi:10.1108/MF-05-2017-0167

Khan, A., Shaikh, M., Shah, A. B., Zahid, I., & Shaikh, F. M. (2017). Impact of Financing Decisions on Firm's Performance: An Empirical Study of Pakistani Listed Firm's in KSE. *International Journal of Management and Information Technology, 12*(1).

Khidmat, W. B., Khan, M. A., & Ullah, H. (2020). The effect of board diversity on firm performance: Evidence from Chinese listed companies. *Indian Journal of Corporate Governance*, *13*(1), 9–33. doi:10.1177/0974686220923793

Kightley & Jędrzejowicz. (n.d.). *Macroeconomic policy response to the Covid-19.* Retrieved from https://www.bis.org/publ/bppdf/bispap122_r.pdf

Killins, R. N. (2019). Firm-specific, industry-specific and macroeconomic factors of life insurers' profitability: Evidence from Canada. *The North American Journal of Economics and Finance*, *101068*. Advance online publication. doi:10.1016/j.najef.2019.101068

Klein, L. S. (2002). *Debt vs. Equity and Asymmetric Information*. Academic Press.

Kliesen, K. L., & Smith, D. C. (2010). *Measuring financial market stress. Economic Synopses.* Federal Reserve Bank of St. Louis.

Kong, Y., Antwi-Adjei, A., & Bawuah, J. (2020). A systematic review of the business case for corporate social responsibility and firm performance. *Corporate Social Responsibility and Environmental Management*, *27*(2), 444–454. doi:10.1002/csr.1838

Koop, G., & Korobilis, D. (2014). A new index of financial conditions. *European Economic Review*, *71*, 101–116. doi:10.1016/j.euroecorev.2014.07.002

Kulkarni, M. S., & Srinivas, V. (n.d.). Investor Attitude Towards Share Markets Post Covid 19 Pandemic. *Journal of Management & Entrepreneurship*, 171.

Kumthakar, S., & Nerlekar, V. (2020). Analytical Study of Investment Patterns and Investment Preferences of Retail Investors Post COVID 19. *Journal of Seybold Report*, (1533), 9211.

Kunreuther, H. a. (2018). *Mastering Catastrophic Risk: How Companies Are Coping with disruption*. Oxford University Press.

Kyere, M., & Ausloos, M. (2019). Corporate governance and firms financial performance in the United Kingdom. *International Journal of Finance & Economics*, 1–15.

KyrolainenP. J.PerttunenJ. (2003). Investors' activity and trading behavior. *Available at* SSRN 302685.

Laborda, R., & Olmo, J. (2021). Volatility spillover between economic sectors in financial crisis prediction: Evidence spanning the great financial crisis and Covid-19 pandemic. *Research in International Business and Finance*, *57*, 101402. doi:10.1016/j.ribaf.2021.101402

Lal, B.S., Sachdeva, P., & Simran, M.T., 2020. Impact of Covid-19 on micro small and medium enterprises (MSMEs): An overview. *International Journal of Multidisciplinary Research and Development*.

Lang, L. H., & Stulz, R. (1992). Contagion and competitive intra-industry effects of bankruptcy announcements: An empirical analysis. *Journal of Financial Economics*, *32*(1), 45–60. doi:10.1016/0304-405X(92)90024-R

Lan, T., Chen, Y., Li, H., Guo, L., & Huang, J. (2021). From driver to enabler: The moderating effect of corporate social responsibility on firm performance. *Economic Research-Ekonomska Istraživanja*, *34*(1), 2240–2262. doi:10.1080/1331677X.2020.1862686

Lee, S. (2007). Private sector participation in the Shanghai water sector. *Water Policy*, *9*(4), 405–423. doi:10.2166/wp.2007.015

Lee, S. B., & Kim, K. J. (1993). Does the October 1987 crash strengthen the co-movements among national stock markets? *Review of Financial Economics*, *3*(1), 89–102. doi:10.1002/j.1873-5924.1993.tb00574.x

Lee, W. C. (2002). Stock market volatility, excess returns, and the role of investor sentiment. *Journal of Banking & Finance*, *26*(12), 2277–2299.

Leszkiewicz, A., Hormann, T., & Krafft, M. (2021). Smart Business and the Social Value of AI. In *Smart Business and Better Management*. Emerald Group Publishing Ltd.

Lewis, A., & Mackenzie, C. (2000). Morals, money, ethical investing and economic psychology. *Human Relations*, *53*(2), 179–191. doi:10.1177/a010699

Li, L., Strahan, P., & Zhang, S. (2020). Bank as lenders of first resort: Evidence from the crisis. *Review of Corporate Finance Studies*, (9), 472–501.

Li, C., & Ongena, S. (2015). Bank loan announcements and borrower stock returns before and during the recent financial crisis. *Journal of Financial Stability*, *21*, 1–12. doi:10.1016/j.jfs.2015.09.006

Li, H., & Chen, P. (2018). Board gender diversity and firm performance: The moderating role of firm size. *Business Ethics (Oxford, England)*, *27*(4), 294–308. doi:10.1111/beer.12188

Li, L. (2018). Private sector participation and performance of county water utilities in China. *China Economic Review*, *52*, 30–53. doi:10.1016/j.chieco.2018.06.001

Li, L., Strahan, P. E., & Zhang, S. (2020). Banks as Lenders of First Resort: Evidence from the COVID-19 Crisis. *The Review of Corporate Finance Studies*, *9*(3), 472–500. doi:10.1093/rcfs/cfaa009

Lin, B., & Su, T. (2021). Does COVID-19 open a Pandora's box of changing the connectedness in energy commodities? *Research in International Business and Finance*, *56*, 101360. doi:10.1016/j.ribaf.2020.101360 PMID:36540766

Lin, D., & Lin, L. (2016). How does Corporate Governance Affect Free Cash Flow? *Journal of Applied Finance & Banking.*, *6*(3), 145–156.

Lins, K. V., Servaes, H., & Tamayo, A. (2017). Social capital, trust, and firm performance: The value of corporate social responsibility during the financial crisis. *The Journal of Finance*, 1785–1824.

Liu, F., Kong, D., Xiao, Z., Zhang, X., Zhou, A., & Qi, J. (2022). Effect of economic policies on the stock and bond market under the impact of COVID-19. *Journal of Safety Science and Resilience*, *3*(1), 24–38. doi:10.1016/j.jnlssr.2021.10.006

Liu, Y., Wei, Z., & Xie, F. (2014). Do women directors improve firm performance in China? *Journal of Corporate Finance*, *28*(C), 169–184. doi:10.1016/j.jcorpfin.2013.11.016

Liu, Z., Huynh, T. L. D., & Dai, P. F. (2021). The impact of COVID-19 on the stock market crash risk in China. *Research in International Business and Finance*, *57*, 101419. doi:10.1016/j.ribaf.2021.101419 PMID:34744246

Li, X., Cheng, B., & Xu, H. (2021). Time-Based Corporate-Social-Responsibility Evaluation Model Taking Chinese Listed Forestry Companies as an Example. *Sustainability*, *13*(14), 7971. doi:10.3390u13147971

Li, X., Li, B., Wei, G., Bai, L., Wei, Y., & Liang, C. (2021). Return connectedness among commodity and financial assets during the COVID-19 pandemic: Evidence from China and the US. *Resources Policy*, *73*, 102166. doi:10.1016/j.resourpol.2021.102166 PMID:34539034

Low, D. C., Roberts, H., & Whiting, R. H. (2015). Board gender diversity and firm performance: Empirical evidence from Hong Kong, South Korea, Malaysia and Singapore. *Pacific-Basin Finance Journal, 35*(A), 381-401.

Low, S. P., Liu, J., & Sio, S. (2010). Business continuity management in large construction companies in Singapore. *Disaster Prevention and Management*, *19*(2), 219–232. doi:10.1108/09653561011038011

Loy, T. R., & Rupertus, H. (2020). How Does the Stock Market Value Female Directors? International Evidence. *Business & Society*, *00*(0), 1–38.

Lu, D., & Bao, Y. (2018). *Board gender diversity and firm performance: Evidence from Chinese Firms*. Retrieved from https://www.semanticscholar.org/paper/Board-Gender-Diversity-and-Firm-Performance-%3A-from-Lu-Bao/f607cc4569ff4bc2dcdb97 8e4bba5a9338ed02f2

Lueg, K., & Lueg, R. (2020). Detecting green-washing or substantial organizational communication: A Model for testing two-way interaction between risk and sustainability reporting. *Sustainability*, *12*(6), 1–9. doi:10.3390u12062520

Lukasz RawdanowiczD. P. (2021, June 22). Retrieved from https://cepr.org/voxeu/columns/covid-19-and-corporate-sector -where-we-stand

Luo, A. (2019, July 18). *Content Analysis: A Step-by-Step Guide with Examples*. Retrieved from https://www.scribbr.com/methodology/content-analysis/

Magd, H., & Karyamsetty, H. (2021). Assessing the Significance of Corporate Social Responsibility Actions to Achieve Sustainable Business and Organizational Performance during the COVID-19 Pandemic in Oman. *Global Business and Management Research*, *13*(3).

Magkonis, G., & Tsopanakis, A. (2020). The financial connectedness between Eurozone core and periphery: A disaggregated view. *Macroeconomic Dynamics*, *24*(7), 1674–1699. doi:10.1017/S1365100518000998

Manuel, T., & Herron, T. L. (2020). An ethical perspective of business CSR and the COVID-19 pandemic. *Society and Business Review, 15*(3), 235-253.

Maruti Suzuki India Limited. (n.d.). https://www.marutisuzuki.com/

McCarthy, N. (2020). COVID-19's Impact On Tourism: Which Countries Are The Most Vulnerable? *Forbes*. Retrieved from https://www.forbes.com/sites/niallmccarthy/2020/05/05/covid-19s-impact-on-tourism-which-countries-are-the-most-vulnerabl e-infographic/?sh=641bfa6d1906

McKibbin & Fernando. (2020, March 2). *The Global Macroeconomic Impacts of COVID-19: Seven scenarios*. Retrieved from https://www.brookings.edu/wp-content/uploads/2020/03/2020030 2_covid19.pdf

Mehran, H., Morrison, A.D., & Shapiro, J.D. (2011). *Corporate governance and banks: What have we learned from the financial crisis?* FRB of New York Staff Report, (502).

Mehta & Shah. (2012). Preference of Investors for Indian Mutual Funds and its performance evaluation. *Pacific Business Review International*, *5*(3), 62–76.

Mensi, W., Al-Yahyaee, K. H., Vo, X. V., & Kang, S. H. (2020). Dynamic spillover and connectedness between oil futures and European Bonds. *The North American Journal of Economics and Finance*, 101342.

Mensi, W., Reboredo, J. C., & Ugolini, A. (2021). Price-switching spillovers between gold, oil, and stock markets: Evidence from the USA and China during the COVID-19 pandemic. *Resources Policy*, *73*, 102217. doi:10.1016/j.resourpol.2021.102217 PMID:36567727

Mercy Ogunnusi, T. O.-A. (2021). Lessons learned from the impact of COVID-19 on the global construction industry. *Journal of Engineering, Design and Technology*.

Merlo, P. D.-D. (2013). *Probabilistic and statistical methods of risk analysis in the investments effectiveness evaluation and their application in business practice*. Academic Press.

Metawa, N., Hassan, M. K., Metawa, S., & Safa, M. F. (2019). Impact of behavioral factors on investors' financial decisions: Case of the Egyptian stock market. *International Journal of Islamic and Middle Eastern Finance and Management*, *12*(1), 30–35.

Michael Halling, J. Y. (2020). How Did COVID-19 Affect Firms' Access to Public Capital Markets. *The Review of Corporate Finance Studies*, *9*(3), 501–533.

Mili, M., Sahut, J.-M., & Teulon, F. (2017). Do corporate governance and ownership structure impact dividend policy in emerging markets during the financial crisis? *Journal of Applied Accounting Research*, *18*(3), 274–293. doi:10.1108/JAAR-07-2014-0079

Miller, T., & del Carmen Triana, M. (2009). Demographic diversity in the boardroom: Mediators of the board diversity firm performance relationship. *Journal of Management Studies*, *46*(5), 755–786. doi:10.1111/j.1467-6486.2009.00839.x

Milliken, F. J., & Martins, L. L. (1996). Searching for common threads: Understanding the multiple effects of diversity in organizational groups. *Academy of Management Review*, *21*(2), 402–433. doi:10.2307/258667

Mini. (2020). A study on the awareness of mutual funds investment in India. *International Journal of Scientific & Technology Research, 9*(1).

Minoiu, C., Kang, C., Subrahmanian, V. S., & Berea, A. (2015). Does financial connectedness predict crises? *Quantitative Finance*, *15*(4), 607–624. doi:10.1080/14697688.2014.968358

Mint. (2020). *Covid impact on MSMEs*. Available at https://www.livemint.com/opinion/online-views/opinion-covid-and-its-impact-on-economy-and-msmes-11603604611652.html

Mirza, N. H. (2020). The impact of human capital efficiency on Latin American mutual funds during Covid-19 outbreak. *Schweizerische Zeitschrift für Volkswirtschaft und Statistik*, *156*(1), 16.

Mishra, S., & Suar, D. (2010). Does corporate social responsibiliinfluencethe e the firm performance of Indian companies? *Journal of Business Ethics*, *95*(4), 571–601. doi:10.100710551-010-0441-1

Mistry & Vyas. (2021). Factors Affecting Capital structure decision: Empirical evidence from Indian oil and gas sector. *International Journal of Financial Management, 11*(2), 13-18.

Mitalbhayani. (2017). A study of recent trends in Indian Mutual Fund Industry. *International Research Journal of Engineering and Technology, 4*(4).

Money Control. (n.d.). www.moneycontrol.com

Monin, P. J. (2019). The OFR financial stress index. *Risks*, *7*(1), 25. doi:10.3390/risks7010025

Moore, S. (n.d.). *News-Medical.net – An AZonetwork site.* https://www.news-medical.net/amp/health/History-of-COVID-19.aspx

Mudamakin, A. K. B., Wulandari, A. A., & Poeh, M. M. (2022). Capital Structure Analysis of Manufacturing Firms Listed on the Indonesia Stock Exchange (Idx) in the Covid-19 Pandemic Era. *International Conference on Applied Science and Technology on Social Science 2021, 647*, 256-259.

Muellbauer, J. (2020, April). *The coronavirus pandemic and US consumption.* Retrieved from VoxEU.org: https://voxeu.org/article/coronavirus-pandemic-and-us-consumption

Mueller, A., & Sensini, L. (2021). Determinants of financing decisions of SMEs: Evidence from hotel industry. *International Journal of Business and Management*, *16*(3), 117–127.

Muñoz, R. M., Fernández, M. V., & Salinero, Y. (2021). Sustainability, Corporate Social Responsibility, and Performance in the Spanish Wine Sector. *Sustainability*, *13*(1), 7. doi:10.3390u13010007

Murungi, D. (2014). *Relationship between macroeconomic variables and financial performance of insurance companies in Kenya*. Academic Press.

Myers, S. C., & Majluf, N. S. (1984). Corporate financing and investment decisions when firms have information the investors do not have. *NBER Working Paper Series, 1396*(38), 3295-3296.

Myers, S. C. (1984). The capital structure puzzle. *The Journal of Finance*, *39*(3), 574–592.

Naeem, M. A., Qureshi, S., Rehman, M. U., & Balli, F. (2022). COVID-19 and cryptocurrency market: Evidence from quantile connectedness. *Applied Economics*, *54*(3), 280–306. doi:10.1080/00036846.2021.1950908

Narayan, P. K., Devpura, N., & Wang, H. (2020). Japanese currency and stock market—What happened during the COVID-19 pandemic? *Economic Analysis and Policy*, *68*, 191–198. doi:10.1016/j.eap.2020.09.014 PMID:33012962

Nelson, R. A. (1989). On the Measurement of Capacity Utilization. *The Journal of Industrial Economics*, 273–286.

Neves, M. E., Serrasqueiro, Z., Dias, A., & Hermano, C. (2020). Capital structure decisions in a period of economic intervention: Empirical evidence of Portuguese companies with panel data. *International Journal of Accounting & Information Management*, *28*(3), 465–495.

Nguyen, T., Locke, S., & Reddy, K. (2015). Does boardroom gender diversity matter? Evidence from a transitional economy. *International Review of Economics & Finance*, *37*(C), 184–202. doi:10.1016/j.iref.2014.11.022

Nunnally, J. (1960). The place of statistics in psychology. *Educational and Psychological Measurement*, *20*(4), 641–650. doi:10.1177/001316446002000401

Nurlaela, S., Mursito, B., Kustiyah, E., Istiqomah, I., & Hartono, S. (2019). Asset turnover, capital structure and financial performance consumption industry company in Indonesia Stock Exchange. *International Journal of Economics and Financial Issues*, *9*(3), 297–301. doi:10.32479/ijefi.8185

Odera, E. O. (2011). *The behaviour and financial performance of individual investors in Kenya* [Doctoral dissertation]. University of Nairobi.

OECD. (2020). *Tourism Policy Responses to the Coronavirus (Covid 19)*. Retrieved from https://www.oecd.org/coronavirus/policy-responses/tourism-policy-responses-to-the-coronavirus-covid-19-6466aa20/

OECD. (2021). *The COVID-19 crisis and banking system resilience: simulation of losses on non-performing loans and policy implications*. OECD.

OECD. (2022, June 24). *Corporate Finance in Asia and the COVID-19 Crisis*. Retrieved from Corporate Finance in Asia and the COVID-19 Crisis: https://www.oecd-ilibrary.org/sites/87861cf0-en/index.html?itemId=/content/publication/87861cf0-en

Oet, M. V., Dooley, J. M., & Ong, S. J. (2015). The financial stress index: Identification of systemic risk conditions. *Risks*, *3*(3), 420–444. doi:10.3390/risks3030420

Oh. (2020). *Financial management operations under the COVID-19 pandemic: The Korean Experience*. iadb.org

Olstein, M., Jennings, J., & Geist, R. (2009). *Improving water utility capital efficiency*. Water Research Foundation.

Ozili, P., & Arun, T. (2020). *Spillover of COVID-19: Impact on the Global Economy (No. 99317)*. University Library of Munich.

Pagach, D., & Wieczorek, M. (2020). The Challenges and Opportunities for ERM Post COVID 19: Agenda for future research. *Journal of Risk and Financial Management*.

Paisarn, W., Chancharat, N., & Chancharat, S. (2021). Factors Influencing Retail Investors' Trading Behaviour in the Thai Stock Market. *Australasian Accounting, Business and Finance Journal*, *15*(2), 26–37. doi:10.14453/aabfj.v15i2.3

Panjaitan, R., & Simbolon, I. P. (2020). Financing and Herd behavior in financial crises: Invesstment decision. *International Journal of Economics and Business Administration*, *8*(4), 1089–1096.

Park, C. Y., & Mercado, R. V. Jr. (2014). Determinants of financial stress in emerging market economies. *Journal of Banking & Finance*, *45*, 199–224. doi:10.1016/j.jbankfin.2013.09.018

Parrotta, J. L., & Johnson, P. J. (1998). The impact of financial attitudes and knowledge on financial management and satisfaction of recently married individuals. *Financial Counseling and Planning*, *9*(2), 59.

Patel & Divyesh. (2020). *COVID-19 and Corporate Governance (India): Practical Issues, Implications and New Relief Measures*. Academic Press.

Patnaik, A. (2022). Measuring Demand and Supply Shocks From COVID-19: An Industry-Level Analysis for India. *Margin: The Journal of Applied Economic Research*, 76-105. doi:10.1177/09738010211067392

Pearson, C. M. (1998). Reframing Crisis Management. *Academy of Management Review*, *23*(1), 59–76. doi:10.5465/amr.1998.192960

Peda, P., Grossi, G., & Liik, M. (2013). Do ownership and size affect the performance of water utilities? Evidence from Estonian municipalities. *The Journal of Management and Governance*, *17*(2), 237–259. doi:10.100710997-011-9173-6

Perryman, A. A., Fernando, G. D., & Tripathy, A. (2016). Do gender differences persist? An examination of gender diversity on firm performance, risk, and executive compensation. *Journal of Business Research*, *69*(2), 579–586. doi:10.1016/j.jbusres.2015.05.013

Peymankar, M., Davari, M., & Ranjbar, M. (2021). Maximizing the expected net present value in a project with uncertain cash flows. *European Journal of Operational Research*, *294*(2), 442–452. doi:10.1016/j.ejor.2021.01.039

Pfeffer, J., & Salancik, G. R. (1978). *The external control of organizations: A resource dependence perspective*. Harper & Row.

Pinzaru, F. &. (2020). *The Impact of The COVID-19 Pandemic on Business. A Preliminary Overview*. Academic Press.

Polat, O. (2019). Systemic risk contagion in FX market: A frequency connectedness and network analysis. *Bulletin of Economic Research*, *71*(4), 585–598. doi:10.1111/boer.12197

Polat, O. (2020). Measuring dynamic connectedness networks in energy commodities: Evidence from the D-Y and frequency connectedness approaches. *OPEC Energy Review*, *44*(4), 404–428. doi:10.1111/opec.12188

Polat, O., & Ozkan, I. (2019). Transmission mechanisms of financial stress into economic activity in Turkey. *Journal of Policy Modeling*, *41*(2), 395–415. doi:10.1016/j.jpolmod.2019.02.010

Porumboiu, C. (2020). *The importance of emerging industries: The case of biopharma*. European Business Perspective, Springer Open.

Post, C., & Byron, K. (2015). Women on boards and firm financial performance: A meta-analysis. *Academy of Management Journal*, *58*(5), 1546–1571. doi:10.5465/amj.2013.0319

Puy, D., & Rawdanowicz, L. (2021, June 21). *Covid-19 and the corporate sector: Where we stand.* Retrieved from https://voxeu.org/article/covid-19-and-corporate-sector-wher e-we-stand

Rai, K., Dua, S., & Yadav, M. (2019). Association of financial attitude, financial behaviour and financial knowledge towards financial literacy: A structural equation modeling approach. *FIIB Business Review*, *8*(1), 51–60. doi:10.1177/2319714519826651

Rai, K., & Garg, B. (2021). Dynamic correlations and volatility spillovers between stock price and exchange rate in BRIICS economies: Evidence from the COVID-19 outbreak period. *Applied Economics Letters*, 1–8.

RBI. (2020). *Report of the expert committee on resolution framework for COVID-19 related stress.* Retrieved from https://rbidocs.rbi.org.in/rdocs/PublicationReport/Pdfs/EXPE RTCOMMITTEED58A96778C5E4799AE0E3FCC13DC67F2.PDF

Rebucci, A., Hartley, J. S., & Jiménez, D. (2021). *An event study of COVID-19 central bank quantitative easing in advanced and emerging economies.* NBER Working Paper 27339.

Remund, D. L. (2010). Financial literacy explicated: The case for a clearer definition in an increasingly complex economy. *The Journal of Consumer Affairs*, *44*(2), 276–295. doi:10.1111/ j.1745-6606.2010.01169.x

Reza, R. (2017). *An Investigation of water investment performance: Analysis of the global water industry* [PhD Thesis]. Griffith University. Retrieved from https://research-repository.griffith. edu.au/handle/10072/371256

Romano, G., & Guerrini, A. (2014). The effects of ownership, board size and board composition on the performance of Italian water utilities. *Utilities Policy*, *31*, 18–28. doi:10.1016/j.jup.2014.06.002

Romano, G., Guerrini, A., & Leardini, C. (2015). Exploring the link between corporate governance and efficiency of Italian water utilities. *Agua y Territorio*, *6*(6), 123–132. doi:10.17561/at.v0i6.2815

Roy, S. (2020). *Economic impact of Covid 19.* Academic Press.

Sabetti, J. M. (2010, May 13). *Corporate Finance During COVID-19: Considerations For Raising Capital During A Time Of Crisis.* Retrieved from Corporate Finance During COVID-19: Considerations For Raising Capital During A Time Of Crisis: https://www.mondaq.com/canada/securities/932868/corporate-fi nance-during-covid-19-considerations-for-raising-capital-dur ing-a-time-of-crisis

Sahoo, J. (2021). Financial stress index, growth and price stability in India: Some recent evidence. *Transnational Corporations Review*, *13*(2), 222–236. doi:10.1080/19186444.2020.1768789

Sakurai, Y., & Kurosaki, T. (2020). How has the relationship between oil and the US stock market changed after the Covid-19 crisis? *Finance Research Letters*, *37*, 101773. doi:10.1016/j.frl.2020.101773 PMID:33046963

Salam, A. F., Ikmat, H., Haquei, I., Badariah, F., Nurjaya, E., Manan, A., ... Purwanto, A. (2021). The influence of share ownership, funding decisions, CSR and financial performance of Food Industry. *Annals of RSCB*, *25*(4), 12698–12710.

Salam, M. A., & Bajaba, S. (2021). Corporate social responsibility during the COVID-19 pandemic: A sequential mediation analysis. *Social Responsibility Journal.*

Salman, A., & Ali, Q. (2021). Covid-19 and its impact on the stock market in GCC. *Journal of Sustainable Finance & Investment*, 1-17.

Samitas, A., Kampouris, E., & Polyzos, S. (2022). Covid-19 pandemic and spillover effects in stock markets: A financial network approach. *International Review of Financial Analysis*, *80*, 102005. doi:10.1016/j.irfa.2021.102005 PMID:36536788

Santa, J. F. (2021). Financial crisis and capital structure decisions. *BMEP*, 67-96.

Santos, A., & Cincera, M. (2021). Determinants of financing constraints. *Small Business Economics*, 1-13. doi:10.1007/s11187-021-00449-w

Sarwar, S., Tiwari, A. K., & Tingqiu, C. (2020). Analyzing volatility spillovers between oil market and Asian stock markets. *Resources Policy*, *66*, 101608. doi:10.1016/j.resourpol.2020.101608

Saturwa, H. N., Suharno, S., & Ahmad, A. A. (2021). The impact of Covid-19 pandemic on MSMEs. *Jurnal Ekonomi Dan Bisnis*, *24*(1), 65–82. doi:10.24914/jeb.v24i1.3905

Schoemaker, P. J., & Russo, J. E. (2016). *Decision Making*. The Palgrave Encyclopaedia of Strategic Management. doi:10.1057/978-1-349-94848-2

Seetanah, B. S. (2014). *Capital structure and firm performance: Evidence from an emerging economy*. Academic Press.

Seetharaman, G. (2020, March 14). How different sectors of the economy are bearing the brunt of the coronavirus outbreak. *The Economic Times.*

Seraj, A. H. A., Alzain, E., & Alshebami, A. S. (2022, September 30). The roles of financial literacy and overconfidence in investment decisions in Saudi Arabia. *Frontiers in Psychology*, *13*, 1005075. doi:10.3389/fpsyg.2022.1005075 PMID:36248580

Sethi, A., & Verma, P. (2018). Role of MSME's In Economic Growth Of India. *Journal of Ravishankar University*, *24*(1), 19–26. doi:10.52228/JRUA.2018-24-1-4

Shafi, M., Liu, J., & Ren, W. (2020). Impact of COVID-19 pandemic on micro, small, and medium-sized enterprises in Pakistan. *Research in Globalization*, *2*(2), 1–15. doi:10.1016/j.resglo.2020.100018

Shahzad, S. J. H., Naeem, M. A., Peng, Z., & Bouri, E. (2021). Asymmetric volatility spillover among Chinese sectors during COVID-19. *International Review of Financial Analysis*, *75*, 101754. doi:10.1016/j.irfa.2021.101754 PMID:36568735

Sharma, P. D. P., & Rao, D. N. (2014). A Study of Risk Orientation of Retail Investors in Indian Mutual Fund Industry with Special Reference to Rajasthan, India. India.

Sharma, Y. S. (2020, July 25). Research on Pandemics Special Issue of the Journal Emerging Markets Finance and Trade. *Emerging Markets Finance & Trade*, 2133–2137. https://www.tandfonline.com/

Sha, S. S. (2020). Part A: Special Section on COVID-19 Research. *Emerging Markets Finance & Trade*, *56*(15), 3551–3553.

Shelly, R., Sharma, T., & Bawa, S. S. (2020). Role of micro, small and medium enterprises in Indian economy. *International Journal of Economics and Financial Issues*, *10*(5), 84–91. doi:10.32479/ijefi.10459

Shohini Roy, D. D. (2020). *Economic Impact of Covid 19 Pandemic*. Retrieved from https://www.researchgate.net/publication/343222400_ECONOMIC_IMPACT_OF_COVID-19_PANDEMIC

Shrader, C. B., Blackburn, V. B., & Iles, P. (1997). Women in management and firm financial value: An exploratory study. *Journal of Managerial Issues*, *9*(3), 355–372.

Si, D. K., Li, X. L., Xu, X., & Fang, Y. (2021). The risk spillover effect of the COVID-19 pandemic on energy sector: Evidence from China. *Energy Economics*, *102*, 105498. doi:10.1016/j.eneco.2021.105498 PMID:34898735

Simpson, W. G., Carter, D., & D'Souza, F. P. (2010). What do we know about women on boards? *Journal of Applied Finance (JAF)*, *20*(2), 27–39.

Singh, L. B., Mondal, S. R., & Das, S. (2020). Human resource practices & their observed significance for Indian SMEs. *Revista ESPACIOS, 41*(7).

Singh, V., & Vinnicombe, S. (2004). Why so few women directors in top UK boardrooms? Evidence and theoretical explanations. *Corporate Governance*, *12*(4), 479–488. doi:10.1111/j.1467-8683.2004.00388.x

Siregar, R. Y., Gunawan, A. H., & Saputro, A. N. (2021). Impact of the COVID-19 shock on banking and corporate sector vulnerabilities in Indonesia. *Bulletin of Indonesian Economic Studies*, *57*(2), 147–173. doi:10.1080/00074918.2021.1956397

Sivaprasad & Mathew. (2021). Corporate Governance. *The International Journal of Business in Society*.

Skagerlund, K., Lind, T., Strömbäck, C., Tinghög, G., & Västfjäll, D. (2018). Financial literacy and the role of numeracy–How individuals' attitude and affinity with numbers influence financial literacy. *Journal of Behavioral and Experimental Economics*, *74*, 18–25. doi:10.1016/j.socec.2018.03.004

SMB. (2021). *Government schemes to help MSMEs tide over COVID-19 woes*. Available at https://yourstory.com/smbstory/government-schemes-help-msmes-tide-over-covid-lockdown/amp

Smirlock, M. (1985). Evidence on the (Non) Relationship between Concentration and Profitability in Banking. *Journal of Money, Credit, and Banking*, *17*(1), 69-83.

So, M. K., Tiwari, A., Chu, A. M., Tsang, J. T., & Chan, J. N. (2020). Visualizing COVID-19 pandemic risk through network connectedness. *International Journal of Infectious Diseases*, *96*, 558–561. doi:10.1016/j.ijid.2020.05.011 PMID:32437929

Soni, P. (2021, January 6). *Effects of COVID-19 lockdown phases in India: an atmospheric perspective*. Retrieved from https://www.ncbi.nlm.nih.gov/pmc/articles/PMC7785398/

Sonobe, T., Takeda, A., Yoshida, S., & Truong, H. T. (2021). *The impacts of the Covid-19 pandemic on micro, small, and medium enterprises in Asia and their digitalization responses*. Academic Press.

Sridevi. (2018). Performance Analysis of Mutual Funds- A Study On Selected Mid Cap And Small Cap Funds. *International Journal of Business And Management Invention*, *7*(7).

Stiles, P., & Taylor, B. (2001). *Boards at work: how directors view their roles and responsibilities*. Oxford University Press.

Stolbov, M., & Shchepeleva, M. (2016). Financial stress in emerging markets: Patterns, real effects, and cross-country spillovers. *Review of Development Finance*, *6*(1), 71–81. doi:10.1016/j.rdf.2016.05.004

Strömbäck, C., Lind, T., Skagerlund, K., Västfjäll, D., & Tinghög, G. (2017). Does self-control predict financial behavior and financial well-being? *Journal of Behavioral and Experimental Finance*, *14*, 30–38. doi:10.1016/j.jbef.2017.04.002

Sullivan, C., Cohen, A., Jean-Marc Faurès, J., & Santini, G. (2008). *The rural water livelihoods index*. FAO Working Paper.

Sundarajan, V. a. (2002). Islamic financial institutions and products in the global Financial System: Key Issues in Risk Management and Challenges Ahead. *IMF Working Paper*, *2*, 1–27.

Supriadi, L. S., & Peng, L. S. (2018). Business Continuity Management (BCM). In *Business Continuity Management in Construction. Management in the Built Environment* (pp. 41–73). Springer. doi:10.1007/978-981-10-5487-7_3

Susmel, R., & Engle, R. F. (1994). Hourly volatility spillovers between international equity markets. *Journal of International Money and Finance*, *13*(1), 3–25. doi:10.1016/0261-5606(94)90021-3

Tajfel, H. (1981). *Human groups and social categories*. Cambridge University Press.

Talwar, M., Talwar, S., Kaur, P., Tripathy, N., & Dhir, A. (2021). Has financial attitude impacted the trading activity of retail investors during the COVID-19 pandemic? *Journal of Retailing and Consumer Services*, *58*, 102341. doi:10.1016/j.jretconser.2020.102341

Tampakoudis, I., Noulas, A., & Kiosses, N. (2022). The market reaction to syndicated loan announcements before and during the COVID-19 pandemic and the role of corporate governance. *Research in International Business and Finance*, *60*, 1–25. doi:10.1016/j.ribaf.2021.101602 PMID:34975188

Tata Capital. (2021). *What Would Be the Role of SMEs in Changing India's Economic*. Author.

Terjesen, S., Sealy, R., & Singh, V. (2009). Women directors on corporate boards: A review and research agenda. *Corporate Governance*, *17*(3), 320–337. doi:10.1111/j.1467-8683.2009.00742.x

Thanh, T. L., Huan, N. Q., & Hong, T. T. T. (2021). Effects of corporate social responsibility on SMEs' performance in an emerging market. *Cogent Business & Management*, *8*(1), 1878978. doi:10.1080/23311975.2021.1878978

The COVID-19 Corporate Response Tracker: How America's Largest Employers Are Treating Stakeholders Amid the Coronavirus Crisis. (n.d.). Retrieved from https://justcapital.com/reports/the-covid-19-corporate-response-tracker-how-americas-largest-employers-are-treating-stakeholders-amid-the-coronavirus-crisis/

The Investopedia Team. (2022, May 17). *Investopedia*. https://www.investopedia.com/ask/answers/03/062003.asp

Thukral, E. (2021). COVID-19: Small and medium enterprises challenges and responses with creativity, innovation and entrepreneurship. *Strategic Change*, *30*(2), 153–158. doi:10.1002/jsc.2399

Titman, S., & Wessels, R. (1988). The determinants of capital structure Choice. *The Journal of Finance*, *43*(1), 1–19.

Toma, M. (2003). *Finanţe şi gestiune financiară*. Economica.

Tongkong, S. (2012). Key factors influencing capital structure decision and its speed of adjustment of Thai listed real estate companies. *Procedia: Social and Behavioral Sciences*, *40*, 716–720.

Úbeda-García, M., Claver-Cortés, E., Marco-Lajara, B., & Zaragoza-Sáez, P. (2021). Corporate social responsibility and firm performance in the hotel industry. The mediating role of green human resource management and environmental outcomes. *Journal of Business Research*, *123*(C), 57–69. doi:10.1016/j.jbusres.2020.09.055

Umar, Z., & Gubareva, M. (2021). Faith-based investments and the Covid-19 pandemic: Analyzing equity volatility and media coverage time-frequency relations. *Pacific-Basin Finance Journal*, *67*, 101571. doi:10.1016/j.pacfin.2021.101571

Umar, Z., Riaz, Y., & Zaremba, A. (2021). Spillover and risk transmission in the components of the term structure of eurozone yield curve. *Applied Economics*, *53*(18), 2141–2157. doi:10.1080/00036846.2020.1856322

UN. (2015). *Water and sustainable development*. Retrieved from https://www.un.org/waterforlifedecade/water_and_sustainable_development.shtml

Usman, M. (2019). The Impact of Capital Structure on Financial Performance of Consumer Goods Industry in Nigeria. *Open Journal of Accounting*, *8*, 47–62.

Vafaei, A., Ahmed, K., & Mather, P. (2015). Board diversity and financial performance in the top 500 Australian firms'. *Australian Accounting Review*, *75*(25), 413–427. doi:10.1111/auar.12068

van Roye, B. (2014). Financial stress and economic activity in Germany. *Empirica*, *41*(1), 101–126. doi:10.100710663-013-9224-0

van Wees, H. H. (2020). Global health beyond geographical boundaries: Reflections from global health education. *BMJ Global Health*, *5*(5), 3.

Venclova, K., & Urbancova. (2013). Advantages and disadvantages of Business Continuity Management. *International Journal of Industrial and Systems Engineering*, *7*(4).

Vuong. (2022). Investor sentiment, corporate social responsibility, and financial performance: Evidence from Japanese companies, Borsa Istanbul Review, 22(5), 911-924.

Wang, D. (2010). Corporate investment, financing, and dividend policies in the high-tech industry. *Journal of Business Research*, *63*(5), 486–489. doi:10.1016/j.jbusres.2009.04.006

Wang, G. J., Xie, C., Zhao, L., & Jiang, Z. Q. (2018). Volatility connectedness in the Chinese banking system: Do state-owned commercial banks contribute more? *Journal of International Financial Markets, Institutions and Money*, *57*, 205–230. doi:10.1016/j.intfin.2018.07.008

Wang, H., Wu, W., & Zheng, S. (2011). An econometric analysis of private sector participation in China's urban water supply. *Utilities Policy*, *19*(3), 134–14. doi:10.1016/j.jup.2011.01.004

Wang, Y., Pan, Z., & Wu, C. (2018). Volatility spillover from the US to international stock markets: A heterogeneous volatility spillover GARCH model. *Journal of Forecasting*, *37*(3), 385–400. doi:10.1002/for.2509

weforum. (2020). *Impact of COVID-19 on the Global Financial System*. Retrieved from https://www3.weforum.org/docs/WEF_Impact_of_COVID_19_on_the_Global_Financial_System_2020.pdf

Wei, A. P., Peng, C. L., Huang, H. C., & Yeh, S. P. (2020). Effects of corporate social responsibility on firm performance: Does customer satisfaction matter? *Sustainability*, *12*(18), 7545. doi:10.3390u12187545

Wei, Z., Luo, Y., Huang, Z., & Guo, K. (2020). Spillover effects of RMB exchange rate among B&R countries: Before and during COVID-19 event. *Finance Research Letters*, *37*, 101782. doi:10.1016/j.frl.2020.101782 PMID:33013238

Wen, T., & Wang, G. J. (2020). Volatility connectedness in global foreign exchange markets. *Journal of Multinational Financial Management*, *54*, 100617. doi:10.1016/j.mulfin.2020.100617

Wilaiporn, P., Nongnit, C., & Surachai, C. (2021). *Factors Influencing Retail Investors' Trading Behaviour in the Thai Stock Market.* Academic Press.

World Economic Forum. (2016). *China has a water crisis - how can it be solved?* Retrieved from https://www.weforum.org/agenda/2016/04/china-has-a-water-crisis-how-can-it-be-solved/

World Health Organisation. (2020, April 27). https://www.who.int/news/item/27-04-2020-who-timeline---covid-19

Wronska-Bukalska, E., & Mazurkiewicz, K. (2018). Corporate Capital Structure Changes during financial crisis: Case of Polish Companies. *Managing Global Transitions - International Research Journal, 16*(1), 19-35. doi:10.26492/1854-6935.16_1

Wronska-Bukalska, E., & Mazurkiewicz, K. (2018). Corproate capital structure changes during crisis times: Case of Polish companies. *Managing Global Transitions - International Research Journal, 16*(1), 19-35.

Wu, F. (2020). Stock market integration in East and Southeast Asia: The role of global factors. *International Review of Financial Analysis*, *67*, 101416. doi:10.1016/j.irfa.2019.101416

Wyman, O. (2020). *To Recovery and Beyond the future of travel & tourism in the wake of COVID 19.* Retrieved from https://wttc.org/Portals/0/Documents/Reports/2020/To%20Recovery%20and%20Beyond-The%20Future%20of%20Travel%20Tourism%20in%20the%20Wake%20of%20COVID-19.pdf?ver=2021-02-25-183120-543

Xiang, Rasoo, Hang, Javid, Javed, & Artene. (2021, May 6). *The Effect of COVID-19 Pandemic on Service Sector Sustainability and Growth.* Retrieved from https://www.frontiersin.org/articles/10.3389/fpsyg.2021.633597/full

Xu, Q., & Abbasov, S. (2021). Impact of COVID-19 pandemic on small and medium sized enterprises (SMEs) in Azerbaijan. *Open Journal of Business and Management*, *9*(6), 2759–2771. doi:10.4236/ojbm.2021.96153

Yang, M., Bento, P., & Akbar, A. (2019). Does CSR influence firm performance indicators? Evidence from Chinese pharmaceutical enterprises. *Sustainability*, *11*(20), 5656. doi:10.3390u11205656

Ying, M., Tikuye, G. A., & Shan, H. (2021). Impacts of firm performance on Corporate Social Responsibility Practices: The mediation role of Corporate Governance in Ethiopia corporate business. *Sustainability*, *13*(17), 9717. doi:10.3390u13179717

Yong, C. C., Yew, S. Y., & Wee, C. K. (2018). Financial knowledge, attitude and behaviour of young working adults in Malaysia. *Institutions and Economies, 10*(4).

Yoon, S. M., Al Mamun, M., Uddin, G. S., & Kang, S. H. (2019). Network connectedness and net spillover between financial and commodity markets. *The North American Journal of Economics and Finance*, *48*, 801–818. doi:10.1016/j.najef.2018.08.012

Yu, A. L., & Liu, D. L. (2006). *The privatization of water supply in China*. Retrieved from https://www.business-humanrights.org/en/latest-news/pdf-the-privatization-of-water-supply-in-china/

Yuesti, A., Ni, W. R., & Suryandari, N. N. A. (2020). Financial literacy in the COVID-19 pandemic: Pressure conditions in Indonesia. *Entrepreneurship and Sustainability Issues*, *8*(1), 884–898. doi:10.9770/jesi.2020.8.1(59)

Zamfir, M., Manea, M. D., & Ionescu, L. (2016). Return on investment – Indicator for measuring the profitability of invested capital, *Valahian. Journal of Economic Studies (Glasgow, Scotland)*, *0*(21), 79–86.

Zhang, D., & Broadstock, D. C. (2018). Global financial crisis and rising connectedness in the international commodity markets. *International Review of Financial Analysis*, 101239.

Zhang, D., Hu, M., & Ji, Q. (2020). Financial markets under the global pandemic of COVID- 19. *Finance Research Letters*, *36*, 101528. doi:10.1016/j.frl.2020.101528 PMID:32837360

Zhang, H., Chen, J., & Shao, L. (2021). Dynamic spillovers between energy and stock markets and their implications in the context of COVID-19. *International Review of Financial Analysis*, *77*, 101828. doi:10.1016/j.irfa.2021.101828 PMID:36570866

Zhang, Y. (2021). Corporate Responses to COVID-19: A Nonmarket Strategy Approach. *Sociological Perspectives*, *64*(5), 1032–1057.

Žižlavský, O. (2014). Net present value approach: Method for economic assessment of innovation projects. *Procedia: Social and Behavioral Sciences*, *156*, 506–512. doi:10.1016/j.sbspro.2014.11.230

Zou, P. H. (2020). The impact of the COVID-19 pandemic on firms: a survey in Guangdong Province. *China. Glob Health Res Policy*, *5*, 41.

Zubair, S., Kabir, R., & Huang, X. (2020). Does the financial crisis change the effect of financing on investment? Evidence from private SMEs. *Journal of Business Research, 110*, 456-463. doi:10.1016/j.jbusres.2020.01.063

Zubair, S., Kabir, R., & Huang, X. (2020). Does the financial crisis change the effect of financing or investment? Evidence from private SMEs. *Journal of Business Research*, (110), 456–463.

About the Contributors

Siraj Kariyilaparambu Kunjumuhammed is an Assistant Professor of Finance at the Modern College of Business and Science, Sultanate of Oman. He received his Ph.D. from Cochin University of Science and Technology, India and postgraduate degrees in Management (MBA) and Commerce (M.Com). Dr. Siraj has over 18 years of academic, research, consulting, and administrative experience. Dr. Siraj is an ISO 9001: 2015 Lead Auditor and a Certified Risk Professional from British Standards Institute. Dr. Siraj is also empaneled in the list of external reviewers at the Oman Authority for Academic Accreditation and Quality Assurance of Education (OAAAQA), Sultanate of Oman. He held positions as Head of the Business Studies department at the University of Technology and Applied Science, Oman, and as Management Consultant in Global Services, before joining MCBS. Dr. Siraj has extensive QA consulting experience as an External Reviewer in Institutional and Program Accreditation, OAAAQA, as Head of the Policy Management Committee and Member of the Strategic Planning and Review Committee, as Member of Self Assessment Team, and as part of various committees on ISA Standards at the University of Technology and Applied Science in Ibra and Muscat, as a member in Quality Assurance and Accreditation Committee and Policy Management Committee in Modern College of Business & Science. He has extensive experience in strategic and operational planning, policy management, development of KPIs, and entity reviews. He also edited a book on Global Perspectives on Quality Assurance and Accreditation in Higher Education Institutions, IGI, United States. LinkedIn Profile: www.linkedin.com/in/sirajkk.462f0264-282e-4ad2-8719-c09ec6daa615

Nithya Ramachandran is a senior lecturer in the Department of Business Studies, University of Technology and Applied Sciences (Ibra), Sultanate of Oman. She is a Commerce & Management graduate, holding PhD (2011) in Commerce from Bharathiar University, Coimbatore, India. An accomplished academician with over 18 + years of teaching and research experience in the areas of Accounting, Finance and Entrepreneurship. She is a speaker in national and international conferences, an author for several publications and faculty mentor for research projects. She has been a part of the core research team of Global Research 2020 on 'Organisational Excellence Framework 2020'. She strongly believes that education can bring socio-economic change in every human. Keeping this in mind, her guidance to students enhances their academic and technical competence. She is a coordinator for Quality and Operational Research (QOR) Newsletter, USA. Attempting to concentrate on research, gained her the position of Research and Consultancy Committee Coordinator in her affiliated university.

* * *

Essia Ries Ahmed is currently working as an assistant professor at the University of Nizwa. He received his Ph.D. from University Malaysia Perlis (UniMap), and a master's degree in Accounting from Universiti Sains Malaysia (USM). He has published articles in several Scopus Journals, and proceedings and presented papers at both national and international conferences. Dr. Essia Ries Ahmed is a reviewer and member of the editorial board in several journals.

Anitha Nair is working as Senior Lecturer in Modern College of Business and Science. As a Faculty Member, she has more than 14 years of experience in the field of teaching, both in India and Oman.

Brinda Kalyani P. R. is active academic researcher and passionate professor for the last 27 years. She has a doctoral degree and is pursuing CMA under ICMA. She has completed her training on Case Methodology as pedagogy in Management Education from IIM Kozhikode. She has published a monograph and was Dean for a national level Management Institute in India. She also chaired a session in the Oman International Business Conference held at Sultan Qaboos University, in Feb 2011.She has wonderful teaching record for a three decade span, in India and Oman. Presently she is an Associate Professor at Sri Krishna Arts and Science College, Coimbatore, India.

Onur Polat is an Associate Professor at the Department of Public Finance in Bilecik University. He is also a part-time Lecturer at Cankaya University at the department of Economics. He holds a Ph.D. in Economics (2017) from Hacettepe University and, also an M.Sc. in Financial Mathematics (2009) from the Middle East Technical University. He conducted a research project titled "The Impacts of Energy Price Shocks on Financial Stability: A Non- Parametric Approach" at the Economics Department in Illinois State University between 2016/10 and 2017/10. Dr. Polat's research interests cover Quantitative Finance, International Finance, Financial Econometrics, Energy Economics, Computational and Statistical modeling,

Metaheuristics, and Heuristics. The results of his research have been published in relevant journals indexed in databases like JCR, Scopus, or ABS such as Journal of Policy Modeling, Borsa Istanbul Review, Bulletin of Economic Research, Operations Research Perspectives, Studies in Economics and Finance, International Journal of Economics and Business Research, and Eastern Journal of European Studies. Dr. Polat has participated in different conferences on national and international levels.

Rajibur Reza is working at Department of Accounting, Finance and Economics, Griffith University as a Research Assistant and Sessional Academic. He is also a Casual academic at School of Business & Law, CQ University, Australia. He obtained a PhD in Finance from Griffith University, Australia. His primary research interests are in the areas of banking and insurance, corporate governance, ownership structure, financial wellbeing, water accounting and auditing, and water finance and investment.

Kabaly P. Subramanian is an Assistant Professor at Faculty of Business Studies-MBA Program, Arab Open University, Oman. He holds MBA and PhD in Management. He is a member of British Academy of Management (UK) and Indian Society for Training and Development (ISTD), Strategic partner of Blue Ocean Strategy Regional Centre (Malaysia). Dr. Kabaly P Subramanian has been in Learning & Development for the past 20 years. His Research and Teaching interests lies at the intersection of Business Strategy, Business Innovation and Digital Transformation of Businesses. Dr. Kabaly has published in indexed journals and conferences. He is presently leading a team of researchers in investigating Digital Transformation of Higher Education Institutions, funded by The Research Council, Oman. Dr. Kabaly is in the Editorial board of several academic research journals. Dr. Kabaly P Subramanian has trained more than 1000 Business leaders, Entrepreneurs and Executives in Strategy, Innovation and Digital Transformation. He has consulted large, medium, and small enterprises on Strategy, Innovation and Digital Transformation initiatives. Presently Dr. Kabaly is consulting a large corporate in Oman on their Digital Transformation Strategy. Recently Dr. Kabaly graduated from Columbia Business School, US and MIT, US in their jointly offered PG program in Digital Business through Emeritus Institute of Management, Singapore. He has attended number of Faculty Development Programs (FDP) and Management Development Programs (MDP) in institutions which includes IIM-K, IIM-B, TAPMI (India), UCSI (Malaysia) and Oxford University (UK). Dr. Kabaly involved in social initiatives which includes supporting educational Institutions and startups. Prior to Arab Open University, Dr. Kabaly P Subramanian worked with National Institute of Human Resources Development, University of Madras affiliated college (India) as Assistant Professor and as Head of Academic Section in Regional College of Technology,

Ministry of Manpower, Sultanate of Oman (Presently University of Technology and Applied Sciences, Oman) He has attended and presented his research in several International Conferences and Journals in US, UK, India, Oman, UAE, Kuwait, Georgia and Malaysia and won best research paper award.

Lan Sun is a Lecturer in Finance at School of Business & Law, CQ University, Australia. She holds a Ph.D. from Curtin University and MAF and MBA from the University of Newcastle, Australia. She has teaching experience across universities including University of New England, the University of Newcastle, Curtin, and New York University Sydney Campus with a focus on business finance, corporate finance, international accounting, financial accounting and auditing. She was a Senior Lecturer from University of New England and received the VC Commendation for the finance unit taught in UNE. Her research interests cover financial reporting quality, earnings management, corporate governance, executive compensation, market efficiency, fair value, sustainable finance and investing, etc.

Index

A

Analysis 14, 17, 21, 25-26, 28, 32, 38-40, 42-46, 61-63, 65, 76-77, 83, 87-88, 92, 96-97, 111-113, 118, 132, 170, 173, 175, 177-178, 180-185, 192-194, 196-197, 200-201, 210, 224, 226-229, 236-237

B

Behavior 8, 23, 27, 49-50, 53, 59, 65, 94, 100, 129-130, 132, 145-148, 173, 187, 192-193
Business Continuity 1-9, 11, 13-14, 16-19, 51, 118, 120-121, 156-158

C

Capital Structure 3, 6, 8, 19, 48-50, 52-56, 58-67, 96, 122, 224-229, 236-237
Channel Financing 204
Comparison 12, 116, 132, 206, 213, 227-228, 230-236
Connectedness Networks 21, 44
Corporate Finance 1-3, 6, 8-9, 13-19, 48-50, 53, 59-61, 65, 93-95
Corporate Governance 17-19, 69-72, 74-77, 80, 82, 90-95, 97, 149-154, 156-159, 161-162, 164-169, 183, 186, 226-227
Corporate Social Responsibility 67, 73, 112, 151, 156-157, 163, 165-166, 170-171, 173-175, 181-182, 184-186
COVID-19 1-3, 7-13, 15-23, 27-28, 32, 36-46, 48-50, 55-57, 60-67, 91, 99-101, 104, 107, 109-114, 116, 122-124, 127-132, 134, 136, 140, 142-150, 156, 159-166, 169-170, 182, 184-185, 187, 203-205, 207-210, 212-214, 216-217, 222-223, 227, 237

D

Debt-Ridden Operational Economy 203-204
Demand 1-2, 5, 7-11, 13-14, 49-51, 56, 59-61, 99, 101, 103-104, 109-111, 113, 116, 130, 160, 189, 203-205, 208-209, 212, 214, 217
Diebold-Yilmaz 21, 23, 25

E

Economy 2, 9, 11, 22, 37, 44, 55, 66, 69, 71, 96, 99-103, 106, 110, 113, 131, 147, 160, 168, 204-206, 208-210, 214-215, 223, 226
Employees 4-5, 7, 69, 103, 107-109, 146, 154-155, 158, 161, 163-164, 166-168, 173, 205, 207, 209, 214
Employment 5, 11, 59, 99, 107, 203, 205-206, 209-210, 214, 216
ENPV 117, 124, 126-127

F

Female Executives 68, 70-71, 76-80, 82-83, 86-87, 89-90
Financial Attitude 129-130, 132, 134, 136, 140-142, 145, 147-148

Financial Connectedness 21-23, 25-27, 39, 43-44
Financial Crisis 1-2, 7-9, 11, 16-19, 21-22, 25, 39-41, 43, 46, 48, 53-55, 57-58, 60-61, 64, 66-67, 70, 112, 120, 128, 169, 187
Financial Decision 115, 121, 198
Financial Performance 63, 65-68, 70-71, 74, 76-79, 84, 86-97, 147, 151-152, 158, 161, 171, 173-174, 184, 205, 226, 237
Financial Stress Index 21, 23, 44-45
Financing 3, 5, 10, 13-14, 48-50, 52-60, 62, 64-67, 69, 115-117, 120-123, 126-128, 151, 154, 160, 204, 210, 229
Firm Performance 13, 17, 62, 66, 72-76, 78, 92-96, 112, 170-171, 174-175, 181-186, 237
Firms 3, 5-6, 8-15, 17-18, 41, 48-51, 53-62, 64-65, 67, 71, 73-76, 84, 88, 93, 95, 97, 100, 102-109, 128, 136, 144, 170, 172, 177, 183-184, 205-210, 212-216, 218, 226-227, 237
Frequency Connectedness 21, 23, 27, 31, 33, 44

G

Gender Diversity 68-80, 82-84, 86-90, 92-96
Government 3, 11-12, 15, 48, 69-72, 75, 100-101, 103, 105-107, 109, 120, 145, 151-152, 158, 164-165, 168, 190-191, 200, 204-211, 213-214, 216, 221, 223

I

Indian Oil 164-165, 226, 237
Industry 7, 14, 28, 40, 49, 51, 53-54, 57-59, 65-66, 69-71, 77, 90-91, 94, 96, 99, 101-105, 107-110, 113, 128, 134, 147, 151-152, 155, 186, 190-192, 201, 203, 209, 211, 213, 225-226, 232, 237
Investment Decision 115, 117-118, 121, 194
Investors 6-7, 9, 14-15, 23, 25, 49-50, 55-56, 59, 65, 69, 71, 94, 105, 121, 130-132, 134-136, 141-144, 146-148, 158, 164, 168, 171, 187-194, 196, 198-201
Investors Behavior 129

L

Leverage 3, 48-49, 52-55, 58-60, 76, 79, 218, 224, 227, 229-231, 235-236
Lockdowns 2, 99-101, 103-105, 107-108

M

Maruti Suzuki India Limited 224-225, 227-237
Mutual Funds 65, 187-194, 196, 198-202

N

Normal Period 127, 228, 230-236

O

Oman 1, 48, 99, 115, 129, 131-132, 134, 136, 171, 175, 182-183, 185, 203

P

Pandemic 1-3, 5-17, 19-23, 27-28, 32, 35-51, 56-57, 60-64, 66-67, 91, 99-115, 120, 126, 128-132, 134, 136, 142-146, 148-150, 154-167, 169-170, 184-185, 187, 204, 206, 208, 212, 214, 216-217, 222-225, 227-228, 230-237
Pandemic Period 27-28, 50, 224-225, 227-228, 230-236

R

Ratio 49, 52-55, 58-59, 79-80, 106, 224, 226-227, 229-236
Retail Investors 130-132, 134, 136, 144, 147-148

S

Spillovers 21, 23, 26-30, 35-37, 39-42, 44-46
Supply 1-2, 5-8, 10, 13-14, 49-50, 57, 60-61, 68-69, 71-72, 97, 101-104, 107-111,

113, 116, 130, 157, 160, 165, 167, 189, 203-205, 212, 214, 217
Supply Chain 1-2, 5-6, 50, 104, 107-108, 157, 160, 167, 204-205, 214, 217
Systematic Risk 22, 36

T

Tata Motors 149, 162
Trading Activity 129, 131-132, 134-136, 138, 141-144, 148
Transitory Connectedness Networks 21

V

Value Chains 203-204, 212, 216

W

Water Companies 68-72, 76-82, 84, 88-91
Women on Board 68, 70, 75-77, 79-80, 84

www.ingramcontent.com/pod-product-compliance
Lightning Source LLC
LaVergne TN
LVHW061539290926
849162LV00004B/844

* 9 7 8 1 6 6 8 4 5 3 4 2 1 *